CHARLES LAMB

1775–1834

SELECTED ESSAYS, LETTERS, AND POEMS
BY CHARLES LAMB

SELECTED ESSAYS
LETTERS
POEMS

CHARLES LAMB

Edited with an Introduction by
J. LEWIS MAY

COLLINS
LONDON AND GLASGOW

GENERAL EDITOR: G. F. MAINE

First published
THE ESSAYS OF ELIA 1823
LAST ESSAYS OF ELIA 1833

This edition 1953

Printed in Holland by
Drukkerij Holland N.V., Amsterdam

CHARLES LAMB

CHARLES LAMB was born on the 10th of February 1775 in London, where his father John Lamb was clerk and servant to Mr. Samuel Salt, a Bencher of the Inner Temple. John Lamb had married Elizabeth Field by whom he had seven children. Only three survived childhood—Charles being the youngest.

The Lamb household being extremely poor, little money could be spared for the education of the children. After some elementary schooling, Charles, through the influence of Mr. Salt, was admitted to Christ's Hospital (School) in 1782 where he remained for seven years and formed his friendship with Coleridge which was to last a lifetime. Lamb was a good Latin scholar but because of the poverty of his family and of a defect in his speech was denied the opportunity of an academic education.

Around 1791 he obtained a post in South Sea House (where his brother John already held an appointment), and in 1792 was promoted to a clerkship in the accountant's office of the East India Company, in whose service he was to continue until 1825. This post gave him economic security, on a modest scale, for the whole of his life. Moreover the nature and routine of his office work proved most beneficial to the process of intellectual gestation; in other words it allowed him time to pursue his own thoughts.

On the death of Samuel Salt in 1792 the Lambs had to give up their home in the Temple and moved into lodgings in Little Queen's Street where they struggled along on Charles' small salary and his sister Mary's earnings from needlework. In 1794 Charles Lamb was able to resume his close contact with Coleridge (who until then had been up at Cambridge), and under his influence began to write sonnets, four of which appeared in the *Morning Chronicle* and were published later in Coleridge's volume *Poems on various subjects*.

The years 1795–96 brought terrible tragedy into Lamb's life. Towards the end of 1795 he had a fit of temporary insanity which necessitated his confinement for several weeks in an asylum. In September 1796 Mary, in a sudden out-burst of psychotic rage, stabbed her mother to death with a table-knife. Certified insane, Mary was taken to a mental home in Islington and Charles, with his old father, moved into lodgings in the immediate neighbourhood. On her release from the asylum she was placed under her brother's guardianship, and in 1799—after their father's death—joined Charles in his lodgings. Henceforth their lives were to be inseparably linked together, Charles devoting himself to the care of his unfortunate sister who all through her life was to suffer from recurring fits of mania.

During the last three years of the century, Lamb resumed his literary activities, writing a number of poems, the poetical drama *John Woodvil* and the prose narrative *Rosamond Gray*. In 1800 he began to try journalism as a means of adding to his income. He wrote short articles, criticism, witty para-graphs and puns for the *Morning Post*, the *Albion*, and later for the *Morning Chronicle*. One of his essays, *The Londoner*, which appeared in the *Morning Post*, attracted considerable atten-tion. In 1805 he was commissioned by William Godwin to write Shakespeare's plays in the form of tales for children. He undertook the task jointly with Mary, she doing the comedies and he the tragedies. The *Tales from Shakespeare* were published in 1807 and met with great success. As the result Charles and Mary were commissioned to write two other children's books: *Mrs Leicester's School* (1807) and *Poetry for Children* (1809), and Charles also wrote a children's version of the *Odyssey*, published in 1808 as *The Adventures of Ulysses*, and later, for Longman's, edited selections from Elizabethan dramatists.

From 1800 to 1817 Charles had lived, together with Mary, in the Temple. During this period he had gradually im-proved his material position, gathered many friends around him, and made a name for himself as a critic and writer of essays. (Most of his early essays had appeared in the *Reflector* and from 1813 on in Leigh Hunt's *Examiner*). In 1817 brother and sister moved to lodgings in Covent Garden. The follow-ing year Charles' collected writings in prose and verse were published in two volumes with a preface by Coleridge. Two years later (1820) began Lamb's association with the *London Magazine* (then under the editorship of John Scott) for which, during the following five years, he was to write the essays—under the pen-name 'Elia'—on which his fame mainly rests. The first series, (covering the years 1820–22) appeared in collected form in 1823 under the title *Essays of Elia*; the second series (1823–25), as well as a number of essays written for other magazines, was published in volume form in 1833, as *The Last Essays of Elia*.

In 1823 Lamb and his sister moved out of London to a cottage in Islington. In 1825 came his retirement from the East India Company, who generously awarded him a pension of £450 a year. The year 1827 saw another change of residence, this time to a furnished cottage at Enfield where Charles and Mary lived as boarders. In 1833 came the final move to Edmonton. The last ten years of Lamb's life were brightened by the presence of a young girl Emma Isola, an orphan whom he adopted and to whose education he and Mary devoted themselves. Lamb's literary output, after his retirement and the closing down of the *London Magazine* (1826) gradually diminished to occasional essays and sketches which appeared in *The New Monthly Magazine*, *The Spectator*, *The Englishman's Magazine* and *Athenaeum*.

He died after a short illness on December 27th 1834, having outlived his friend Coleridge by six months.

H. d. R.

CONTENTS

Miscellaneous Essays

Letters

Poems

Bibliography

INTRODUCTION

Lamb's Place in Literature

LITERATURE is a comprehensive term. In its wider connotation, it might signify anything from 'Printed Matter' to *Paradise Lost*. Even if we were to restrict it to such works as are deemed to be of permanent value, the definition would still be vague, for it would include two definitely contrasted kinds of composition, two distinct orders or categories, which differ from each other, not in degree but in nature, and which have nothing in common save that words are the medium of them both.

Take the opening sentence of an acknowledged masterpiece in its kind, Gibbon's *Decline and Fall*; it reads, 'In the second century of the Christian era, the Empire of Rome comprehended the fairest parts of the earth.' I imagine that no great harm would be done to that, whether in sense or rhythm, if we substituted 'Roman Empire' for 'Empire of Rome' and 'regions of the earth' for 'parts of the earth.'

But now, consider these three lines of Wordsworth:

> the fierce confederate storm
> Of sorrow barricadoed evermore
> Within the walls of Cities.

Into that, introduce the slightest possible variation; omit one letter and for 'barricadoed', say 'barricaded'. 'Well; the meaning is the same,' the practical, matter-of-fact reader will declare. The dictionary meaning, no doubt; but the poetical meaning, no. That seemingly trifling, that infinitesimal, alteration has wrought irreparable damage to the whole ethereal structure; the spell is broken, the charm has fled.

This quality of inviolability, this quality which forbids that even the smallest detail, a single letter, a single vowel-sound should be tampered with on pain of marring the whole, is the distinctive characteristic of high poetry. It would not, for example, need a very sensitive ear to perceive how the magic of,

> A voice so thrilling ne'er was heard
> In spring-time from the Cuckoo-bird,
> Breaking the silence of the seas
> Among the farthest Hebrides . . . .

would be utterly destroyed if, in the last line, we substituted 'furthest' for 'farthest'; a closed vowel for an open one.

But this inviolability, the attribute of perfection, which belongs to poetry of the highest order, belongs also to some prose, to prose which, like poetry, is the product of the creative imagination, to prose which, in everything but form, *is* poetry, its office being, not to impart information, or to formulate ideas, or to enunciate theories, but to inspire visions, to awaken dreams. Its ultimate appeal is to the feelings, the emotions, rather than to the understanding; to the heart rather than to the head.

Such are the essays of Charles Lamb. Prose in form, they are in reality poetry, and to be judged as poetry. The error into which his detractors have fallen has been to misapprehend his category, to judge him by the canons applicable to prose instead of by those appropriate to poetry. 'How laughable,' says Mark Pattison, 'are the attempts of the commentators to interpret a line in Virgil as they would a sentence in Aristotle's *Physics*.' And how laughable the attempts made by some critics to interpret Lamb as if he were an Emerson or a Lord Macaulay. Yet the first few lines of the first essay should have told these gentlemen into whose presence they had come; what manner of writer they had to deal with. The aptness and originality of the epithets— 'a *grave* court' .... '*thinly peopled* with a few *straggling* clerks' and so on—things like these should have opened their eyes; but if not, if they were still undeceived, then the haunting beauty of such a phrase as 'dusty maps of Mexico, dim as dreams, and soundings of the Bay of Panama,' should have enlightened even the most unperceptive, the most purblind among them.

Or take, again, such a passage as this from *The Old and the New Schoolmaster*:

'Rest to the souls of those fine old Pedagogues; the breed, long since extinct, of the the Lilys and the Linacres; who believing that all learning was contained in the languages which they taught, and despising every other acquirement as superficial and useless, came to their task as to a sport. Passing from infancy to age, they dreamed away all their days as in a grammar-school. Revolving in a perpetual cycle of declensions, conjugations, syntaxes and prosodies; renewing constantly the occupations which had charmed their studious childhood; rehearsing continually the part of the past; life must have slipped from them at last like one day.'

That reveals to us more of the spirit of those old grammar-school worthies than pages of formal biography would have done. *Life must have slipped from them at last like one day.* Is not that as magical in its way as those words (for the most part Anglo-Saxon and monosyllabic) with which Prospero sums up his philosophy of life in *The Tempest,*

> We are such stuff
> As dreams are made on, and our little life
> Is rounded with a sleep.

For Elia, in kind if not in stature, is of the breed of Shakespeare. Is there not 'One glory of the sun, another glory of the moon, and another glory of the stars?'

'I have no ear!' said Lamb of himself; but, as we turn his pages, what phrases of incomparable felicity, of inimitable cadence we encounter. 'No ear?' Then listen:

'Stones of old Mincing Lane which I have worn with my daily pilgrimage for six-and-thirty years, to the footsteps of what toilworn clerk are your everlasting flints now vocal?'

Or to this, in a letter to George Dyer:

'Alas! can we ring the bells backward? Can we unlearn the arts that pretend to civilize, and then burn the world? There is a march of science; but who shall beat the drums for its retreat?'

'If you were called upon to part with all the essays save one, which would you keep?' I have sometimes wondered what answer I should make if such a question were put to me. If I fixed on *The South Sea House,* I should immediately conceive a terrible longing for *The Old Benchers.* Then how could I possibly do without *Amicus Redivivus?,* or *Dream Children?,* or *Old China?*—and so on, till the whole tale, down to the last *Popular Fallacy,* was complete. It was no doubt because he too was aware of the impossibility of selecting any essays in particular that the Editor of the present volume very wisely decided to include them all.

'Many things,' says Mr Middleton Murry, 'are written, few are remembered, and of those few, few are remembered *passionately,* as though to forget them were to die.' A pregnant, a valuable utterance because, as in a flash, it indicates the chasm between the two categories of literature on which I

have been insisting. One might forget this or that passage of
Macaulay, let us say, or of Hume, or of Herbert Spencer and
yet manage to rub along tolerably enough without them. But
to whom would the world not seem an immeasurably poorer
place, a desert, nay, a tomb, were he to lose such a thing as—

> daffodils
> That come before the swallow dares and take
> The winds of March with beauty ....

or as this, from *The Old Benchers of the Inner Temple*:

'What an antique air had the now almost effaced sun-
dials, with their moral inscriptions, seeming coevals with
that Time which they measured, and to take their revelations
of its flight immediately from heaven, holding correspondence
with the fountain of light! How would the dark line steal
imperceptibly on, watched by the eye of childhood, eager to
detect its movement, never catched, nice as an evanescent
cloud, or the first arrest of sleep....'

At which point, some Ariel, or perhaps his Guardian
Angel prompted him to add:

> Ah! yet doth beauty like a dial-hand
> Steal from his figure and no pace perceived!

Surely the ultimate perfection of the art of quotation is
reached when, as here, the thing quoted and the text which
is its setting, the jewel and the casket, mutually heighten one
another—'The marriage of true minds.'

Lamb, then, is a poet, and to be read as a poet. Hear, now,
what a poet has to say of him:

'The exquisite humour, the womanly tenderness which
inform and imbue each other with perfect life and faultless
grace, beyond reach of any art but that which itself is
nature; the matchless refinement of his criticism, the incomparable spontaneity of his style; all this it is easy, if it is
not impertinent to praise; the something within or beyond
all these, which possibly may appeal to few, can assuredly be
defined by none.'

Swinburne is right, and that mysterious 'something' is in
fact the poetry, and poetry defies definition.

We draw near to the heart and soul of such writers as
Charles Lamb not by reading *about* them, but by reading
them, for their works *are themselves*. Within and beyond their

14

words, beyond the surface-meaning, beyond the music of them, there is, for those whose ears are attuned to hear it, an 'unheard melody,' clear, entrancing, yet completely incommunicable.

Well; books come and go, clever, ingenious, informative, entertaining, provocative, brilliant, and so on; they 'have their day and cease to be.' Histories slip out of date; philosophies out of fashion; works of science, constantly superseded by fresh discoveries, are obsolescent as soon as born; but the great, the choice creations of the human spirit—these abide. 'The gardens of the Muses keep the privilege of the Golden Age; they ever flourish and are in league with Time.' Amid the flowers in those unfading gardens, some may be more splendid, but none are sweeter, or more lovable, none exhale a more delicate perfume, than those born of the genius of Charles Lamb.

J. LEWIS MAY

THE ESSAYS OF ELIA

The South-Sea House

READER, in thy passage from the Bank—where thou hast
been receiving thy half-yearly dividends (supposing thou art
a lean annuitant like myself)—to the Flower Pot, to secure a
place for Dalston, or Shacklewell, or some other thy suburban retreat northerly,—didst thou never observe a melancholy-looking, handsome brick and stone edifice, to the left—
where Threadneedle Street abuts upon Bishopsgate? I dare
say thou hast often admired its magnificent portals ever
gaping wide, and disclosing to view a grave court, with
cloisters, and pillars, with few or no traces of goers-in or
comers-out—a desolation something like Balclutha's. *

This was once a house of trade,—a centre of busy interests. The throng of merchants was here—the quick pulse
of gain—and here some forms of business are still kept up,
though the soul be long since fled. Here are still to be seen
stately porticos; imposing staircases; offices roomy as the
state apartments in palaces—deserted, or thinly peopled with
a few straggling clerks; the still more sacred interiors of
court and committee-rooms, with venerable faces of beadles,
doorkeepers—directors seated in form on solemn days (to
proclaim a dead dividend), at long worm-eaten tables, that
have been mahogany, with tarnished gilt-leather coverings,
supporting massy silver inkstands long since dry;—the oaken
wainscots hung with pictures of deceased governors and sub-
governors, of Queen Anne, and the two first monarchs of the
Brunswick dynasty:—huge charts, which subsequent discoveries have antiquated; dusty maps of Mexico, dim as
dreams,—and soundings of the Bay of Panama! The long
passages hung with buckets, appended, in idle row, to walls,
whose substance might defy any, short of the last, conflagration;—with vast ranges of cellarage under all, where
dollars and pieces-of-eight once lay, an 'unsunned heap,' for
Mammon to have solaced his solitary heart withal,—long
since dissipated, or scattered into air at the blast of the
breaking of that famous BUBBLE.——

* I passed by the walls of Balclutha, and they were desolate.—OSSIAN.

Such is the SOUTH-SEA HOUSE. At least, such it was forty years ago, when I knew it,—a magnificent relic! What alterations may have been made in it since, I have had no opportunities of verifying. Time, I take for granted, has not freshened it. No wind has resuscitated the face of the sleeping waters. A thicker crust by this time stagnates upon it. The moths, that were then battering upon its obsolete ledgers and daybooks, have rested from their depredations, but other light generations have succeeded, making fine fretwork among their single and double entries. Layers of dust have accumulated (a superfœtation of dirt!) upon the old layers, that seldom used to be disturbed, save by some curious finger, now and then, inquisitive to explore the mode of bookkeeping in Queen Anne's reign; or, with less hallowed curiosity, seeking to unveil some of the mysteries of that tremendous HOAX whose extent the petty peculators of our day look back upon with the same expression of incredulous admiration, and hopeless ambition of rivalry, as would become the puny face of modern conspiracy contemplating the Titan size of Vaux's superhuman plot.

Peace to the manes of the BUBBLE! Silence and destitution are upon thy walls, proud house, for a memorial!

Situated as thou art, in the very heart of stirring and living commerce,—amid the fret and fever of speculation—with the Bank, and the 'Change, and the India House about thee, in the hey-day of present prosperity, with their important faces, as it were, insulting thee, their *poor neighbour out of business*—to the idle and merely contemplative,—to such as me, old house! there is a charm in thy quiet: a cessation—a coolness from business—an indolence almost cloistral—which is delightful! With what reverence have I paced thy great bare rooms and courts at eventide! They spoke of the past:—the shade of some dead accountant, with visionary pen in ear, would flit by me, stiff as in life. Living accounts and accountants puzzle me. I have no skill in figuring. But thy great dead tomes, which scarce three degenerate clerks of the present day could lift from their enshrining shelves—with their old fantastic flourishes, and decorative rubric interlacings—their sums in triple columniations, set down with formal superfluity of ciphers—with pious sentences at the beginning, without which our religious ancestors never ventured to open a book of business, or bill of lading—the costly vellum covers of some of them almost persuading us that we are got into some *better library*,—are very agreeable and edifying spectacles. I can look upon these defunct dragons with complacency. Thy heavy odd-shaped ivory-handled penknives (our ancestors had everything on a larger scale than we have hearts for) are as good as anything from Herculaneum. The pounce-boxes of our days have gone retrograde.

The very clerks which I remember in the South-Sea House —I speak of forty years back—had an air very different from those in the public offices that I have had to do with since. They partook of the genius of the place!

They were mostly (for the establishment did not admit of superfluous salaries) bachelors. Generally (for they had not much to do) persons of a curious and speculative turn of mind. Old-fashioned, for a reason mentioned before. Humourists, for they were of all descriptions; and, not having been brought together in early life (which has a tendency to assimilate the members of corporate bodies to each other), but, for the most part, placed in this house in ripe or middle age, they necessarily carried into it their separate habits and oddities, unqualified, if I may so speak, as into a common stock. Hence they formed a sort of Noah's ark. Odd fishes. A lay-monastery. Domestic retainers in a great house, kept more for show than use. Yet pleasant fellows, full of chat— and not a few among them had arrived at considerable proficiency on the German flute.

The cashier at that time was one Evans, a Cambro-Briton. He had something of the choleric complexion of his countrymen stamped on his visage, but was a worthy sensible man at bottom. He wore his hair, to the last, powdered and frizzed out, in the fashion which I remember to have seen in caricatures of what were termed, in my young days, *Maccaronies*. He was the last of that race of beaux. Melancholy as a gib-cat over his counter all the forenoon, I think I see him, making up his cash (as they call it) with tremulous fingers, as if he feared every one about him was a defaulter; in his hypochondry ready to imagine himself one; haunted, at least, with the idea of the possibility of his becoming one; his tristful visage clearing up a little over his roast neck of veal at Anderton's at two (where his picture still hangs, taken a little before his death by desire of the master of the coffee-house, which he had frequented for the last five-and-twenty years), but not attaining the meridian of its animation till evening brought on the hour of tea and visiting. The simultaneous sound of his well-known rap at the door with the stroke of the clock announcing six, was a topic of never-failing mirth in the families which this dear old bachelor gladdened with his presence. Then was his *forte*, his glorified hour! How would he chirp, and expand, over a muffin! How would he dilate into secret history! His countryman, Pennant himself, in particular, could not be more eloquent than he in relation to old and new London—the site of old theatres, churches, streets gone to decay—where Rosamond's Pond stood—the Mulberry gardens—and the Conduit in Cheap— with many a pleasant anecdote, derived from paternal tradition, of those grotesque figures which Hogarth has immortalised in his picture of *Noon*,—the worthy descendants of those heroic confessors, who, flying to this country, from the wrath of Louis the Fourteenth and his dragoons, kept alive the flame of pure religion in the sheltering obscurities of Hog Lane, and the vicinity of the Seven Dials!

Deputy, under Evans, was Thomas Tame. He had the air and stoop of a nobleman. You would have taken him for one, had you met him in one of the passages leading to Westminster Hall. By stoop, I mean that gentle bending of the body forwards, which, in great men, must be supposed to be the effect of an habitual condescending attention to the applications of their inferiors. While he held you in converse, you felt strained to the height in the colloquy. The conference over, you were at leisure to smile at the comparative insignificance of the pretensions which had just awed you. His intellect was of the shallowest order. It did not reach to a saw or a proverb. His mind was in its original state of white paper. A sucking-babe might have posed him. What was it then? Was he rich? Alas, no! Thomas Tame was very poor. Both he and his wife looked outwardly gentlefolks, when I fear all was not well at all times within. She had a neat meagre person, which it was evident she had not sinned in over-pampering; but in its veins was noble blood. She traced her descent, by some labyrinth of relationship, which I never thoroughly understood,—much less can explain with any heraldic certainty at this time of day,—to the illustrious, but unfortunate house of Derwentwater. This was the secret of

Thomas's stoop. This was the thought—the sentiment—the bright solitary star of your lives,—ye mild and happy pair,—which cheered you in the night of intellect, and in the obscurity of your station! This was to you instead of riches, instead of rank, instead of glittering attainments: and it was worth them all together. You insulted none with it; but while you wore it as a piece of defensive armour only, no insult likewise could reach you through it. *Decus et solamen.*

Of quite another stamp was the then accountant, John Tipp. He neither pretended to high blood, nor, in good truth, cared one fig about the matter. He 'thought an accountant the greatest character in the world, and himself the greatest accountant in it.' Yet John was not without his hobby. The fiddle relieved his vacant hours. He sang, certainly, with other notes than to the Orphean lyre. He did, indeed, scream and scrape most abominably. His fine suite of official rooms in Threadneedle Street, which, without anything very substantial appended to them, were enough to enlarge a man's notions of himself that lived in them (I know not who is the occupier of them now), resounded fortnightly to the notes of a concert of 'sweet breasts,' as our ancestors would have called them, culled from club-rooms and orchestras—chorus-singers—first and second violoncellos—double-basses—and clarionets—who ate his cold mutton, and drank his punch, and praised his ear. He sate like Lord Midas among them. But at the desk Tipp was quite another sort of creature. Thence all ideas, that were purely ornamental, were banished. You could not speak of anything romantic without rebuke. Politics were excluded. A newspaper was thought too refined and abstracted. The whole duty of man consisted in writing off dividend warrants. The striking of the annual balance in the company's books (which, perhaps, differed from the balance of last year in the sum of £25 : 1 : 6) occupied his days and nights for a month previous. Not that Tipp was blind to the deadness of *things* (as they call them in the city) in his beloved house, or did not sigh for a return of the old stirring days when South-Sea hopes were young—(he was indeed equal to the wielding of any of the most intricate accounts of the most flourishing company in these or those days):—but to a genuine accountant the difference of proceeds is as nothing. The fractional farthing is as dear to his heart as the thousands which stand before it. He is the true actor, who, whether his part be a prince or a peasant, must act it with like intensity. With Tipp form was everything. His life was formal. His actions seemed ruled with a ruler. His pen was not less erring than his heart. He made the best executor in the world; he was plagued with incessant executorships accordingly, which excited his spleen and soothed his vanity in equal ratios. He would swear (for Tipp swore) at the little orphans, whose rights he would guard with a tenacity like the grasp of the dying hand that commended their interests to his protection. With all this there was about him a sort of timidity—(his few enemies used to give it a worse name)—a something which in reverence to the dead, we will place, if you please, a little on this side of the heroic. Nature certainly had been pleased to endow John Tipp with a sufficient measure of the principle of self-preservation. There is a cowardice which we do not despise, because it has nothing base or treacherous in its elements; it betrays itself, not you: it is mere temperament; the absence of the romantic and the enterprising; it sees a lion in the way, and will not, with Fortinbras, 'greatly find quarrel in a straw,' when some supposed honour is at stake. Tipp never mounted the box of a stage-coach in his life; or leaned against the rails of a balcony; or walked upon the ridge of a parapet; or looked down a precipice; or let off a gun; or went upon a water-party; or would willingly let you go, if he could have helped it: neither was it recorded of him, that for lucre, or for intimidation, he ever forsook friend or principle.

Whom next shall we summon from the dusty dead, in whom common qualities become uncommon? Can I forget thee, Henry Man, the wit, the polished man of letters, the *author*, of the South-Sea House? who never enteredst thy office in a morning, or quittedst it in mid-day—(what didst *thou* in an office?)—without some quirk that left a sting! Thy gibes and thy jokes are now extinct, or survive but in two forgotten volumes, which I had the good fortune to rescue from a stall in Barbican, not three days ago, and found thee terse, fresh, epigrammatic, as alive. Thy wit is a little gone by in these fastidious days—thy topics are staled by the 'new-born gauds' of the time:—but great thou used to be in Public Ledgers, and in Chronicles, upon Chatham, and Shelburne, and Rockingham, and Howe, and Burgoyne, and Clinton, and the war which ended in the tearing from Great

Britain her rebellious colonies,—and Keppel, and Wilkes, and Sawbridge, and Bull, and Dunning, and Pratt, and Richmond,—and such small politics.——

A little less facetious, and a great deal more obstreperous, was fine rattling, rattle-headed Plumer. He was descended, —not in a right line, reader (for his lineal pretensions, like his personal, favoured a little of the sinister bend)—from the Plumers of Hertfordshire. So tradition gave him out; and certain family features not a little sanctioned the opinion. Certainly old Walter Plumer (his reputed author) had been a rake in his days, and visited much in Italy, and had seen the world. He was uncle, bachelor-uncle, to the fine old whig still living, who has represented the county in so many successive parliaments, and has a fine old mansion near Ware. Walter flourished in George the Second's days, and was the same who was summoned before the House of Commons about a business of franks, with the old Duchess of Marlborough. You may read of it in Johnson's Life of Cave. Cave came off cleverly in that business. It is certain our Plumer did nothing to discountenance the rumour. He rather seemed pleased whenever it was, with all gentleness, insinuated. But, besides his family pretensions, Plumer was an engaging fellow, and sang gloriously.——

Not so sweetly sang Plumer as thou sangest, mild, child-like, pastoral M——; a flute's breathing less divinely whispering than thy Arcadian melodies, when, in tones worthy of Arden, thou didst chant that song sung by Amiens to the banished Duke, which proclaims the winter wind more lenient than for a man to be ungrateful. Thy sire was old surly M——, the unapproachable churchwarden of Bishopsgate. He knew not what he did, when he begat thee, like spring, gentle offspring of blustering winter:—only unfortunate in thy ending, which should have been mild, conciliatory, swan-like.——

Much remains to sing. Many fantastic shapes rise up, but they must be mine in private:—already I have fooled the reader to the top of his bent;—else could I omit that strange creature Woollett, who existed in trying the question, and *bought litigations?*—and still stranger, inimitable, solemn Hepworth, from whose gravity Newton might have deduced the law of gravitation. How profoundly would he nib a pen— with what deliberation would he wet a wafer!——

25

But it is time to close—night's wheels are rattling fast over me—it is proper to have done with this solemn mockery.

Reader, what if I have been playing with thee all this while?—peradventure the very *names*, which I have summond up before thee, are fantastic—insubstantial—like Henry Pimpernel, and old John Naps of Greece:——

Be satisfied that something answering to them has had a being. Their importance is from the past.

Oxford in the Vacation

CASTING a preparatory glance at the bottom of this article— as the wary connoisseur in prints, with cursory eye (which, while it reads, seems as though it read not), never fails to consult the *quis sculpsit* in the corner, before he pronounces some rare piece to be a Vivares, or a Woollet—— methinks I hear you exclaim, reader, *Who is Elia*?

Because in my last I tried to divert thee with some half-forgotten humours of some old clerks defunct, in an old house of business, long since gone to decay, doubtless you have already set me down in your mind as one of the self-same college—a votary of the desk—a notched and cropt scrivener—one that sucks his sustenance, as certain sick people are said to do, through a quill.

Well, I do agnize something of the sort. I confess that it is my humour, my fancy—in the forepart of the day, when the mind of your man of letters requires some relaxation—(and none better than such as at first sight seems most abhorrent from his beloved studies)—to while away some good hours of my time in the contemplation of indigos, cottons, raw silks, piece-goods, flowered or otherwise. In the first place * * * * and then it sends you home with such increased appetite to your books * * * not to say, that your outside sheets, and waste wrappers of foolscap, do receive into them, most kindly and naturally, the impression of sonnets, epigrams, *essays*—so that the very parings of a counting-house are, in some sort, the settings up of an author. The enfranchised quill, that has plodded all the morning among the cart-rucks of figures and ciphers, frisks and curvets so at its ease over the flowery carpet-ground of a midnight dissertation.—It feels its promotion. * * * So that you see, upon the whole, the literary dignity of *Elia* is very little, if at all, compromised in the condescension.

Not that, in my anxious detail of the many commodities incidental to the life of a public office, I would be thought blind to certain flaws, which a cunning carper might be able to pick in this Joseph's vest. And here I must have leave, in the fulness of my soul, to regret the abolition, and doing-away-with altogether, of those consolatory interstices and sprinklings of freedom, through the four seasons,—the *red-letter days*, now become, to all intents and purposes, *dead-letter days*. There was Paul, and Stephen, and Barnabas—

Andrew and John, men famous in old times

—we were used to keep all their days holy as long back as I was at school at Christ's. I remember their effigies, by the same token, in the old Basket Prayer-Book. There hung Peter in his uneasy posture——holy Bartlemy in the troublesome act of flaying, after the famous Marsyas by Spagnoletti.——I honoured them all, and could almost have wept the defal-cation of Iscariot—so much did we love to keep holy memories sacred:—only methought I a little grudged at the coalition of the *better Jude* with Simon—clubbing (as it were) their sanctities together to make up one poor gaudy-day between them—as an economy unworthy of the dispensation.

These were bright visitations in a scholar's and a clerk's life—'far off their coming shone.'—I was as good as an al-manac in those days. I could have told you such a saint's day falls out next week, or the week after. Peradventure the Epiphany, by some periodical infelicity, would, once in six years, merge in a Sabbath. Now am I little better than one of the profane. Let me not be thought to arraign the wisdom of my civil superiors, who have judged the further observation of these holy tides to be papistical, superstitious. Only in a custom of such long standing, methinks, if their Holinesses the Bishops had, in decency, been first sounded——but I am wading out of my depths. I am not the man to decide the limits of civil and ecclesiastical authority——I am plain Elia—no Selden, nor Archbishop Usher—though at present in the thick of their books, here in the heart of learning, under the shadow of the mighty Bodley.

I can here play the gentleman, enact the student. To such

a one as myself, who has been defrauded in his young years of
the sweet food of academic institution, nowhere is so pleasant, to while away a few idle weeks at, as one or other of
the Universities. Their vacation, too, at this time of the year,
falls in so pat with *ours*. Here I can take my walks un-
molested, and fancy myself of what degree or standing I
please. I seem admitted *ad eundem*. I fetch up past opportunities. I can rise at the chapel-bell, and dream that it rings
for *me*. In moods of humility I can be a Sizar, or a Servitor.
When the peacock vein rises, I strut a Gentleman Commoner. In graver moments I proceed Master of Arts. Indeed
I do not think I am much unlike that respectable character.
I have seen your dim-eyed vergers, and bed-makers in
spectacles, drop a bow or a curtsy, as I pass, wisely mistaking
me for something of the sort. I go about in black, which
favours the notion. Only in Christ Church reverend qua-
drangle, I can be content to pass for nothing short of a
Seraphic Doctor.

The walks at these times are so much one's own,—the tall
trees of Christ's, the groves of Magdalen! The halls deserted,
and with open doors inviting one to slip in unperceived, and
pay a devoir to some Founder, or noble or royal Benefactress
(that should have been ours), whose portrait seems to smile
upon their overlooked beadsman, and to adopt me for their
own. Then, to take a peep in by the way at the butteries, and
sculleries, redolent of antique hospitality: the immense caves
of kitchens, kitchen fireplaces, cordial recesses; ovens whose
first pies were baked four centuries ago; and spits which have
cooked for Chaucer! Not the meanest minister among the
dishes but is hallowed to me through his imagination, and
the Cook goes forth a Manciple.

Antiquity! thou wondrous charm, what art thou? that,
being nothing, art everything! When thou *wert*, thou wert
not antiquity—then thou wert nothing, but hadst a remoter
antiquity, as thou calledst it, to look back to with blind
veneration; thou thyself being to thyself flat, jejune, *modern*!
What mystery lurks in this retroversion? or what half
Januses * are we, that cannot look forward with the same
idolatry with which we for ever revert! The mighty future is
as nothing, being everything! the past is everything, being
nothing!

* Januses of one face.—Sir Thomas Browne.

What were thy *dark ages*? Surely the sun rose as brightly then as now, and man got him to his work in the morning. Why is it we can never hear mention of them without an accompanying feeling as though a palpable obscure had dimmed the face of things, and that our ancestors wandered to and fro groping!

Above all thy rarities, old Oxenford, what do most arride and solace me, are thy repositories of mouldering learning, thy shelves——

What a place to be in is an old library! It seems as though all the souls of all the writers, that have bequeathed their labours to these Bodleians, were reposing here, as in some dormitory, or middle state. I do not want to handle, to profane the leaves, their winding-sheets. I could as soon dislodge a shade. I seem to inhale learning, walking amid their foliage; and the odour of their old moth-scented coverings is fragrant as the first bloom of those sciential apples which grew amid the happy orchard.

Still less have I curiosity to disturb the elder repose of MSS. Those *variæ lectiones*, so tempting to the more erudite palates, do but disturb and unsettle my faith. I am no Herculanean raker. The credit of the three witnesses might have slept unimpeached for me. I leave these curiosities to Porson, and to G. D.—whom, by the way, I found busy as a moth over some rotten archive, rummaged out of some seldom-explored press, in a nook at Oriel. With long poring he is grown almost into a book. He stood as passive as one by the side of the old shelves. I longed to new-coat him in russia, and assign him his place. He might have mustered for a tall Scapula.

D. is assiduous in his visits to these seats of learning. No inconsiderable portion of his moderate fortune, I apprehend, is consumed in journeys between them and Clifford's Innen where, like a dove on the asp's nest, he has long taken up his unconscious abode, amid an incongruous assembly of attorneys' clerks, apparitors, promoters, vermin of the law, among whom he sits 'in calm and sinless peace.' The fangs of the law pierce him not—the winds of litigation blow over his humble chambers—the hard sheriff's officer moves his hat as he passes—legal nor illegal discourtesy touches him—none thinks of offering violence or injustice to him—you would as soon 'strike an abstract idea.'

D. has been engaged, he tells me, through a course of laborious years, in an investigation into all curious matter connected with the two Universities; and has lately lit upon a MS. collection of charters, relative to C——, by which he hopes to settle some disputed points—particularly that long controversy between them as to priority of foundation. The ardour with which he engages in these liberal pursuits, I am afraid, has not met with all the encouragement it deserved, either here, or at C——. Your caputs, and heads of colleges, care less than anybody else about these questions.—Contented to suck the milky fountains of their Alma Maters, without inquiring into the venerable gentlewomen's years, they rather hold such curiosities to be impertinent—unreverend. They have their good glebe lands *in manu*, and care not much to rake into the title-deeds. I gather at least so much from other sources, for D. is not a man to complain.

D. started like an unbroke heifer when I interrupted him. *A priori* it was not very probable that we should have met in Oriel. But D. would have done the same, had I accosted him on the sudden in his own walks in Clifford's Inn, or in the Temple. In addition to a provoking shortsightedness (the effect of late studies and watchings at the midnight oil) D. is the most absent of men. He made a call the other morning at our friend M.'s in Bedford Square; and, finding nobody at home, was ushered into the hall, where, asking for pen and ink, with great exactitude of purpose he enters me his name in the book—which ordinarily lies about in such places, to record the failures of the untimely or unfortunate visitor—and takes his leave with many ceremonies and professions of regret. Some two or three hours after, his walking destinies returned him into the same neighbourhood again, and again the quiet image of the fireside circle at M.'s—Mrs. M. presiding at it like a Queen Lar, with pretty A. S. at her side—striking irresistibly on his fancy, he makes another call (forgetting that they were 'certainly not to return from the country before that day week') and disappointed a second time, inquires for pen and paper as before: again the book is brought, and in the line just above that in which he is about to print his second name (his re-script)—his first name (scarce dry) looks out upon him like another Sosia, or as if a man should suddenly encounter his own duplicate!—The effect may be conceived. D. made many a good resolution against any such lapses in future. I hope he will not keep them too rigorously.

For with G. D.—to be absent from the body is sometimes (not to speak it profanely) to be present with the Lord. At the very time when, personally encountering thee he passes on with no recognition—or, being stopped, starts like a thing surprised—at that moment, reader, he is on Mount Tabor—or Parnassus—or co-sphered with Plato—or, with Harrington, framing 'immortal commonwealths'—devising some plan of amelioration to thy country, or thy species—— peradventure meditating some individual kindness or courtesy, to be done to *thee thyself*, the returning consciousness of which made him to start so guiltily at thy obtruded personal presence.

D. is delightful anywhere, but he is at the best in such places as these. He cares not much for Bath. He is out of his element at Buxton, at Scarborough, or Harrowgate. The Cam and the Isis are to him 'better than all the waters of Damascus.' On the Muses' hill he is happy, and good as one of the Shepherds on the Delectable Mountains; and when he goes about with you to show you the halls and colleges, you think you have with you the Interpreter at the House Beautiful.

Christ's Hospital
Five-and-thirty Years Ago

IN Mr. Lamb's *Works*, published a year or two since, I find a magnificent eulogy on my old school, * such as it was, or now appears to him to have been, between the years 1782 and 1789. It happens very oddly that my own standing at Christ's was nearly corresponding with his; and, with all gratitude to him for his enthusiasm for the cloisters, I think he has contrived to bring together whatever can be said in praise of them, dropping all the other side of the argument most ingeniously.

I remember L. at school, and can well recollect that he had some peculiar advantages, which I and others of his schoolfellows had not. His friends lived in town, and were near at hand; and he had the privilege of going to see them

* Recollections of Christ's Hospital.

almost as often as he wished, through some invidious distinction, which was denied to us. The present worthy subtreasurer to the Inner Temple can explain how that happened. He had his tea and hot rolls in a morning, while we were battening upon our quarter of a penny loaf—our *crug*—moistened with attenuated small beer, in wooden piggins, smacking of the pitched leathern jack it was poured from. Our Monday's milk porritch, blue and tasteless, and the pease soup of Saturday, coarse and choking, were enriched for him with a slice of 'extraordinary bread and butter,' from the hot loaf of the Temple. The Wednesday's mess of millet, somewhat less repugnant—(we had three banyan to four meat days in the week)—was endeared to his palate with a lump of double-refined, and a smack of ginger (to make it go down the more glibly) or the fragrant cinnamon. In lieu of our *half-pickled* Sundays, or *quite fresh* boiled beef on Thursdays (strong as *caro equina*), with detestable marigolds floating in the pail to poison the broth—our scanty mutton scrags on Friday—and rather more savoury, but grudging, portions of the same flesh, rotten-roasted or rare, on the Tuesdays (the only dish which excited our appetites, and disappointed our stomachs, in almost equal proportion)—he had his hot plate of roast veal, or the more tempting griskin (exotics unknown to our palates), cooked in the paternal kitchen (a great thing), and brought him daily by his maid or aunt! I remember the good old relative (in whom love forbade pride) squatting down upon some odd stone in a bynook of the cloisters, disclosing the viands (of higher regale than those cates which the ravens ministered to the Tishbite); and the contending passions of L. at the unfolding. There was love for the bringer; shame for the thing brought, and the manner of its bringing; sympathy for those who were too many to share in it; and, at top of all, hunger (eldest, strongest of the passions!) predominant, breaking down the stony fences of shame, and awkwardness, and a troubling overconsciousness.

I was a poor friendless boy. My parents, and those who should care for me, were far away. Those few acquaintances of theirs, which they could reckon upon being kind to me in the great city, after a little forced notice, which they had the grace to take of me on my first arrival in town, soon grew tired of my holiday visits. They seemed to them to recur too

often, though I thought them few enough; and another, they all failed me, and I felt myself alone hundred playmates.

O the cruelty of separating a poor lad from homestead! The yearnings which I used to have towa those unfledged years! How, in my dreams, would my town (far in the west) come back, with its church, and and faces! How I would wake weeping, and in the angui my heart exclaim upon sweet Calne in Wiltshire!

To this late hour of my life, I trace impressions left by t. recollections of those friendless holidays. The long warm day of summer never return but they bring with them a gloom from the haunting memory of those *whole-day leaves*, when, by some strange arrangement, we were turned out for the live-long day, upon our own hands, whether we had friends to go to or none. I remember those bathing excursions to the New River which L. recalls with such relish, better, I think, than he can—for he was a home-seeking lad, and did not much care for such water pastimes:—How merrily we would sally forth into the fields; and strip under the first warmth of the sun; and wanton like young dace in the streams; getting us appetites for noon, which those of us that were penniless (our scanty morning crust long since exhausted) had not the means of allaying—while the cattle, and the birds, and the fishes were at feed about us and we had nothing to satisfy our cravings—the very beauty of the day, and the exercise of the pastime, and the sense of liberty, setting a keener edge upon them! How faint and languid, finally, we would return, towards night-fall, to our desired morsel, half-rejoicing, half-reluctant, that the hours of our uneasy liberty had expired!

It was worse in the days of winter, to go prowling abou the streets objectless—shivering at cold windows of prir shops, to extract a little amusement; or haply, as a last re in the hopes of a little novelty, to pay a fifty-times repe visit (where our individual faces should be as well kno the warden as those of his own charges) to the Lion Tower—to whose levee, by courtesy immemorial, prescriptive title to admission.

L.'s governor (so we called the patron who pre the foundation) lived in a manner under his p Any complaint which he had to make was

attended to. This was understood at Christ's, and was an effectual screen to him against the severity of masters, or worse tyranny of the monitors. The oppressions of these young brutes are heart-sickening to call to recollection. I have been called out of my bed, and *waked for the purpose*, in the coldest winter nights—and this not once, but night after night—in my shirt, to receive the discipline of a leathern thong, with eleven other sufferers, because it pleased my callow overseer, when there has been any talking heard after we were gone to bed, to make the six last beds in the dormitory, where the youngest children of us slept, answerable for an offence they neither dared to commit nor had the power to hinder. The same execrable tyranny drove the younger part of us from the fires, when our feet were perishing with snow; and, under the cruellest penalties, forbade the indulgence of a drink of water when we lay in sleepless summer nights fevered with the season and the day's sports.

There was one H——, who, I learned, in after days was seen expiating some maturer offence in the hulks. (Do I flatter myself in fancying that this might be the planter of that name, who suffered—at Nevis, I think, or St. Kitts—some few years since? My friend Tobin was the benevolent instrument of bringing him to the gallows.) This petty Nero actually branded a boy who had offended him with a red-hot iron; and nearly starved forty of us with exacting contributions, to the one half of our bread, to pamper a young ass, which, incredible as it may seem, with the connivance of the nurse's daughter (a young flame of his) he had contrived to smuggle in, and keep upon the leads of the *ward*, as they called our dormitories. This game went on for better than a week, till the foolish beast, not able to fare well but he must cry roast meat—happier than Caligula's minion, could he have kept his own counsel—but, foolisher, alas! than any of his species in the fables—waxing fat, and kicking, in the fulness of bread, one unlucky minute would needs proclaim his good fortune to the world below; and, laying out his simple throat, blew such a ram's-horn blast, as (toppling down the walls of his own Jericho) set concealment any longer at defiance. The client was dismissed, with certain attentions, to Smithfield; but I never understood that the matron underwent any censure on the occasion. This was in the stewardship of L.'s admired Perry.

Under the same *facile* administration, can L. have forgotten the cool impunity with which the nurses used to carry away openly, in open platters, for their own tables, one out of two of every hot joint, which the careful matron had been seeing scrupulously weighed out for our dinners? These things were daily practised in that magnificent apartment which L. (grown connoisseur since, we presume) praises so highly for the grand paintings 'by Verrio, and others,' with which it is 'hung round and adorned.' But the sight of sleek, well-fed blue-coat boys in pictures was, at that time, I believe, little consolatory to him, or us, the living ones, who saw the better part of our provisions carried away before our faces by harpies; and ourselves reduced (with the Trojan in the hall of Dido)

> To feed our mind with idle portraiture.

L. has recorded the repugnance of the school to *gags*, or the fat of fresh beef boiled; and sets it down to some superstition. But these unctuous morsels are never grateful to young palates (children are universally fat-haters), and in strong, coarse, boiled meats, *unsalted*, are detestable. A *gag-eater* in our time was equivalent to a *goule*, and held in equal detestation——suffered under the imputation:

> . . . . 'Twas said
> He ate strange flesh.

He was observed, after dinner, carefully to gather up the remnants left at his table (not many nor very choice fragments, you may credit me)—and, in an especial manner, these disreputable morsels, which he would convey away and secretly stow in the settle that stood at his bedside. None saw when he ate them. It was rumoured that he privately devoured them in the night. He was watched, but no traces of such midnight practices were discoverable. Some reported that on leave-days he had been seen to carry out of the bounds a large blue check handkerchief, full of something. This then must be the accursed thing. Conjecture next was at work to imagine how he could dispose of it. Some said he sold it to the beggars. This belief generally prevailed. He went about moping. None spake to him. No one would play with him. He was excommunicated; put out of the pale of the school. He was too powerful a boy to be beaten, but he underwent every mode of that negative punishment which is more grievous than many stripes. Still he persevered. At length he was observed by two of his schoolfellows, who were determined to get at the secret, and had traced him one leave-day for the purpose, to enter a large worn-out building, such as there exist specimens of in Chancery Lane, which are let out to various scales of pauperism, with open door and a common staircase. After him they silently slunk in, and followed by stealth up four flights, and saw him tap at a poor wicket, which was opened by an aged woman, meanly clad. Suspicion was now ripened into certainty. The informers had secured their victim. They had him in their toils. Accusation was formally preferred, and retribution most signal was looked for. Mr. Hathaway, the then steward (for this happened a little after my time), with that patient sagacity which tempered all his conduct, determined to investigate the matter before he proceeded to sentence. The result was that the supposed mendicants, the receivers or purchasers of the mysterious scraps, turned out to be the parents of——, an honest couple come to decay—whom this seasonable supply had, in all probability, saved from mendicancy; and that this young stork, at the expense of his own good name, had all this while been only feeding the old birds!—The governors on this occasion, much to their honour, voted a present relief to the family of ——, and presented him with a silver medal. The lesson which the steward read upon RASH JUDGMENT, on the occasion of publicly delivering the medal to ——, I believe would not be lost upon his auditory.—I had left school then, but I well remember ——. He was a tall, shambling youth, with a cast in his eye, not at all calculated to conciliate hostile prejudices. I have since seen him carrying a baker's basket. I think I heard he did not do quite so well by himself as he had done by the old folks.

I was a hypochondriac lad; and the sight of a boy in fetters, upon the day of my first putting on the blue clothes, was not exactly fitted to assuage the natural terrors of initiation. I was of tender years, barely turned of seven; and had only read of such things in books, or seen them but in dreams. I was told he had *run away*. This was the punishment for the first offence.—As a novice I was soon after taken to see the dungeons. These were little, square, Bedlam cells, where a boy could just lie at his length upon straw and a blanket—a mattress, I think, was afterwards substituted—with a peep of light, let in askance, from a prison-orifice at top, barely enough to read by. Here the poor boy was locked in by himself all day, without sight of any but the porter who brought him his bread and water—who *might not speak to him;*—or of the beadle, who came twice a week to call him out to receive his periodical chastisement, which was almost welcome, because it separated him for a brief interval from solitude:—and here he was shut up by himself *of nights* out of the reach of any sound, to suffer whatever horrors the weak nerves, and superstition incident to his time of life, might subject him to. * This was the penalty for the second offence. Wouldst thou like, reader, to see what became of him in the next degree?

The culprit, who had been a third time an offender, and whose expulsion was at this time deemed irreversible, was brought forth, as at some solemn *auto da fe*, arrayed in uncouth and most appalling attire—all trace of his late 'watchet weeds' carefully effaced, he was exposed in a jacket resembling those which London lamplighters formerly delighted in, with a cap of the same. The effect of this divestiture was such as the ingenious devisers of it could have anticipated. With his pale and frighted features, it was as if some of those disfigurements in Dante had seized upon him. In this disguisement he was brought into the hall (*L.'s favourite state-room*), where awaited him the whole number of his schoolfellows, whose joint lessons and sports he was thenceforth to share no more; the awful presence of the steward, to be seen for the last time; of the executioner beadle, clad in his state robe for the occasion; and of two faces more, of direr import, because never but in these extremities visible. These were governors; two of whom by choice, or charter, were always accustomed to officiate at these *Ultima Supplicia;* not to mitigate (so at least we understood it), but to enforce the uttermost stripe. Old Bamber Gascoigne, and Peter Aubert, I remember, were colleagues on one occasion, when the beadle turning rather pale, a glass of brandy was ordered to prepare him for the mysteries. The

* One or two instances of lunacy, or attempted suicide, accordingly, at length convinced the governors of the impolicy of this part of the sentence, and the midnight torture to the spirits was dispensed with.—This fancy of dungeons for children was a sprout of Howard's brain; for which (saving the reverence due to Holy Paul) methinks I could willingly spit upon his statue.

scourging was, after the old Roman fashion, long and stately. The lictor accompanied the criminal quite round the hall. We were generally too faint, with attending to the previous disgusting circumstances, to make accurate report with our eyes of the degree of corporal suffering inflicted. Report, of course, gave out the back knotty and livid. After scourging, he was made over, in his *San Benito*, to his friends, if he had any (but commonly such poor runagates were friendless), or to his parish officer, who, to enhance the effect of the scene, had his station allotted to him on the outside of the hall gate.

These solemn pageantries were not played off so often as to spoil the general mirth of the community. We had plenty of exercise and recreation *after* school hours; and, for myself, I must confess, that I was never happier than *in* them. The Upper and the Lower Grammar Schools were held in the same room; and an imaginary line only divided their bounds. Their character was as different as that of the inhabitants on the two sides of the Pyrenees. The Rev. James Boyer was the Upper Master; but the Rev. Matthew Field presided over that portion of the apartment of which I had the good fortune to be a member. We lived a life as careless as birds. We talked and did just what we pleased, and nobody molested us. We carried an accidence, or a grammar, for form; but, for any trouble it gave us, we might take two years in getting through the verbs deponent, and another two in forgetting all that we had learned about them. There was now and then the formality of saying a lesson, but if you had not learned it, a brush across the shoulders (just enough to disturb a fly) was the sole remonstrance. Field never used the rod; and in truth he wielded the cane with no great good-will—holding it 'like a dancer.' It looked in his hands rather like an emblem than an instrument of authority; and an emblem, too, he was ashamed of. He was a good, easy man, that did not care to ruffle his own peace, nor perhaps set any great consideration upon the value of juvenile time. He came among us, now and then, but often stayed away whole days from us; and when he came it made no difference to us—he had his private room to retire to, the short time he stayed, to be out of the sound of our noise. Our mirth and uproar went on. We had classics of our own, without being beholden to 'insolent Greece or haughty Rome,' that passed current

among us—Peter Wilkins—the Adventures of the Hon.
Captain Robert Boyle—the Fortunate Bluecoat Boy—and the
like. Or we cultivated a turn for mechanic and scientific
operations; making little sundials of paper; or weaving those
ingenious parentheses called *cat-cradles;* or making dry peas to
dance upon the end of a tin pipe; or studying the art military
over that laudable game 'French and English,' and a hundred other such devices to pass away the time—mixing the
useful with the agreeable—as would have made the souls of
Rousseau and John Locke chuckle to have seen us.

Matthew Field belonged to that class of modest divines
who affect to mix in equal proportion the *gentleman,* the
scholar, and the *Christian;* but, I know not how, the first
ingredient is generally found to be the predominating dose in
the composition. He was engaged in gay parties, or with his
courtly bow at some episcopal levee, when he should have
been attending upon us. He had for many years the classical
charge of a hundred children, during the four or five first
years of their education, and his very highest form seldom
proceeded further than two or three of the introductory
fables of Phædrus. How things were suffered to go on thus, I
cannot guess. Boyer, who was the proper person to have
remedied these abuses, always affected, perhaps felt, a delicacy in interfering in a province not strictly his own. I have
not been without my suspicions, that he was not altogether
displeased at the contrast we presented to his end of the
school. We were a sort of Helots to his young Spartans. He
would sometimes, with ironic deference, send to borrow a rod
of the Under Master, and then, with Sardonic grin, observe
to one of his upper boys, 'how neat and fresh the twigs
looked.' While his pale students were battering their brains
over Xenophon and Plato, with a silence as deep as that
enjoyed by the Samite, we were enjoying ourselves at our
ease in our little Goshen. We saw a little into the secrets of
his discipline, and the prospect did but the more reconcile us
to our lot. His thunders rolled innocuous for us: his storms
came near, but never touched us; contrary to Gideon's
miracle, while all around were drenched, our fleece was
dry. * His boys turned out the better scholars; we, I suspect,
have the advantage in temper. His pupils cannot speak of
him without something of terror allaying their gratitude; the

* Cowley.

39

remembrance of Field comes back with all the soothing images of indolence, and summer slumbers, and work like play, and innocent idleness, and Elysian exemptions, and life itself a 'playing holiday.'

Though sufficiently removed from the jurisdiction of Boyer, we were near enough (as I have said) to understand a little of his system. We occasionally heard sounds of the *Ululantes*, and caught glances of Tartarus. B. was a rabid pedant. His English style was crampt to barbarism. His Easter anthems (for his duty obliged him to those periodical flights) were grating as scrannel pipes. *—He would laugh, ay, and heartily, but then it must be at Flaccus's quibble about *Rex* —— or at the *tristis serveritas in vultu*, or *inspicere in patinas*, of Terence—thin jests, which at their first broaching could hardly have had *vis* enough to move a Roman muscle. —He had two wigs, both pedantic, but of different omen. The one serene, smiling, fresh powdered, betokening a mild day. The other, an old, discoloured, unkempt, angry caxon, denoting frequent and bloody execution. Woe to the school, when he made his morning appearance in his *passy*, or *passionate wig*. No comet expounded surer.—J. B. had a heavy hand. I have known him double his knotty fist at a poor trembling child (the maternal milk hardly dry upon its lips) with a 'Sirrah, do you presume to set your wits at me?'—Nothing was more common than to see him make a headlong entry into the schoolroom, from his inner recess, or library, and, with turbulent eye, singling out a lad, roar out, 'Od's my life, sirrah' (his favourite adjuration), 'I have a great mind to whip you,'—then, with as sudden a retracting impulse, fling back into his lair—and, after a cooling lapse of some minutes (during which all but the culprit had totally forgotten the context) drive headlong out again, piecing out his imperfect sense, as if it had been some Devil's Litany, with the expletory yell—'*and I* WILL, *too.*'—In his gentler moods, when the *rabidus furor* was assuaged, he had resort to an ingenious method, peculiar, for what I have heard, to

---

* In this and everything B. was the antipodes of his coadjutor. While the former was digging his brains for crude anthems, worth a pig-nut, F. would be recreating his gentlemanly fancy in the more flowery walks of the Muses. A little dramatic effusion of his, under the name of Vertumnus and Pomona, is not yet forgotten by the chroniclers of that sort of literature. It was accepted by Garrick, but the town did not give it their sanction.—B. used to say of it, in a way of half-compliment, half-irony, that it was *too classical for representation*.

himself, of whipping the boy, and reading the Debates, at the same time; a paragraph, and a lash between; which in those times, when parliamentory oratory was most at a height and flourishing in these realms, was not calculated to impress the patient with a veneration for the diffuser graces of rhetoric.

Once, and but once, the uplifted rod was known to fall ineffectual from his hand—when droll squinting W—— having been caught putting the inside of the master's desk to a use for which the architect had clearly not designed it, to justify himself, with great simplicity averred, that *he did not know that the thing had been forewarned.* This exquisite irrecognition of any law antecedent to the *oral* or *declaratory*, struck so irresistibly upon the fancy of all who heard it (the pedagogue himself not excepted)—that remission was unavoidable.

L. has given credit to B.'s great merits as an instructor. Coleridge, in his literary life, has pronounced a more intelligible and ample encomium on them. The author of the Country Spectator doubts not to compare him with the ablest teachers of antiquity. Perhaps we cannot dismiss him better than with the pious ejaculation of C.—when he heard that his old master was on his deathbed: 'Poor J. B.!—may all his faults be forgiven; and may he be wafted to bliss by little cherub boys all head and wings, with no *bottoms* to reproach his sublunary infirmities.'

Under him were many good and sound scholars bred.— First Grecian of my time was Lancelot Pepys Stevens, kindest of boys and men, since Co-grammar-master (and inseparable companion) with Dr. T——e. What an edifying spectacle did this brace of friends present to those who remembered the anti-socialities of their predecessors!—You never met the one by chance in the street without a wonder, which was quickly dissipated by the almost immediate subappearance of the other. Generally arm-in-arm, these kindly coadjutors lightened for each other the toilsome duties of their profession, and when, in advanced age, one found it convenient to retire, the other was not long in discovering that it suited him to lay down the fasces also. Oh, it is pleasant, as it is rare, to find the same arm linked in yours at forty, which at thirteen helped it to turn over the *Cicero De Amicitiâ,* or some tale of Antique Friendship, which the young

41

heart even then was burning to anticipate!—Co-Grecian with S. was Th——, who has since executed with ability various diplomatic functions at the Northern courts. Th—— was a tall, dark, saturnine youth, sparing of speech, with raven locks.—Thomas Fanshaw Middleton followed him (now Bishop of Calcutta), a scholar and a gentleman in his teens. He has the reputation of an excellent critic; and is author (besides the Country Spectator) of a Treatise on the Greek Article, against Sharpe. M. is said to bear his mitre high in India, where the *regni novitas* (I dare say) sufficiently justifies the bearing. A humility quite as primitive as that of Jewel or Hooker might not be exactly fitted to impress the minds of those Anglo-Asiatic diocesans with a reverence for home institutions, and the church which those fathers watered. The manners of M. at school, though firm, were mild and unassuming.—Next to M. (if not senior to him) was Richards, author of the Aboriginal Britons, the most spirited of the Oxford Prize Poems; a pale, studious Grecian. —Then followed poor S——, ill-fated M——! of these the Muse is silent.

> Finding some of Edward's race
> Unhappy, pass their annals by.

Come back into memory, like as thou wert in the day-spring of thy fancies, with hope like a fiery column before thee—the dark pillar not yet turned—Samuel Taylor Coleridge—Logician, Metaphysician, Bard!—How have I seen the casual passer through the Cloisters stand still, entranced with admiration (while he weighed the disproportion between the *speech* and the *garb* of the young Mirandula), to hear thee unfold, in thy deep and sweet intonations, the mysteries of Jamblichus, or Plotinus (for even in those years thou waxedst not pale at such philosophic draughts), or reciting Homer in his Greek, or Pindar——while the walls of the old Grey Friars re-echoed to the accents of the *inspired charity-boy*!—Many were the 'wit-combats' (to dally awhile with the words of old Fuller) between him and C. V. Le G——, 'which two I behold like a Spanish great galleon, and an English man-of-war; Master Coleridge, like the former, was built far higher in learning, solid, but slow in his performances. C. V. L., with the English man-of-war, lesser in bulk, but lighter in sailing, could turn with all tides, tack about, and take advantage of all winds, by the quickness of his wit and invention.'

Nor shalt thou, their compeer, be quickly forgotten, Allen, with the cordial smile, and still more cordial laugh, with which thou wert wont to make the old Cloisters shake, in thy cognition of some poignant jest of theirs; of the anticipation of some more material, and, peradventure practical one, of thine own. Extinct are those smiles, with that beautiful countenance, with which (for thou wert the *Nireus formosus* of the school), in the days of thy maturer waggery, thou didst disarm the wrath of infuriated town-damsel, who, incensed by provoking pinch, turning tigress-like round, suddenly converted by thy angel-look, exchanged the half-formed terrible '*bl*——,' for a gentler greeting— '*bless thy handsome face!*'

Next follow two, who ought to be now alive, and the friends of Elia—the junior Le G—— and F——; who impelled, the former by a roving temper, the latter by too quick a sense of neglect—ill capable of enduring the slights poor Sizars are sometimes subject to in our seats of learning—exchanged their Alma Mater for the camp; perishing, one by climate, and one on the plains of Salamanca:—Le G——, sanguine, volatile, sweet-natured; F——, dogged, faithful, anticipative of insult, warm-hearted, with something of the old Roman height about him.

Fine, frank-hearted Fr——, the present master of Hertford, with Marmaduke T——, mildest of Missionaries—and both my good friends still—close the catalogue of Grecians in my time.

The two Races of Men

THE human species, according to the best theory I can form of it, is composed of two distinct races, *the men who borrow, and the men who lend.* To these two original diversities may be reduced all those impertinent classifications of Gothic and Celtic tribes, white men, black men, red men. All the dwellers upon earth, 'Parthians, and Medes, and Elamites,' flock hither, and do naturally fall in with one or other of these primary distinctions. The infinite superiority of the former,

43

which I choose to designate as the *great race*, is discernible in their figure, port, and a certain instinctive sovereignty. The latter are born degraded. 'He shall serve his brethren.' There is something in the air of one of this cast, lean and suspicious; contrasting with the open, trusting, generous manners of the other.

Observe who have been the greatest borrowers of all ages—Alcibiades—Falstaff—Sir Richard Steele—our late incomparable Brinsley—what a family likeness in all four!

What a careless, even deportment hath your borrower! what rosy gills! what a beautiful reliance on Providence doth he manifest,—taking no more thought than lilies! What contempt for money,—accounting it (yours and mine especially) no better than dross! What a liberal confounding of those pedantic distinctions of *meum* and *tuum!* or rather, what a noble simplification of language (beyond Tooke), resolving these supposed opposites into one clear, intelligible pronoun adjective!—What near approaches doth he make to the primitive *community*,—to the extent of one half of the principle at least.

He is the true taxer who 'calleth all the world up to be taxed'; and the distance is as vast between him and *one of us*, as subsisted between the Augustan Majesty and the poorest obolary Jew that paid it tribute-pittance at Jerusalem!—His exactions, too, have such a cheerful, voluntary air! So far removed from your sour parochial or state-gatherers,—those ink-horn varlets, who carry their want of welcome in their faces! He cometh to you with a smile, and troubleth you with no receipt; confining himself to no set season. Every day is his Candlemas, or his Feast of Holy Michael. He applieth the *lene tormentum* of a pleasant look to your purse,—which to that gentle warmth expands her silken leaves, as naturally as the cloak of the traveller, for which sun and wind contended! He is the true Propontic which never ebbeth! The sea which taketh handsomely at each man's hand. In vain the victim, whom he delighteth to honour, struggles with destiny; he is in the net. Lend therefore cheerfully, O man ordained to lend—that thou lose not in the end, with thy worldly penny, the reversion promised. Combine not preposterously in thine own person the penalties of Lazarus and of Dives!—but, when thou seest the proper authority coming, meet it smilingly, as it were half-way. Come, a handsome sacrifice!

See how light *he* makes of it! Strain not courtesies with a
noble enemy.

Reflections like the foregoing were forced upon my mind
by the death of my old friend, Ralph Bigod, Esq., who parted
this life, on Wednesday evening; dying, as he had lived,
without much trouble. He boasted himself a descendant from
mighty ancestors of that name, who heretofore held ducal
dignities in this realm. In his actions and sentiments he
belied not the stock to which he pretended. Early in life he
found himself invested with ample revenues; which, with
that noble disinterestedness which I have noticed as inherent
in men of the *great race*, he took almost immediate measures
entirely to dissipate and bring to nothing: for there is something revolting in the idea of a king holding a private purse;
and the thoughts of Bigod were all regal. Thus furnished by
the very act of disfurnishment; getting rid of the cumbersome luggage of riches, more apt (as one sings)

> To slacken virtue, and abate her edge,
> Than prompt her to do aught may merit praise,—

he set forth, like some Alexander, upon his great enterprise,
'borrowing and to borrow!'

In his periegesis, or triumphant progress throughout this
island, it has been calculated that he laid a tythe part of the
inhabitants under contribution. I reject this estimate as
greatly exaggerated:—but having had the honour of
accompanying my friend divers times, in his perambulations
about this vast city, I own I was greatly struck at first with
the prodigious number of faces we met who claimed a sort
of respectful acquaintance with us. He was one day so
obliging as to explain the phenomenon. It seems, these were
his tributaries; feeders of his exchequer; gentlemen, his good
friends (as he was pleased to express himself), to whom he
had occasionally been beholden for a loan. Their multitudes
did no way disconcert him. He rather took a pride in num-
bering them; and, with Comus, seemed pleased to be
'stocked with so fair a herd.'

With such sources, it was a wonder how he contrived to
keep his treasury always empty. He did it by force of an
aphorism, which he had often in his mouth, that 'money kept
longer than three days stinks.' So he made use of it while it
was fresh. A good part he drank away (for he was an excel-

¹ent toss-pot); some he gave away, the rest he threw away, literally tossing and hurling it violently from him—as boys do burrs, or as if it had been infectious,—into ponds, or ditches, or deep holes, inscrutable cavities of the earth;—or he would bury it (where he would never seek it again) by a river's side under some bank, which (he would facetiously observe) paid no interest—but out away from him it must go peremptorily, as Hagar's offspring into the wilderness, while it was sweet. He never missed it. The streams were perennial which fed his fisc. When new supplies became necessary, the first person that had the felicity to fall in with him, friend or stranger, was sure to contribute to the deficiency. For Bigod had an *undeniable* way with him. He had a cheerful, open exterior, a quick jovial eye, a bald forehead, just touched with grey (*cana fides*). He anticipated no excuse, and found none. And, waiving for a while my theory as to the *great race*, I would put it to the most untheorising reader, who may at times have disposable coin in his pockets, whether it is not more repugnant to the kindliness of his nature to refuse such a one as I am describing, than to say *no* to a poor petitionary rogue (your bastard borrower), who, by his mumping visnomy, tells you, that he expects nothing better; and, therefore, whose preconceived notions and expectations you do in reality so much less shock in the refusal.

When I think of this man; his fiery glow of heart; his swell of feeling; how magnificent, how *ideal* he was; how great at the midnight hour; and when I compare with him the companions with whom I have associated since, I grudge the saving of a few idle ducats, and think that I am fallen into the society of *lenders*, and *little* men.

To one like Elia, whose treasures are rather cased in leather covers than closed in iron coffers, there is a class of alienators more formidable than that which I have touched upon; I mean your *borrowers of books*—those mutilators of collections, spoilers of the symmetry of shelves, and creators of odd volumes. There is Comberbatch, matchless in his depredations!

That foul gap in the bottom shelf facing you, like a great eye-tooth knocked out—(you are now with me in my little back study in Bloomsbury, reader!)—with the huge Switzer-like tomes on each side (like the Guildhall giants, in their reformed posture, guardant of nothing), once held the tallest of my folios, *Opera Bonaventuræ*, choice and massy divinity, to which its two supporters (school divinity also, but of a lesser calibre,—Bellarmine, and Holy Thomas), showed but as dwarfs,—itself an Ascapart!—*that* Comberbatch abstracted upon the faith of a theory he holds, which is more easy, I confess, for me to suffer by than to refute, namely, that 'the title to property in a book (my Bonaventure, for instance), is in exact ratio to the claimant's powers of understanding and appreciating the same.' Should he go on acting upon this theory, which of our shelves is safe?

The slight vacuum in the left-hand case—two shelves from the ceiling—scarcely distinguishable but by the quick eye of a loser—was whilom the commodious resting-place of Browne on Urn Burial. C. will hardly allege that he knows more about that treatise than I do, who introduced it to him, and was indeed the first (of the moderns) to discover its beauties—but so have I known a foolish lover to praise his mistress in the presence of a rival more qualified to carry her off than himself. Just below, Dodsley's dramas want their fourth volume, where Vittoria Corombona is! The remainder nine are as distasteful as Priam's refuse sons when the Fates *borrowed* Hector. Here stood the Anatomy of Melancholy, in sober state. There loitered the Compleat Angler; quiet as in life, by some stream side. In yonder nook, John Buncle, a widower-volume, with 'eyes closed,' mourns his ravished mate.

One justice I must do my friend, that if he sometimes, like the sea, sweeps away a treasure, at another time, sea-like, he throws up as rich an equivalent to match it. I have a small under-collection of this nature (my friend's gatherings in his various calls), picked up, he has forgotten at what odd places, and deposited with as little memory at mine. I take in these orphans, the twice-deserted. These proselytes of the gate are welcome as the true Hebrews. There they stand in conjunction; natives, and naturalised. The latter seem as little disposed to inquire out their true lineage as I am.—I charge no warehouse-room for these deodands, nor shall ever put myself to the ungentlemanly trouble of advertising a sale of them to pay expenses.

To lose a volume to C. carries some sense and meaning in it. You are sure that he will make one hearty meal on your viands, if he can give no account of the platter after it. But what moved thee, wayward, spiteful K., to be so importunate to carry off with thee, in spite of tears and adjurations to thee to forbear, the Letters of that princely woman, the thrice noble Margaret Newcastle?—knowing at the time, and knowing that I knew also, thou most assuredly wouldst never turn over one leaf of the illustrious folio:—what but the mere spirit of contradiction, and childish love of getting the better of thy friend?—Then, worst cut of all! to transport it with thee to the Gallican land—

Unworthy land to harbour such a sweetness,
A virtue in which all ennobling thoughts dwelt,
Pure thoughts, kind thoughts, high thoughts, her sex's wonder!

——hadst thou not thy play-books, and books of jests and fancies, about thee, to keep thee merry, even as thou keepest all companies with thy quips and mirthful tales? Child of the Green-room, it was unkindly done of thee. Thy wife, too, that part-French, better-part Englishwoman!—that *she* could fix upon no other treatise to bear away, in kindly token of remembering us, than the works of Fulke Greville, Lord Brook—of which no Frenchman, nor woman of France, Italy, or England, was ever by nature constituted to comprehend a tittle!—*Was there not Zimmerman on Solitude?*

Reader, if haply thou art blest with a moderate collection, be shy of showing it; or if thy heart overfloweth to lend them, lend thy books; but let it be to such a one as S. T. C.—he will return them (generally anticipating the time appointed) with usury; enriched with annotations tripling their value. I have had experience. Many are these precious MSS. of his—(in *matter* oftentimes, and almost in *quantity* not unfrequently, vying with the originals) in no very clerkly hand—legible in my Daniel; in old Burton; in Sir Thomas Browne; and those abstruser cogitations of the Greville, now, alas! wandering in Pagan lands. I counsel thee, shut not thy heart, nor thy library, against S. T. C.

New Year's Eve

EVERY man hath two birthdays: two days, at least, in every year, which set him upon revolving the lapse of time, as it affects his mortal duration. The one is that which in an especial manner he termeth *his*. In the gradual desuetude of old observances, this custom of solemnising our proper birthday hath nearly passed away, or is left to children, who reflect nothing at all about the matter, nor understand anything in it beyond cake and orange. But the birth of a New Year is of an interest too wide to be pretermitted by king or cobbler. No one ever regarded the first of January with indifference. It is that from which all date their time and count upon what is left. It is the nativity of our common Adam.

Of all sound of all bells—(bells, the music nighest bordering upon heaven)—most solemn and touching is the peal which rings out the Old Year. I never hear it without a gathering-up of my mind to a concentration of all the images that have been diffused over the past twelvemonth; all I have done or suffered, performed or neglected—in that regretted time. I begin to know its worth, as when a person dies. It takes a personal colour; nor was it a poetical flight in a contemporary, when he exclaimed,

I saw the skirts of the departing Year.

It is no more than what in sober sadness every one of us seems to be conscious of, in that awful leave-taking. I am sure I felt it, and all felt it with me, last night; though some of my companions affected rather to manifest an exhilaration at the birth of the coming year, than any very tender regrets for the decease of its predecessor. But I am none of those who

Welcome the coming, speed the parting guest.

I am naturally, beforehand, shy of novelties; new books, new faces, new years,—from some mental twist which makes it difficult in me to face the prospective. I have almost ceased to hope; and am sanguine only in the prospects of other

49

(former) years. I plunge into foregone visions and conclusions. I encounter pell-mell with past disappointments. I
am armour-proof against old discouragements. I forgive, or
overcome in fancy, old adversaries. I play over again *for love*,
as the gamesters phrase it, games, for which I once paid so
dear. I would scarce now have any of those untoward
accidents and events of my life reversed. I would no more
alter them than the incidents of some well-contrived novel.
Methinks it is better that I should have pined away seven of
my goldenest years, when I was thrall to the fair hair, and
fairer eyes of Alice W——n, than that so passionate a love-
adventure should be lost. It was better that our family should
have missed that legacy, which old Dorrell cheated us of,
than that I should have at this moment two thousand pounds
in banco, and be without the idea of that specious old rogue.

In a degree beneath manhood, it is my infirmity to look
back upon those early days. Do I advance a paradox, when I
say, that, skipping over the intervention of forty years, a man
may have leave to love *himself*, without the imputation of
self-love?

If I know aught of myself, no one whose mind is intro-
spective—and mine is painfully so—can have a less respect
for his present identity than I have for the man Elia. I know
him to be light, and vain, and humoursome; a notorious
* * * ; addicted to * * * * ; averse from counsel, neither
taking it nor offering it;— * * * besides; a stammering
buffoon; what you will; lay it on, and spare not: I subscribe
to it all, and much more than thou canst be willing to lay at
his door;—but for the child Elia, that 'other me,' there, in
the background—I must take leave to cherish the remembrance of that young master—with as little reference, I
protest, to this stupid changeling of five-and-forty, as if it had
been a child of some other house, and not of my parents. I
can cry over its patient small-pox at five, and rougher medi-
caments. I can lay its poor fevered head upon the sick pillow
at Christ's, and wake with it in surprise at the gentle posture
of maternal tenderness hanging over it, that unknown had
watched its sleep. I know how it shrank from any the least
colour of falsehood. God help thee, Elia, how art thou
changed!—Thou art sophisticated.—I know how honest, how
courageous (for a weakling) it was—how religious, how
imaginative, how hopeful! From what have I not fallen, if

the child I remember was indeed myself,—and not some dissembling guardian, presenting a false identity, to give the rule to my unpractised steps, and regulate the tone of my moral being!

That I am fond of indulging, beyond a hope of sympathy, in such retrospection, may be the symptom of some sickly idiosyncrasy. Or is it owing to another cause: simply, that being without wife or family, I have not learned to project myself enough out of myself; and having no offspring of my own to dally with, I turn back upon memory, and adopt my own early idea, as my heir and favourite? If these speculations seem fantastical to thee, reader (a busy man perchance), if I tread out of the way of thy sympathy, and am singularly conceited only, I retire, impenetrable to ridicule, under the phantom cloud of Elia.

The elders, with whom I was brought up, were of a character not likely to let slip the sacred observance of any old institution; and the ringing out of the Old Year was kept by them with circumstances of peculiar ceremony.—In those days the sound of those midnight chimes, though it seemed to raise hilarity in all around me, never failed to bring a train of pensive imagery into my fancy. Yet I then scarce conceived what it meant, or thought of it as a reckoning that concerned me. Not childhood alone, but the young man till thirty, never feels practically that he is mortal. He knows it indeed, and, if need were, he could preach a homily on the fragility of life; but he brings it not home to himself, any more than in a hot June we can appropriate to our imagination the freezing days of December. But now, shall I confess a truth?—I feel these audits but too powerfully. I begin to count the probabilities of my duration, and to grudge at the expenditure of moments and shortest periods, like misers' farthings. In proportion as the years both lessen and shorten, I set more count upon their periods, and would fain lay my ineffectual finger upon the spoke of the great wheel. I am not content to pass away 'like a weaver's shuttle.' Those metaphors solace me not, nor sweeten the unpalatable draught of mortality. I care not to be carried with the tide, that smoothly bears human life to eternity; and reluct at the inevitable course of destiny. I am in love with this green earth; the face of town and country; the unspeakable rural solitudes, and the sweet security of streets. I would set up my tabernacle here. I am content to stand still at the age to which I am arrived; I, and my friends: to be no younger, no richer, no handsomer. I do not want to be weaned by age; or drop, like mellow fruit, as they say, into the grave.—Any alteration, on this earth of mine, in diet or in lodging, puzzles and discomposes me. My household-gods plant a terrible fixed foot, and are not rooted up without blood. They do not willingly seek Lavinian shores. A new state of being staggers me.

Sun, and sky, and breeze, and solitary walks, and summer holidays, and the greenness of fields, and the delicious juices of meats and fishes, and society, and the cheerful glass, and candle-light, and fireside conversations, and innocent vanities, and jests, and *irony itself*—do these things go out with life?

Can a ghost laugh, or shake his gaunt sides, when you are pleasant with him?

And you, my midnight darlings, my Folios! must I part with the intense delight of having you (huge armfuls) in my embraces? Must knowledge come to me, if it come at all, by some awkward experiment of intuition, and no longer by this familiar process of reading?

Shall I enjoy friendships there, wanting the smiling indications which point me to them here,—the recognisable face—the 'sweet assurance of a look'?—

In winter this intolerable disinclination to dying—to give it its mildest name—does more especially haunt and beset me. In a genial August noon, beneath a sweltering sky, death is almost problematic. At those times do such poor snakes as myself enjoy an immortality. Then we expand and burgeon. Then we are as strong again, as valiant again, as wise again, and a great deal taller. The blast that nips and shrinks me, puts me in thoughts of death. All things allied to the insubstantial, wait upon that master feeling; cold, numbness, dreams, perplexity; moonlight itself, with its shadowy and spectral appearances,—that cold ghost of the sun, or Phœbus' sickly sister, like that innutritious one denounced in the Canticles:—I am none of her minions—I hold with the Persian.

Whatsoever thwarts, or puts me out of my way, brings death into my mind. All partial evils, like humours, run into that capital plague-sore.—I have heard some profess an indifference to life. Such hail the end of their existence as a port of refuge; and speak of the grave as of some soft arms, in which they may slumber as on a pillow. Some have wooed death—but out upon thee, I say, thou foul, ugly phantom! I detest, abhor, execrate, and (with Friar John) give thee to six score thousand devils, as in no instance to be excused or tolerated, but shunned as an universal viper; to be branded, proscribed, and spoken evil of! In no way can I be brought to digest thee, thou thin, melancholy *Privation*, or more frightful and confounding *Positive!*

Those antidotes, prescribed against the fear of thee, are altogether frigid and insulting, like thyself. For what satisfaction hath a man, that he shall 'lie down with kings and emperors in death,' who in his lifetime never greatly coveted the society of such bed-fellows?—or, forsooth, that 'so shall the fairest face appear'?—why, to comfort me, must Alice W—n be a goblin? More than all, I conceive disgust at those impertinent and misbecoming familiarities inscribed upon your ordinary tombstones. Every dead man must take upon himself to be lecturing me with his odious truism, that 'Such as he now is I must shortly be.' Not so shortly, friend, perhaps as thou imaginest. In the meantime I am alive. I move about. I am worth twenty of thee. Know thy betters! Thy New Years' days are past. I survive, a jolly candidate for 1821. Another cup of wine—and while that turncoat bell, that just now mournfully chanted the obsequies of 1820 departed, with changed notes lustily rings in a successor, let us attune to its peal the song made on a like occasion, by hearty, cheerful Mr. Cotton.

THE NEW YEAR

Hark, the cock crows, and yon bright star
Tells us, the day himself's not far;
And see where, breaking from the night,
He gilds the western hills with light.
With him old Janus doth appear,
Peeping into the future year,
With such a look as seems to say,
The prospect is not good that way.
Thus do we rise ill sights to see,
And 'gainst ourselves to prophesy;

When the prophetic fear of things
A more tormenting mischief brings,
More full of soul-tormenting gall
Than direst mischiefs can befall.
But stay! but stay! methinks my sight,
Better inform'd by clearer light,
Discerns sereneness in that brow,
That all contracted seem'd but now.
His revers'd face may show distaste,
And frown upon the ills are past;
But that which this way looks is clear,
And smiles upon the New-born Year.
He looks too from a place so high,
The year lies open to his eye;
And all the moments open are
To the exact discoverer.
Yet more and more he smiles upon
The happy revolution.

Why should we then suspect or fear
The influences of a year,
So smiles upon us the first morn,
And speaks us good so soon as born?
Plague on't! the last was ill enough,
This cannot but make better proof;
Or, at the worst, as we brush'd through
The last, why so we may this too;
And then the next in reason shou'd
Be superexcellently good:
For the worst ills (we daily see)
Have no more perpetuity
Than the best fortunes that do fall;
Which also bring us wherewithal
Longer their being to support,
Than those do of the other sort:
And who has one good year in three,
And yet repines a destiny,
Appears ungrateful in the case,
And merits not the good he has.
Then let us welcome the New Guest
With lusty brimmers of the best:
Mirth always should Good Fortune meet,
And renders e'en Disaster sweet:
And though the Princess turn her back,
Let us but line ourselves with sack,

> We better shall by far hold out,
> Till the next Year she face about.

How say you, reader—do not these verses smack of the rough magnanimity of the old English vein? Do they not fortify like a cordial; enlarging the heart, and productive of sweet blood, and generous spirits, in the concoction? Where be those puling fears of death, just now expressed or affected? —Passed like a cloud—absorbed in the purging sunlight of clear poetry—clean washed away by a wave of genuine Helicon, your only Spa for these hypochondries—And now another cup of the generous! and a merry New Year, and many of them to you all, my masters!

Mrs. Battle's Opinions on Whist

'A CLEAR fire, a clean hearth, and the rigour of the game.' This was the celebrated *wish* of old Sarah Battle (now with God), who, next to her devotions, loved a good game of whist. She was none of your lukewarm gamesters, your half-and-half players, who have no objection to take a hand, if you want one to make up a rubber; who affirm that they have no pleasure in winning; that they like to win one game and lose another; that they can while away an hour very agreeably at a card-table, but are indifferent whether they play or no; and will desire an adversary, who has slipped a wrong card, to take it up and play another. These insufferable triflers are the curse of a table. One of these flies will spoil a whole pot. Of such it may be said that they do not play at cards, but only play at playing at them.

Sarah Battle was none of that breed. She detested them, as I do, from her heart and soul, and would not, save upon a striking emergency, willingly seat herself at the same table with them. She loved a thorough-paced partner, a determined enemy. She took, and gave, no concessions. She hated favours. She never made a revoke, nor ever passed it over in her adversary without exacting the utmost forfeiture. She fought a good fight: cut and thrust. She held not her good sword (her cards) 'like a dancer.' She sate bolt upright; and neither showed you her cards, nor desired to see yours. All people have their blind side—their superstitions; and I have heard her declare, under the rose, that hearts was her favourite suit.

I never in my life—and I knew Sarah Battle many of the best years of it—saw her take out her snuff-box when it was her turn to play; or snuff a candle in the middle of a game; or ring for a servant, till it was fairly over. She never introduced, or connived at, miscellaneous conversation during its process. As she emphatically observed, cards were cards; and if I ever saw unmingled distaste in her fine last-century countenance, it was at the airs of a young gentleman of a literary turn, who had been with difficulty persuaded to take a hand; and who, in his excess of candour, declared, that he thought there was no harm in unbending the mind now and then, after serious studies, in recreations of that kind! She could not bear to have her noble occupation, to which she wound up her faculties, considered in that light. It was her business, her duty, the thing she came into the world to do,—and she did it. She unbent her mind afterwards over a book.

Pope was her favourite author: his Rape of the Lock her favourite work. She once did me the favour to play over with me (with the cards) his celebrated game of Ombre in that poem; and to explain to me how far it agreed with, and in what points it would be found to differ from, tradrille. Her illustrations were apposite and poignant; and I had the pleasure of sending the substance of them to Mr. Bowles; but I suppose they came too late to be inserted among his ingenious notes upon that author.

Quadrille, she has often told me, was her first love; but whist had engaged her maturer esteem. The former, she said, was showy and specious, and likely to allure young persons. The uncertainty and quick shifting of partners—a thing which the constancy of whist abhors; the dazzling supremacy and regal investiture of Spadille—absurd, as she justly observed, in the pure aristocracy of whist, where his crown and garter gave him no proper power above his brother-nobility of the Aces;—the giddy vanity, so taking to the inexperienced, of playing alone; above all, the overpowering attractions of a *Sans Prendre Vole*,—to the triumph of which there is certainly nothing parallel or approaching, in the contingencies of whist;—all these, she would say, make quadrille a game of captivation to the young and enthusiastic. But whist was the *solider* game: that was her word. It was a long meal; not, like quadrille, a feast of snatches. One or two rubbers might co-extend in duration with an evening. They gave time to form rooted friendships, to cultivate steady enmities. She despised the chance-started, capricious, and ever-fluctuating alliances of the other. The skirmishes of quadrille, she would say, reminded her of the petty ephemeral embroilments of the little Italian states, depicted by Machiavel: perpetually changing postures and connexions; bitter foes to-day, sugared darlings to-morrow; kissing and scratching in a breath;—but the wars of whist were comparable to the long, steady, deep-rooted, rational antipathies of the great French and English nations.

A grave simplicity was what she chiefly admired in her favourite game. There was nothing silly in it, like the nob in cribbage—nothing superfluous. No *flushes*—that most irrational of all pleas that a reasonable being can set up:—that any one should claim four by virtue of holding cards of the same mark and colour, without reference to the playing of the game, or the individual worth or pretensions of the cards themselves! She held this to be a solecism; as pitiful an ambition at cards as alliteration is in authorship. She despised superficiality, and looked deeper than the colours of things.—Suits were soldiers, she would say, and must have an uniformity of array to distinguish them: but what should we say to a foolish squire, who should claim a merit from dressing up his tenantry in red jackets, that never were to be marshalled—never to take the field?—She even wished that whist were more simple than it is; and, in my mind, would have stripped it of some appendages, which, in the state of human frailty, may be venially, and even commendably, allowed of. She saw no reason for the deciding of the trump by the turn of the card. Why not one suit always trumps?—Why two colours, when the mark of the suits would have sufficiently distinguished them without it?—

'But the eye, my dear Madam, is agreeably refreshed with the variety. Man is not the creature of pure reason—he must have his senses delightfully appealed to. We see it in Roman Catholic countries, where the music and the paintings draw in many to worship, whom your Quaker spirit of unsensualising would have kept out.—You yourself have a pretty collection of paintings—but confess to me, whether, walking in your gallery at Sandham, among those clear Vandykes, or among the Paul Potters in the ante-room, you ever felt your bosom glow with an elegant delight, at all comparable to *that* you have it in your power to experience most evenings over a well-arranged assortment of the court-cards?—the pretty antic habits, like heralds in a procession—the gay triumph-assuring scarlets—the contrasting deadly-killing sables—the "hoary majesty of spades"—Pam in all his glory!—

'All these might be dispensed with; and with their naked names upon the drab pasteboard, the game might go on very well pictureless. But the *beauty* of cards would be extinguished for ever. Stripped of all that is imaginative in them, they must degenerate into mere gambling. Imagine a dull deal board, or drum head, to spread them on, instead of that nice verdant carpet (next to nature's), fittest arena for those courtly combatants to play their gallant jousts and turneys in!—Exchange those delicately-turned ivory markers—(work of Chinese artist, unconscious of their symbol,—or as profanely slighting their true application as the arrantest Ephesian journeyman that turned out those little shrines for the goddess)—exchange them for little bits of leather (our ancestors' money) or chalk and a slate!'—

The old lady, with a smile, confessed the soundness of my logic; and to her approbation of my arguments on her favourite topic that evening, I have always fancied myself indebted for the legacy of a curious cribbage-board, made of the finest Sienna marble, which her maternal uncle (old Walter Plumer, whom I have elsewhere celebrated) brought with him from Florence:—this, and a trifle of five hundred pounds, came to me at her death.

The former bequest (which I do not least value) I have kept with religious care; though she herself, to confess a truth, was never greatly taken with cribbage. It was an essentially vulgar game, I have heard her say,—disputing with her uncle, who was very partial to it. She could never heartily bring her mouth to pronounce '*Go*'—or '*That's a go.*' She called it an ungrammatical game. The pegging teased her. I once knew her to forfeit a rubber (a five-dollar stake) because she would not take advantage of the turn-up knave, which would have given it her, but which she must have claimed by the disgraceful tenure of declaring '*two for his heels.*' There is something extremely genteel in this sort of self-denial. Sarah Battle was a gentlewoman born.

Piquet she held the best game at the cards for two persons, though she would ridicule the pedantry of the terms—such as pique—repique—the capot—they savoured (she thought) of affectation. But games for two, or even three, she never greatly cared for. She loved the quadrate, or square. She would argue thus:—Cards are warfare: the ends are gain with glory. But cards are war, in disguise of a sport: when single adversaries encounter, the ends proposed are too palpable. By themselves it is too close a fight; with spectators it is not much bettered. No looker-on can be interested, except for a bet, and then it is a mere affair of money; he cares not for your luck *sympathetically*, or for your play.—Three are still worse; a mere naked war of every man against every man, as in cribbage, without league or alliance; or a rotation of petty and contradictory interests, a succession of heartless leagues, and not much more hearty infractions of them, as in tradrille.—But in square games (*she meant whist*), all that is possible to be attained in card-playing is accomplished. There are the incentives of profit with honour, common to every species—though the *latter* can be but very imperfectly enjoyed in those other games, where the spectator is only feebly a participator. But the parties in whist are spectators and principals too. They are a theatre to themselves, and a looker-on is not wanted. He is rather worse than nothing, and an impertinence. Whist abhors neutrality, or interests beyond its sphere. You glory in some surprising stroke of skill or fortune, not because a cold—or even an interested— bystander witnesses it, but because your *partner* sympathises in the contingency. You win for two. You triumph for two. Two are exalted. Two again are mortified; which divides their disgrace, as the conjunction doubles (by taking off the invidiousness) your glories. Two losing to two are better reconciled, than one to one in that close butchery. The hostile feeling is weakened by multiplying the channels. War becomes a civil game. By such reasonings as these the old lady was accustomed to defend her favourite pastime.

No inducement could ever prevail upon her to play at any game, where chance entered into the composition, *for nothing*. Chance, she would argue—and here again, admire the subtlety of her conclusion;—chance is nothing, but where something else depends upon it. It is obvious that cannot be *glory*. What rational cause of exultation could it give to a man to turn up size ace a hundred times together by himself? or before spectators, where no stake was depending. Make a lottery of a hundred thousand tickets with but one fortunate number—and what possible principle of our nature, except stupid wonderment, could it gratify to gain that number as many times successively, without a prize? Therefore she disliked the mixture of chance in backgammon, where it was not played for money. She called it foolish, and those people idiots, who were taken with a lucky hit under such circumstances. Games of pure skill were as little to her fancy. Played for a stake, they were a mere system of over-reaching. Played for glory, they were a mere setting of one man's wit—his memory, or combination-faculty rather—against another's; like a mock-engagement at a review, bloodless and profitless. She could not conceive a *game* wanting the spritely infusion of chance, the handsome excuses of good fortune. Two people playing at chess in a corner of a room, while whist was stirring in the centre, would inspire her with insufferable horror and ennui. Those well-cut similitudes of Castles, and Knights, the *imagery* of the board, she would argue (and I think in this case justly), were entirely misplaced and senseless. Those hard head-contests can in no instance ally with the fancy. They reject form and colour. A pencil and dry slate (she used to say) were the proper arena for such combatants.

To those puny objectors against cards, as nurturing the bad passions, she would retort, that man is a gaming animal. He must be always trying to get the better in something or other:—that this passion can scarcely be more safely expended than upon a game at cards: that cards are a temporary illusion; in truth, a mere drama; for we do but *play* at being mightily concerned, where a few idle shillings are at stake, yet, during the illusion, we *are* as mightily concerned as those whose stake is crowns and kingdoms. They are a sort of dream-fighting; much ado; great battling, and little bloodshed; mighty means for disproportioned ends; quite as diverting, and a great deal more innoxious, than many of those more serious *games* of life, which men play, without esteeming them to be such.—

With great deference to the old lady's judgment in these matters, I think I have experienced some moments in my life, when playing at cards *for nothing* has even been agreeable. When I am in sickness, or not in the best spirits, I sometimes call for the cards, and play a game at piquet *for love* with my cousin Bridget—Bridget Elia.

I grant there is something sneaking in it; but with a toothache, or a sprained ankle,—when you are subdued and humble,—you are glad to put up with an inferior spring of action.

There is such a thing in nature, I am convinced, as *sick whist*.

I grant it is not the highest style of man—I deprecate the manes of Sarah Battle—she lives not, alas! to whom I should apologise.

At such times, those *terms* which my old friend objected to, come in as something admissible.—I love to get a tierce or a quatorze, though they mean nothing. I am subdued to an inferior interest. Those shadows of winning amuse me.

That last game I had with my sweet cousin (I capotted her)—(dare I tell thee, how foolish I am?)—I wished it might have lasted for ever, though we gained nothing, and lost nothing, though it was a mere shade of play: I would be content to go on in that idle folly for ever. The pipkin should be ever boiling, that was to prepare the gentle lenitive to my foot, which Bridget was doomed to apply after the game was over: and, as I do not much relish appliances, there it should ever bubble. Bridget and I should be ever playing.

A Chapter on Ears

I HAVE no ear.—Mistake me not, reader—nor imagine that I am by nature destitute of those exterior twin appendages, hanging ornaments, and (architecturally speaking) handsome volutes to the human capital. Better my mother had never borne me.—I am, I think, rather delicately than copiously provided with those conduits; and I feel no disposition to envy the mule for his plenty, or the mole for her exactness, in those ingenious labyrinthine inlets—those indispensable side-intelligencers.

Neither have I incurred, or done anything to incur, with Defoe, that hideous disfigurement, which constrained him to draw upon assurance—to feel 'quite unabashed,' and at ease upon that article. I was never, I thank my stars, in the pillory; nor, if I read them aright, is it within the compass of my destiny, that I ever should be.

When therefore I say that I have no ear, you will understand me to mean—*for music.* To say that this heart never melted at the concord of sweet sounds, would be a foul self-libel. '*Water parted from the sea*' never fails to move it strangely. So does '*In infancy.*' But they were used to be sung at her harpsichord (the old-fashioned instrument in vogue in those days) by a gentlewoman—the gentlest, sure, that ever merited the appellation—the sweetest—why should I hesitate to name Mrs. S——, once the blooming Fanny Weatheral of the Temple—who had power to thrill the soul of Elia, small imp as he was, even in his long coats; and to make him glow, tremble, and blush with a passion, that not faintly indicated the dayspring of that absorbing sentiment which was afterwards destined to overwhelm and subdue his nature quite for Alice W——n.

I even think that *sentimentally* I am disposed to harmony. But *organically* I am incapable of a tune. I have been practising '*God save the King*' all my life; whistling and humming of it over to myself in solitary corners; and am not yet arrived, they tell me, within many quavers of it. Yet hath the loyalty of Elia never been impeached.

I am not without suspicion, that I have an undeveloped faculty of music within me. For thrumming, in my wild way, on my friend A.'s piano, the other morning, while he was engaged in an adjoining parlour,—on his return he was pleased to say, '*he thought it could not be the maid!*' On his first surprise at hearing the keys touched in somewhat an airy and masterful way, not dreaming of me, his suspicions had lighted on *Jenny.* But a grace, snatched from a superior refinement, soon convinced him that some being—technically perhaps deficient, but higher informed from a principle common to all the fine arts—had swayed the keys to a mood which Jenny, with all her (less cultivated) enthusiasm, could never have elicited from them. I mention this as a proof of my friend's penetration, and not with any view of disparaging Jenny.

Scientifically I could never be made to understand (yet have I taken some pains) what a note in music is; or how one note should differ from another. Much less in voices can I distinguish a soprano from a tenor. Only sometimes the thorough-bass I contrive to guess at, from its being super-eminently harsh and disagreeable. I tremble, however, for my misapplication of the simplest terms of *that* which I disclaim. While I profess my ignorance, I scarce know what to *say* I am ignorant of. I hate, perhaps, by misnomers. *Sostenuto* and *adagio* stand in the like relation of obscurity to me; and *Sol, Fa, Mi, Re*, is as conjuring as *Baralipton*.

It is hard to stand alone in an age like this,—(constituted to the quick and critical perception of all harmonious combinations, I verily believe, beyond all preceding ages, since Jubal stumbled upon the gamut,) to remain, as it were, singly unimpressible to the magic influences of an art, which is said to have such an especial stroke at soothing, elevating, and refining the passions.—Yet, rather than break the candid current of my confessions, I must avow to you, that I have received a great deal more pain than pleasure from this so cried-up faculty.

I am constitutionally susceptible of noises. A carpenter's hammer, in a warm summer noon, will fret me into more than midsummer madness. But those unconnected, unset sounds are nothing to the measured malice of music. The ear is passive to those single strokes; willingly enduring stripes while it hath no task to con. To music it cannot be passive. It will strive—mine at least will—spite of its inaptitude, to thrid the maze; like an unskilled eye painfully poring upon hieroglyphics. I have sat through an Italian Opera, till, for sheer pain, and inexplicable anguish, I have rushed out into the noisiest places of the crowded streets, to solace myself with sounds, which I was not obliged to follow, and get rid of the distracting torment of endless, fruitless, barren attention! I take refuge in the unpretending assemblage of honest common-life sounds;—and the purgatory of the Enraged Musician becomes my paradise.

I have sat at an Oratorio (that profanation of the purposes of the cheerful playhouse) watching the faces of the auditory in the pit (what a contrast to Hogarth's Laughing Audience!) immovable, or affecting some faint emotion—till (as some have said, that our occupations in the next world will be but a shadow of what delighted us in this) I have imagined myself in some cold Theatre in Hades, where some of the *forms* of the earthly one should be kept up, with none of the *enjoyment;* or like that

> ——Party in a parlour
> All silent, and all damned.

Above all, those insufferable concertos, and pieces of music, as they are called, do plague and embitter my apprehension.—Words are something; but to be exposed to an endless battery of mere sounds; to be long a dying; to lie stretched upon a rack of roses; to keep up languor by unintermitted effort; to pile honey upon sugar, and sugar upon honey, to an interminable tedious sweetness; to fill up sound with feeling, and strain ideas to keep pace with it; to gaze on empty frames, and be forced to make the pictures for yourself; to read a book, *all stops*, and be obliged to supply the verbal matter; to invent extempore tragedies to answer to the vague gestures of an inexplicable rambling mime—these are faint shadows of what I have undergone from a series of the ablest-executed pieces of this empty *instrumental music.*

I deny not, that in the opening of a concert, I have experienced something vastly lulling and agreeable:—afterwards followeth the languor and the oppression.—Like that disappointing book in Patmos; or, like the comings on of melancholy, described by Burton, doth music make her first insinuating approaches:—'Most pleasant it is to such as are melancholy given to walk alone in some solitary grove, betwixt wood and water, by some brook side, and to meditate upon some delightsome and pleasant subject, which shall affect him most, *amabilis insania*, and *mentis gratissimus error.* A most incomparable delight to build castles in the air, to go smiling to themselves, acting an infinite variety of parts, which they suppose, and strongly imagine, they act, or that they see done.—So delightsome these toys at first, they could spend whole days and nights without sleep, even whole years, in such contemplations, and fantastical meditations, which are like so many dreams, and will hardly be drawn from them—winding and unwinding themselves as so many clocks, and still pleasing their humours, until at the last the SCENE TURNS UPON A SUDDEN, and they being now habitated to such meditations and solitary places, can endure no company, can think of nothing but harsh and distasteful subjects. Fear, sorrow, suspicion, *subrusticus pudor*, discontent, cares, and weariness of life, surprise them on a sudden and they can think of nothing else; continually suspecting, no sooner are their eyes open, but this infernal plague of melancholy seizeth on them, and terrifies their souls, representing some dismal object to their minds; which now, by no means, no labour, no persuasions, they can avoid, they cannot be rid of, they cannot resist.'

Something like this 'SCENE TURNING' I have experienced at the evening parties, at the house of my good Catholic friend *Nov*——; who, by the aid of a capital organ, himself the most finished of players, converts his drawing-room into a chapel, his week days into Sundays, and these latter into minor heavens. *

When my friend commences upon one of those solemn anthems, which peradventure struck upon my heedless ear, rambling in the side aisles of the dim Abbey, some five-and-thirty years since, waking a new sense, and putting a soul of old religion into my young apprehension—(whether it be *that*, in which the Psalmist, weary of the persecutions of bad men, wisheth to himself dove's wings—or *that other*, which, with a like measure of sobriety and pathos, inquireth by what means the young man shall best cleanse his mind)—a holy calm pervadeth me.—I am for the time

——rapt above earth,
And possess joys not promised at my birth.

But when this master of the spell, not content to have laid a soul prostrate, goes on, in his power, to inflict more bliss than lies in her capacity to receive,—impatient to overcome her 'earthly' with his 'heavenly,'—still pouring in, for protracted hours, fresh waves and fresh from the sea of sound, or from that inexhausted *German* ocean, above which, in triumphant progress, dolphin-seated, ride those Arions *Haydn* and *Mozart*, with their attendant Tritons, *Bach*, *Beethoven*, and a countless tribe, whom to attempt to reckon up would but plunge me again in the deeps,—I stagger under the weight of harmony, reeling to and fro at my wits' end;—clouds, as of frankincense, oppress me—priests, altars, cen-

---

* I have been there, and still would go;
'Tis like a little heaven below.—Dr. WATTS.

sers, dazzle before me—the genius of *his* religion hath me in her toils—a shadowy triple tiara invests the brow of my friend, late so naked, so ingenuous—he is Pope,—and by him sits, like as in the anomaly of dreams, a she-Pope too,— tri-coroneted like himself!—I am converted, and yet a Protestant;—at once *malleus hereticorum*, and myself grand heresiarch: or three heresies centre in my person:—I am Marcion, Ebion, and Cerinthus—Gog and Magog—what not?—till the coming in of the friendly supper-tray dissipates the figment, and a draught of true Lutheran beer (in which chiefly my friend shows himself no bigot) at once reconciles me to the rationalities of a purer faith; and restores to me the genuine unterrifying aspects of my pleasant-countenanced host and hostess.

All Fools' Day

THE compliments of the season to my worthy masters, and a merry first of April to us all!

Many happy returns of this day to you—and you—and *you*, Sir—nay, never frown, man, nor put a long face upon the matter. Do not we know one another? what need of ceremony among friends? we have all a touch of *that same*—you understand me—a speck of the motley. Beshrew the man who on such a day as this, the *general festival*, should affect to stand aloof. I am none of those sneakers. I am free of the corporation, and care not who knows it. He that meets me in the forest to-day, shall meet with no wise-acre, I can tell him. *Stultus sum*. Translate me that, and take the meaning of it to yourself for your pains. What! man, we have four quarters of the globe on our side, at the least computation.

Fill us a cup of that sparkling gooseberry—we will drink no wise, melancholy, politic port on this day—and let us troll the catch of Amiens—*duc ad me—duc ad me*—how goes it?

> Here shall he see
> Gross fools as he.

Now would I give a trifle to know, historically and authentically, who was the greatest fool that ever lived. I would certainly give him in a bumper. Marry, of the present breed, I think I could without much difficulty name you the party.

Remove your cap a little further, if you please: it hides my bauble. And now each man bestride his hobby, and dust away his bells to what tune he pleases. I will give you, for my part,

—————The crazy old church clock,
And the bewildered chimes.

Good master Empedocles, you are welcome. It is long since you went a salamander-gathering down Ætna. Worse than samphire-picking by some odds. 'Tis a mercy your worship did not singe your mustachios.

Ha! Cleombrotus! and what salads in faith did you light upon at the bottom of the Mediterranean? You were founder, I take it, of the disinterested sect of the Calenturists.

Gebir, my old free-mason, and prince of plasterers at Babel, bring in your trowel, most Ancient Grand! You have claim to a seat here at my right hand, as patron of the stammerers. You left your work, if I remember Herodotus correctly, at eight hundred million toises, or thereabout, above the level of the sea. Bless us, what a long bell you must have pulled, to call your top workmen to their nuncheon on the low grounds of Shinar. Or did you send up your garlic and onions by a rocket? I am a rogue if I am not ashamed to show you our Monument on Fish Street Hill, after your altitudes. Yet we think it somewhat.

What, the magnanimous Alexander in tears?—cry, baby, put its finger in its eye, it shall have another globe, round as an orange, pretty moppet!

Mister Adams—'odso, I honour, your coat—pray do us the favour to read to us that sermon, which you lent to Mistress Slipslop—the twenty and second in your portmanteau there—on Female Incontinence—the same—it will come in most irrelevantly and impertinently seasonable to the time of the day.

Good Master Raymund Lully, you look wise. Pray correct that error.——

Duns, spare your definitions. I must fine you a bumper, or a paradox. We will have nothing said or done syllogistically this day. Remove those logical forms, waiter, that no gentleman break the tender shins of his apprehension stumbling across them.

Master Stephen, you are late.—Ha! Cokes, is it you?—
Aguecheek, my dear knight, let me pay my devoir to you.—
Master Shallow, your worship's poor servant to command.—
Master Silence, I will use few words with you.—Slender, it
will go hard if I edge not you in somewhere.—You six will
engross all the poor wit of the company to-day.—I know it,
I know it.

Ha! honest R——, my fine old Librarian of Ludgate, time
out of mind, art thou here again? Bless thy doublet, it is not
over-new, threadbare as thy stories:—what dost thou flitting
about the world at this rate?—Thy customers are extinct,
defunct, bed-rid, have ceased to read long ago.—Thou goest
still among them, seeing if, peradventure, thou canst hawk a
volume or two.—Good Granville S——, thy last patron, is
flown.

> King Pandion, he is dead,
> All thy friends are lapt in lead—

Nevertheless, noble R——, come in, and take your seat
here, between Armado and Quisada; for in true courtesy, in
gravity, in fantastic smiling to thyself, in courteous smiling
upon others, in the goodly ornature of well-apparelled speech,
and the commendation of wise sentences, thou art nothing
inferior to those accomplished Dons of Spain. The spirit of
chivalry forsake me for ever, when I forget thy singing the
song of Macheath, which declares that he might be *happy
with either*, situated between those two ancient spinsters—
when I forget the inimitable formal love which thou didst
make, turning now to the one, and now to the other, with
that Malvolian smile—as if Cervantes, not Gay, had written
it for his hero; and as if thousands of periods must revolve,
before the mirror of courtesy could have given his invidious
preference between a pair of so goodly-propertied and
meritorious-equal damsels. * * * *

To descend from these altitudes, and not to protract our
Fools' Banquet beyond its appropriate day,—for I fear the
second of April is not many hours distant—in sober verity I
will confess a truth to thee, reader. I love a *Fool*—as naturally, as if I were of kith and kin to him. When a child, with
child-like apprehensions, that dived not below the surface of
the matter, I read those *Parables*—not guessing at the involved wisdom—I had more yearnings towards that simple

architect, that built his house upon the sand, than I entertained for his more cautious neighbour: I grudged at the hard censure pronounced upon the quiet soul that kept his talent; and—prizing their simplicity beyond the more provident, and, to my apprehension, somewhat *unfeminine* wariness of their competitors—I felt a kindliness, that almost amounted to a *tendre*, for those five thoughtless virgins.—I have never made an acquaintance since, that lasted: or a friendship, that answered; with any that had not some tincture of the absurd in their characters. I venerate an honest obliquity of understanding. The more laughable blunders a man shall commit in your company, the more tests he giveth you, that he will not betray or overreach you. I love the safety which a palpable hallucination warrants; the security which a word out of season ratifies. And take my word for this, reader, and say a fool told it you, if you please, that he who hath not a dram of folly in his mixture, hath pounds of much worse matter in his composition. It is observed, that 'the foolisher the fowl or fish,—woodcocks—dotterels—cods'-heads, etc., the finer the flesh thereof,' and what are commonly the world's received fools, but such whereof the world is not worthy? and what have been some of the kindliest patterns of our species, but so many darlings of absurdity, minions of the goddess, and her white boys?—Reader, if you wrest my words beyond their fair construction, it is you, and not I, that are the *April Fool*.

A Quakers' Meeting

Still-born Silence! thou that art
Flood-gate of the deeper heart!
Offspring of a heavenly kind!
Frost o' the mouth, and thaw o' the mind!
Secrecy's confidant, and he
Who makes religion mystery!
Admiration's speaking'st tongue!
Leave, thy desert shades among,
Reverend hermits' hallow'd cells,
Where retired devotion dwells!
With thy enthusiasms come,
Seize our tongues, and strike us dumb! *

READER, would'st thou know what true peace and quiet mean; would'st thou find a refuge from the noises and clamours of the multitude; would'st thou enjoy at once solitude and society; would'st thou possess the depth of thine own spirit in stillness, without being shut out from the consolatory faces of thy species; would'st thou be alone and yet accompanied; solitary, yet not desolate; singular, yet not without some to keep thee in countenance; a unit in aggregate; a simple in composite:—come with me into a Quakers' Meeting.

Dost thou love silence deep as that 'before the winds were made'? go not out into the wilderness, descend not into the profundities of the earth; shut not up thy casements; nor pour wax into the little cells of thy ears, with little-faith'd self-mistrusting Ulysses.—Retire with me into a Quakers' Meeting.

For a man to refrain even from good words, and to hold his peace, it is commendable; but for a multitude it is great mastery.

What is the stillness of the desert compared with this place? what the uncommunicating muteness of fishes?—here the goddess reigns and revels.—'Boreas, and Cesias, and Argestes loud,' do not with their interconfounding uproars more augment the brawl—nor the waves of the blown Baltic with their clubbed sounds—than their opposite (Silence her sacred self) is multiplied and rendered more intense by numbers, and by sympathy. She too hath her deeps, that call

* From *Poems of all Sorts*, by Richard Fleckno, 1653.

unto deeps. Negation itself hath a positive more and less; and
closed eyes would seem to obscure the great obscurity of
midnight.

There are wounds which an imperfect solitude cannot
heal. By imperfect I mean that which a man enjoyeth by
himself. The perfect is that which he can sometimes attain in
crowds, but nowhere so absolutely as in a Quakers' Meeting.
—Those first hermits did certainly understand this principle,
when they retired into Egyptian solitudes, not singly, but in
shoals, to enjoy one another's want of conversation. The
Carthusian is bound to his brethren by this agreeing spirit of
incommunicativeness. In secular occasions, what so pleasant
as to be reading a book through a long winter evening, with a
friend sitting by—say, a wife—he, or she, too (if that be
probable), reading another, without interruption, or oral
communication?—can there be no sympathy without the
gabble of words?—away with this inhuman, shy, single,
shade-and-cavern-haunting solitariness. Give me, Master
Zimmermann, a sympathetic solitude.

To pace alone in the cloisters or side aisles of some cathedral, times-tricken;

> Or under hanging mountains,
> Or by the fall of fountains;

is but a vulgar luxury compared with that which those enjoy
who come together for the purposes of more complete,
abstracted solitude. This is the loneliness 'to be felt.'—The
Abbey Church of Westminster hath nothing so solemn, so
spirit-soothing, as the naked walls and benches of a Quakers'
Meeting. Here are no tombs, no inscriptions.

> ————Sands, ignoble things,
> Dropt from the ruined sides of kings—

but here is something which throws Antiquity herself into
the foreground—SILENCE—eldest of things—language of old
Night—primitive discourser—to which the insolent decays
of mouldering grandeur have but arrived by a violent, and,
as we may say, unnatural progression.

> How reverend is the view of these hushed heads,
> Looking tranquillity!

Nothing-plotting, nought-caballing, unmischievous synod!

71

convocation without intrigue! parliament without debate! what a lesson dost thou read to council, and to consistory!— if my pen treat of you lightly—as haply it will wander—yet my spirit hath gravely felt the wisdom of your custom, when sitting among you in deepest peace, which some outwelling tears would rather confirm than disturb, I have reverted to the times of your beginnings, and the sowings of the seed by Fox and Dewesbury.—I have witnessed that which brought before my eyes your heroic tranquillity, inflexible to the rude jests and serious violence of the insolent soldiery, republican or royalist, sent to molest you—for ye sate betwixt the fires of two persecutions, the outcast and offscouring of church and presbytery.—I have seen the reeling sea-ruffian, who had wandered into your receptacle with the avowed intention of disturbing your quiet, from the very spirit of the place receive in a moment a new heart, and presently sit among ye as a lamb amidst lambs. And I remember Penn before his accusers, and Fox in the bail-dock, where he was lifted up in spirit, as he tells us, and 'the Judge and the Jury became as dead men under his feet.'

Reader, if you are not acquainted with it, I would recommend to you, above all church-narratives, to read Sewel's History of the Quakers. It is in folio, and is the abstract of the journals of Fox and the primitive Friends. It is far more edifying and affecting than anything you will read of Wesley and his colleagues. Here is nothing to stagger you, nothing to make you mistrust, no suspicion of alloy, no drop or dreg of the worldly or ambitious spirit. You will here read the true story of that much-injured, ridiculed man (who perhaps hath been a by-word in your mouth)—James Naylor: what dreadful sufferings, with what patience, he endured, even to the boring through of his tongue with red-hot irons, without a murmur; and with what strength of mind, when the delusion he had fallen into, which they stigmatised for blasphemy, had given way to clearer thoughts, he could renounce his error, in a strain of the beautifullest humility, yet keep his first grounds, and be a Quaker still!—so different from the practice of your common converts from enthusiasm, who, when they apostatize, *apostatize all*, and think they can never get far enough from the society of their former errors, even to the renunciation of some saving truths, with which they had been mingled, not implicated.

Get the writings of John Woolman by heart; and love the early Quakers.

How far the followers of these good men in our days have kept to the primitive spirit, or in what proportion they have substituted formality for it, the Judge of Spirits can alone determine. I have seen faces in their assemblies upon which the dove sate visibly brooding. Others, again, I have watched, when my thoughts should have been better engaged, in which I could possibly detect nothing but a blank inanity. But quiet was in all, and the disposition to unanimity, and the absence of the fierce controversial workings.— If the spiritual pretensions of the Quakers have abated, at least they make few pretences. Hypocrites they certainly are not, in their preaching. It is seldom, indeed, that you shall see one get up amongst them to hold forth. Only now and then a trembling, female, generally *ancient*, voice is heard— you cannot guess from what part of the meeting it proceeds —with a low, buzzing, musical sound, laying out a few words which 'she thought might suit the condition of some present,' with a quaking diffidence, which leaves no possibility of supposing that anything of female vanity was mixed up, where the tones were so full of tenderness, and a restraining modesty.—The men, for what I have observed, speak seldomer.

Once only, and it was some years ago, I witnessed a sample of the old Foxian orgasm. It was a man of giant stature, who, as Wordsworth phrases it, might have danced 'from head to foot equipt in iron mail.' His frame was of iron, too. But *he* was malleable. I saw him shake all over with the spirit—I dare not say of delusion. The strivings of the outer man were unutterable—he seemed not to speak, but to be spoken from. I saw the strong man bowed down, and his knees to fail—his joints all seemed loosening—it was a figure to set off against Paul preaching—the words he uttered were few, and sound —he was evidently resisting his will—keeping down his own word-wisdom with more mighty effort than the world's orators strain for theirs. 'He had been a WIT in his youth,' he told us, with expressions of a sober remorse. And it was not till long after the impression had begun to wear away that I was enabled, with something like a smile, to recall the striking incongruity of the confession—understanding the term in its worldly acceptation with the frame and

73

physiognomy of the person before me. His brow would have scared away the Levities—the Jocos Risus-que—faster than the Loves fled the face of Dis at Enna.—By *wit*, even in his youth, I will be sworn he understood something far within the limits of an allowable liberty.

More frequently the Meeting is broken up without a word having been spoken. But the mind has been fed. You go away with a sermon not made with hands. You have been in the milder caverns of Trophonius; or as in some den, where that fiercest and savagest of all wild creatures, the TONGUE, that unruly member, has strangely lain tied up and captive. You have bathed with stillness.—O, when the spirit is sore fretted, even tired to sickness of the janglings and nonsense-noises of the world, what a balm and a solace it is to go and seat yourself for a quiet half-hour upon some undisputed corner of a bench, among the gentle Quakers!

Their garb and stillness conjoined, present a uniformity, tranquil and herd-like—as in the pasture—'forty feeding like one.' —

The very garments of a Quaker seem incapable of receiving a soil; and cleanliness in them to be something more than the absence of its contrary. Every Quakeress is a lily; and when they come up in bands to their Whitsun-conferences, whitening the easterly streets of the metropolis, from all parts of the United Kingdom, they show like troops of the Shining Ones.

The Old and the New Schoolmaster

MY reading has been lamentably desultory and immethodical. Odd, out of the way, old English plays, and treatises, have supplied me with most of my notions, and ways of feeling. In everything that relates to *science*, I am a whole Encyclopædia behind the rest of the world. I should have scarcely cut a figure among the franklins, or country gentlemen, in King John's days. I know less geography than a school-boy of six weeks' standing. To me a map of old Ortelius is as authentic as Arrowsmith. I do not know whereabout Africa merges into Asia; whether Ethiopia lie in one or other of these great divisions; nor can form the remotest conjecture of the position of New South Wales, or Van Diemen's Land. Yet do I hold a correspondence with a very dear friend in the first-named of these two Terræ Incognitæ. I have no astronomy. I do not know where to look for the Bear, or Charles's Wain; the place of any star; or the name of any of them at sight. I guess at Venus only by her brightness—and if the sun on some portentous morn were to make his first appearance in the West, I verily believe, that, while all the world were gasping in apprehension about me, I alone should stand unterrified, from sheer incuriosity and want of observation. Of history and chronology I possess some vague points, such as one cannot help picking up in the course of miscellaneous study; but I never deliberately sat down to a chronicle, even of my own country. I have most dim apprehensions of the four great monarchies; and sometimes the Assyrian, sometimes the Persian, floats as *first*, in my fancy. I make the wi dest conjectures concerning Egypt and her shepherd kings. My friend *M.*, with great painstaking, got me to think I understood the first proposition in Euclid, but gave me over in despair at the second. I am entirely unacquainted with the modern languages; and, like a better man than myself, have 'small Latin and less Greek.' I am a stranger to the shapes and texture of the commonest trees, herbs, flowers—not from the circumstance of my being town-born—for I should have brought the same inobservant spirit into the world with me, had I first seen it 'on Devon's leafy shores,'—and am no less at a loss among purely town-objects, tools, engines, mechanic processes.—Not that I affect ignorance—but my head has not many mansions, nor spacious; and I have been obliged to fill it with such cabinet curiosities as it can hold without aching. I sometimes wonder, how I have passed by probation with so little discredit in the world, as I have done, upon so meagre a stock. But the fact is, a man way do very well with a very little knowledge, and scarce be found out, in mixed company; everybody is so much more ready to produce his own, than to call for a display of your acquisitions. But in a *tête-à-tête* there is no shuffling. The truth will out. There is nothing which I dread so much, as the being left alone for a quarter of an hour with a sensible, well-informed man, that does not know me. I lately got into a dilemma of this sort.—

In one of my daily jaunts between Bishopsgate and Shack-

lewell, the coach stopped to take up a staid-looking gentleman, about the wrong side of thirty, who was giving his
parting directions (while the steps were adjusting), in a tone
of mild authority, to a tall youth, who seemed to be neither
his clerk, his son, nor his servant, but something partaking of
all three. The youth was dismissed, and we drove on. As we
were the sole passengers, he naturally enough addressed his
conversation to me; and we discussed the merits of the fare,
the civility and punctuality of the driver; the circumstance of
an opposition coach having been lately set up, with the probabilities of its success—to all which I was enabled to return
pretty satisfactory answers, having been drilled into this kind
of etiquette by some years' daily practice of riding to and fro
in the stage aforesaid—when he suddenly alarmed me by a
startling question, whether I had seen the show of prize
cattle that morning in Smithfield? Now, as I had not seen it,
and do not greatly care for such sort of exhibitions, I was
obliged to return a cold negative. He seemed a little mortified, as well as astonished, at my declaration, as (it appeared)
he was just come fresh from the sight, and doubtless had
hoped to compare notes on the subject. However, he assured
me that I had lost a fine treat, as it far exceeded the show of
last year. We were now approaching Norton Folgate, when
the sight of some shop-goods *ticketed* freshened him up into a
dissertation upon the cheapness of cottons this spring. I was
now a little in heart, as the nature of my morning avocations
had brought me into some sort of familiarity with the raw
material; and I was surprised to find how eloquent I was
becoming on the state of the India market—when, presently,
he dashed my incipient vanity to the earth at once, by inquiring whether I had ever made any calculations as to the
value of the rental of all the retail shops in London. Had he
asked of me, what song the Syrens sang, or what name Achilles
assumed when he hid himself among women, I might, with
Sir Thomas Browne, have hazarded a 'wide solution.' * My
companion saw my embarrassment, and, the almshouses
beyond Shoreditch just coming in view, with great good-
nature and dexterity shifted his conversation to the subject of
public charities; which led to the comparative merits of
provisions for the poor in past and present times, with
observations on the old monastic institutions, and charitable

* Urn Burial.

orders; but, finding me rather dimly impressed with some glimmering notions from old poetic associations, than strongly fortified with any speculations reducible to calculation on the subject, he gave the matter up; and, the country beginning to open more and more upon us, as we approached the turnpike at Kingsland (the destined termination of his journey), he put a home thrust upon me, in the most unfortunate position he could have chosen, by advancing some queries relative to the North Pole Expedition. While I was muttering out something about the Panorama of those strange regions (which I had actually seen), by way of parrying the question, the coach stopping relieved me from any further apprehensions. My companion getting out, left me in the comfortable possession of my ignorance; and I heard him, as he went off, putting questions to an outside passenger, who had alighted with him, regarding an epidemic disorder, that had been rife about Dalston, and which my friend assured him had gone through five or six schools in that neighbourhood. The truth now flashed upon me, that my companion was a schoolmaster; and that the youth, whom he had parted from at our first acquaintance, must have been one of the bigger boys, or the usher.—He was evidently a kind-hearted man, who did not seem so much desirous of provoking discussion by the questions which he put, as of obtaining information at any rate. It did not appear that he took any interest, either, in such kind of inquiries, for their own sake; but that he was in some way bound to seek for knowledge. A greenish-coloured coat, which he had on, forbade me to surmise that he was a clergyman. The adventure gave birth to some reflections on the difference between persons of his profession in past and present times.

Rest to the souls of those fine old Pedagogues; the breed, long since extinct, of the Lilys, and the Linacres: who believing that all learning was contained in the languages which they taught, and despising every other acquirement as superficial and useless, came to their task as to a sport! Passing from infancy to age, they dreamed away all their days as in a grammar-school. Revolving in a perpetual cycle of declensions, conjugations, syntaxes, and prosodies; renewing constantly the occupations which had charmed their studious childhood; rehearsing continually the part of the past; life must have slipped from them at last like one day. They were always in their first garden, reaping harvests of their golden time, among their *Flori* and their *Spici-legia;* in Arcadia still, but kings; the ferule of their sway not much harsher, but of like dignity with that mild sceptre attributed to king Basileus; the Greek and Latin, their stately Pamela and their Philoclea; with the occasional duncery of some untoward tyro, serving for a refreshing interlude of a Mopsa, or a clown Damœtas!

With what a savour doth the Preface to Colet's, or (as it is sometimes called) Paul's Accidence, set forth! 'To exhort every man to the learning of grammar, that intendeth to attain the understanding of the tongues, wherein is contained a great treasury of wisdom and knowledge, it would seem but vain and lost labour; for so much as it is known, that nothing can surely be ended, whose beginning is either feeble or faulty; and no building be perfect whereas the foundation and groundwork is ready to fall, and unable to uphold the burden of the frame.' How well doth this stately preamble (comparable to those which Milton commendeth as 'having been the usage to prefix to some solemn law, then first promulgated by Solon or Lycurgus') correspond with and illustrate that pious zeal for conformity, expressed in a succeeding clause, which would fence about grammar-rules with the severity of faith-articles!—'as for the diversity of grammars, it is well profitably taken away by the king majesties wisdom, who foreseeing the inconvenience, and favourably providing the remedie, caused one kind of grammar by sundry learned men to be diligently drawn, and so to be set out, only everywhere to be taught for the use of learners, and for the hurt in changing of schoolmaisters.' What a *gusto* in that which follows: 'wherein it is profitable that he [the pupil] can orderly decline his noun and his verb.' *His* noun!

The fine dream is fading away fast; and the least concern of a teacher in the present day is to inculcate grammar-rules.

The modern schoolmaster is expected to know a little of everything, because his pupil is required not to be entirely ignorant of anything. He must be superficially, if I may so say, omniscient. He is to know something of pneumatics; of chemistry; of whatever is curious or proper to excite the attention of the youthful mind; an insight into mechanics is desirable, with a touch of statistics; the quality of soils, etc., botany, the constitution of his country, *cum multis aliis*. You may get a notion of some part of his expected duties by consulting the famous Tractate on Education, addressed to Mr. Hartlib.

All these things—these, or the desire of them—he is expected to instil, not by set lessons from professors, which he may charge in the bill, but at school intervals, as he walks the streets, or saunters through green fields (those natural instructors), with his pupils. The least part of what is expected from him is to be done in school-hours. He must insinuate knowledge at the *mollia tempora fandi*. He must seize every occasion—the season of the year—the time of the day—a passing cloud—a rainbow—a waggon of hay—a regiment of soldiers going by—to inculcate something useful. He can receive no pleasure from a casual glimpse of Nature, but must catch at it as an object of instruction. He must interpret beauty into the picturesque. He cannot relish a beggar-man, or a gipsy, for thinking of the suitable improvement. Nothing comes to him, not spoiled by the sophisticating medium of moral uses. The Universe—that Great Book, as it has been called—is to him, indeed, to all intents and purposes, a book out of which he is doomed to read tedious homilies to distasting schoolboys.—Vacations themselves are none to him, he is only rather worse off than before; for commonly he has some intrusive upper-boy fastened upon him at such times; some cadet of a great family; some neglected lump of nobility, or gentry; that he must drag after him to the play, to the Panorama, to Mr. Bartley's Orrery, to the Panopticon, or into the country, to a friend's house, or his favourite watering-place. Wherever he goes this uneasy shadow attends him. A boy is at his board, and in his path, and in all his movements. He is boy-rid, sick of perpetual boy.

Boys are capital fellows in their own way, among their mates; but they are unwholesome companions for grown people. The restraint is felt no less on the one side than on the other.—Even a child, that 'plaything for an hour,' tires *always*. The noises of children, playing their own fancies—as I now hearken to them, by fits, sporting on the green before my window, while I am engaged in these grave speculations at my neat surburban retreat at Shacklewell—by distance made more sweet—inexpressibly take from the labour of my task. It is like writing to music. They seem to modulate my periods. They ought at least to do so—for in the voice of that tender age there is a kind of poetry, far unlike the harsh prose-accents of man's conversation.—I should but spoil their sport, and diminish my own sympathy for them, by mingling in their pastime.

I would not be domesticated all my days with a person of very superior capacity to my own—not, if I know myself at all, from any considerations of jealousy or self-comparison, for the occasional communion with such minds has constituted the fortune and felicity of my life—but the habit of too constant intercourse with spirits above you, instead of raising you, keeps you down. Too frequent doses of original thinking from others, restrain what lesser portion of that faculty you may possess of your own. You get entangled in another man's mind, even as you lose yourself in another man's grounds. You are walking with a tall varlet, whose strides out-pace yours to lassitude. The constant operation of such potent agency would reduce me, I am convinced, to imbecility. You may derive thoughts from others; your way of thinking, the mould in which your thoughts are cast, must be your own. Intellect may be imparted, but not each man's intellectual frame.—

As little as I should wish to be always thus dragged upward, as little (or rather still less) is it desirable to be stunted downwards by your associates. The trumpet does not more stun you by its loudness, than a whisper teases you by its provoking inaudibility.

Why are we never quite at our ease in the presence of a schoolmaster?—because we are conscious that he is not quite at his ease in ours. He is awkward, and out of place, in the society of his equals. He comes like Gulliver from among his little people, and he cannot fit the stature of his understanding to yours. He cannot meet you on the square. He wants a point given him, like an indifferent whist-player. He is so used to teaching, that he wants to be teaching *you*. One of these professors, upon my complaining that these little sketches of mine were anything but methodical, and that I was unable to make them otherwise, kindly offered to instruct me in the method by which young gentlemen in *his* seminary were taught to compose English themes. The jests of a schoolmaster are coarse, or thin. They do not *tell* out of school. He is under the restraint of a formal or didactive hypocrisy in company, as a clergyman is under a moral one. He can no more let his intellect loose in society than the other can his inclinations.—He is forlorn among his coevals; his juniors cannot be his friends.

'I take blame to myself,' said a sensible man of this profession, writing to a friend respecting a youth who had quitted his school abruptly, 'that your nephew was not more attached to me. But persons in my situation are more to be pitied than can well be imagined. We are surrounded by young, and, consequently, ardently affectionate hearts, but *we* can never hope to share an atom of their affections. The relation of master and scholar forbids this. *How pleasing this must be to you, how I envy your feelings!* my friends will sometimes say to me, when they see young men whom I have educated return after some years' absence from school, their eyes shining with pleasure, while they shake hands with their old master, bringing a present of game to me, or a toy to my wife, and thanking me in the warmest terms for my care of their education. A holiday is begged for the boys; the house is a scene of happiness; I, only, am sad at heart.— This fine-spirited and warm-hearted youth, who fancies he repays his master with gratitude for the care of his boyish years—this young man—in the eight long years I watched over him with a parent's anxiety, never could repay me with one look of genuine feeling. He was proud, when I praised; he was submissive, when I reproved him; but he did never *love* me—and what he now mistakes for gratitude and kindness for me, is but the pleasant sensation which all persons feel at revisiting the scenes of their boyish hopes and fears; and the seeing on equal terms the man they were accustomed to look up to with reverence. My wife, too,' this interesting correspondent goes on to say, 'my once darling Anna, is the wife of a schoolmaster.—When I married her— knowing that the wife of a schoolmaster ought to be a busy notable creature, and fearing that my gentle Anna would ill supply the loss of my dear bustling mother, just then dead, who never sat still, was in every part of the house in a moment, and whom I was obliged sometimes to threaten to fasten down in a chair, to save her from fatiguing herself to death—I expressed my fears that I was bringing her into a way of life unsuitable to her; and she, who loved me tenderly, promised for my sake to exert herself to perform the duties of her new situation. She promised, and she has kept her word. What wonders will not woman's love perform?—My house is managed with a propriety and decorum unknown in other schools; my boys are well fed, look healthy, and have every proper accommodation; and all this performed with a careful economy, that never descends to meanness. But I have lost my gentle *helpless* Anna! When we sit down to enjoy an hour of repose after the fatigue of the day, I am compelled to listen to what have been her useful (and they are really useful) employments through the day, and what she proposes for her to-morrow's task. Her heart and her features are changed by the duties of her situation. To the boys, she never appears other than the *master's wife*, and she looks up to me as the *boys' master;* to whom all show of love and affection would be highly improper, and unbecoming the dignity of her situation and mine. Yet *this* my gratitude forbids me to hint to her. For my sake she submitted to be this altered creature, and can I reproach her for it?'—For the communication of this letter I am indebted to my cousin Bridget.

Imperfect Sympathies

I am of a constitution so general, that it consorts and sympathizeth with all things; I have no antipathy, or rather idiosyncrasy in anything. Those natural repugnancies do not touch me, nor do I behold with prejudice the French, Italian, Spaniard, or Dutch.—*Religio Medici.*

THAT the author of the Religio Medici, mounted upon the airy stilts of abstraction, conversant about notional and conjectural essences; in whose categories of Being the possible took the upper hand of the actual; should have overlooked the impertinent individualities of such poor concretions as mankind, is not much to be admired. It is rather to be wondered at, that in the genus of animals he should have condescended to distinguish that species at all. For myself—earth-bound and fettered to the scene of my activities,—

Standing on earth, not rapt above the sky,

I confess that I do feel the differences of mankind, national or individual, to an unhealthy excess. I can look with no indifferent eye upon things or persons. Whatever is, is to me a matter of taste or distaste; or when once it becomes indifferent, it begins to be disrelishing. I am, in plainer words, a bundle of prejudices—made up of likings and dislikings—the veriest thrall to sympathies, apathies, antipathies. In a certain sense, I hope it may be said of me that I am a lover of my species. I can feel for all indifferently, but I cannot feel towards all equally. The more purely-English word that expresses sympathy, will better explain my meaning. I can be a friend to a worthy man, who upon another account cannot be my mate or *fellow*. I cannot *like* all people alike. *

I have been trying all my life to like Scotchmen, and am obliged to desist from the experiment in despair. They cannot like me—and in truth, I never knew one of that nation who attempted to do it. There is something more plain and ingenuous in their mode of proceeding. We know one another at first sight. There is an order of imperfect intellects (under which mine must be content to rank) which in its constitution is essentially anti-Caledonian. The owners of the sort of faculties I allude to, have minds rather suggestive than comprehensive. They have no pretences to much clearness or precision in their ideas, or in their manner of expressing them. Their intellectual wardrobe (to confess fairly) has few whole pieces in it. They are content with fragments and scattered pieces of Truth. She presents no full front to them— a feature or side-face at the most. Hints and glimpses, germs and crude essays at a system, is the utmost they pretend to.

---

* I would be understood as confining myself to the subject of *imperfect sympathies*. To nations or classes of men there can be no direct antipathy. There may be individuals born and constellated so opposite to another individual nature, that the same sphere cannot hold them. I have met with my moral antipodes, and can believe the story of two persons meeting (who never saw one another before in their lives) and instantly fighting.

————We by proof find there should be
'Twixt man and man such an antipathy,
That though he can show no just reason why
For any former wrong or injury,
Can neither find a blemish in his fame,
Nor aught in face or feature justly blame,
Can challenge or accuse him of no evil,
Yet notwithstanding hates him as a devil.

The lines are from old Heywood's 'Hierarchie of Angels,' and he subjoins a curious story in confirmation, of a Spaniard who attempted to assassinate a King Ferdinand of Spain, and being put to the rack could give no other reason for the deed but an inveterate antipathy which he had taken to the first sight of the King.

————The cause which to that act compell'd him
Was, he ne'er loved him since he first beheld him.

They beat up a little game peradventure—and leave it to knottier heads, more robust constitutions, to run it down. The light that lights them is not steady and polar, but mutable and shifting: waxing, and again waning. Their conversation is accordingly. They will throw out a random word in or out of season, and be content to let it pass for what it is worth. They cannot speak always as if they were upon their oath—but must be understood, speaking or writing, with some abatement. They seldom wait to mature a proposition, but e'en bring it to market in the green ear. They delight to impart their defective discoveries as they arise, without waiting for their full development. They are no systematizers, and would but err more by attempting it. Their minds, as I said before, are suggestive merely. The brain of a true Caledonian (if I am not mistaken) is constituted upon quite a different plan. His Minerva is born in panoply. You are never admitted to see his ideas in their growth—if, indeed, they do grow, and are not rather put together upon principles of clock-work. You never catch his mind in an undress. He never hints or suggests anything, but unlades his stock of ideas in perfect order and completeness. He brings his total wealth into company, and gravely unpacks it. His riches are always about him. He never stoops to catch a glittering something in your presence to share it with you, before he quite knows whether it be true touch or not. You cannot cry *halves* to anything that he finds. He does not find, but bring. You never witness his first apprehension of a thing. His understanding is always at its meridian—you never see the first dawn, the early streaks.—He has no falterings of self-suspicion. Surmises, guesses, misgivings, half-intuitions, semi-consciousnesses, partial illuminations, dim instincts, embryo conceptions, have no place in his brain, or vocabulary. The twilight of dubiety never falls upon him. Is he orthodox—he has no doubts. Is he an infidel—he has none either. Between the affirmative and the negative there is no border-land with him. You cannot hover with him upon the confines of truth, or wander in the maze of a probable argument. He always keeps the path. You cannot make excursions with him—for he sets you right. His taste never fluctuates. His morality never abates. He cannot compromise, or understand middle actions. There can be but a right and a wrong. His conversation is as a book. His affirmations have the sanctity of an oath. You must speak upon the square with him. He stops a metaphor like a suspected person in an enemy's country. 'A healthy book!'—said one of his countrymen to me, who had ventured to give that appellation to John Buncle,—'Did I catch rightly what you said? I have heard of a man in health, and of a healthy state of body, but I do not see how that epithet can be properly applied to a book.' Above all, you must beware of indirect expressions before a Caledonian. Clap an extinguisher upon your irony, if you are unhappily blest with a vein of it. Remember you are upon your oath. I have a print of a graceful female after Leonardo da Vinci, which I was showing off to Mr. * * * * After he had examined it minutely, I ventured to ask him how he liked MY BEAUTY (a foolish name it goes by among my friends)—when he very gravely assured me, that 'he had considerable respect for my character and talents' (so he was pleased to say), 'but had not given himself much thought about the degree of my personal pretensions.' The misconception staggered me, but did not seem much to disconcert him.—Persons of this nation are particularly fond of affirming a truth—which nobody doubts. They do not so properly affirm, as annunciate it. They do indeed appear to have such a love of truth (as if, like virtue, it were valuable for itself) that all truth becomes equally valuable, whether the proposition that contains it be new or old, disputed, or such as is imposssible to become a subject of disputation. I was present not long since at a party of North Britons, where a son of Burns was expected; and happened to drop a silly expression (in my South British way), that I wished it were the father instead of the son—when four of them started up at once to inform me, that 'that was impossible, because he was dead.' An impracticable wish, it seems, was more than they could conceive. Swift has hit off this part of their character, namely their love of truth, in his biting way, but with an illiberality that necessarily confines the passage to the margin. * The tediousness of these

* There are some people who think they sufficiently acquit themselves, and entertain their company, with relating facts of no consequence, not at all out of the road of such common incidents as happen every day; and this I have observed more frequently among the Scots than any other nation, who are very careful not to omit the minutest circumstances of time or place; which kind of discourse, if it were not a little relieved by the uncouth terms and phrases, as well as accent and gesture, peculiar to that country, would be hardly tolerable.—*Hints towards an Essay on Conversation*.

people is certainly provoking. I wonder if they ever tire one another!—In my early life I had a passionate fondness for the poetry of Burns. I have sometimes foolishly hoped to ingratiate myself with his countrymen by expressing it. But I have always found that a true Scot resents your admiration of his compatriot, even more than he would your contempt of him. The latter he imputes to your 'imperfect acquaintance with many of the words which he uses'; and the same objection makes it a presumption in you to suppose that you can admire him.—Thomson they seem to have forgotten. Smollett they have neither forgotten nor forgiven, for his delineation of Rory and his companion, upon their first introduction to our metropolis.—Speak of Smollett as a great genius, and they will retort upon you Hume's History compared with *his* Continuation of it. What if the historian had continued Humphrey Clinker?

I have, in the abstract, no disrespect for Jews. They are a piece of stubborn antiquity, compared with which Stonehenge is in its nonage. They date beyond the pyramids. But I should not care to be in habits of familiar intercourse with any of that nation. I confess that I have not the nerves to enter their synagogues. Old prejudices cling about me. I cannot shake off the story of Hugh of Lincoln. Centuries of injury, contempt, and hate, on the one side,—of cloaked revenge, dissimulation, and hate, on the other, between our and their fathers, must and ought to affect the blood of the children. I cannot believe it can run clear and kindly yet; or that a few fine words, such as candour, liberality, the light of a nineteenth century, can close up the breaches of so deadly a disunion. A Hebrew is nowhere congenial to me. He is least distasteful on 'Change—for the mercantile spirit levels all distinctions, as all are beauties in the dark. I boldly confess that I do not relish the approximation of Jew and Christian, which has become so fashionable. The reciprocal endearments have, to me, something hypocritical and unnatural in them. I do not like to see the Church and Synagogue kissing and congeeing in awkward postures of an affected civility. If *they* are converted, why do they not come over to us altogether? Why keep up a form of separation, when the life of it is fled? If they can sit with us at table, why do they keck at our cookery? I do not understand these half convertites. Jews christianizing—Christians judaizing—

puzzle me. I like fish or flesh. A moderate Jew is a more confounding piece of anomaly than a wet Quaker. The spirit of the synagogue is essentially *separative*. B—— would have been more in keeping if he had abided by the faith of his forefathers. There is a fine scorn in his face, which nature meant to be of——Christians. The Hebrew spirit is strong in him, in spite of his proselytism. He cannot conquer the Shibboleth. How it breaks out, when he sings, 'The Children of Israel passed through the Red Sea!' The auditors, for the moment, are as Egyptians to him, and he rides over our necks in triumph. There is no mistaking him. B—— has a strong expression of sense in his countenance, and it is confirmed by his singing. The foundation of his vocal excellence is sense. He sings with understanding, as Kemble delivered dialogue. He would sing the Commandments, and give an appropriate character to each prohibition. His nation, in general, have not over-sensible countenances. How should they?—but you seldom see a silly expression among them.— Gain, and the pursuit of gain, sharpen a man's visage. I never heard of an idiot being born among them.—Some admire the Jewish female-physiognomy. I admire it—but with trembling. Jael had those full dark inscrutable eyes.

In the Negro countenance you will often meet with strong traits of benignity. I have felt yearnings of tenderness towards some of these faces—or rather masks—that have looked out kindly upon one in casual encounters in the streets and highways. I love what Fuller beautifully calls— these 'images of God cut in ebony.' But I should not like to associate with them, to share my meals and my good-nights with them—because they are black.

I love Quaker ways, and Quaker worship. I venerate the Quaker principles. It does me good for the rest of the day when I meet any of their people in my path. When I am ruffled or disturbed by any occurrence, the sight, or quiet voice of a Quaker, acts upon me as a ventilator, lightening the air, and taking off a load from the bosom. But I cannot like the Quakers (as Desdemona would say) 'to live with them.' I am all over sophisticated—with humours, fancies, craving hourly sympathy. I must have books, pictures, theatres, chit-chat, scandal, jokes, ambiguities, and a thousand whim-whams, which their simpler taste can do without. I should starve at their primitive banquet. My appetites are too high for the salads which (according to Evelyn) Eve dressed for the angel, my gusto too excited

> To sit a guest with Daniel at his pulse.

The indirect answers which Quakers are often found to return to a question put to them may be explained, I think, without the vulgar assumption, that they are more given to evasion and equivocating than other people. They naturally look to their words more carefully, and are more cautious of committing themselves. They have a peculiar character to keep up on his head. They stand in a manner upon their veracity. A Quaker is by law exempted from taking an oath. The custom of resorting to an oath in extreme cases, sanctified as it is by all religious antiquity, is apt (it must be confessed) to introduce into the laxer sort of minds the notion of two kinds of truth—the one applicable to the solemn affairs of justice, and the other to the common proceedings of daily intercourse. As truth bound upon the conscience by an oath can be but truth, so in the common affirmations of the shop and the market-place a latitude is expected, and conceded upon questions wanting this solemn covenant. Something less than truth satisfies. It is common to hear a person say, 'You do not expect me to speak as if I were upon my oath.' Hence a great deal of incorrectness and inadvertancy, short of falsehood, creeps into ordinary conversation; and a kind of secondary or laic-truth is tolerated, where clergy-truth—oath-truth, by the nature of the circumstances, is not required. A Quaker knows none of this distinction. His simple affirmation being received, upon the most sacred occasions, without any further test, stamps a value upon the words which he is to use upon the most indifferent topics of life. He looks to them, naturally, with more severity. You can have of him no more than his word. He knows, if he is caught tripping in a casual expression, he forfeits, for himself at least, his claim to the invidious exemption. He knows that his syllables are weighed—and how far a consciousness of this particular watchfulness, exerted against a person, has a tendency to produce indirect answers, and a diverting of the question by honest means, might be illustrated, and the practice justified, by a more sacred example than is proper to be adduced upon this occasion. The admirable presence of mind, which is notorious in Quakers upon all contingencies, might be traced to this imposed self-watchfulness—if it did not seem rather an humble and secular scion of that old stock of religious constancy, which never bent or faltered, in the Primitive Friends, or gave way to the winds of persecution, to the violence of judge or accuser, under trials and racking examinations. 'You will never be the wiser, if I sit here answering your questions till midnight,' said one of those upright Justicers to Penn, who had been putting law-cases with a puzzling subtlety. 'Thereafter as the answers may be,' retorted the Quaker. The astonishing composure of this people is sometimes ludicrously displayed in lighter instances.—I was traveling in a stage-coach with three male Quakers, buttoned up in the straitest nonconformity of their sect. We stopped to bait at Andover, where a meal, partly tea apparatus, partly supper, was set before us. My friends confined themselves to the tea-table. I in my way took supper. When the landlady brought in the bill, the eldest of my companions discovered that she had charged for both meals. This was resisted. Mine hostess was very clamorous and positive. Some mild arguments were used on the part of the Quakers, for which the heated mind of the good lady seemed by no means a fit recipient. The guard came in with his usual peremptory notice. The Quakers pulled out their money and formally tendered it—so much for tea—I, in humble imitation, tendering mine—for the supper which I had taken. She would not relax in her demand. So they all three quietly put up their silver, as did myself, and marched out of the room, the eldest and gravest going first, with myself closing up the rear, who thought I could not do better than follow the example of such grave and warrantable personages. We got in. The steps went up. The coach drove off. The murmurs of mine hostess, not very indistinctly or ambiguously pronounced, became after a time inaudible—and now my conscience, which the whimsical scene had for a while suspended, beginning to give some twitches, I waited, in the hope that some justification would be offered by these serious persons for the seeming injustice of their conduct. To my great surprise not a syllable was dropped on the subject. They sat as mute as at a meeting. At length the eldest of them broke silence, by inquiring of his next neighbour, 'Hath thee heard how indigos go at the India House?' and the question operated as a soporific on my moral feeling as far as Exeter.

Witches, and Other Night Fears

WE are too hasty when we set down our ancestors in the gross for fools, for the monstrous inconsistencies (as they seem to us) involved in their creed of witchcraft. In the relations of this visible world we find them to have been as rational, and shrewd to detect an historic anomaly, as ourselves. But when once the invisible world was supposed to be opened, and the lawless agency of bad spirits assumed, what measures of probability, of decency, of fitness, or proportion—of that which distinguishes the likely from the palpable absurd— could they have to guide them in the rejection or admission of any particular testimony?—That maidens pined away, wasting inwardly as their waxen images consumed before a fire—that corn was lodged, and cattle lamed—that whirl-winds uptore in diabolic revelry the oaks of the forest—or that spits and kettles only danced a fearful innocent vagary about some rustic's kitchen when no wind was stirring—were all equally probable where no law of agency was understood. That the prince of the powers of darkness, passing by the flower and pomp of the earth, should lay preposterous siege to the weak fantasy of indigent eld—has neither likelihood nor unlikelihood *a priori* to us, who have no measure to guess at his policy, or standard to estimate what rate those anile souls may fetch in the devil's market. Nor, when the wicked are expressly symbolised by a goat, was it to be wondered at so much, that *he* should come sometimes in that body, and assert his metaphor.—That the intercourse was opened at all between both worlds was perhaps the mistake—but that once assumed, I see no reason for disbelieving one attested story of this nature more than another on the score of absurdity. There is no law to judge of the lawless, or canon by which a dream may be criticised.

I have sometimes thought that I could not have existed in the days of received witchcraft; that I could not have slept in a village where one of those reputed hags dwelt. Our ancestors were bolder, or more obtuse. Amidst the universal belief that these wretches were in league with the author of all evil, holding hell tributary to their muttering, no simple Justice of the Peace seems to have scrupled issuing, or silly Headborough serving, a warrant upon them—as if they should subpœna Satan!—Prospero in his boat, with his books and wand about him, suffers himself to be conveyed away at the mercy of his enemies to an unknown island. He might have raised a storm or two, we think, on the passage. His acquiescence is in exact analogy to the non-resistance of witches to the constituted powers.—What stops the Fiend in Spenser from tearing Guyon to pieces—or who had made it a condition of his prey that Guyon must take assay of the glorious bait—we have no guess. We do not know the laws of that country.

From my childhood I was extremely inquisitive about witches and witch-stories. My maid, and more legendary aunt, supplied me with good store. But I shall mention the accident which directed my curiosity originally into this channel. In my father's book-closet the History of the Bible by Stackhouse occupied a distinguished station. The pictures with which it abounds—one of the ark, in particular, and another of Solomon's temple, delineated with all the fidelity of ocular admeasurement, as if the artist had been upon the spot—attracted my childish attention. There was a picture, too, of the Witch raising up Samuel, which I wish that I had never seen. We shall come to that hereafter. Stackhouse is in two huge tomes—and there was a pleasure in removing folios of that magnitude, which, with infinite straining, was as much as I could manage, from the situation which they occupied upon an upper shelf. I have not met with the work from that time to this, but I remember it consisted of Old Testament stories, orderly set down, with the *objection* appended to each story, and the *solution* of the objection regularly tacked to that. The *objection* was a summary of whatever difficulties had been opposed to the credibility of the history, by the shrewdness of ancient or modern infidelity, drawn up with an almost complimentary excess of candour. The *solution* was brief, modest, and satisfactory. The bane and antidote were both before you. To doubts so put, and so quashed, there seemed to be an end for ever. The dragon lay dead, for the foot of the veriest babe to trample on. But—like as was rather feared than realised from that slain monster in Spenser—from the womb of those crushed errors young dragonets would creep, exceeding the prowess of so tender a Saint George as myself to vanquish. The habit of expecting objections to every passage set me upon starting more objections, for the glory of finding a solution of my own for them. I became staggered and perplexed, a sceptic in long-coats. The pretty Bible stories which I had read, or heard read in church, lost their purity and sincerity of impression, and were turned into so many historic or chronologic theses to be defended against whatever impugners. I was not to disbelieve them, but—the next thing to that—I was to be quite sure that some one or other would or had disbelieved them. Next to making a child an infidel is the letting him know that there are infidels at all. Credulity is the man's weakness, but the child's strength. O, how ugly sound scriptural doubts from the mouth of a babe and a suckling!—I should have lost myself in these mazes, and have pined away, I think, with such unfit sustenance as these husks afforded, but for a fortunate piece of ill-fortune which about this time befell me. Turning over the picture of the ark with too much haste, I unhappily made a breach in its ingenious fabric—driving my inconsiderate fingers right through the two larger quadrupeds—the elephant and the camel—that stare (as well they might) out of the two last windows next the steerage in that unique piece of naval architecture. Stackhouse was henceforth locked up, and became an interdicted treasure. With the book, the *objections* and *solutions* gradually cleared out of my head, and have seldom returned since in any force to trouble me.—But there was one impression which I had imbibed from Stackhouse which no lock or bar could shut out, and which was destined to try my childish nerves rather more seriously.—That detestable picture!

I was dreadfully alive to nervous terrors. The night-time, solitude, and the dark, were my hell. The sufferings I endured in this nature would justify the expression. I never laid my head on my pillow, I suppose, from the fourth to the seventh or eighth year of my life—so far as memory serves in things so long ago—without an assurance, which realised its own prophecy, of seeing some frightful spectre. Be old Stackhouse then acquitted in part, if I say, that to his picture of the Witch raising up Samuel—(O that old man covered with a mantle!)—I owe—not my midnight terrors, the hell of my infancy—but the shape and manner of their visitation.

It was he who dressed up for me a hag that nightly sate upon my pillow—a sure bedfellow, when my aunt or my maid was far from me. All day long, while the book was permitted me, I dreamed waking over his delineation, and at night (if I may use so bold an expression) awoke into sleep, and found the vision true. I durst not, even in the day-light, once enter the chamber where I slept, without my face turned to the window, aversely from the bed where my witch-ridden pillow was. Parents do not know what they do when they leave tender babes alone to go to sleep in the dark. The feeling about for a friendly arm—the hoping for a familiar voice—when they wake screaming—and find none to soothe them—what a terrible shaking it is to their poor nerves! The keeping them up till midnight, through candle-light and the unwholesome hours, as they are called,—would, I am satisfied, in a medical point of view, prove the better caution.—That detestable picture, as I have said, gave the fashion to my dreams—if dreams they were—for the scene of them was invariably the room in which I lay. Had I never met with the picture, the fears would have come self-pictured in some shape or other—

Headless bear, black man, or ape—

but, as it was, my imaginations took that form.—It is not book, or picture, or the stories of foolish servants, which create these terrors in children. They can at most but give them a direction. Dear little T. H., who of all children has been brought up with the most scrupulous exclusion of every taint of superstition—who was never allowed to hear of goblin or apparition, or scarcely to be told of bad men, or to read or hear of any distressing story—finds all this world of fear, from which he has been so rigidly excluded *ab extra*, in his own 'thick-coming fancies'; and from his little midnight pillow, this nurse-child of optimism will start at shapes, unborrowed of tradition, in sweats to which the reveries of the cell-damned murderer are tranquillity.

Gorgons, and Hydras, and Chimæras dire—stories of Celæno and the Harpies—may reproduce themselves in the brain of superstition—but they were there before. They are transcripts, types—the archetypes are in us, and eternal. How else should the recital of that, which we know in a waking sense to be false, come to affect us at all?—or

——Names, whose sense we see not,
Fray us with things that be not?

Is it that we naturally conceive terror from such objects, considered in their capacity of being able to inflict upon us bodily injury?—O, least of all! These terrors are of older standing. They date beyond body—or, without the body, they would have been the same. All the cruel, tormenting, defined devils in Dante—tearing, mangling, choking, stifling, scorching demons—are they one half so fearful to the spirit of a man, as the simple idea of a spirit unembodied following him—

> Like one that on a lonesome road
> Doth walk in fear and dread,
> And having once turn'd round, walks on
> And turns no more his head;
> Because he knows a frightful fiend
> Doth close behind him tread.*

That the kind of fear here treated of is purely spiritual— that it is strong in proportion as it is objectless upon earth— that it predominates in the period of sinless infancy—are difficulties, the solution of which might afford some probable insight into our ante-mundane condition, and a peep at least into the shadowland of pre-existence.

My night-fancies have long ceased to be afflictive. I confess an occasional nightmare; but I do not, as in early youth, keep a stud of them. Fiendish faces, with the extinguished taper, will come and look at me; but I know them for mockeries, even while I cannot elude their presence, and I fight and grapple with them. For the credit of my imagination, I am almost ashamed to say how tame and prosaic my dreams are grown. They are never romantic, seldom even rural. They are of architecture and of buildings—cities abroad, which I have never seen and hardly have hoped to see. I have traversed, for the seeming length of a natural day, Rome, Amsterdam, Paris, Lisbon—their churches, palaces, squares, market-places, shops, suburbs, ruins, with an inexpressible sense of delight—a map-like distinctness of trace — and a daylight vividness of vision, that was all but being awake.—I have formerly travelled among the Westmoreland

* Mr. Coleridge's Ancient Mariner.

fells—my highest Alps,—but they are objects too mighty for the grasp of my dreaming recognition; and I have again and again awoke with ineffectual struggles of the inner eye, to make out a shape, in any way whatever, of Helvellyn. Methought I was in that country, but the mountains were gone. The poverty of my dreams mortifies me. There is Coleridge, at his will can conjure up icy domes, and pleasure-houses for Kubla Khan, and Abyssinian maids, and songs of Abara, and caverns,

Where Alph, the sacred river, runs,

to solace his night solitudes—when I cannot muster a fiddle. Barry Cornwall has his tritons and his nereids gambolling before him in nocturnal visions, and proclaiming sons born to Neptune—when my stretch of imaginative activity can hardly, in the night season, raise up the ghost of a fish-wife. To set my failures in somewhat a mortifying light— it was after reading the noble Dream of this poet, that my fancy ran strong upon these marine spectra; and the poor plastic power, such as it is, within me set to work, to humour my folly in a sort of dream that very night. Methought I was upon the ocean billows at some sea nuptials, riding and mounted high, with the customary train sounding their conchs before me (I myself, you may be sure, the *leading god*), and jollily we went careering over the main, till just where Ino Leucothea should have greeted me (I think it was Ino) with a white embrace, the billows gradually subsiding, fell from a sea roughness to a sea calm, and thence to a river motion, and that river (as happens in the familiarisation of dreams) was no other than the gentle Thames, which landed me in the wafture of a placid wave or two, alone, safe and inglorious, somewhere at the foot of Lambeth palace.

The degree of the soul's creativeness in sleep might furnish no whimsical criterion of the quantum of poetical faculty resident in the same soul waking. An old gentleman, a friend of mine, and a humourist, used to carry this notion so far, that when he saw any stripling of his acquaintance ambitious of becoming a poet, his first question would be,— 'Young man, what sort of dreams have you?' I have so much faith in my old friend's theory, that when I feel that idle vein returning upon me, I presently subside into my proper element of prose, remembering those eluding nereids, and that inauspicious inland landing.

Valentine's Day

HAIL to thy returning festival, old Bishop Valentine! Great is thy name in the rubric, thou venerable Archflamen of Hymen! Immortal Go-between; who and what manner of person art thou? Art thou but a *name*, typifying the restless principle which impels poor humans to seek perfection in union? or wert thou indeed a mortal prelate, with thy tippet and thy rochet, thy apron on, and decent lawn sleeves? Mysterious personage! like unto thee, assuredly, there is no other mitred father in the calendar; not Jerome, nor Ambrose, nor Cyril; nor the consigner of undipt infants to eternal torments, Austin, whom all mothers hate; nor he who hated all mothers, Origen; nor Bishop Bull, nor Archbishop Parker, nor Whitgift. Thou comest attended with thousands and ten thousands of little Loves, and the air is

Brush'd with the hiss of rustling wings.

Singing Cupids are thy choristers and thy precentors; and instead of the crosier, the mystical arrow is borne before thee.

In other words, this is the day on which those charming little missives, ycleped Valentines, cross and intercross each other at every street and turning. The weary and all forspent twopenny postman sinks beneath a load of delicate embarrassments, not his own. It is scarcely credible to what an extent this ephemeral courtship is carried on in this loving town, to the great enrichment of porters, and detriment of knockers and bell wires. In these little visual interpretations, no emblem is so common as the *heart*,—that little three-cornered exponent of all our hopes and fears,—the bestuck and bleeding heart; it is twisted and tortured into more allegories and affectations than an opera-hat. What authority we have in history or mythology for placing the head-quarters and metropolis of God Cupid in this anatomical seat rather than in any other, is not very clear; but we have got it, and it will serve as well as any other. Else we might easily imagine, upon some other system which might have prevailed for anything which our pathology knows to the contrary, a lover addressing his mistress, in perfect simplicity of feeling, 'Madam, my *liver* and fortune are entirely at your disposal'; or putting a delicate question, 'Amanda, have you a *midriff* to bestow?' But custom has settled these things, and awarded the seat of sentiment to the aforesaid triangle, while its less fortunate neighbours wait at animal and anatomical distance.

Not many sounds in life, and I include all urban and all rural sounds, exceed in interest a *knock at the door*. It 'gives a very echo to the throne where hope is seated.' But its issues seldom answer to this oracle within. It is so seldom that just the person we want to see comes. But of all the clamorous visitations the welcomest in expectation is the sound that ushers in, or seems to usher in, a Valentine. As the raven himself was hoarse that announced the fatal entrance of Duncan, so the knock of the postman on this day is light, airy, confident, and befitting one that bringeth good tidings. It is less mechanical than on other days; you will say, 'That is not the post, I am sure.' Visions of Love, of Cupids, of Hymens!—delightful eternal common-places, which 'having been will always be'; which no school-boy nor school-man can write away; having your irreversible throne in the fancy and affections—what are your transports, when the happy maiden, opening with careful finger, careful not to break the emblematic seal, bursts upon the sight of some well-designed allegory, some type, some youthful fancy, not without verses—

> Lovers all,
> A madrigal,

or some such device, not over abundant in sense—young Love disclaims it,—and not quite silly—something between wind and water, a chorus where the sheep might almost join the shepherd, as they did, or as I apprehend they did, in Arcadia.

All Valentines are not foolish; and I shall not easily forget thine, my kind friend (if I may have leave to call you so) E. B.—E. B. lived opposite a young maiden whom he had often seen, unseen, from his parlour window in C—e Street. She was all joyousness and innocence, and just of an age to enjoy receiving a Valentine, and just of a temper to bear the disappointment of missing one with good-humour. E. B. is an artist of no common powers; in the fancy parts of designing, perhaps inferior to none; his name is known at the bottom of many a well-executed vignette in the way of his profession, but no further; for E. B. is modest, and the world meets nobody half-way. E. B. meditated how he could repay this young maiden for many a favour which she had done him unknown; for when a kindly face greets us, though but passing by, and never knows us again, nor we it, we should feel it as an obligation: and E. B. did. This good artist set himself at work to please the damsel. It was just before Valentine's day three years since. He wrought, unseen and unsuspected, a wondrous work. We need not say it was on the finest gilt paper with borders—full, not of common hearts and heartless allegory, but all the prettiest stories of love from Ovid, and older poets than Ovid (for E. B. is a scholar). There was Pyramus and Thisbe, and be sure Dido was not forgot, nor Hero and Leander, and swans more than sang in Cayster, with mottoes and fanciful devices, such as beseemed —a work, in short, of magic. Iris dipt the woof. This on Valentine's eve he commended to the all-swallowing indiscriminate orifice—(O ignoble trust!)—of the common post; but the humble medium did its duty, and from his watchful stand, the next morning he saw the cheerful messenger knock, and by and by the precious charge delivered. He saw, unseen, the happy girl unfold the Valentine, dance about, clap her hands, as one after one the pretty emblems unfolded themselves. She danced about, not with light love, or foolish expectations, for she had no lover; or, if she had, none she knew that could have created those bright images which delighted her. It was more like some fairy present; a God-send, as our familiarly pious ancestors termed a benefit received where the benefactor was unknown. It would do her no harm. It would do her good for ever after. It is good to love the unknown. I only give this as a specimen of E.B. and his modest way of doing a concealed kindness.

Good morrow to my Valentine, sings poor Ophelia; and no better wish, but with better auspices, we wish to all faithful lovers, who are not too wise to despise old legends, but are content to rank themselves humble diocesans of old Bishop Valentine and his true church.

My Relations

I AM arrived at that point of life at which a man may account it a blessing, as it is a singularity, if he have either of his parents surviving. I have not that felicity—and sometimes think feelingly of a passage in Browne's Christian Morals, where he speaks of a man that hath lived sixty or seventy years in the world. 'In such a compass of time,' he says, 'a man may have a close apprehension what it is to be forgotten, when he hath lived to find none who could remember his father, or scarcely the friends of his youth, and may sensibly see with what a face in no long time OBLIVION will look upon himself.'

I had an aunt, a dear and good one. She was one whom single blessedness had soured to the world. She often used to say, that I was the only thing in it which she loved; and, when she thought I was quitting it, she grieved over me with mother's tears. A partiality quite so exclusive my reason cannot altogether approve. She was from morning till night poring over good books, and devotional exercises. Her favourite volumes were, Thomas à Kempis, in Stanhope's translation; and a Roman Catholic Prayer Book, with the *matins* and *complines* regularly set down,—terms which I was at that time too young to understand. She persisted in reading them, although admonished daily concerning their Papistical tendency; and went to church every Sabbath as a good Protestant should do. These were the only books she studied; though, I think at one period of her life, she told me, she had read with great satisfaction the Adventures of an Unfortunate Young Nobleman. Finding the door of the chapel in Essex Street open one day—it was in the infancy of that heresy— she went in, liked the sermon, and the manner of worship, and frequented it at intervals for some time after. She came not for doctrinal points, and never missed them. With some little asperities in her constitution, which I have above hinted at, she was a steadfast, friendly being, and a fine *old Christian*. She was a woman of strong sense, and a shrewd mind— extraordinary at a *repartee;* one of the few occasions of her breaking silence—else she did not much value wit. The only secular employment I remember to have seen her engaged in, was, the splitting of French beans, and dropping them into a china basin of fair water. The odour of those tender vegetables to this day comes back upon my sense, redolent of soothing recollections. Certainly it is the most delicate of culinary operations.

Male aunts, as somebody calls them, I had none—to remember. By the uncle's side I may be said to have been born an orphan. Brother, or sister, I never had any—to know them. A sister, I think, that should have been Elizabeth, died in both our infancies. What a comfort, or what a care, may I not have missed in her!—But I have cousins sprinkled about in Hertfordshire—besides *two*, with whom I have been all my life in habits of the closest intimacy, and whom I may term cousins *par excellence*. These are James and Bridget Elia. They are older than myself by twelve, and ten, years; and neither of them seems disposed, in matters of advice and guidance, to waive any of the prerogatives which primogeniture confers. May they continue still in the same mind; and when they shall be seventy-five, and seventy-three, years old (I cannot spare them sooner), persist in treating me in my grand climacteric precisely as a stripling, or younger brother!

James is an inexplicable cousin. Nature hath her unities, which not every critic can penetrate: or, if we feel, we cannot explain them. The pen of Yorick, and of none since his, could have drawn J. E. entire—those fine Shandean lights and shades, which make up his story. I must limp after in my poor antithetical manner, as the fates have given me grace and talent. J. E. then—to the eye of a common observer at least— seemeth made up of contradictory principles. The genuine child of impulse, the frigid philosopher of prudence—the phlegm of my cousin's doctrine is invariably at war with his temperament, which is high sanguine. With always some fire-new project in his brain, J.E. is the systematic opponent of innovation, and crier down of everything that has not stood the test of age and experiment. With a hundred fine notions chasing one another hourly in his fancy, he is startled at the least approach to the romantic in others: and, de-termined by his own sense in everything, commends *you* to the guidance of common sense on all occasions.—With a touch of the eccentric in all which he does, or says, he is only anxious that *you* should not commit yourself by doing anything absurd or singular. On my once letting slip at table, that I was not fond of a certain popular dish, he begged me at any rate not to *say* so—for the world would think me mad. He disguises a passionate fondness for works of high art (whereof he hath amassed a choice collection), under the pretext of buying only to sell again—that his enthusiasm may give no encouragement to yours. Yet, if it were so, why does that piece of tender, pastoral Domenichino hang still by his wall?—is the ball of his sight much more dear to him?—or what picture-dealer can talk like him?

Whereas mankind in general are observed to warp their speculative conclusions to the bent of their individual humours, *his* theories are sure to be in diametrical opposition to his conclusions. He is courageous as Charles of Sweden, upon instinct; chary of his person upon principle, as a travelling Quaker. He has been preaching up to me, all my life, the doctrine of bowing to the great—the necessity of forms, and manner, to a man's getting on in the world. He himself never aims at either, that I can discover,—and has a spirit that would stand upright in the presence of the Cham of Tartary. It is pleasant to hear him discourse of patience —extolling it as the truest wisdom—and to see him during the last seven minutes that his dinner is getting ready. Nature never ran up in her haste a more restless piece of workmanship than when she moulded this impetuous cousin—and Art never turned out a more elaborate orator than he can display himself to be, upon his favourite topic of the advantages of quiet and contentedness in the state, whatever it be, that we are placed in. He is triumphant on this theme, when he has you safe in one of those short stages that ply for the western road, in a very obstructing manner, at the foot of John Murray's Street—where you get in when it is empty, and are expected to wait till the vehicle hath completed her just freight—a trying three-quarters of an hour to some people. He wonders at your fidgetiness,—'where could we be better than we are, *thus sitting, thus consulting?*' —'prefers, for his part, a state of rest to locomotion,'—with an eye all the while upon the coachman,—till at length, waxing out of all patience, at *your want of it*, he breaks out into a pathetic remonstrance at the fellow for detaining us so long over the time which he had professed, and declares peremptorily, that 'the gentleman in the coach is determined to get out, if he does not drive on that instant.'

Very quick at inventing an argument, or detecting a sophistry, he is incapable of attending *you* in any chain of arguing. Indeed, he makes wild work with logic; and seems to jump at most admirable conclusions by some process, not at all akin to it. Consonantly enough to this, he hath been heard to deny, upon certain occasions, that there exists such a faculty at all in man as *reason;* and wondereth how man came first to have a conceit of it—enforcing his negation with all the might of *reasoning* he is master of. He has some speculative notions against laughter and will maintain that laughing is not natural to *him*—when peradventure the next moment his lungs shall crow like Chanticleer. He says some of the best things in the world—and declareth that wit is his aversion. It was he who said, upon seeing the Eton boys at play in their grounds—*What a pity to think, that these fine* ingenuous lads in a few years will be changed into frivolous *Members of Parliament*!

His youth was fiery, glowing, tempestuous—and in age he discovereth no symptom of cooling. This is that which I admire in him. I hate people who meet Time half-way. I am for no compromise with that inevitable spoiler. While he lives, J.E. will take his swing.—It does me good, as I walk towards the street of my daily avocation, on some fine May morning, to meet him marching in a quite opposite direction, with a jolly handsome presence, and shining sanguine face, that indicate some purchase in his eye—a Claude—or a Hobbima—for much of his enviable leisure is consumed at Christie's and Phillips's—or where not, to pick up pictures, and such gauds. On these occasions he mostly stoppeth me, to read a short lecture on the advantage a person like me possesses above himself, in having his time occupied with business which he *must* do—assureth me that he often feels it hang heavy on his hands—wishes he had fewer holidays—and goes off—Westward Ho!—chanting a tune, to Pall Mall—perfectly convinced that he has convinced me—while I proceed in my opposite direction tuneless.

It is pleasant, again, to see this Professor of Indifference doing the honours of his new purchase, when he has fairly housed it. You must view it in every light, till *he* has found the best—placing it at this distance, and at that, but always suiting the focus of your sight to his own. You must spy at it through your fingers, to catch the aërial perspective—though you assure him that to you the landscape shows much more agreeable without that artifice. Woe be to the luckless wight who does not only not respond to his rapture, but who should drop an unseasonable intimation of preferring one of his anterior bargains to the present!—The last is always his best hit—his 'Cynthia of the minute.'—Alas! how many a mild Madonna have I known to *come in*—a Raphael!—keep its ascendancy for a few brief moons—then, after certain intermedial degradations, from the front drawing-room to the back gallery, thence to the dark parlour,—adopted in turn by each of the Carracci, under successive lowering ascriptions of filiation, mildly breaking its fall—consigned to the oblivious lumber-room, *go out* at last a Lucca Giordano, or plain Carlo Maratti!—which things when I beheld—musing upon the chances and mutabilities of fate below, hath made me to reflect upon the altered condition of great personages, or that woeful Queen of Richard the Second—

> ———set forth in pomp,
> She came adorned hither like sweet May.
> Sent back like Hallowmass or shortest day.

With great love for *you*, J.E. hath but a limited sympathy with what you feel or do. He lives in a world of his own, and makes slender guesses at what passes in your mind. He never pierces the marrow of your habits. He will tell an old-established play-goer, that Mr. Such-a-one, of So-and-so (naming one of the theatres), is a very lively comedian—as a piece of news! He advertised me but the other day of some pleasant green lanes which he had found out for me, *knowing me to be a great walker*, in my own immediate vicinity —who have haunted the identical spot any time these twenty years!—He has not much respect for that class of feelings which goes by the name of sentimental. He applies the definition of real evil to bodily sufferings exclusively—and rejecteth all others as imaginary. He is affected by the sight, or the bare supposition, of a creature in pain, to a degree which I have never witnessed out of womankind. A constitutional acuteness to this class of sufferings may in part account for this. The animal tribe in particular he taketh under his especial protection. A broken-winded or spur-galled horse is sure to find an advocate in him. An over-loaded ass is his client for ever. He is the apostle to the brute kind—the never-failing friend of those who have none to care for them. The contemplation of a lobster boiled, or eels skinned *alive*, will wring him so, that 'all for pity he could die.' It will take the savour from his palate, and the rest from his pillow, for days and nights. With the intense feeling of Thomas Clarkson, he wanted only the steadiness of pursuit, and unity of purpose, of that 'true yoke-fellow with Time,' to have effected as much for the *Animal* as *he* hath done for the *Negro Creation*. But my uncontrollable cousin is but imperfectly formed for purposes which demand co-operation. He cannot wait. His amelioration plans must be ripened in a day. For this reason he has cut but an equivo-cal figure in benevolent societies, and combinations for the alleviation of human sufferings. His zeal constantly makes him to outrun, and put out, his coadjutors. He thinks of relieving,—while they think of debating. He was black-balled out of a society for the Relief of * * * * * * * * * * *, because the fervour of his humanity toiled beyond the formal apprehension, and creeping processes, of his associates. I shall always consider this distinction as a patent of nobility in the Elia family!

Do I mention these seeming inconsistencies to smile at, or upbraid, my unique cousin? Marry, heaven, and all good manners, and the understanding that should be between kinsfolk, forbid!—With all the strangenesses of this *strangest of the Elias*—I would not have him in one jot or tittle other than he is; neither would I barter or exchange my wild kinsman for the most exact, regular, and every way consistent kinsman breathing.

In my next, reader, I may perhaps give you some account of my cousin Bridget—if you are not already surfeited with cousins—and take you by the hand, if you are willing to go with us, on an excursion which we made a summer or two since, in search of *more cousins*—

Through the green plains of pleasant Hertfordshire.

Mackery End, in Hertfordshire

BRIDGET ELIA has been my housekeeper for many a long year. I have obligations to Bridget, extending beyond the period of memory. We house together, old bachelor and maid, in a sort of double singleness; with such tolerable comfort, upon the whole, that I, for one, find in myself no sort of disposition to go out upon the mountains, with the rash king's offspring, to bewail my celibacy. We agree pretty well in our tastes and habits—yet so, as 'with a difference.' We are generally in harmony, with occasional bickerings—as it should be among near relations. Our sympathies are rather understood than expressed; and once upon my dissembling a tone in my voice more kind than ordinary, my cousin burst into tears, and complained that I was altered. We are both great readers in different directions. While I am hanging over (for the thousandth time) some passage in old Burton, or one of his strange contemporaries, she is abstracted in some modern tale, or adventure, whereof our common reading-table is daily fed with assiduously fresh supplies. Narrative teases me. I have little concern in the progress of events. She must have a story—well, ill, or in-differently told—so there be life stirring in it, and plenty of good or evil accidents. The fluctuations of fortune in fiction—and almost in real life—have ceased to interest, or operate but dully upon me. Out-of-the-way humours and opinions—heads with some diverting twist in them—the oddities of authorship, please me most. My cousin has a native disrelish of anything that sounds odd or bizarre. Nothing goes down with her that is quaint, irregular, or out of the road of common sympathy. She 'holds Nature more clever.' I can pardon her blindness to the beautiful obliquities of the Religio Medici; but she must apologise to me for certain disrespectful insinuations, which she has been pleased to throw out latterly, touching the intellectuals of a dear favourite of mine, of the last century but one—the thrice noble, chaste, and virtuous, but again somewhat fantastical and original-brained, generous Margaret Newcastle.

It has been the lot of my cousin, oftener perhaps than I could have wished, to have had for her associates and mine, free-thinkers—leaders, and disciples, of novel philosophies and systems; but she neither wrangles with, nor accepts, their opinions. That which was good and venerable to her, when a child, retains its authority over her mind still. She never juggles or plays tricks with her understanding.

We are both of us inclined to be a little too positive; and I have observed the result of our disputes to be almost uniformly this—that in matters of fact, dates, and circumstances, it turns out, that I was in the right, and my cousin in the wrong. But where we have differed upon moral points; upon something proper to be done, or let alone; whatever heat of opposition, or steadiness of conviction, I set out with, I am sure always, in the long-run, to be brought over to her way of thinking.

I must touch upon the foibles of my kinswoman with a gentle hand, for Bridget does not like to be told of her faults. She hath an awkward trick (to say no worse of it) of reading in company: at which times she will answer *yes* for *no* to a question, without fully understanding its purport—which is provoking, and derogatory in the highest degree to the dignity of the putter of the said question. Her presence of mind is equal to the most pressing trials of life, but will sometimes desert her upon trifling occasions. When the purpose requires it, and is a thing of moment, she can speak to it greatly; but in matters which are not stuff of the conscience, she hath been known sometimes to let slip a word less seasonably.

Her education in youth was not much attended to; and she happily missed all that train of female garniture which passeth by the name of accomplishments. She was tumbled early, by accident or design, into a spacious closet of good old English reading, without much selection or prohibition, and browsed at will upon that fair and wholesome pasturage. Had I twenty girls, they should be brought up exactly in this fashion. I know not whether their chance in wedlock might not be diminished by it; but I can answer for it, that it makes (if the worst come to the worst) most incomparable old maids.

In a season of distress, she is the truest comforter; but in the teasing accidents, and minor perplexities, which do not call out the *will* to meet them, she sometimes maketh matters worse by an excess of participation. If she does not always divide your trouble, upon the pleasanter occasions of life she is sure always to treble your satisfaction. She is excellent to be at a play with, or upon a visit; but best, when she goes a journey with you.

We made an excursion together a few summers since, into Hertfordshire, to beat up the quarters of some of our less-known relations in that fine corn country.

The oldest thing I remember is Mackery End; or Mackarel End, as it is spelt, perhaps more properly, in some old maps of Hertfordshire; a farm-house,—delightfully situated within a gentle walk from Wheathampstead. I can just remember having been there, on a visit to a great-aunt, when I was a child, under the care of Bridget; who, as I have said, is older than myself by some ten years. I wish that I could throw into a heap the remainder of our joint existences; that we might share them in equal division. But that is impossible. The house was at that time in the occupation of a substantial yeoman, who had married my grandmother's sister. His name was Gladman. My grandmother was Bruton, married to a Field. The Gladmans and the Brutons are still flourishing in that part of the county, but the Fields are almost extinct. More than forty years had elapsed since the visit I speak of; and, for the greater portion of that period, we had lost sight of the other two branches also. Who or what sort of persons inherited Mackery End—kindred or strange folk—we were afraid almost to conjecture, but determined some day to explore.

By somewhat a circuitous route, taking the noble park at Luton in our way from St. Albans, we arrived at the spot of our anxious curiosity about noon. The sight of the old farm-house, though every trace of it was effaced from my recollection, affected me with a pleasure which I had not experienced for many a year. For though I had forgotten it, *we* had never forgotten being there together, and we had been talking about Mackery End all our lives, till memory on my part became mocked with a phantom of itself, and I thought I knew the aspect of a place, which, when present, O how unlike it was to *that*, which I had conjured up so many times instead of it!

Still the air breathed balmily about it; the season was in 'the heart of June,' and I could say with the poet,

But thou, that didst appear so fair
To fond imagination,
Dost rival in the light of day
Her delicate creation!

Bridget's was more a waking bliss than mine, for she easily remembered her old acquaintance again—some altered features, of course, a little grudged at. At first, indeed, she was ready to disbelieve for joy; but the scene soon re-confirmed itself in her affections—and she traversed every outpost of the old mansion, to the wood-house, the orchard, the place where the pigeon-house had stood (house and birds were alike flown)—with a breathless impatience of recognition, which was more pardonable perhaps than decorous at the age of fifty odd. But Bridget in some things is behind her years.

The only thing left was to get into the house—and that was a difficulty which to me singly would have been insurmountable; for I am terribly shy in making myself known to strangers and out-of-date kinsfolk. Love, stronger than scruple, winged my cousin in without me; but she soon returned with a creature that might have sat to a sculptor for the image of Welcome. It was the youngest of the Gladmans; who, by marriage with a Bruton, had become mistress of the old mansion. A comely brood are the Brutons. Six of them, females, were noted as the handsomest young women in the county. But this adopted Bruton, in my mind, was better than they all—more comely. She was born too late to have remembered me. She just recollected in early life to have had her cousin Bridget once pointed out to her, climbing a stile. But the name of kindred, and of cousinship, was enough. Those slender ties, that prove slight as gossamer in the rending atmosphere of a metropolis, bind faster, as we found it, in hearty, homely, loving Hertfordshire. In five minutes we were as thoroughly acquainted as if we had been born and bred up together; were familiar, even to the calling each other by our Christian names. So Christians should call one another. To have seen Bridget, and her—it was like the meeting of the two scriptural cousins! There was a grace and dignity, an amplitude of form and stature, answering to her mind, in this farmer's wife, which would have shined in a palace—or so we thought it. We were made welcome by husband and wife equally—we, and our friend that was with us.—I had almost forgotten him—but B.F. will not so soon forget that meeting, if peradventure he shall read this on the far distant shores where the kangaroo haunts. The fatted calf was made ready or rather was already so, as if in anticipation of our coming; and, after an appropriate glass of native wine, never let me forget with what honest pride this hospitable cousin made us proceed to Wheathampstead, to introduce us (as some new-found rarity) to her mother and sister Gladmans, who did indeed know something more of us, at a time when she almost knew nothing.—With what corresponding kindness we were received by them also—how Bridget's memory, exalted by the occasion, warmed into a thousand half-obliterated recollections of things and persons, to my utter astonishment, and her own—and to the astoundment of B.F., who sat by, almost the only thing that was not a cousin there,—old effaced images of more than half-forgotten names and circumstances still crowding back upon her, as words written in lemon come out upon exposure to a friendly warmth,—when I forget all this, then may my country cousins forget me; and Bridget no more remember, that in the days of weakling infancy I was her tender charge—as I have been her care in foolish manhood since—in those pretty pastoral walks, long ago, about Mackery End, in Hertfordshire.

My First Play

AT the north end of Cross Court there yet stands a portal, of some architectural pretensions, though reduced to humble use, serving at present for an entrance to a printing-office. This old door-way, if you are young, reader, you may not know was the identical pit entrance to old Drury—Garrick's Drury—all of it that is left. I never pass it without shaking some forty years from off my shoulders, recurring to the evening when I passed through it to see *my first play*. The afternoon had been wet, and the condition of our going (the elder folks and myself) was, that the rain should cease. With what a beating heart did I watch from the window the puddles, from the stillness of which I was taught to prognosticate the desired cessation! I seem to remember the last spurt, and the glee with which I ran to announce it.

We went with orders, which my godfather F. had sent us. He kept the oil shop (now Davies's) at the corner of Feather-stone Buildings, in Holborn. F. was a tall grave person, lofty in speech, and had pretensions above his rank. He associated in those days with John Palmer, the comedian, whose gait and bearing he seemed to copy; if John (which is quite as likely) did not rather borrow somewhat of his manner from my godfather. He was also known to, and visited by, Sheridan. It was to his house in Holborn that young Brinsley brought his first wife on her elopement with him from a boarding-school at Bath—the beautiful Maria Linley. My parents were present (over a quadrille table) when he arrived in the evening with his harmonious charge. From either of these connexions it may be inferred that my godfather could command an order for the then Drury Lane theatre at pleasure—and, indeed, a pretty liberal issue of those cheap billets, in Brinsley's easy autograph, I have heard him say was the sole remuneration which he had received for many years' nightly illumination of the orchestra and various avenues of that theatre—and he was content it should be so. The honour of Sheridan's familiarity—or supposed familiarity —was better to my godfather than money.

F. was the most gentlemanly of oilmen; grandiloquent, yet courteous. His delivery of the commonest matters of fact was Ciceronian. He had two Latin words almost constantly in his mouth (how odd sounds Latin from an oilman's lips!), which my better knowledge since has enabled me to correct. In strict pronunciation they should have been sounded *vice versâ*—but in those young years they impressed me with more awe than they would now do, read aright from Seneca or Varro—in his own peculiar pronunciation, monosyllabically elaborated, or Anglicised, into something like *verse verse*. By an imposing manner, and the help of these distorted syllables, he climbed (but that was little) to the highest parochial honours which St. Andrew's has to bestow.

He is dead—and thus much I thought due to his memory, both for my first orders (little wondrous talismans!—slight keys, and insignificant to outward sight, but opening to me more than Arabian paradises!) and moreover that by his testamentary beneficence I came into possession of the only landed property which I could ever call my own—situate near the road-way village of pleasant Puckeridge, in Hertfordshire. When I journeyed down to take possession, and planted foot on my own ground, the stately habits of the donor descended upon me, and I strode (shall I confess the vanity?) with larger paces over my allotment of three-quarters of an acre with its commodious mansion in the midst, with the feeling of an English freeholder that all betwixt sky and centre was my own. The estate has passed into more prudent hands, and nothing but an agrarian can restore it.

In those days were pit orders. Beshrew the uncomfortable manager who abolished them!—with one of these we went. I remember the waiting at the door—not that which is left —but between that and an inner door in shelter—O when shall I be such an expectant again!—with the cry of nonpareils, an indispensable play-house accompaniment in those days. As near as I can recollect, the fashionable pronunciation of the theatrical fruiteresses then was, 'Chase some oranges, chase some numparels, chase a bill of the play';— chase *pro* chuse. But when we got in, and I beheld the green curtain that veiled a heaven to my imagination, which was soon to be disclosed—the breathless anticipations I endured! I had seen something like it in the plate prefixed to Troilus and Cressida, in Rowe's Shakespeare—the tent scene with Diomede—and a sight of that plate can always bring back in a measure the feeling of that evening.—The boxes at that time, full of well-dressed women of quality, projected over the pit: and the pilasters reaching down were adorned with a glistering substance (I know not what) under glass (as it seemed), resembling—a homely fancy—but I judged it to be sugar-candy—yet, to my raised imagination, divested of its homelier qualities, it appeared a glorified candy!—The orchestra lights at length arose, those 'fair Auroras'! Once the bell sounded. It was to ring out yet once again—and, incapable of the anticipation, I reposed my shut eyes in a sort of resignation upon the maternal lap. It rang the second time. The curtain drew up—I was not past six years old, and the play was Artaxerxes!

I had dabbled a little in the Universal History—the ancient part of it—and here was the court of Persia.—It was being admitted to a sight of the past. I took no proper interest in the action going on, for I understood not its import—but I heard the word Darius, and I was in the midst of Daniel. All feeling was absorbed in vision. Gorgeous vests, gardens, palaces, princesses, passed before me. I knew not players. I was in Persepolis for the time, and the burning idol of their devotion almost converted me into a worshipper. I was awe-struck, and believed those significations to be something more than elemental fires. It was all enchantment and a dream. No such pleasure has since visited me but in dreams.—Harlequin's invasion followed; where, I remember, the transformation of the magistrates into reverend beldams seemed to me a piece of grave historic justice, and the tailor carrying his own head to be as sober a verity as the legend of St. Denys.

The next play to which I was taken was the Lady of the Manor, of which, with the exception of some scenery, very faint traces are left in my memory. It was followed by a pantomime, called Lun's Ghost—a satiric touch, I apprehend, upon Rich, not long since dead—but to my apprehension (too sincere for satire), Lun was as remote a piece of antiquity as Lud—the father of a line of Harlequins—transmitting his dagger of lath (the wooden sceptre) through countless ages. I saw the primeval Motley come from his silent tomb in a ghastly vest of white patchwork, like the apparition of a dead rainbow. So Harlequins (thought I) look when they are dead.

My third play followed in quick succession. It was the Way of the World. I think I must have sat at it as grave as a judge; for, I remember, the hysteric affections of good Lady Wishfort affected me like some solemn tragic passion. Robinson Crusoe followed; in which Crusoe, man Friday, and the parrot were as good and authentic as in the story.—The clownery and pantaloonery of these pantomimes have clean passed out of my head. I believe, I no more laughed at them, than at the same age I should have been disposed to laugh at the grotesque Gothic heads (seeming to me then replete with devout meaning) that gape, and grin, in stone around the inside of the old Roman Church (my church) of the Templars.

I saw these plays in the season 1781-2, when I was from six to seven years old. After the intervention of six or seven other years (for at school all play-going was inhibited) I again entered the doors of a theatre. That old Artaxerxes

evening had never done ringing in my fancy. I expected the
same feelings to come again with the same occasion. But
we differ from ourselves less at sixty and sixteen, than the
latter does from six. In that interval what had I not lost! At
the first period I knew nothing, understood nothing, dis-
criminated nothing. I felt all, loved all, wondered all—

Was nourished, I could not tell how—

I had left the temple a devotee, and was returned a rationalist.
The same things were there materially; but the emblem,
the reference, was gone!—The green curtain was no longer
a veil, drawn between two worlds, the unfolding of which was
to bring back past ages to present a 'royal ghost,'—but a
certain quantity of green baize, which was to separate the
audience for a given time from certain of their fellow-men
who were to come forward and pretend those parts. The
lights—the orchestra lights—came up a clumsy machinery.
The first ring, and the second ring, was now but a trick of
the prompter's bell—which had been, like the note of the
cuckoo, a phantom of a voice, no hand seen or guessed at
which ministered to its warning. The actors were men and
women painted. I thought the fault was in them; but it was
in myself, and the alteration which those many centuries—of
six short twelvemonths—had wrought in me.—Perhaps it was
fortunate for me that the play of the evening was but an
indifferent comedy, as it gave me time to crop some unreasonable expectations, which might have interfered with
the genuine emotions with which I was soon after enabled to
enter upon the first appearance to me of Mrs. Siddons in
Isabella. Comparison and retrospection soon yielded to the
present attraction of the scene; and the theatre became to
me, upon a new stock, the most delightful of recreations.

Modern Gallantry

In comparing modern with ancient manners, we are pleased
to compliment ourselves upon the point of gallantry; a certain
obsequiousness, or deferential respect, which we are supposed
to pay to females, as females.

I shall believe that this principle actuates our conduct,

when I can forget, that in the nineteenth century of the era from which we date our civility, we are but just beginning to leave off the very frequent practice of whipping females in public, in common with the coarsest male offenders.

I shall believe it to be influential, when I can shut my eyes to the fact, that in England women are still occasionally —hanged.

I shall believe in it, when actresses are no longer subject to be hissed off a stage by gentlemen.

I shall believe in it, when Dorimant hands a fish-wife across the kennel; or assists the apple-woman to pick up her wandering fruit, which some unlucky dray has just dissipated.

I shall believe in it, when the Dorimants in humbler life, who would be thought in their way notable adepts in this refinement, shall act upon it in places where they are not known, or think themselves not observed—when I shall see the traveller for some rich tradesman part with his admired box-coat, to spread it over the defenceless shoulders of the poor woman, who is passing to her parish on the roof of the same stage-coach with him, drenched in the rain—when I shall no longer see a woman standing up in the pit of a London theatre, till she is sick and faint with the exertion, with men about her, seated at their ease, and jeering at her distress; till one, that seems to have more manners or conscience than the rest, significantly declares 'she should be welcome to his seat, if she were a little younger and handsomer.' Place this dapper warehouseman, or that rider, in a circle of their own female acquaintance, and you shall confess you have not seen a politer-bred man in Lothbury.

Lastly, I shall begin to believe that there is some such principle influencing our conduct, when more than one-half of the drudgery and coarse servitude of the world shall cease to be performed by women.

Until that day comes, I shall never believe this boasted point to be anything more than a conventional fiction; a pageant got up between the sexes, in a certain rank, and at a certain time of life, in which both find their account equally.

I shall be even disposed to rank it among the salutary fictions of life, when in polite circles I shall see the same attentions paid to age as to youth, to homely features as to handsome, to coarse complexions as to clear—to the woman, as she is a woman, not as she is a beauty, a fortune, or a title.

I shall believe it to be something more than a name, when a well-dressed gentleman in a well-dressed company can advert to the topic of *female old age* without exciting, and intending to excite, a sneer:—when the phrases 'antiquated virginity,' and such a one has 'overstood her market,' pronounced in good company, shall raise immediate offence in man, or woman, that shall hear them spoken.

Joseph Paice, of Bread Street Hill, merchant, and one of the Directors of the South-Sea Company—the same to whom Edwards, the Shakespeare commentator, has addressed a fine sonnet—was the only pattern of consistent gallantry I have met with. He took me under his shelter at an early age, and bestowed some pains upon me. I owe to his precepts and example whatever there is of the man of business (and that is not much) in my composition. It was not his fault that I did not profit more. Though bred a Presbyterian, and brought up a merchant, he was the finest gentleman of his time. He had not *one* system of attention to females in the drawing-room, and *another* in the shop, or at the stall. I do not mean that he made no distinction. But he never lost sight of sex, or overlooked it in the casualties of a disadvantageous situation. I have seen him stand bareheaded—smile if you please—to a poor servant-girl, while she has been inquiring of him the way to some street—in such a posture of unforced civility, as neither to embarrass her in the acceptance, nor himself in the offer, of it. He was no dangler, in the common acceptation of the word, after women: but he reverenced and upheld, in every form in which it came before him, *womanhood*. I have seen him—nay, smile not—tenderly escorting a market-woman, whom he had encountered in a shower, exalting his umbrella over her poor basket of fruit, that it might receive no damage, with as much carefulness as if she had been a Countess. To the reverend form of Female Eld he would yield the wall (though it were to an ancient beggar-woman) with more ceremony than he can afford to show our grandams. He was the Preux Chevalier of Age; the Sir Calidore, or Sir Tristan, to those who have no Calidores or Tristans to defend them. The roses, that had long faded thence, still bloomed for him in those withered and yellow cheeks.

He was never married, but in his youth he paid his addresses to the beautiful Susan Winstanley—old Winstanley's daughter of Clapton—who dying in the early days of their courtship, confirmed in him the resolution of perpetual bachelorship. It was during their short courtship, he told me, that he had been one day treating his mistress with a profusion of civil speeches—the common gallantries—to which kind of thing she had hitherto manifested no repugnance—but in this instance with no effect. He could not obtain from her a decent acknowledgment in return. She rather seemed to resent his compliments. He could not set it down to caprice, for the lady had always shown herself above that littleness. When he ventured on the following day, finding her a little better humoured, to expostulate with her on her coldness of yesterday, she confessed, with her usual frankness, that she had no sort of dislike to his attentions; that she could even endure some high-flown compliments; that a young woman placed in her situation had a right to expect all sort of civil things said to her; that she hoped she could digest a dose of adulation, short of insincerity, with as little injury to her humility as most young women; but that—a little before he had commenced his compliments—she had overheard him by accident, in rather rough language, rating a young woman, who had not brought home his cravats quite to the appointed time, and she thought to herself, 'As I am Miss Susan Winstanley, and a young lady—a reputed beauty, and known to be a fortune—I can have my choice of the finest speeches from the mouth of this very fine gentleman who is courting me,—but if I had been poor Mary Such-a-one (*naming the milliner*)—and had failed of bringing home the cravats to the appointed hour—though perhaps I had sat up half the night to forward them—what sort of compliments should I have received then?—And my woman's pride came to my assistance; and I thought, that if it were only to do *me* honour, a female, like myself, might have received handsomer usage: and I was determined not to accept any fine speeches, to the compromise of that sex, the belonging to which was after all my strongest claim and title to them.'

I think the lady discovered both generosity, and a just way of thinking, in this rebuke which she gave her lover; and I have sometimes imagined, that the uncommon strain of courtesy, which through life regulated the actions and behaviour of my friend towards all of womankind indiscriminately, owed its happy origin to this seasonable lesson from the lips of his lamented mistress.

I wish the whole female world would entertain the same notion of these things that Miss Winstanley showed. Then we should see something of the spirit of consistent gallantry; and no longer witness the anomaly of the same man—a pattern of true politeness to a wife—of cold contempt, or rudeness, to a sister—the idolater of his female mistress—the disparager and despiser of his no less female aunt, or unfortunate—still female—maiden cousin. Just so much respect as a woman derogates from her own sex, in whatever condition placed—her hand-maid, or dependant—she deserves to have diminished from herself on that score; and probably will feel the diminution, when youth, and beauty, and advantages, not inseparable from sex, shall lose of their attraction. What a woman should demand of a man in courtship, or after it, is first—respect for her as she is a woman;—and next to that —to be respected by him above all other women. But let her stand upon her female character as upon a foundation; and let the attentions, incident to individual preference, to so many pretty additaments and ornaments—as many, and as fanciful, as you please—to that main structure. Let her first lesson be with sweet Susan Winstanley—to *reverence her sex.*

The Old Benchers of the Inner Temple

I was born, and passed the first seven years of my life, in the Temple. Its church, its halls, its gardens, its fountain, its river, I had almost said—for in those young years, what was this king of rivers to me but a stream that watered our pleasant places?—these are of my oldest recollections. I repeat, to this day, no verses to myself more frequently, or with kindlier emotion, than those of Spenser, where he speaks of this spot.

> There when they came, whereas those bricky towers,
> The which on Themmes brode aged back doth ride,
> Where now the studious lawyers have their bowers,
> There whylome wont the Templer knights to bide,
> Till they decayed through pride.

Indeed, it is the most elegant spot in the metropolis. What a transition for a countryman visiting London for the first time—the passing from the crowded Strand or Fleet Street, by unexpected avenues, into its magnificent ample squares, its classic green recesses! What a cheerful, liberal look hath that portion of it, which, from three sides, overlooks the greater garden; that goodly pile

Of building strong, albeit of Paper hight,

confronting with massy contrast, the lighter, older, more fantastically shrouded one, named of Harcourt, with the cheerful Crown Office Row (place of my kindly engendure), right opposite the stately stream, which washes the garden-foot with her yet scarcely trade-polluted waters, and seems but just weaned from her Twickenham Naïades! a man would give something to have been born in such places. What a collegiate aspect has that fine Elizabethan hall, where the fountain plays, which I have made to rise and fall, how many times! to the astoundment of the young urchins, my contemporaries, who, not being able to guess at its recondite machinery, were almost tempted to hail the wondrous work as magic! What an antique air had the now almost effaced sundials, with their moral inscriptions, seeming coevals with that Time which they measured, and to take their revelations of its flight immediately from heaven, holding correspondence with the fountain of light! How would the dark line steal imperceptibly on, watched by the eye of childhood, eager to detect its movement, never catched, nice as an evanescent cloud, or the first arrests of sleep!

Ah! yet doth beauty like a dial hand
Steal from his figure, and no pace perceived!

What a dead thing is a clock, with its ponderous embowelments of lead and brass, its pert or solemn dulness of communication, compared with the simple altar-like structure, and silent heart-language of the old dial! It stood as the garden god of Christian gardens. Why is it almost everywhere vanished? If its business-use be superseded by more elaborate inventions, its moral uses, its beauty, might have pleaded for its continuance. It spoke of moderate labours, of pleasures not protracted after sun-set, of temperance, and good hours. It was the primitive clock, the horologe of the

first world. Adam could scarce have missed it in Paradise.
It was the measure appropriate for sweet plants and flowers
to spring by, for the birds to apportion their silver warblings
by, for flocks to pasture and be led to fold by. The shepherd
'carved it out quaintly in the sun'; and, turning philosopher
by the very occupation, provided it with mottoes more
touching than tomb-stones. It was a pretty device of the
gardener, recorded by Marvell, who, in the days of artificial
gardening, made a dial out of herbs and flowers. I must
quote his verses a little higher up, for they are full, as all
his serious poetry was, of a witty delicacy. They will not come
in awkwardly, I hope, in a talk of fountains and sun-dials.
He is speaking of sweet garden scenes:—

> What wondrous life is this I lead!
> Ripe apples drop about my head.
> The luscious clusters of the vine
> Upon my mouth do crush their wine.
> The nectarine, and curious peach,
> Into my hands themselves do reach.
> Stumbling on melons, as I pass,
> Insnared with flowers, I fall on grass.
> Meanwhile the mind from pleasure less
> Withdraws into its happiness.
> The mind, that ocean, where each kind
> Does straight its own resemblance find;
> Yet it creates, transcending these,
> Far other worlds and other seas;
> Annihilating all that's made
> To a green thought in a green shade.
> Here at the fountain's sliding foot,
> Or at some fruit-tree's mossy root,
> Casting the body's vest aside,
> My soul into the boughs does glide;
> There, like a bird, it sits and sings,
> Then wets and claps its silver wings,
> And, till prepared for longer flight,
> Waves in its plumes the various light.
> How well the skilful gardener drew,
> Of flowers and herbs, this dial new!
> Where, from above, the milder sun
> Does through a fragrant zodiac run:
> And, as it works, the industrious bee
> Computes its time as well as we.

How could such sweet and wholesome hours
Be reckon'd, but with herbs and flowers?*

The artificial fountains of the metropolis are, in like manner, fast vanishing. Most of them are dried up or bricked over. Yet, where one is left, as in that little green nook behind the South-Sea House, what a freshness it gives to the dreary pile! Four little winged marble boys used to play their virgin fancies, spouting out ever fresh streams from their innocent-wanton lips in the square of Lincoln's Inn, when I was no bigger than they were figured. They are gone, and the spring choked up. The fashion, they tell me, is gone by, and these things are esteemed childish. Why not, then, gratify children, by letting them stand? Lawyers, I suppose, were children once. They are awakening images to them at least. Why must everything smack of man and mannish? Is the world all grown up? Is childhood dead? Or is there not in the bosoms of the wisest and the best some of the child's heart left, to respond to its earliest enchantments? The figures were grotesque. Are the stiff-wigged living figures, that still flitter and chatter about that area, less Gothic in appearance? or is the splutter of their hot rhetoric one-half so refreshing and innocent as the little cool playful streams those exploded cherubs uttered?

They have lately gothicised the entrance to the Inner Temple, and the library front; to assimilate them, I suppose, to the body of the hall, which they do not at all resemble. What is become of the winged horse that stood over the former? a stately arms! and who has removed those frescoes of the Virtues, which Italianised the end of the Paper Buildings?—my first hint of allegory! They must account to me for these things, which I miss so greatly.

The terrace is, indeed, left, which we used to call the parade; but the traces are passed away of the footsteps which made its pavement awful! It is become common and profane. The old benchers had it almost sacred to themselves, in the forepart of the day at least. They might not be sided or jostled. Their air and dress asserted the parade. You left wide spaces betwixt you when you passed them. We walk on even terms with their successors. The roguish eye of J——ll, ever ready to be delivered of a jest, almost invites

* From a copy of verses entitled The Garden.

a stranger to vie a repartee with it. But what insolent familiar durst have mated Thomas Coventry?—whose person was a quadrate, his step massy and elephantine, his face square as the lion's, his gait peremptory and path-keeping, indivertible from his way as a moving column, the scarecrow of his inferiors, the browbeater of equals and superiors, who made a solitude of children wherever he came, for they fled his insufferable presence, as they would have shunned an Elisha bear. His growl was as thunder in their ears, whether he spake to them in mirth or in rebuke; his invitatory notes being, indeed, of all, the most repulsive and horrid. Clouds of snuff, aggravating the natural terrors of his speech, broke from each majestic nostril, darkening the air. He took it, not by pinches, but a palmful at once,—diving for it under the mighty flaps of his old-fashioned waistcoat pocket; his waistcoat red and angry, his coat dark rappee, tinctured by dye original, and by adjuncts, with buttons of obsolete gold. And so he paced the terrace.

By his side a milder form was sometimes to be seen; the pensive gentility of Samuel Salt. They were coevals, and had nothing but that and their benchership in common. In politics Salt was a whig, and Coventry a staunch tory. Many a sarcastic growl did the latter cast out—for Coventry had a rough spinous humour—at the political confederates of his associate, which rebounded from the gentle bosom of the latter like cannon-balls from wool. You could not ruffle Samuel Salt.

S. had the reputation of being a very clever man, and of excellent discernment in the chamber practice of the law. I suspect his knowledge did not amount to much. When a case of difficult disposition of money, testamentary or otherwise, came before him, he ordinarily handed it over, with a few instructions, to his man Lovel, who was a quick little fellow, and would despatch it out of hand by the light of natural understanding, of which he had an uncommon share. It was incredible what repute for talents S. enjoyed by the mere trick of gravity. He was a shy man; a child might pose him in a minute—indolent and procrastinating to the last degree. Yet men would give him credit for vast application, in spite of himself. He was not to be trusted with himself with impunity. He never dressed for a dinner party but he forgot his sword—they wore swords then—or some other necessary part of his equipage. Lovel had his eye upon him on all these occasions, and ordinarily gave him his cue. If there was anything which he could speak unseasonably, he was sure to do it.—He was to dine at a relative's of the unfortunate Miss Blandy on the day of her execution;—and L., who had a wary foresight of his probable hallucinations, before he set out schooled him, with great anxiety, not in any possible manner to allude to her story that day. S. promised faithfully to observe the injunction. He had not been seated in the parlour, where the company was expecting the dinner summons, four minutes, when, a pause in the conversation ensuing, he got up, looked out of window, and pulling down his ruffles—an ordinary motion with him—observed, 'it was a gloomy day,' and added, 'Miss Blandy must be hanged by this time, I suppose.' Instances of this sort were perpetual. Yet S. was thought by some of the greatest men of his time a fit person to be consulted, not alone in matters pertaining to the law, but in the ordinary niceties and embarrassments of conduct—from force of manner entirely. He never laughed. He had the same good fortune among the female world,—was a known toast with the ladies, and one or two are said to have died for love of him—I suppose, because he never trifled or talked gallantry with them, or paid them, indeed, hardly common attentions. He had a fine face and person, but wanted, methought, the spirit that should have shown them off with advantage to the women. His eye lacked lustre.—Not so, thought Susan P——; who, at the advanced age of sixty, was seen, in the cold evening time, unaccompanied, wetting the pavement of B——d Row, with tears that fell in drops which might be heard, because her friend had died that day—he, whom she had pursued with a hopeless passion for the last forty years —a passion which years could not extinguish or abate; nor the long-resolved, yet gently-enforced, puttings-off of unrelenting bachelorhood dissuade from its cherished purpose. Mild Susan P——, thou hast now thy friend in heaven!

Thomas Coventry was a cadet of the noble family of that name. He passed his youth in contracted circumstances, which gave him early those parsimonious habits which in after life never forsook him, so that with one windfall or another, about the time I knew him he was master of four or five hundred thousand pounds; nor did he look or walk worth a moidore less. He lived in a gloomy house opposite the pump in Serjeant's Inn, Fleet Street. J., the counsel, is doing self-imposed penance in it, for what reason I divine not, at this day. C. had an agreeable seat at North Cray, where he seldom spent above a day or two at a time in the summer; but preferred, during the hot months, standing at his window in this damp, close, well-like mansion, to watch, as he said, 'the maids drawing water all day long.' I suspect he had his within-door reasons for the preference. *Hic currus et arma fuêre*. He might think his treasures more safe. His house had the aspect of a strong-box. C. was a close hunks—a hoarder rather than a miser—or, if a miser, none of the mad Elwes breed, who have brought discredit upon a character which cannot exist without certain admirable points of steadiness and unity of purpose. One may hate a true miser, but cannot, I suspect, so easily despise him. By taking care of the pence he is often enabled to part with the pounds, upon a scale that leaves us careless generous fellows halting at an immeasurable distance behind. C. gave away £30,000 at once in his lifetime to a blind charity. His housekeeping was severely looked after, but he kept the table of a gentleman. He would know who came in and who went out of his house, but his kitchen chimney was never suffered to freeze.

Salt was his opposite in this, as in all—never knew what he was worth in the world; and having but a competency for his rank, which his indolent habits were little calculated to improve, might have suffered severely if he had not had honest people about him. Lovel took care of everything. He was at once his clerk, his good servant, his dresser, his friend, his 'flapper,' his guide, stop-watch, auditor, treasurer. He did nothing without consulting Lovel, or failed in anything without expecting and fearing his admonishing. He put himself almost too much in his hands, had they not been the purest in the world. He resigned his title almost to respect as a master, if L. could ever have forgotten for a moment that he was a servant.

I knew this Lovel. He was a man of an incorrigible and losing honesty. A good fellow withal, and 'would strike.' In the cause of the oppressed he never considered inequalities, or calculated the number of his opponents. He once wrested a sword out of the hand of a man of quality that had drawn upon him, and pommelled him severely with the hilt of it.

The swordsman had offered insult to a female—an occasion upon which no odds against him could have prevented the interference of Lovel. He would stand next day bareheaded to the same person modestly to excuse his interference—for L. never forgot rank where something better was not concerned. L. was the liveliest little fellow breathing, had a face as gay as Garrick's, whom he was said greatly to resemble (I have a portrait of him which confirms it), possessed a fine turn for humorous poetry—next to Swift and Prior—moulded heads in clay or plaster of Paris to admiration, by the dint of natural genius merely; turned cribbage boards, and such small cabinet toys, to perfection; took a hand at quadrille or bowls with equal facility; made punch better than any man of his degree in England; had the merriest quips and conceits; and was altogether as brimful of rogueries and inventions as you could desire. He was a brother of the angle, moreover, and just such a free, hearty, honest companion as Mr. Izaak Walton would have chosen to go a-fishing with. I saw him in his old age and the decay of his faculties, palsy-smitten, in the last sad stage of human weakness—'a remnant most forlorn of what he was,'—yet even then his eye would light up upon the mention of his favourite Garrick. He was greatest, he would say, in Bayes—'was upon the stage nearly throughout the whole performance, and as busy as a bee.' At intervals, too, he would speak of his former life, and how he came up a little boy from Lincoln, to go to service, and how his mother cried at parting with him, and how he returned, after some years' absence, in his smart new livery, to see her, and she blessed herself at the change, and could hardly be brought to believe that it was 'her own bairn.' And then, the excitement subsiding, he would weep, till I have wished that sad second-childhood might have a mother still to lay its head upon her lap. But the common mother of us all in no long time after received him gently into hers.

With Coventry, and with Salt, in their walks upon the terrace, most commonly Peter Pierson would join to make up a third. They did not walk linked arm-in-arm in those days—'as now our stout triumvirs sweep the streets,'—but generally with both hands folded behind them for state, or with one at least behind, the other carrying a cane. P. was a benevolent, but not a prepossessing man. He had that in his face which you could not term unhappiness; it rather implied an incapacity of being happy. His cheeks were colourless, even to whiteness. His look was uninviting; resembling (but without his sourness) that of our great philanthropist. I know that he *did* good acts, but I could never make out what he *was*. Contemporary with these, but subordinate, was Daines Barrington—another oddity—he walked burly and square—in imitation, I think, of Coventry —howbeit he attained not to the dignity of his prototype. Nevertheless, he did pretty well, upon the strength of being a tolerable antiquarian, and having a brother a bishop. When the account of his year's treasurership came to be audited the following singular charge was unanimously disallowed by the bench: 'Item, disbursed Mr. Allen, the gardener, twenty shillings for stuff to poison the sparrows, by my orders.' Next to him was old Barton—a jolly negation, who took upon him the ordering of the bills of fare for the parliament chamber, where the benchers dine—answering to the combination rooms at College—much to the easement of his less epicurean brethren. I know nothing more of him. —Then Read, and Twopeny—Read, good-humoured and personable—Twopeny, good-humoured, but thin, and felicitous in jests upon his own figure. If T. was thin, Wharry was attenuated and fleeting. Many must remember him (for he was rather of later date) and his singular gait, which was performed by three steps and a jump regularly succeeding. The steps were little efforts, like that of a child beginning to walk; the jump comparatively vigorous, as a foot to an inch. Where he learned this figure, or what occasioned it, I could never discover. It was neither graceful in itself, nor seemed to answer the purpose any better than common walking. The extreme tenuity of his frame, I suspect, set him upon it. It was a trial of poising. Twopeny would often rally him upon his leanness, and hail him as Brother Lusty; but W. had no relish of a joke. His features were spiteful. I have heard that he would pinch his cat's ears extremely when anything had offended him. Jackson—the omniscient Jackson he was called—was of this period. He had the reputation of possessing more multifarious knowledge than any man of his time. He was the Friar Bacon of the less literate portion of the Temple. I remember a pleasant passage of the cook applying to him, with much formality of apology, for instructions how to write

THE ESSAYS OF ELIA

down *edge* bone of beef in his bill of commons. He was supposed to know, if any man in the world did. He decided the orthography to be—as I have given it—fortifying his authority with such anatomical reasons as dismissed the manciple (for the time) learned and happy. Some do spell it yet, perversely, *aitch* bone, from a fanciful resemblance between its shape and that of the aspirate so denominated. I had almost forgotten Mingay with the iron hand—but he was somewhat later. He had lost his right hand by some accident, and supplied it with a grappling-hook, which he wielded with a tolerable adroitness. I detected the substitute before I was old enough to reason whether it were artificial or not. I remember the astonishment it raised in me. He was a blustering, loud-talking person; and I reconciled the phenomenon to my ideas as an emblem of power—somewhat like the horns in the forehead of Michael Angelo's Moses. Baron Maseres, who walks (or did till very lately) in the costume of the reign of George the Second, closes my imperfect recollections of the old benchers of the Inner Temple.

Fantastic forms, whither are ye fled? Or, if the like of you exist, why exist they no more for me? Ye inexplicable, half-understood appearances, why comes in reason to tear away the preternatural mist, bright or gloomy, that enshrouded you? Why make ye so sorry a figure in my relation, who made up to me—to my childish eyes—the mythology of the Temple? In those days I saw Gods, as 'old men covered with a mantle,' walking upon the earth. Let the dreams of classic idolatry perish,—extinct be the fairies and fairy trumpery of legendary fabling, in the heart of childhood there will, for ever, spring up a well of innocent or wholesome superstition—the seeds of exaggeration will be busy there, and vital—from every-day forms educing the unknown and the uncommon. In that little Goshen there will be light when the grown world flounders about in the darkness of sense and materiality. While childhood, and while dreams, reducing childhood, shall be left, imagination shall not have spread her holy wings totally to fly the earth.

P.S.—I have done injustice to the soft shade of Samuel Salt. See what it is to trust to imperfect memory, and the erring notices of childhood! Yet I protest I always thought that he had been a bachelor! This gentleman, R.N. informs me, married young, and losing his lady in childbed, within the first year of their union, fell into a deep melancholy, from the effects of which, probably, he never thoroughly recovered. In what a new light does this place his rejection (O call it by a gentler name!) of mild Susan P——, unravelling into beauty certain peculiarities of this very shy and retiring character! Henceforth let no one receive the narratives of Elia for true records! They are, in truth, but shadows of fact—verisimilitudes, not verities—or sitting but upon the remote edges and outskirts of history. He is no such honest chronicler as R.N., and would have done better perhaps to have consulted that gentleman before he sent these incondite reminiscences to press. But the worthy sub-treasurer—who respects his old and his new masters—would but have been puzzled at the indecorous liberties of Elia. The good man wots not, peradventure, of the licence which *Magazines* have arrived at in this plain-speaking age, or hardly dreams of their existence beyond the *Gentleman's*—his furthest monthly excursions in this nature having been long confined to the holy ground of *Urban's* obituary. May it be long before his own name shall help to swell those columns of Inner Temple, cherish him kindly, for he is himself the kindliest of human creatures. Should infirmities overtake him—he is yet in green and vigorous senility—make allowances for them, remembering that 'ye yourselves are old.' So may the Winged Horse, your ancient badge and cognisance, still flourish! so may future Hookers and Seldens illustrate your church and chambers! so may the sparrows, in default of more melodious quirirsters, unpoisoned hop about your walks; so may the fresh-coloured and cleanly nursery-maid, who, by leave, airs her playful charge in your stately gardens, drop her prettiest blushing curtsy as ye pass, reductive of juvenescent emotion! so may the younkers of this generation eye you, pacing your stately terrace, with the same superstitious veneration with which the child Elia gazed on the Old Worthies that solemnised the parade before ye!

Grace Before Meat

THE custom of saying grace at meals had, probably, its origin in the early times of the world, and the hunter-state of man, when dinners were precarious things, and a full meal was something more than a common blessing! when a belly-full was a wind-fall, and looked like a special providence. In the shouts and triumphal songs with which, after a season of sharp abstinence, a lucky booty of deer's or goat's flesh would naturally be ushered home, existed, perhaps, the germ of the modern grace. It is not otherwise easy to be understood, why the blessing of food—the act of eating—should have had a particular expression of thanksgiving annexed to it, distinct from that implied and silent gratitude with which we are expected to enter upon the enjoyment of the many other various gifts and good things of existence.

I own that I am disposed to say grace upon twenty other occasions in the course of the day besides my dinner. I want a form for setting out upon a pleasant walk, for a moonlight ramble, for a friendly meeting, or a solved problem. Why have we none for books, those spiritual repasts—a grace before Milton—a grace before Shakespeare—a devotional exercise proper to be said before reading the Faëry Queen? —but the received ritual having prescribed these forms to the solitary ceremony of manduction, I shall confine my observations to the experience which I have had of the grace, properly so called; commending my new scheme for extension to a niche in the grand philosophical, poetical, and perchance in part heretical, liturgy, now compiling by my friend Homo Humanus, for the use of a certain snug congregation of Utopian Rabelæsian Christians, no matter where assembled.

The form, then, of the benediction before eating has its beauty at a poor man's table, or at the simple and unprovocative repast of children. It is here that the grace becomes exceedingly graceful. The indigent man, who hardly knows whether he shall have a meal next day or not, sits down to his fare with a present sense of the blessing, which can be but feebly acted by the rich, into whose minds the conception of wanting a dinner could never, but by some extreme theory, have entered. The proper end of food—the animal sustenance—is barely contemplated by them. The poor man's bread is his daily bread, literally his bread for the day. Their courses are perennial.

Again, the plainest diet seems the fittest to be preceded by the grace. That which is least stimulative to appetite, leaves the mind most free for foreign considerations. A man may feel thankful, heartily thankful, over a dish of plain mutton with turnips, and have leisure to reflect upon the ordinance and institution of eating; when he shall confess a perturbation of mind, inconsistent with the purposes of the grace, at the presence of venison or turtle. When I have sate (a *rarus hospes*) at rich men's tables, with the savoury soup and messes steaming up the nostrils, and moistening the lips of the guests with desire and a distracted choice, I have felt the introduction of that ceremony to be unseasonable. With the ravenous orgasm upon you, it seems impertinent to interpose a religious sentiment. It is a confusion of purpose to mutter out praises from a mouth that waters. The heats of epicurism put out the gentle flame of devotion. The incense which rises round is pagan, and the belly-god intercepts it for his own. The very excess of the provision beyond the needs, takes away all sense of proportion between the end and means. The giver is veiled by his gifts. You are startled at the injustice of returning thanks—for what?—for having too much, while so many starve. It is to praise the Gods amiss.

I have observed this awkwardness felt, scarce consciously perhaps, by the good man who says the grace. I have seen it in clergymen and others—a sort of shame—a sense of the co-presence of circumstances which unhallow the blessing. After a devotional tone put on for a few seconds, how rapidly the speaker will fall into his common voice! helping himself or his neighbour, as if to get rid of some uneasy sensation of hypocrisy. Not that the good man was a hypocrite, or was not most conscientious in the discharge of the duty; but he felt in his inmost mind the incompatibility of the scene and the viands before him with the exercise of a calm and rational gratitude.

I hear somebody exclaim,—Would you have Christians sit

down at table, like hogs to their troughs, without remembering the Giver?—no—I would have them sit down as Christians, remembering the Giver, and less like hogs. Or if their appetites must run riot, and they must pamper themselves with delicacies for which east and west are ransacked, I would have them postpone their benediction to a fitter season, when appetite is laid; when the still small voice can be heard, and the reason of the grace returns—with temperate diet and restricted dishes. Gluttony and surfeiting are no proper occasions for thanksgiving. When Jeshurun waxed fat, we read that he kicked. Virgil knew the harpy-nature better, when he put into the mouth of Celæno anything but a blessing. We may be greatly sensible of the deliciousness of some kinds of food beyond others, though that is a meaner and inferior gratitude: but the proper object of the grace is sustenance, not relishes; daily bread, not delicacies; the means of life, and not the means of pampering the carcass. With what frame or composure, I wonder, can a city chaplain pronounce his benediction at some great Hall-feast, when he knows that his last concluding pious word—and that, in all probability, the sacred name which he preaches—is but the signal for so many impatient harpies to commence their foul orgies, with as little sense of true thankfulness (which is temperance) as those Virgilian fowl! It is well if the good man himself does not feel his devotions a little clouded, those foggy sensuous steams mingling with and polluting the pure altar sacrifice.

The severest satire upon full tables and surfeits is the banquet which Satan, in the *Paradise Regained*, provides for a temptation in the wilderness:

> A table richly spread in regal mode
> With dishes piled, and meats of noblest sort
> And savour; beasts of chase, or fowl of game,
> In pastry built, or from the spit, or boiled,
> Gris-amber-steamed; all fish from sea or shore,
> Freshet or purling brook, for which was drained
> Pontus, and Lucrine bay, and Afric coast.

The Tempter, I warrant you, thought these cates would go down without the recommendatory preface of a benediction. They are like to be short graces where the devil plays the host. I am afraid the poet wants his usual decorum

in this place. Was he thinking of the old Roman luxury, or
of a gaudy day at Cambridge? This was a temptation fitter
for a Heliogabalus. The whole banquet is too civic and
culinary, and the accompaniments altogether a profanation
of that deep, abstracted holy scene. The mighty artillery
of sauces, which the cook-fiend conjures up, is out of proportion to the simple wants and plain hunger of the guest.
He that disturbed him in his dreams, from his dreams might
have been taught better. To the temperate fantasies of the
famished Son of God, what sort of feasts presented themselves?
—He dreamed indeed,

> ——As appetite is wont to dream,
> Of meats and drinks, nature's refreshment sweet.

But what meats?—

> Him thought, he by the brook of Cherith stood,
> And saw the ravens with their horny beaks
> Food to Elijah bringing even and morn;
> Though ravenous, taught to abstain from what they brought;
> He saw the prophet also how he fled
> Into the desert and how there he slept
> Under a juniper; then how awaked
> He found his supper on the coals prepared,
> And by the angel was bid rise and eat,
> And ate the second time after repose,
> The strength whereof sufficed him forty days:
> Sometimes, that with Elijah he partook,
> Or as a guest with Daniel at his pulse.

Nothing in Milton is finelier fancied than these temperate
dreams of the divine Hungerer. To which of these two
visionary banquets, think you, would the introduction of
what is called the grace have been the most fitting and
pertinent?

Theoretically I am no enemy to graces; but practically
I own that (before meat especially) they seem to involve
something awkward and unseasonable. Our appetites, of one
or another kind, are excellent spurs to our reason, which
might otherwise but feebly set about the great ends of
preserving and continuing the species. They are fit blessings
to be contemplated at a distance with a becoming gratitude;
but the moment of appetite (the judicious reader will ap-

prehend me) is, perhaps, the least fit season for that exercise. The Quakers, who go about their business of every description with more calmness than we, have more title to the use of these benedictory prefaces. I have always admired their silent grace, and the more because I have observed their applications to the meat and drink following to be less passionate and sensual than ours. They are neither gluttons nor wine-bibbers as a people. They eat, as a horse bolts his chopped hay, with indifference, calmness, and cleanly circumstances. They neither grease nor slop themselves. When I see a citizen in his bib and tucker, I cannot imagine it a surplice.

I am no Quaker at my food. I confess I am not indifferent to the kinds of it. Those unctuous morsels of deer's flesh were not made to be received with dispassionate services. I hate a man who swallows it, affecting not to know what he is eating. I suspect his taste in higher matters. I shrink instinctively from one who professes to like minced veal. There is a physiognomical character in the tastes for food. C——holds that a man cannot have a pure mind who refuses apple-dumplings. I am not certain but he is right. With the decay of my first innocence, I confess a less and less relish daily for those innocuous cates. The whole vegetable tribe have lost their gust with me. Only I stick to asparagus, which still seems to inspire gentle thoughts. I am impatient and querulous under culinary disappointments, as to come home at the dinner-hour, for instance, expecting some savoury mess, and to find one quite tasteless and sapidless. Butter ill melted —that commonest of kitchen failures—puts me beside my tenor.—The author of the Rambler used to make inarticulate animal noises over a favourite food. Was this the music quite proper to be preceded by the grace? or would the pious man have done better to postpone his devotions to a season when the blessing might be contemplated with less perturbation? I quarrel with no man's tastes, nor would set my thin face against those excellent things, in their way, jollity and feasting. But as these exercises, however laudable, have little in them of grace or gracefulness, a man should be sure, before he ventures so to grace them, that while he is pretending his devotions otherwhere, he is not secretly kissing his hand to some great fish—his Dagon—with a special consecration of no ark but the fat tureen before him. Graces are the sweet preluding strains to the banquets of angels and children; to the roots and severer repasts of the Chartreuse; to the slender, but not slenderly acknowledged, refection of the poor and humble man: but at the heaped-up boards of the pampered and the luxurious they become of dissonant mood, less timed and tuned to the occasion, methinks, than the noise of those better befitting organs would be which children hear tales of, at Hog's Norton. We sit too long at our meals, or are too curious in the study of them, or too disordered in our application to them, or engross too great a portion of those good things (which should be common) to our share, to be able with any grace to say grace. To be thankful for what we grasp exceeding our proportion, is to add hypocrisy to injustice. A lurking sense of this truth is what makes the performance of this duty so cold and spiritless a service at most tables. In houses where the grace is as indispensable as the napkin, who has not seen that never-settled question arise, as to *who shall say it?* while the good man of the house and the visitor clergyman, or some other guest belike of next authority, from years or gravity, shall be bandying about the office between them as a matter of compliment, each of them not unwilling to shift the awkward burthen of an equivocal duty from his own shoulders?

I once drank tea in company with two Methodist divines of different persuasions, whom it was my fortune to introduce to each other for the first time that evening. Before the first cup was handed round, one of these reverend gentlemen put it to the other, with all due solemnity, whether he chose to *say anything*. It seems it is the custom with some sectaries to put up a short prayer before this meal also. His reverend brother did not at first quite apprehend him, but upon an explanation, with little less importance he made answer that it was not a custom known in his church: in which courteous evasion the other acquiescing for good manner's sake, or in compliance with a weak brother, the supplementary or tea-grace was waived altogether. With what spirit might not Lucian have painted two priests, of *his* religion, playing into each other's hands the compliment of performing or omitting a sacrifice,—the hungry God meantime, doubtful of his incense, with expectant nostrils hovering over the two flamens, and (as between two stools) going away in the end without his supper.

A short form upon these occasions is felt to want reverence; a long one, I am afraid, cannot escape the charge of impertinence. I do not quite approve of the epigrammatic conciseness with which that equivocal wag (but my pleasant schoolfellow) C.V.L., when importuned for a grace, used to inquire, first slyly leering down the table, 'Is there no clergyman here?'—significantly adding, 'Thank G—.' Nor do I think our form at school quite pertinent, where we were used to preface our bald bread-and-cheese-suppers with a preamble, connecting with that humble blessing a recognition of benefits the most awful and overwhelming to the imagination which religion has to offer. *Non tunc illis erat locus.* I remember we were put to it to reconcile the phrase 'good creatures,' upon which the blessing rested, with the fare set before us, wilfully understanding that expression in a low and animal sense,— till some one recalled a legend, which told how, in the golden days of Christ's, the young Hospitallers were wont to have smoking joints of roast meat upon their nightly boards, till some pious benefactor, commiserating the decencies, rather than the palates, of the children, commuted our flesh for garments, and gave us—*horresco referens*—trousers instead of mutton.

Dream Children : a Reverie

CHILDREN love to listen to stories about their elders, when *they* were children; to stretch their imagination to the conception of a traditionary great-uncle, or grandame, whom they never saw. It was in this spirit that my little ones crept about me the other evening to hear about their great-grandmother Field, who lived in a great house in Norfolk (a hundred times bigger than that in which they and papa lived) which had been the scene—so at least it was generally believed in that part of the country—of the tragic incidents which they had lately become familiar with from the ballad of the Children in the Wood. Certain it is that the whole story of the children and their cruel uncle was to be seen fairly carved out in wood upon the chimney-piece of the great hall, the whole story down to the Robin Redbreasts; till a foolish rich person pulled it down to set up a marble one of modern invention in its stead, with no story upon it. Here Alice put out one of her dear mother's looks, too tender to be called upbraiding. Then I went on to say, how religious and how good their great-grandmother Field was, how beloved and respected by everybody, though she was not indeed the mistress of this great house, but had only the charge of it (and yet in some respects she might be said to be the mistress of it too) committed to her by the owner, who preferred living in a newer and more fashionable mansion which he had purchased somewhere in the adjoining county; but still she lived in it in a manner as if it had been her own, and kept up the dignity of the great house in a sort while she lived, which afterwards came to decay, and was nearly pulled down, and all its old ornaments stripped and carried away to the owner's other house, where they were set up, and looked as awkward as if some one were to carry away the old tombs they had seen lately at the Abbey, and stick them up in Lady C.'s tawdry gilt drawing-rrom. Here John smiled, as much as to say, 'that would be foolish indeed.' And then I told how, when she came to die, her funeral was attended by a concourse of all the poor, and some of the gentry too, of the neighbour-hood for many miles round, to show their respect for her memory, because she had been such a good and religious woman; so good indeed that she knew all the Psaltery by heart, ay, and a great part of the Testament besides. Here little Alice spread her hands. Then I told what a tall, upright graceful person their great-grandmother Field once was; and how in her youth she was esteemed the best dancer—here Alice's little right foot played an involuntary movement, till, upon my looking grave, it desisted—the best dancer, I was saying, in the county, till a cruel disease, called a cancer, came, and bowed her down with pain; but it could never bend her good spirits, or make them stoop, but they were still upright, because she was so good and religious. Then I told how she was used to sleep by herself in a lone chamber of the great lone house; and how she believed that an appa-rition of two infants was to be seen at midnight gliding up and down the great staircase near where she slept, but she said 'those innocents would do her no harm'; and how frightened I used to be, though in those days I had my maid to sleep with me, because I was never half so good or religious as she—and yet I never saw the infants. Here John expanded all his eyebrows and tried to look courageous. Then I told how good she was to all her grandchildren, having us to the great house in the holidays, where I in particular used to spend many hours by myself, in gazing upon the old busts of the twelve Cæsars, that had been Emperors of Rome, till the old marble heads would seem to live again, or I to be turned into marble with them; how I never could be tired with roaming about that huge mansion, with its vast empty rooms, with their worn-out hangings, fluttering tapestry, and carved oaken panels, with the gilding almost rubbed out —sometimes in the spacious old-fashioned gardens, which I had almost to myself, unless when now and then a solitary gardening man would cross me—and how the nectarines and peaches hung upon the walls, without my ever offering to pluck them, because they were forbidden fruit, unless now and then,—and because I had more pleasure in strolling about among the old melancholy-looking yew-trees, or the firs, and picking up the red berries, and the fir-apples, which were good for nothing but to look at—or in lying about upon the fresh grass with all the fine garden smells around me—or basking in the orangery, till I could almost fancy myself ripening too along with the oranges and the limes in that grateful warmth—or in watching the dace that darted to and fro in the fish-pond, at the bottom of the garden, with here and there a great sulky pike hanging midway down the water in silent state, as if it mocked at their impertinent friskings,—I had more pleasure in these busy-idle diversions than in all the sweet flavours of peaches, nectarines, oranges, and such-like common baits of children. Here John slyly deposited back upon the plate a bunch of grapes, which, not unobserved by Alice, he had meditated dividing with her, and both seemed willing to relinquish them for the present as irrelevant. Then, in somewhat a more heightened tone, I told how, though their great-grandmother Field loved all her grandchildren, yet in an especial manner she might be said to love their uncle, John L——, because he was so handsome and spirited a youth, and a king to the rest of us; and, instead of moping about in solitary corners, like some of us, he would mount the most mettlesome horse he could get, when but an imp no bigger than themselves, and make it carry him half over the county in a morning, and join the hunters when there were any out—and yet he loved the old great house and gardens too, but had too much spirit to be always pent up within their boundaries—and how their uncle grew up to man's estate as brave as he was handsome, to the admiration of everybody, but of their great-grandmother Field most especially; and how he used to carry me upon his back when I was a lame-footed boy—for he was a good bit older than me—many a mile when I could not walk for pain;—and how in after life he became lame-footed too, and I did not always (I fear) make allowances enough for him when he was impatient, and in pain, nor remember sufficiently how considerate he had been to me when I was lame-footed; and how when he died, though he had not been dead an hour, it seemed as if he had died a great while ago, such a distance there is betwixt life and death; and how I bore his death as I thought pretty well at first, but afterwards it haunted and haunted me; and though I did not cry or take it to heart as some do, and as I think he would have done if I had died, yet I missed him all day long, and knew not till then how much I had loved him. I missed his kindness, and I missed his crossness, and wished him to be alive again, to be quarrelling with him (for we quarrelled sometimes), rather than not have him again, and was as uneasy without him, as he their poor uncle must have been when the doctor took off his limb.—Here the children fell a-crying, and asked if their little mourning which they had on was not for uncle John, and they looked up, and prayed me not to go on about their uncle, but to tell them some stories about their pretty dead mother. Then I told how for seven long years, in hope sometimes, sometimes in despair, yet persisting ever, I courted the fair Alice W——n; and, as much as children could understand, I explained to them what coyness, and difficulty, and denial, meant in maidens —when suddenly, turning to Alice, the soul of the first Alice looked out at her eyes with such a reality of re-presentment, that I became in doubt which of them stood there before me, or whose that bright hair was; and while I stood gazing, both the children gradually grew fainter to my view, receding, and still receding, till nothing at last but two mournful features were seen in the uttermost distance, which, without speech, strangely impressed upon me the effects of speech: 'We are not of Alice, nor of thee, nor are we children at all. The children of Alice call Bartrum father. We are nothing;

less than nothing, and dreams. We are only what might have been, and must wait upon the tedious shores of Lethe millions of ages before we have existence, and a name'——and immediately awaking, I found myself quietly seated in my bachelor arm-chair, where I had fallen asleep, with the faithful Bridget unchanged by my side—but John L. (or James Elia) was gone for ever.

Distant Correspondents

IN A LETTER TO B.F., ESQ., AT SYDNEY,

NEW SOUTH WALES

MY DEAR F.—When I think how welcome the sight of a letter from the world where you were born must be to you in that strange one to which you have been transplanted, I feel some compunctious visitings at my long silence. But, indeed, it is no easy effort to set about a correspondence at our distance. The weary world of waters between us oppresses the imagination. It is difficult to conceive how a scrawl of mine should ever stretch across it. It is a sort of presumption to expect that one's thoughts should live so far. It is like writing for posterity; and reminds me of one of Mrs. Rowe's superscriptions, 'Alcander to Strephon in the shades.' Cowley's Post-Angel is no more than would be expedient in such an intercourse. One drops a packet at Lombard Street, and in twenty-four hours a friend in Cumberland gets it as fresh as if it came in ice. It is only like whispering through a long trumpet. But suppose a tube let down from the moon, with yourself at one end and *the man* at the other; it would be some balk to the spirit of conversation, if you knew that the dialogue exchanged with that interesting theosophist would take two or three revolutions of a higher luminary in its passage. Yet, for aught I know, you may be some parasangs nigher that primitive idea—Plato's man—than we in England here have the honour to reckon ourselves.

Epistolary matter usually compriseth three topics; news, sentiment, and puns. In the latter, I include all non-serious subjects; or subjects serious in themselves, but treated after my fashion, non-seriously.—And first, for news. In them the most desirable circumstance, I suppose, is that they shall be

true. But what security can I have that what I now send you
for truth shall not, before you get it, unaccountably turn into
a lie? For instance, our mutual friend P. is at this present
writing—*my Now*—in good health, and enjoys a fair share
of worldly reputation. You are glad to hear it. This is natural
and friendly. But at this present reading—*your Now*—he may
possibly be in the Bench, or going to be hanged, which in
reason ought to abate something of your transport (*i.e.* at
hearing he was well, etc.), or at least considerably to modify
it. I am going to the play this evening, to have a laugh with
Munden. You have no theatre, I think you told me, in your
land of d——d realities. You naturally lick your lips, and
envy me my felicity. Think but a moment, and you will
correct the hateful emotion. Why, it is Sunday morning with
you, and 1823. This confusion of tenses, this grand solecism
of *two presents*, is in a degree common to all postage. But if I
sent you word to Bath or Devizes, that I was expecting the
aforesaid treat this evening, though at the moment you
received the intelligence my full feast of fun would be over,
yet there would be for a day or two after, as you would well
know, a smack, a relish left upon my mental palate, which
would give rational encouragement for you to foster a portion,
at least, of the disagreeable passion, which it was in part my
intention to produce. But ten months hence, your envy or
your sympathy would be as useless as a passion spent upon
the dead. Not only does truth, in these long intervals, un-
essence herself, but (what is harder) one cannot venture a
crude fiction, for the fear that it may ripen into a truth upon
the voyage. What a wild improbable banter I put upon you,
some three years since,——of Will Weatherall having married
a servant-maid! I remember gravely consulting you how we
were to receive her—for Will's wife was in no case to be
rejected; and your no less serious replication in the matter;
how tenderly you advised an abstemious introduction of
literary topics before the lady, with a caution not to be too
forward in bringing on the carpet matters more within the
sphere of her intelligence; your deliberate judgment, or
rather wise suspension of sentence, how far jacks, and spits,
and mops, could, with propriety, be introduced as subjects;
whether the conscious avoiding of all such matters in discourse
would not have a worse look than the taking of them casually
in our way; in what manner we should carry ourselves to

our maid Becky, Mrs. William Weatherall being by; whether we should show more delicacy, and a truer sense of respect for Will's wife, by treating Becky with our customary chiding before her, or by an unusual deferential civility paid to Becky, as to a person of great worth, but thrown by the caprice of fate into a humble station. There were difficulties, I remember, on both sides, which you did me the favour to state with the precision of a lawyer, united to the tenderness of a friend. I laughed in my sleeve at your solemn pleadings, when lo! while I was valuing myself upon this flam put upon you in New South Wales, the devil in England, jealous possibly of any lie-children not his own, or working after my copy, has actually instigated our friend (not three days since) to the commission of a matrimony, which I had only conjured up for your diversion. William Weatherall has married Mrs. Cotterel's maid. But to take it in its truest sense, you will see, my dear F., that news from me must become history to you; which I neither profess to write, nor indeed care much for reading. No person, under a diviner, can, with any prospect of veracity, conduct a correspondence at such an arm's length. Two prophets, indeed, might thus interchange intelligence with effect; the epoch of the writer (Habakkuk) falling in with the true present time of the receiver (Daniel); but then we are no prophets.

Then as to sentiment. It fares little better with that. This kind of dish, above all, requires to be served up hot, or sent off in water-plates, that your friend may have it almost as warm as yourself. If it have time to cool, it is the most tasteless of all cold meats. I have often smiled at a conceit of the late Lord C. It seems that travelling somewhere about Geneva, he came to some pretty green spot, or nook, where a willow, or something, hung so fantastically and invitingly over a stream—was it?—or a rock?—no matter—but the stillness and the repose, after a weary journey, 'tis likely, in a languid moment of his Lordship's hot, restless life, so took his fancy that he could imagine no place so proper, in the event of his death, to lay his bones in. This was all very natural and excusable as a sentiment, and shows his character in a very pleasing light. But when from a passing sentiment it came to be an act; and when, by a positive testamentary disposal, his remains were actually carried all that way from England; who was there, some desperate sentimentalists excepted, that did not ask the question, Why could not his Lordship have found a spot as solitary, a nook as romantic, a tree as green and pendent, with a stream as emblematic to his purpose, in Surrey, in Dorset, or in Devon? Conceive the sentiment boarded up, freighted, entered at the Custom House (startling the tide-waiters with the novelty), hoisted into a ship. Conceive it pawed about and handled between the rude jests of tarpaulin ruffians—a thing of its delicate texture— the salt bilge wetting it till it became as vapid as a damaged lustring. Suppose it in material danger (mariners have some superstition about sentiments) of being tossed over in a fresh gale to some propitiatory shark (spirit of Saint Gothard, save us from a quietus so foreign to the deviser's purpose!), but it has happily evaded a fishy consummation. Trace it then to its lucky landing—at Lyons shall we say?—I have not the map before me—jostled upon four men's shoulders —baiting at this town—stopping to refresh at t'other village —waiting a passport here, a license there; the sanction of the magistracy in this district, the concurrence of the ecclesiastics in that canton; till at length it arrives at its destination, tired out and jaded, from a brisk sentiment into a feature of silly pride or tawdry senseless affectation. How few sentiments, my dear F., I am afraid we can set down, in the sailor's phrase, as quite seaworthy.

Lastly, as to the agreeable levities, which, though contemptible in bulk, are the twinkling corpuscula which should irradiate a right friendly epistle—your puns and small jests are, I apprehend, extremely circumscribed in their sphere of action. They are so far from a capacity of being packed up and sent beyond sea, they will scarce endure to be transported by hand from this room to the next. Their vigour is as the instant of their birth. Their nutriment for their brief existence is the intellectual atmosphere of the by-standers: or this last is the fine slime of Nilus—the *melior lutus*—whose maternal recipiency is as necessary as the *sol pater* to their equivocal generation. A pun hath a hearty kind of present ear-kissing smack with it; you can no more transmit it in its pristine flavour than you can send a kiss.—Have you not tried in some instances to palm off a yesterday's pun upon a gentleman, and has it answered? Not but it was new to his hearing, but it did not seem to come new from you. It did not hitch in. It was like picking up at a village ale-house a two-days'-old newspaper. You have not seen it before, but you resent the stale thing as an affront. This sort of merchandise above all requires a quick return. A pun, and its recognitory laugh, must be co-instantaneous. The one is the brisk lightning, the other the fierce thunder. A moment's interval, and the link is snapped. A pun is reflected from a friend's face as from a mirror. Who would consult his sweet visnomy, if the polished surface were two or three minutes (not to speak of twelve months, my dear F.) in giving back its copy?

I cannot image to myself whereabout you are. When I try to fix it, Peter Wilkins's island comes across me. Sometimes you seem to be in the *Hades* of *Thieves*. I see Diogenes prying among you with his perpetual fruitless lantern. What must you be willing by this time to give for the sight of an honest man! You must almost have forgotten how *we* look. And tell me what your Sydneyites do? are they th**v*ng all day long? Merciful heaven! what property can stand against such a depredation! The kangaroos—your Aborigines—do they keep their primitive simplicity un-Europe-tainted, with those little short fore pads, looking like a lesson framed by nature to the pickpocket! Marry, for diving into fobs they are rather lamely provided *a priori;* but if the hue and cry were once up, they would show as fair a pair of hind-shifters as the expertest loco-motor in the colony. We hear the most improbable tales at this distance. Pray is it true that the young Spartans among you are born with six fingers, which spoils their scanning?—It must look very odd, but use reconciles. For their scansion, it is less to be regretted; for if they take it into their heads to be poets, it is odds but they turn out, the greater part of them, vile plagiarists. Is there much difference to see, too, between the son of a th**f and the grandson? or where does the taint stop? Do you bleach in three or in four generations? I have many questions to put, but ten Delphic voyages can be made in a shorter time than it will take to satisfy my scruples. Do you grow your own hemp?—What is your staple trade,—exclusive of the national profession, I mean? Your locksmiths, I take it, are some of your great capitalists.

I am insensibly chatting to you as familiarly as when we used to exchange good-morrows out of our old contiguous windows, in pump-famed Hare Court in the Temple. Why did you ever leave that quiet corner?—Why did I?—with its complement of four poor elms, from whose smoke-dyed barks, the theme of jesting ruralists, I picked my first lady-birds! My heart is as dry as that spring sometimes proves in a thirsty August, when I revert to the space that is between us; a length of passage enough to render obsolete the phrases of our English letters before they can reach you. But while I talk I think you hear me—thoughts dallying with vain surmise—

> Aye me! while thee the seas and sounding shores
> Hold far away.

Come back, before I am grown into a very old man, so as you shall hardly know me. Come, before Bridget walks on crutches. Girls whom you left children have become sage matrons while you are tarrying there. The blooming Miss W—r (you remember Sally W—r) called upon us yesterday, an aged crone. Folks whom you knew die off every year. Formerly, I thought that death was wearing out,—I stood ramparted about with so many healthy friends. The departure of J.W., two springs back, corrected my delusion. Since then the old divorcer has been busy. If you do not make haste to return, there will be little left to greet you, of me, or mine.

The Praise of Chimney-Sweepers

I LIKE to meet a sweep—understand me—not a grown sweeper—old chimney-sweepers are by no means attractive —but one of those tender novices, blooming through their first nigritude, the maternal washings not quite effaced from the cheek—such as come forth with the dawn, or somewhat earlier, with their little professional notes sounding like the *peep peep* of a young sparrow; or liker to the matin lark should I pronounce them, in their aërial ascents not seldom antici-pating the sun-rise?

I have a kindly yearning toward these dim specks—poor blots—innocent blacknesses—

I reverence these young Africans of our own growth— these almost clergy imps, who sport their cloth without assumption; and from their little pulpits (the tops of chimneys), in the nipping air of a December morning, preach a lesson of patience to mankind.

When a child, what a mysterious pleasure it was to witness their operation! to see a chit no bigger than one's-self, enter, one knew not by what process, into what seemed the *fauces Averni*—to pursue him in imagination, as he went sounding on through so many dark stifling caverns, horrid shades! to shudder with the idea that 'now, surely, he must be lost for ever!'—to revive at hearing his feeble shout of discovered daylight—and then (O fulness of delight!) running out of doors, to come just in time to see the sable phenomenon emerge in safety, the brandished weapon of his art victorious like some flag waved over a conquered citadel! I seem to remember having been told, that a bad sweep was once left in a stack with his brush, to indicate which way the wind blew. It was an awful spectacle certainly; not much unlike the old stage direction in Macbeth, where the 'Apparition of a child crowned, with a tree in his hand, rises.'

Reader, if thou meetest one of these small gentry in thy early rambles, it is good to give him a penny. It is better to give him twopence. If it be starving weather, and to the proper troubles of his hard occupation, a pair of kibed heels (no unusual accompaniment) be superadded, the demand on thy humanity will surely rise to a tester.

There is a composition, the ground-work of which I have understood to be the sweet wood yclept sassafras. This wood boiled down to a kind of tea, and tempered with an infusion of milk and sugar, hath to some tastes a delicacy beyond the China luxury. I know not how thy palate may relish it; for myself, with every deference to the judicious Mr. Read, who hath time out of mind kept open a shop (the only one he avers in London) for the vending of this 'wholesome and pleasant beverage,' on the south side of Fleet Street, as thou approachest Bridge Street—*the only Salopian house*—I have never yet adventured to dip my own particular lip in a basin of his commended ingredients—a cautious premonition to the olfactories constantly whispering to me, that my stomach must infallibly, with all due courtesy, decline it. Yet I have seen palates, otherwise not uninstructed in dietetical elegancies, sup it up with avidity.

I know not by what particular conformation of the organ it happens, but I have always found that this composition is surprisingly gratifying to the palate of a young chimney-sweeper—whether the oily particles (sassafras is slightly oleaginous) do attenuate and soften the fuliginous concretions, which are sometimes found (in dissections) to adhere to the roof of the mouth in these unfledged practitioners; or whether Nature, sensible that she had mingled too much of bitter wood in the lot of these raw victims, caused to grow out of the earth her sassafras for a sweet lenitive—but so it is, that no possible taste or odour to the senses of a young chimney-sweeper can convey a delicate excitement comparable to this mixture. Being penniless, they will yet hang their black heads over the ascending steam, to gratify one sense if possible, seemingly no less pleased than those domestic animals—cats—when they purr over a new-found sprig of valerian. There is something more in these sympathies than philosophy can inculcate.

Now albeit Mr. Read boasteth, not without reason, that his is the *only Salopian house;* yet be it known to thee, reader —if thou art one who keepest what are called good hours, thou art haply ignorant of the fact—he hath a race of industrious imitators, who from stalls, and under open sky, dispense the same savoury mess to humbler customers, at that dead time of the dawn, when (as extremes meet) the rake, reeling home from his midnight cups, and the hard-handed artisan leaving his bed to resume the premature labours of the day, jostle, not unfrequently to the manifest disconcerting of the former, for the honours of the pavement. It is the time when, in summer, between the expired and the not yet relumined kitchen-fires, the kennels of our fair metropolis give forth their least satisfactory odours. The rake, who wisheth to dissipate his o'ernight vapours in more grateful coffee, curses the ungenial fume, as he passeth; but the artisan stops to taste, and blesses the fragrant breakfast.

This is *saloop*—the precocious herb-woman's darling—the delight of the early gardener, who transports his smoking cabbages by break of day from Hammersmith to Covent Garden's famed piazzas—the delight, and oh! I fear, too often the envy, of the unpennied sweep. Him shouldst thou haply encounter, with his dim visage pendent over the grateful steam, regale him with a sumptuous basin (it will cost thee but threehalf-pennies) and a slice of delicate bread and butter (an added half-penny)—so may thy culinary fires, eased of the o'er-charged secretions from thy worse-placed hospitalities, curl up a lighter volume to the welkin—so may the descending soot never taint thy costly well-ingredienced soups—nor the odious cry, quick-reaching from street to street, of the *fired chimney*, invite the rattling engines from ten adjacent parishes, to disturb for a casual scintillation thy peace and pocket!

I am by nature extremely susceptible of street affronts; the jeers and taunts of the populace; the low-bred triumph they display over the casual trip, or splashed stocking, of a gentleman. Yet can I endure the jocularity of a young sweep with something more than forgiveness.—In the last winter but one, pacing along Cheapside with my accustomed precipitation when I walk westward, a treacherous slide brought me upon my back in an instant. I scrambled up with pain and shame enough—yet outwardly trying to face it down, as if nothing had happened—when the roguish grin of one of these young wits encountered me. There he stood, pointing me out with his dusky finger to the mob, and to a poor woman (I suppose his mother) in particular, till the tears for the exquisiteness of the fun (so he thought it) worked themselves out at the corners of his poor red eyes, red from many a previous weeping, and soot-inflamed, yet twinkling through all with such a joy, snatched out of desolation, that Hogarth——but Hogarth has got him already (how could he miss him?) in the March to Finchley, grinning at the pieman—there he stood, as he stands in the picture, irremovable, as if the jest was to last for ever—with such a maximum of glee, and minimum of mischief, in his mirth—for the grin of a genuine sweep hath absolutely no malice in it—that I could have been content, if the honour of a gentleman might endure it, to have remained his butt and his mockery till midnight.

I am by theory obdurate to the seductiveness of what are called a fine set of teeth. Every pair of rosy lips (the ladies must pardon me) is a casket presumably holding such jewels; but, methinks, they should take leave to 'air' them as frugally as possible. The fine lady, or fine gentleman, who show me their teeth, show me bones. Yet must I confess, that from the mouth of a true sweep a display (even to ostentation) of those white and shining ossifications, strikes me as an agreeable anomaly in manners, and an allowable piece of foppery. It is, as when

A sable cloud
Turns forth her silver lining on the night.

It is like some remnant of gentry not quite extinct; a badge of better days; a hint of nobility:—and, doubtless, under the obscuring darkness and double night of their forlorn disguisement, oftentimes lurketh good blood, and gentle conditions, derived from lost ancestry, and a lapsed pedigree. The premature apprenticements of these tender victims give but too much encouragement, I fear, to clandestine and almost infantile abductions; the seeds of civility and true courtesy, so often discernible in these young grafts (not otherwise to be accounted for) plainly hint at some forced adoptions; many noble Rachels mourning for their children, even in our days, countenance the fact; the tales of fairy-spiriting may shadow a lamentable verity, and the recovery of the young Montagu be but a solitary instance of good fortune out of many irreparable and hopeless *defiliations*

In one of the state-beds at Arundel Castle, a few years since—under a ducal canopy—(that seat of the Howards is an object of curiosity to visitors, chiefly for its beds, in which the late duke was especially a connoisseur)—encircled with curtains of delicatest crimson, with starry coronets inwoven—folded between a pair of sheets whiter and softer than the lap where Venus lulled Ascanius—was discovered by chance, after all methods of search had failed, at noon-day, fast asleep, a lost chimney-sweeper. The little creature, having somehow confounded his passage among the intricacies of those lordly chimneys, by some unknown aperture had alighted upon this magnificent chamber; and, tired with his tedious explorations, was unable to resist the delicious invitement to repose, which he there saw exhibited; so creeping between the sheets very quietly, laid his black head upon the pillow, and slept like a young Howard.

Such is the account given to the visitors at the Castle.—But I cannot help seeming to perceive a confirmation of what I have just hinted at in this story. A high instinct was at work in the case, or I am mistaken. Is it probable that a poor child of that description, with whatever weariness he might be visited, would have ventured, under such a penalty as he would be taught to expect, to uncover the sheets of a duke's bed, and deliberately to lay himself down between them, when the rug, or the carpet, presented an obvious couch, still far above his pretensions—is this probable, I would ask, if the great power of nature, which I contend for, had not been manifested within him, prompting to the adventure? Doubtless this young nobleman (for such my mind misgives me that he must be) was allured by some memory, not amounting to full consciousness, of his condition in infancy, when he was used to be lapped by his mother, or his nurse, in just such sheets as he there found, into which he was now but creeping back as into his proper *incunabula*, and resting-place.—By no other theory than by this sentiment of a pre-existent state (as I may call it), can I explain a deed so venturous, and, indeed, upon any other system, so indecorous, in this tender, but unseasonable, sleeper.

My pleasant friend JEM WHITE was so impressed with a belief of metamorphoses like this frequently taking place, that in some sort to reverse the wrongs of fortune in these poor changelings, he instituted an annual feast of chimney-sweepers, at which it was his pleasure to officiate as host and waiter. It was a solemn supper held in Smithfield, upon the yearly return of the fair of St. Bartholomew. Cards were issued a week before to the master-sweeps in and about the metropolis, confining the invitation to their younger fry. Now and then an elderly stripling would get in among us, and be good-naturedly winked at; but our main body were infantry. One unfortunate wight, indeed, who, relying upon his dusky suit, had intruded himself into our party, but by tokens was providentially discovered in time to be no chimney-sweeper (all is not soot which look so), was quoited out of the presence with universal indignation, as not having on the wedding garment; but in general the greatest harmony prevailed. The place chosen was a convenient spot among the pens, at the north side of the fair, not so far distant as to be impervious to the agreeable hubbub of that vanity; but remote enough not to be obvious to the interruption of every gaping spectator in it. The guests assembled about seven. In those little temporary parlours three tables were spread with napery, not so fine as substantial, and at every board a comely hostess presided with her pan of hissing sausages. The nostrils of the young rogues dilated at the savour. JAMES WHITE, as head waiter, had charge of the first table; and myself with our trusty companion BIGOD, ordinarily ministered to the other two. There was clambering and jostling, you may be sure, who should get at the first table—for Rochester in his maddest days could not have done the humours of the scene with more spirit than my friend. After some general expression of thanks for the honour the company had done him, his inaugural ceremony was to clasp the greasy waist of old dame Ursula (the fattest of the three), that stood frying and fretting, half-blessing, half-cursing 'the gentleman,' and imprint upon her chaste lips a tender salute, whereat the universal host would set up a shout that tore the concave, while hundreds of grinning teeth startled the night with their brightness. O it was a pleasure to see the sable younkers lick in the unctuous meat, with *his* more unctuous sayings—how he would fit the tit-bits to the puny mouths, reserving the lengthier links for the seniors—how he would intercept a morsel even in the jaws of some young desperado, declaring it 'must to the pan again to be browned, for it was not fit for a gentleman's eating'—how he would recommend this slice of white bread, or that piece of kissing-crust, to a tender juvenile, advising them all to have a care of cracking their teeth, which were their best patrimony,—how genteelly he would deal about the small ale, as if it were wine, naming the brewer, and protesting, if it were not good, he should lose their custom; with a special recommendation to wipe the lip before drinking. Then we had our toasts—'The King,'—'the Cloth,'—which, whether they understood or not, was equally diverting and flattering; —and for a crowning sentiment, which never failed, 'May the Brush supersede the Laurel!' All these, and fifty other fancies which were rather felt than comprehended by his guests, would he utter, standing upon tables, and prefacing every sentiment with a 'Gentlemen, give me leave to propose so and so,' which was a prodigious comfort to those young orphans; every now and then stuffing into his mouth (for it did not do to be squeamish on these occasions) indiscriminate pieces of those reeking sausages, which pleased them mightily, and was the savouriest part, you may believe, of the entertainment.

> Golden lads and lasses must,
> As chimney-sweepers, come to dust—

JAMES WHITE is extinct, and with him these suppers have

long ceased. He carried away with him half the fun of the world when he died—of my world at least. His old clients look for him among the pens; and, missing him, reproach the altered feast of St. Bartholomew, and the glory of Smithfield departed for ever.

A Complaint of the Decay of Beggars in the Metropolis

THE all-sweeping besom of societarian reformation—your only modern Alcides' club to rid the time of its abuses—is uplift with many-handed sway to extirpate the last fluttering tatters of the bugbear MENDICITY from the metropolis. Scrips, wallets, bags—staves, dogs, and crutches—the whole mendicant fraternity, with all their baggage, are fast posting out of the purlieus of this eleventh persecution. From the crowded crossing, from the corners of streets and turnings of alleys, the parting Genius of Beggary is 'with sighing sent.'

I do not approve of this wholesale going to work, this impertinent crusado, or *bellum ad exterminationem*, proclaimed against a species. Much good might be sucked from these Beggars.

They were the oldest and the honourablest form of pauperism. Their appeals were to our common nature; less revolting to an ingenuous mind than to be a suppliant to the particular humours or caprice of any fellow-creature, or set of fellow-creatures, parochial or societarian. Theirs were the only rates uninvidious in the levy, ungrudged in the assessment.

There was a dignity springing from the very depth of their desolation; as to be naked is to be so much nearer to the being a man, than to go in livery.

The greatest spirits have felt this in their reverses; and when Dionysius from king turned schoolmaster, do we feel anything towards him but contempt? Could Vandyke have made a picture of him, swaying a ferula for a sceptre, which would have affected our minds with the same heroic pity, the same compassionate admiration, with which we regard his Belisarius begging for an *obolum?* Would the moral have been more graceful, more pathetic?

The Blind Beggar in the legend—the father of pretty Bessy—whose story doggrel rhymes and alehouse signs cannot so degrade or attenuate but that some sparks of a lustrous spirit will shine through the disguisements—this noble Earl of Cornwall (as indeed he was) and memorable sport of fortune, fleeing from the unjust sentence of his liege lord, stript of all, and seated on the flowering green of Bethnal, with his more fresh and springing daughter by his side, illumining his rags and his beggary—would the child and parent have cut a better figure doing the honours of a counter, or expiating their fallen condition upon the three-foot eminence of some sempstering shop-board?

In tale or history your Beggar is ever the just antipode to your King. The poets and romancical writers (as dear Margaret Newcastle would call them), when they would most sharply and feelingly paint a reverse of fortune, never stop till they have brought down their hero in good earnest to rags and the wallet. The depth of the descent illustrates the height he falls from. There is no medium which can be presented to the imagination without offence. There is no breaking the fall. Lear, thrown from his palace, must divest him of his garments, till he answer 'mere nature'; and Cresseid, fallen from a prince's love, must extend her pale arms, pale with other whiteness than of beauty, supplicating lazar arms with bell and clap-dish.

The Lucian wits knew this very well; and, with a converse policy, when they would express scorn of greatness without the pity, they show us an Alexander in the shades cobbling shoes, or a Semiramis getting up foul linen.

How would it sound in song, that a great monarch had declined his affections upon the daughter of a baker! yet do we feel the imagination at all violated when we read the 'true ballad,' where King Cophetua woos the beggar maid?

Pauperism, pauper, poor man, are expressions of pity, but pity alloyed with contempt. No one properly contemns a Beggar. Poverty is a comparative thing, and each degree of it is mocked by its 'neighbour grice.' Its poor rents and comings-in are soon summed up and told. Its pretences to property are almost ludicrous. Its pitiful attempts to save excite a smile. Every scornful companion can weigh his trifle-bigger purse against it. Poor man reproaches poor man in the street with impolitic mention of his condition, his own being a shade better, while the rich pass by and jeer at both. No rascally comparative insults a Beggar, or thinks of weighing purses with him. He is not in the scale of comparison. He is not under the measure of property. He confessedly hath none, any more than a dog or a sheep. No one twitteth him with ostentation above his means. No one accuses him of pride, or upbraideth him with mock humility. None jostle with him for the wall, or pick quarrels for precedency. No wealthy neighbour seeketh to eject him from his tenement. No man sues him. No man goes to law with him. If I were not the independent gentleman that I am, rather than I would be a retainer to the great, a led captain, or a poor relation, I would choose, out of the delicacy and the true greatness of my mind, to be a Beggar.

Rags, which are the reproach of poverty, are the Beggar's robes, and graceful *insignia* of his profession, his tenure, his full dress, the suit in which he is expected to show himself in public. He is never out of the fashion, or limpeth awkwardly behind it. He is not required to put on court mourning. He weareth all colours, fearing none. His costume hath undergone less change than the Quaker's. He is the only man in the universe who is not obliged to study appearances. The ups and downs of the world concern him no longer. He alone continueth in one stay. The price of stock or land affecteth him not. The fluctuations of agricultural or commercial prosperity touch him not, or at worst but change his customers. He is not expected to become bail or surety for any one. No man troubleth him with questioning his religion or politics. He is the only free man in the universe.

The Mendicants of this great city were so many of her sights, her lions. I can no more spare them than I could the Cries of London. No corner of a street is complete without them. They are as indispensable as the Ballad Singer; and in their picturesque attire as ornamental as the signs of old London. They were the standing morals, emblems, mementoes, dial-mottoes, the spital sermons, the books for children, the salutary checks and pauses to the high and rushing tide of greasy citizenry—

———Look
Upon that poor and broken bankrupt there.

Above all, those old blind Tobits that used to line the wall of Lincoln's Inn Garden, before modern fastidiousness had expelled them, casting up their ruined orbs to catch a ray of pity, and (if possible) of light, with their faithful Dog Guide at their feet,—whither are they fled? or into what corners, blind as themselves, have they been driven, out of the wholesome air and sun-warmth? immersed between four walls in what withering poor-house do they endure the penalty of double darkness, where the chink of the dropt halfpenny no more consoles their forlorn bereavement, far from the sound of the cheerful and hope-stirring tread of the passenger? Where hang their useless staves? and who will farm their dogs?—Have the overseers of St. L——caused them to be shot? or were they tied up in sacks and dropt into the Thames, at the suggestion of B——, the mild rector of——?

Well fare the soul of unfastidious Vincent Bourne, most classical, and at the same time, most English, of the Latinists! —who has treated of this human and quadrupedal alliance, this dog and man friendship, in the sweetest of his poems, the *Epitaphium in Canem*, or, *Dog's Epitaph*. Reader, peruse it; and say, if customary sights, which could call up such gentle poetry as this, were of a nature to do more harm or good to the moral sense of the passengers through the daily thoroughfares of a vast and busy metropolis.

Pauperis hic Iri requiesco Lyciscus, herilis,
Dum vixi, tutela vigil columenque senectæ,
Dux cæco fidus : nec, me ducente, solebat,
Prætenso hinc atque hinc baculo, per iniqua locorum
Incertam explorare viam ; sed fila secutus,
Quæ dubios regerent passus, vestigia tuta
Fixit inoffenso gressu ; gelidumque sedile
In nudo nactus saxo, quâ prætereuntium
Unda frequens confluxit, ibi miserisque tenebras
Lamentis, noctemque oculis ploravit obortam.
Ploravit nec frustra ; obolum dedit alter et alter,
Queis corda et mentem indiderat natura benignam.
Ad latus interea jacui sopitus herile,
Vel mediis vigil in somnis ; ad herilia jussa
Auresque atque animum arrectus, seu frustula amice
Porrexit sociasque dapes, seu longa diei
Tædia perpessus, reditum sub nocte parabat.

Hi mores, hæc vita fuit, dum fata sinebant,
Dum neque languebam morbis, nec inerte senectâ ;
Quæ tandem obrepsit, veterique satellite cæcum
Orbavit dominum : prisci sed gratia facti
Ne tota intereat, longos deleta per annos,
Exiguum hunc Irus tumulum de cespite fecit,
Etsi inopis, non ingratæ, munuscula dextræ ;
Carmine signavitque brevi, dominumque canemque
Quod memoret, fidumque canem dominumque benignum.*

These dim eyes have in vain explored for some months
past a well-known figure, or part of the figure of a man, who
used to glide his comely upper half over the pavements of
London, wheeling along with most ingenious celerity upon
a machine of wood; a spectacle to natives, to foreigners, and
to children. He was of a robust make, with a florid sailor-
like complexion, and his head was bare to the storm and
sunshine. He was a natural curiosity, a speculation to the
scientific, a prodigy to the simple. The infant would stare

* Poor Irus' faithful wolf-dog here I lie,
  That wont to tend my old blind master's steps,
  His guide and guard; nor, while my service lasted,
  Had he occasion for that staff, with which
  He now goes picking out his path in fear
  Over the highways and crossings; but would plant,
  Safe in the conduct of my friendly string,
  A firm foot forward still, till he had reach'd
  His poor seat on some stone, nigh where the tide
  Of passers-by in thickest confluence flow'd:
  To whom with loud and passionate laments
  From morn to eve his dark estate he wail'd.
  Nor wail'd to all in vain: some here and there,
  The well-disposed and good, their pennies gave.
  I meantime at his feet obsequious slept;
  Not all-sleep in sleep, but heart and ear
  Prick'd up at his least motion; to receive
  At his kind hand my customary crumbs,
  And common portion in his feast of scraps;
  Or when night warn'd us homeward, tired and spent
  With our long day and tedious beggary.
  These were my manners, this my way of life,
  Till age and slow disease me overtook,
  And sever'd from my sightless master's side.
  But lest the grace of so good deeds should die,
  Through tract of years in mute oblivion lost,
  This slender tomb of turf hath Irus reared,
  Cheap monument of no ungrudging hand,
  And with short verse inscribed it, to attest,
  In long and lasting union to attest,
  The virtues of the Beggar and his Dog.

at the mighty man brought down to his own level. The common cripple would despise his own pusillanimity, viewing the hale stoutness, and hearty heart, of this half-limbed giant. Few but must have noticed him; for the accident which brought him low took place during the riots of 1780, and he has been a groundling so long. He seemed earth-born, an Antæus, and to suck in fresh vigour from the soil which he neighboured. He was a grand fragment; as good as an Elgin marble. The nature, which should have recruited his reft legs and thighs, was not lost, but only retired into his upper parts, and he was half a Hercules. I heard a tremendous voice thundering and growling, as before an earthquake, and casting down my eyes, it was this mandrake reviling a steed that had started at his portentous appearance. He seemed to want but his just stature to have rent the offending quadruped in shivers. He was as the man-part of a centaur, from which the horse-half had been cloven in some dire Lapithan controversy. He moved on, as if he could have made shift with yet half of the body-portion which was left him. The *os sublime* was not wanting; and he threw out yet a jolly countenance upon the heavens. Forty-and-two years had he driven this out-of-door trade, and now that his hair is grizzled in the service, but his good spirits no way impaired, because he is not content to exchange his free air and exercise for the restraints of a poor-house, he is expiating his contumacy in one of those houses (ironically christened) of Correction.

Was a daily spectacle like this to be deemed a nuisance, which called for legal interference to remove? or not rather a salutary and a touching object to the passers-by in a great city? Among her shows, her museums, and supplies for ever-gaping curiosity (and what else but an accumulation of sights—endless sights—*is* a great city; or for what else is it desirable?) was there not room for one *Lusus* (not *Naturae*, indeed, but) *Accidentium?* What if in forty-and-two-years' going about, the man had scraped together enough to give a portion to his child (as the rumour ran) of a few hundreds —whom had he injured?—whom had he imposed upon? The contributors had enjoyed their *sight* for their pennies. What if after being exposed all day to the heats, the rains, and the frosts of heaven—shuffling his ungainly trunk along in an elaborate and painful motion—he was enabled to retire at night to enjoy himself at a club of his fellow cripples over a dish of hot meat and vegetables, as the charge was gravely brought against him by a clergyman deposing before a House of Commons' Committee—was *this*, or was his truly paternal consideration, which (if a fact) deserved a statue rather than a whipping-post, and is inconsistent, at least, with the exaggeration of nocturnal orgies which he has been slandered with—a reason that he should be deprived of his chosen, harmless, nay edifying, way of life, and be committed in hoary age for a sturdy vagabond?—

There was a Yorick once, whom it would not have shamed to have sate down at the cripples' feast, and to have thrown in his benediction, ay, and his mite too, for a companionable symbol. 'Age, thou hast lost thy breed.'—

Half of these stories about the prodigious fortunes made by begging are (I verily believe) misers' calumnies. One was much talked of in the public papers some time since, and the usual charitable inferences deduced. A clerk in the Bank was surprised with the announcement of a five-hundred-pound legacy left him by a person whose name he was a stranger to. It seems that in his daily morning walks from Peckham (or some village thereabouts) where he lived, to his office, it had been his practice for the last twenty years to drop his halfpenny duly into the hat of some blind Bartimeus, that sate begging alms by the wayside in the Borough. The good old beggar recognised his daily benefactor by the voice only; and, when he died, left all the amassings of his alms (that had been half a century perhaps in the accumulating) to his old Bank friend. Was this a story to purse up people's hearts, and pennies, against giving an alms to the blind?—or not rather a beautiful moral of well-directed charity on the one part, and noble gratitude upon the other?

I sometimes wish I had been that Bank clerk.

I seem to remember a poor old grateful kind of creature, blinking, and looking up with his no eyes in the sun.—

Is it possible I could have steeled my purse against him? Perhaps I had no small change.

Reader, do not be frightened at the hard words imposition, imposture—*give, and ask no questions*. Cast thy bread upon the waters. Some have unawares (like this Bank clerk) entertained angels.

Shut not thy purse-strings always against painted distress. Act a charity sometimes. When a poor creature (outwardly and visibly such) comes before thee, do not stay to inquire whether the 'seven small children,' in whose name he implores thy assistance, have a veritable existence. Rake not into the bowels of unwelcome truth to save a halfpenny. It is good to believe him. If he be not all that he pretendeth, *give*, and under a personate father of a family, think (if thou pleasest) that thou hast relieved an indigent bachelor. When they come with their counterfeit looks, and mumping tones, think them players. You pay your money to see a comedian feign these things, which, concerning these poor people, thou canst not certainly tell whether they are feigned or not.

A Dissertation Upon Pig

MANKIND, says a Chinese manuscript, which my friend M. was obliging enough to read and explain to me, for the first seventy thousand ages ate their meat raw, clawing or biting it from the living animal, just as they do in Abyssinia to this day. This period is not obscurely hinted at by their great Confucius in the second chapter of his Mundane Mutations, where he designates a kind of golden age by the term Chofang, literally the Cooks' Holiday. The manuscript goes on to say, that the art of roasting, or rather broiling (which I take to be the elder brother) was accidentally discovered in the manner following. The swine-herd, Ho-ti, having gone out into the woods one morning, as his manner was, to collect mast for his hogs, left his cottage in the care of his eldest son Bo-bo, a great lubberly boy, who being fond of playing with fire, as younkers of his age commonly are, let some sparks escape into a bundle of straw, which kindling quickly, spread the conflagration over every part of their poor mansion, till it was reduced to ashes. Together with the cottage (a sorry antediluvian make-shift of a building, you may think it), what was of much more importance, a fine litter of new-farrowed pigs, no less than nine in number, perished. China pigs have been esteemed a luxury all over the East, from the remotest periods that we read of. Bo-bo was in the utmost consternation, as you may think, not so much for the sake of the tenement, which his father and he could easily build up again with a few dry branches, and the labour of an hour or two, at any time, as for the loss of the pigs. While he was thinking what he should say to his father, and wringing his hands over the smoking remnants of one of those untimely sufferers, an odour assailed his nostrils, unlike any scent which he had before experienced. What could it proceed from?—not from the burnt cottage—he had smelt that smell before—indeed this was by no means the first accident of the kind which had occurred through the negligence of this unlucky young fire-brand. Much less did it resemble that of any known herb, weed, or flower. A premonitory moistening at the same time overflowed his nether lip. He knew not what to think. He next stooped down to feel the pig, if there were any signs of life in it. He burnt his fingers, and to cool them he applied them in his booby fashion to his mouth. Some of the crumbs of the scorched skin had come away with his fingers, and for the first time in his life (in the world's life indeed, for before him no man had known it) he tasted —*crackling!* Again he felt and fumbled at the pig. It did not burn him so much now, still he licked his fingers from a sort of habit. The truth at length broke into his slow understanding, that it was the pig that smelt so, and the pig that tasted so delicious; and surrendering himself up to the new-born pleasure, he fell to tearing up whole handfuls of the scorched skin with the flesh next it, and was cramming it down his throat in his beastly fashion, when his sire entered amid the smoking rafters, armed with retributory cudgel, and finding how affairs stood, began to rain blows upon the young rogue's shoulders, as thick as hailstones, which Bo-bo heeded not any more than if they had been flies. The tickling pleasure, which he experienced in his lower regions, had rendered him quite callous to any inconveniences he might feel in those remote quarters. His father might lay on, but he could not beat him from his pig, till he had fairly made an end of it, when, becoming a little more sensible of his situation, something like the following dialogue ensued.

'You graceless whelp, what have you got there devouring? Is it not enough that you have burnt me down three houses with your dog's tricks, and be hanged to you! but you must be eating fire, and I know not what—what have you got there, I say?'

'O father, the pig, the pig! do come and taste how nice the burnt pig eats.'

The ears of Ho-ti tingled with horror. He cursed his son, and he cursed himself that ever he should beget a son that should eat burnt pig.

Bo-bo, whose scent was wonderfully sharpened since morning, soon raked out another pig, and fairly rending it asunder, thrust the lesser half by main force into the fists of Ho-ti, still shouting out, 'Eat, eat, eat the burnt pig, father, only taste—O Lord!'—with such-like barbarous ejaculations, cramming all the while as if he would choke.

Ho-ti trembled every joint while he grasped the abominable thing, wavering whether he should not put his son to death for an unnatural young monster, when the crackling scorching his fingers, as it had done his son's, and applying the same remedy to them, he in his turn tasted some of its flavour, which, make what sour mouths he would for a pretence, proved not altogether displeasing to him. In conclusion (for the manuscript here is a little tedious), both father and son fairly set down to the mess, and never left off till they had despatched all that remained of the litter.

Bo-bo was strictly enjoined not to let the secret escape, for the neighbours would certainly have stoned them for a couple of abominable wretches, who could think of improving upon the good meat which God had sent them. Nevertheless, strange stories got about. It was observed that Ho-ti's cottage was burnt down now more frequently than ever. Nothing but fires from this time forward. Some would break out in broad day, others in the night-time. As often as the sow farrowed, so sure was the house of Ho-ti to be in a blaze; and Ho-ti himself, which was the more remarkable, instead of chastising his son, seemed to grow more indulgent to him than ever. At length they were watched, the terrible mystery discovered, and father and son summoned to take their trial at Pekin, then an inconsiderable assize town. Evidence was given, the obnoxious food itself produced in court, and verdict about to be pronounced, when the foreman of the jury begged that some of the burnt pig, of which the culprits stood accused, might be handed into the box. He handled it, and they all handled it; and burning their fingers, as Bo-bo and is father had done before them, and nature prompting to each of them the same remedy, against the face of all the facts, and the clearest charge which judge had ever given,—to the surprise of the whole court, townsfolk, strangers, reporters, and all present—without leaving the box, or any manner of consultation whatever, they brought in a simultaneous verdict of Not Guilty.

The judge, who was a shrewd fellow, winked at the manifest iniquity of the decision: and when the court was dismissed, went privily and bought up all the pigs that could be had for love or money. In a few days his lordship's town-house was observed to be on fire. The thing took wing, and now there was nothing to be seen but fire in every direction. Fuel and pigs grew enormously dear all over the district. The insurance-offices one and all shut up shop. People built slighter and slighter every day, until it was feared that the very science of architecture would in no long time be lost to the world. Thus this custom of firing houses continued, till in process of time, says my manuscript, a sage arose, like our Locke, who made a discovery that the flesh of swine, or indeed of any other animal, might be cooked (*burnt*, as they called it) without the necessity of consuming a whole house to dress it. Then first began the rude form of a gridiron. Roasting by the string or spit came in a century or two later, I forget in whose dynasty. By such slow degrees, concludes the manuscript, do the most useful, and seemingly the most obvious, arts make their way among mankind——

Without placing too implicit faith in the account above given, it must be agreed that if a worthy pretext for so dangerous an experiment as setting houses on fire (especially in these days) could be assigned in favour of any culinary object, that pretext and excuse might be found in ROAST PIG.

Of all the delicacies in the whole *mundus edibilis*, I will maintain it to be the most delicate—*princeps obsoniorum*.

I speak not of your grown porkers—things between pig and pork—those hobbydehoys—but a young and tender suckling—under a moon old—guiltless as yet of the sty— with no original speck of the *amor immunditie*, the hereditary failing of the first parent, yet manifest—his voice as yet not broken, but something between a childish treble and a grumble—the mild forerunner or *præludium* of a grunt.

He must be roasted. I am not ignorant that our ancestors ate them seethed, or boiled—but what a sacrifice to the exterior tegument!

There is no flavour comparable, I will contend, to that of the crisp, tawny, well-watched, not over-roasted, *crackling*, as it is well called—the very teeth are invited to their share of the pleasure at this banquet in overcoming the coy, brittle resistance—with the adhesive oleaginous—O call it not fat! but an indefinable sweetness growing up to it—the tender blossoming of fat—fat cropped in the bud—taken in the shoot—in the first innocence—the cream and quintessence of the child-pig's yet pure food—the lean, no lean, but a kind of animal manna—or, rather, fat and lean (if it must be so) so blended and running into each other, that both together make but one ambrosian result or common substance.

Behold him, while he is 'doing'—it seemeth rather a refreshing warmth, than a scorching heat, that he is so passive to. How equably he twirleth round the string!— Now he is just done. To see the extreme sensibility of that tender age! he hath wept out his pretty eyes—radiant jellies —shooting stars.—

See him in the dish, his second cradle, how meek he lieth! —wouldst thou have had this innocent grow up to the grossness and indocility which too often accompany maturer swinehood? Ten to one he would have proved a glutton, a sloven, an obstinate, disagreeable animal—wallowing in all manner of filthy conversation—from these sins he is happily snatched away——

> Ere sin could blight or sorrow fade,
> Death came with timely care—

his memory is odoriferous—no clown curseth, while his stomach half rejecteth, the rank bacon—no coal-heaver bolteth him in reeking sausages—he hath a fair sepulchre in the grateful stomach of the judicious epicure—and for such a tomb might be content to die.

He is the best of sapors. Pine-apple is great. She is indeed almost too transcendent—a delight, if not sinful, yet so like to sinning that really a tender-conscienced person would do well to pause—too ravishing for mortal taste, she woundeth and excoriateth the lips that approach her—like lovers' kisses, she biteth—she is a pleasure bordering on pain from the fierceness and insanity of her relish—but she stoppeth at the palate—she meddleth not with the appetite—and the coarsest hunger might barter her consistently for a mutton-chop.

Pig—let me speak his praise—is no less provocative of the appetite, than he is satisfactory to the criticalness of the censorious palate. The strong man may batten on him, and the weakling refuseth not his mild juices.

Unlike to mankind's mixed characters, a bundle of virtues and vices, inexplicably intertwisted, and not to be unravelled without hazard, he is—good throughout. No part of him is better or worse than another. He helpeth, as far as his little means extend, all around. He is the least envious of banquets. He is all neighbours' fare.

I am one of those, who freely and ungrudgingly impart a share of the good things of this life which fall to their lot (few as mine are in this kind) to a friend. I protest I take as great an interest in my friend's pleasures, his relishes, and proper satisfactions, as in mine own. 'Presents,' I often say, 'endear Absents.' Hares, pheasants, partridges, snipes, barndoor chickens (those 'tame villatic fowl'), capons, plovers, brawn, barrels of oysters, I dispense as freely as I receive them. I love to taste them, as it were, upon the tongue of my friend. But a stop must be put somewhere. One would not, like Lear, 'give everything.' I make my stand upon pig. Methinks it is an ingratitude to the Giver of all good flavours to extra-domiciliate, or send out of the house slightingly (under pretext of friendship or I know not what) a blessing so particularly adapted, predestined, I may say, to my individual palate.—It argues an insensibility.

I remember a touch of conscience in this kind at school. My good old aunt, who never parted from me at the end of a holiday without stuffing a sweetmeat, or some nice thing into my pocket, had dismissed me one evening with a smoking plum-cake, fresh from the oven. In my way to school (it was over London Bridge) a grey-headed old beggar saluted me (I have no doubt, at this time of day, that he was a counterfeit). I had no pence to console him with, and in the vanity of self-denial and the very coxcombry of charity, schoolboy-like, I made him a present of—the whole cake! I walked on a little, buoyed up, as one is on such occasions, with a sweet soothing of self-satisfaction; but before I had got to the end of the bridge, my better feelings returned, and I burst into tears, thinking how ungrateful I had been to my good aunt, to go and give her good gift away to a stranger that I had never seen before, and who might be a bad man for aught I knew; and then I thought of the pleasure my aunt would be taking in thinking that I—I myself, and not another—would eat her nice cake—and what should I say to her the next time I saw her—how naughty I was to part with her pretty present!—and the odour of that spicy cake came back upon my recollection, and the pleasure and the curiosity I had taken in seeing her make it, and her joy when she sent it to the oven, and how disappointed she would feel that I had never had a bit of it in my mouth at last—and I blamed my impertinent spirit of alms-giving, and out-of-place hypocrisy of goodness; and above all I wished never to see the face again of that insidious, good-for-nothing, old grey impostor.

Our ancestors were nice in their method of sacrificing these tender victims. We read of pigs whipt to death with something of a shock, as we hear of any other obsolete custom. The age of discipline is gone by, or it would be curious to inquire (in a philosophical light merely) what effect this process might have towards intenerating and dulcifying a substance, naturally so mild and dulcet as the flesh of young pigs. It looks like refining a violet. Yet we should be cautious, while we condemn the inhumanity, how we censure the wisdom of the practice. It might impart a gusto.—

I remember an hypothesis, argued upon by the young students, when I was at St. Omer's, and maintained with much learning and pleasantry on both sides, 'Whether, supposing that the flavour of a pig who obtained his death by whipping (*per flagellationem extremam*) superadded a pleasure upon the palate of a man more intense than any possible suffering we can conceive in the animal, is man justified in using that method of putting the animal to death?' I forget the decision.

His sauce should be considered. Decidedly, a few bread crumbs, done up with his liver and brains, and a dash of mild sage. But banish, dear Mrs. Cook, I beseech you, the whole onion tribe. Barbecue your whole hogs to your palate, steep them in shalots, stuff them out with plantations of the rank and guilty garlic; you cannot poison them, or make them stronger than they are—but consider, he is a weakling a flower.

A Bachelor's Complaint of the Behaviour of Married People

As a single man, I have spent a good deal of my time in noting down the infirmities of Married People, to console myself for those superior pleasures, which they tell me I have lost by remaining as I am.

I cannot say that the quarrels of men and their wives ever made any great impression upon me, or had much tendency to strengthen me in those anti-social resolutions, which I took up long ago upon more substantial considerations. What oftenest offends me at the houses of married persons where I visit, is an error of quite a different description;—it is that they are too loving.

Not too loving neither: that does not explain my meaning. Besides, why should that offend me? The very act of separating themselves from the rest of the world, to have the fuller enjoyment of each other's society, implies that they prefer one another to all the world.

But what I complain of is, that they carry this preference so undisguisedly, they perk it up in the faces of us single people so shamelessly, you cannot be in their company a moment without being made to feel, by some indirect hint or open avowal, that *you* are not the object of this preference. Now there are some things which give no offence, while implied or taken for granted merely; but expressed, there is much offence in them. If a man were to accost the first homely-featured or plain-dressed young woman of his acquaintance, and tell her bluntly, that she was not handsome or rich enough for him, and he could not marry her, he would deserve to be kicked for his ill manners; yet no less is implied in the fact, that having access and opportunity of putting the question to her, he has never yet thought fit to do it. The young woman understands this as clearly as if it were put into words; but no reasonable young woman would think of making this the ground of a quarrel. Just as little right have a married couple to tell me by speeches, and looks that are scarce less plain than speeches, that I am not the happy man,—the lady's choice. It is enough that I know I am not: I do not want this perpetual reminding.

The display of superior knowledge or riches may be made sufficiently mortifying; but these admit of a palliative. The knowledge which is brought out to insult me, may accidentally improve me; and in the rich man's houses and pictures,— his parks and gardens, I have a temporary usufruct at least. But the display of married happiness has none of these palliatives: it is throughout pure, unrecompensed, unqualified insult.

Marriage by its best title is a monopoly, and not of the least invidious sort. It is the cunning of most possessors of any exclusive privilege to keep their advantage as much out of sight as possible that their less favoured neighbours, seeing little of the benefit, may the less be disposed to question the right. But these married monopolists thrust the most ob- noxious part of their patent into our faces.

Nothing is to me more distasteful than that entire com- placency and satisfaction which beam in the countenances of a new-married couple,—in that of the lady particularly: it tells you, that her lot is disposed of in this world: that *you* can have no hopes of her. It is true, I have none: nor wishes either, perhaps; but this is one of those truths which ought, as I said before, to be taken for granted, not expressed.

The excessive airs which those people give themselves, founded on the ignorance of us unmarried people, would be more offensive if they were less irrational. We will allow them to understand the mysteries belonging to their own craft better than we, who have not had the happiness to be made free of the company: but their arrogance is not content within these limits. If a single person presume to offer his opinion in their presence, though upon the most indifferent subject, he is immediately silenced as an incompetent person. Nay, a young married lady of my acquaintance, who, the best of the jest was, had not changed her condition above a fortnight before, in a question on which I had the misfortune to differ from her, respecting the properest mode of breeding oysters for the London market, had the assurance to ask with a sneer, how such an old Bachelor as I could pretend to know anything about such matters!

But what I have spoken of hitherto is nothing to the airs these creatures give themselves when they come, as they generally do, to have children. When I consider how little of a rarity children are,—that every street and blind alley swarms with them,—that the poorest people commonly have them in most abundance,—that there are few marriages that are not blest with at least one of these bargains,—how often they turn out ill, and defeat the fond hopes of their parents, taking to vicious courses, which end in poverty, disgrace, the gallows, etc.—I cannot for my life tell what cause for pride there can possibly be in having them. If they were young phœnixes, indeed, that were born but one in a year, there might be a pretext. But when they are so common——

I do not advert to the insolent merit which they assume with their husbands on these occasions. Let *them* look to that. But why *we*, who are not their natural-born subjects, should be expected to bring our spices, myrrh, and incense, —our tribute and homage of admiration,—I do not see.

'Like as the arrows in the hand of the giant, even so are the young children'; so says the excellent office in our Prayer-book appointed for the churching of women. 'Happy is the man that hath his quiver full of them': So say I; but then don't let him discharge his quiver upon us that are weaponless;—let them be arrows, but not to gall and stick us. I have generally observed that these arrows are double-headed: they have two forks, to be sure to hit with one or the other. As for instance, where you come into a house which is full of children, if you happen to take no notice of them (you are thinking of something else, perhaps, and turn a deaf ear to their innocent caresses), you are set down as untractable, morose, a hater of children. On the other hand, if you find them more than usually engaging,—if you are taken with their pretty manners, and set about in earnest to romp and play with them, some pretext or other is sure to be found for sending them out of the room; they are too noisy or boisterous, or Mr.——does not like children. With one or other of these forks the arrow is sure to hit you.

I could forgive their jealousy, and dispense with toying with their brats, if it gives them any pain; but I think it unreasonable to be called upon to *love* them, where I see no occasion,—to love a whole family, perhaps eight, nine, or ten, indiscriminately,—to love all the pretty dears, because children are so engaging!

I know there is a proverb, 'Love me, love my dog'; that is not always so very practicable, particularly if the dog be set upon you to tease you or snap at you in sport. But a dog, or a lesser thing—any inanimate substance, as a keepsake, a watch or a ring, a tree, or the place where we last parted when my friend went away upon a long absence, I can make shift to love, because I love him, and anything that reminds me of him; provided it be in its nature indifferent, and apt to receive whatever hue fancy can give it. But children have a real character, and an essential being of themselves: they are amiable or unamiable *per se;* I must love or hate them as I see cause for either in their qualities. A child's nature is too serious a thing to admit of its being regarded as a mere appendage to another being, and to be loved or hated accordingly: they stand with me upon their own stock, as much as men and women do. Oh! but you will say, sure it is an attractive age,—there is something in the tender years of infancy that of itself charms us? This is the very reason why I am more nice about them. I know that a sweet child is the sweetest thing in nature, not even excepting the delicate creatures which bear them; but the prettier the kind of a thing is, the more desirable it is that it should be pretty of its kind. One daisy differs not much from another in glory; but a violet should look and smell the daintiest.—I was always rather squeamish in my women and children.

But this is not the worst: one must be admitted into their familiarity at least, before they can complain of inattention. It implies visits, and some kind of intercourse. But if the husband be a man with whom you have lived on a friendly footing before marriage—if you did not come in on the wife's side—if you did not sneak into the house in her train, but were an old friend in fast habits of intimacy before their courtship was so much as thought on,—look about you—your tenure is precarious—before a twelvemonth shall roll over your head, you shall find your old friend gradually grow cool and altered towards you, and at last seek opportunities of breaking with you. I have scarce a married friend of my acquaintance, upon whose firm faith I can rely, whose friendship did not commence *after the period of his marriage.* With some limitations, they can endure that; but that the good man should have dared to enter into a solemn league of friendship in which they were not consulted, though it happened before they knew him,—before they that are now man and wife ever met,—this is intolerable to them. Every long friendship, every old authentic intimacy, must be brought into their office to be new stamped with their currency, as a sovereign prince calls in the good old money that was coined in some reign before he was born or thought of, to be new marked and minted with the stamp of his authority, before he will let it pass current in the world. You may guess what luck generally befalls such a rusty piece of metal as I am in these *new mintings*.

Innumerable are the ways which they take to insult and worm you out of their husband's confidence. Laughing at all you say with a kind of wonder, as if you were a queer kind of fellow that said good things, *but an oddity*, is one of the ways;—they have a particular kind of stare for the purpose;—till at last the husband, who used to defer to your judgment, and would pass over some excrescences of understanding and manner for the sake of a general vein of observation (not quite vulgar) which he perceived in you, begins to suspect whether you are not altogether a humorist, —a fellow well enough to have consorted with in his bachelor days, but not quite so proper to be introduced to ladies. This may be called the staring way; and is that which has oftenest been put in practice against me.

Then there is the exaggerating way, or the way of irony; that is, where they find you an object of especial regard with their husband, who is not so easily to be shaken from the lasting attachment founded on esteem which he has conceived towards you, by never qualified exaggerations to cry up all that you say or do, till the good man, who understands well enough that it is all done in compliment to him, grows weary of the debt of gratitude which is due to so much candour, and by relaxing a little on his part, and taking down a peg or two in his enthusiasm, sinks at length to the kindly level of moderate esteem—that 'decent affection and complacent kindness' towards you, where she herself can join in sympathy with him without much stretch and violence to her sincerity.

Another way (for the ways they have to accomplish so desirable a purpose are infinite) is, with a kind of innocent simplicity, continually to mistake what it was which first made their husband fond of you. If an esteem for something excellent in your moral character was that which riveted the chain which she is to break, upon any imaginary discovery of a want of poignancy in your conversation, she will cry, 'I thought, my dear, you described your friend, Mr.——, as a great wit?' If, on the other hand, it was for some supposed charm in your conversation that he first grew to like you, and was content for this to overlook some trifling irregularities in your moral deportment, upon the first notice of any of these she as readily exclaims, 'This, my dear, is your good Mr.——!' One good lady whom I took the liberty of expostulating with for not showing me quite so much respect as I thought due to her husband's old friend, had the candour to confess to me that she had often heard Mr.——speak of me before marriage, and that she had conceived a great desire to be acquainted with me, but that the sight of me had very much disappointed her expectations; for from her husband's representations of me, she had formed a notion that she was to see a fine, tall, officer-like-looking man (I use her very words), the very reverse of which proved to be the truth. This was candid; and I had the civility not to ask her in return, how she came to pitch upon a standard of personal accomplishments for her husband's friends which differed so much from his own; for my friend's dimensions as near as possible approximate to mine; he standing five feet five in his shoes, in which I have the advantage of him by about half an inch; and he no more than myself exhibiting any indications of a martial character in his air or countenance.

These are some of the mortifications which I have encountered in the absurd attempt to visit at their houses. To enumerate them all would be a vain endeavour; I shall therefore just glance at the very common impropriety of which married ladies are guilty,—of treating us as if we were their husbands, and *vice versâ*. I mean, when they use us with familiarity, and their husbands with ceremony. *Testacea*, for instance, kept me the other night two or three hours beyond my usual time of supping, while she was fretting because Mr.——did not come home, till the oysters were all spoiled, rather than she would be guilty of the impoliteness of touching one in his absence. This was reversing the point of good manners: for ceremony is an invention to take off the uneasy feeling which we derive from knowing ourselves to be less the object of love and esteem with a fellow-creature than some other person is. It endeavours to make up, by superior attentions in little points, for that invidious preference which it is forced to deny in the greater. Had *Testacea* kept the oysters back for me, and withstood her husband's importunities to go to supper, she would have acted according to the strict rules of propriety. I know no ceremony that ladies are bound to observe to their husbands, beyond the point of a modest behaviour and decorum: therefore I must protest against the vicarious gluttony of *Cerasia*, who at her own table sent away a dish of Morellas, which I was applying to with great good-will, to her husband at the other end of the table, and recommended a plate of less extraordinary gooseberries to my unwedded palate in their stead. Neither can I excuse the wanton affront of——

But I am weary of stringing up all my married acquaintances by Roman denominations. Let them amend and change their manners, or I promise to record the full-length English of their names, to the terror of all such desperate offenders in future.

On Some of the Old Actors

THE casual sight of an old Play Bill, which I picked up the other day—I know not by what chance it was preserved so long—tempts me to call to mind a few of the Players, who make the principal figure in it. It presents the cast of parts in the Twelfth Night, at the old Drury Lane Theatre two-and-thirty years ago. There is something very touching in these old remembrances. They make us think how we *once* used to read a Play Bill—not, as now peradventure, singling out a favourite performer, and casting a negligent eye over the rest; but spelling out every name, down to the very mutes and servants of the scene;—when it was a matter of no small moment to us whether Whitfield, or Packer, took the part of Fabian; when Benson, and Burton, and Phillimore— names of small account—had an importance, beyond what we can be content to attribute now to the time's best actors. —'Orsino, by Mr. Barrymore.'—What a full Shakespearian sound it carries! how fresh to memory arise the image and the manner of the gentle actor!

Those who have only seen Mrs. Jordan within the last ten or fifteen years, can have no adequate notion of her performance of such parts as Ophelia; Helena, in All's Well that Ends Well; and Viola in this play. Her voice had latterly acquired a coarseness, which suited well enough with her Nells and Hoydens, but in those days it sank, with her steady, melting eye, into the heart. Her joyous parts—in which her memory now chiefly lives—in her youth were outdone by her plaintive ones. There is no giving an account how she delivered the disguised story of her love for Orsino. It was no set speech, that she had foreseen, so as to weave it into an harmonious period, line necessarily following line, to make up the music—yet I have heard it so spoken, or rather *read*, not without its grace and beauty—but, when she had declared her sister's history to be a 'blank,' and that she 'never told her love,' there was a pause, as if the story had ended—and then the image of the 'worm in the bud,' came up as a new suggestion—and the heightened image of 'Patience' still followed after that, as by some growing (and not mechanical) process, thought springing up after thought, I would almost say, as they were watered by her tears. So in those fine lines—

> Write loyal cantons of contemned love—
> Hollow your name to the reverberate hills—

there was no preparation made in the foregoing image for that which was to follow. She used no rhetoric in her passion; or it was nature's own rhetoric, most legitimate then, when it seemed altogether without rule or law.

Mrs. Powel (now Mrs. Renard), then in the pride of her beauty, made an admirable Olivia. She was particularly excellent in her unbending scenes in conversation with the Clown. I have seen some Olivias—and those very sensible actresses too—who in these interlocutions have seemed to set their wits at the jester, and to vie conceits with him in downright emulation. But she used him for her sport, like what he was, to trifle a leisure sentence or two with, and then to be dismissed, and she to be the Great Lady still. She touched the imperious fantastic humour of the character with nicety. Her fine spacious person filled the scene.

The part of Malvolio has, in my judgment, been so often misunderstood, and the *general merits* of the actor, who then played it, so unduly appreciated, that I shall hope for pardon, if I am a little prolix upon these points.

Of all the actors who flourished in my time—a melancholy phrase if taken aright, reader—Bensley had most of the swell of soul, was greatest in the delivery of heroic conceptions, the emotions consequent upon the presentment of a great idea to the fancy. He had the true poetical enthusiasm—the rarest faculty among players. None that I remember possessed even a portion of that fine madness which he threw out in Hotspur's famous rant about glory, or the transports of the Venetian incendiary at the vision of the fired city. His voice had the dissonance, and at times the inspiriting effect, of the trumpet. His gait was uncouth and stiff, but no way embarrassed by affectation; and the thorough-bred gentleman was uppermost in every movement. He seized the moment of passion with greatest truth; like a faithful clock, never striking before the time; never anticipating or leading you to anticipate. He was totally destitute of trick and artifice. He seemed come upon the stage to do the poet's message simply, and he did it with as genuine fidelity as the nuncios in Homer deliver the errands of the gods. He let the passion or the sentiment do its own work without prop or bolstering. He would have scorned to mountebank it; and betrayed none of that *cleverness* which is the bane of serious acting. For this reason, his Iago was the only endurable one which I remember to have seen. No spectator, from his action, could divine more of his artifice than Othello was supposed to do. His confessions in soliloquy alone put you in possession of the mystery. There were no by-intimations to make the audience fancy their own discernment so much greater than that of the Moor—who commonly stands like a great helpless mark, set up for mine Ancient, and a quantity of barren spectators, to shoot their bolts at. The Iago of Bensley did not go to work so grossly. There was a triumphant tone about the character, natural to a general consciousness of power; but none of that petty vanity which chuckles and cannot contain itself upon any little successful stroke of its knavery —as is common with your small villains, and green probationers in mischief. It did not clap or crow before its time. It was not a man setting his wits at a child, and winking all the while at other children, who are mightily pleased at being let into the secret; but a consummate villain entrapping a noble nature into toils, against which no discernment was available, where the manner was as fathomless as the purpose seemed dark, and without motive. The part of Malvolio, in the Twelfth Night, was performed by Bensley, with a richness and a dignity, of which (to judge from some recent castings of that character) the very tradition must be worn out from the stage. No manager in those days would have dreamed of giving it to Mr. Baddeley, or Mr. Parsons; when Bensley was occasionally absent from the theatre, John Kemble thought it no derogation to succeed to the part. Malvolio is not essentially ludicrous. He becomes comic but by accident. He is cold, austere, repelling; but dignified, consistent, and, for what appears, rather of an over-stretched morality. Maria describes him as a sort of Puritan; and he might have worn his gold chain with honour in one of our old roundhead families, in the service of a Lambert, or a Lady Fairfax. But his morality and his manners are misplaced in Illyria. He is opposed to the proper *levities* of the piece, and falls in the unequal contest. Still his pride, or his gravity (call it which you will), is inherent, and native to the man, not mock or affected, which latter only are the fit objects to excite laughter. His quality is at the best unlovely, but neither buffoon nor contemptible. His bearing is lofty, a little above his station, but probably not much above his deserts. We see no reason why he should not have been brave, honourable, accomplished. His careless committal of the ring to the ground (which he was commissioned to restore to Cesario), bespeaks a generosity of birth and feeling. His dialect on all occasions is that of a gentleman, and a man of education. We must not confound him with the eternal old, low steward of comedy. He is master of the household to a great princess; a dignity probably conferred upon him for other respects than age or length of service. Olivia, at the first indication of his supposed madness, declares that she 'would not have him miscarry for half of her dowry.' Does this look as if the character was meant to appear little or insignificant? Once, indeed, she accuses him to his face—of what?—of being 'sick of self-love,'—but with a gentleness and considerateness, which could not have been, if she had not thought that this particular infirmity shaded some virtues. His rebuke to the knight, and his sottish revellers, is sensible and spirited; and when we take into consideration the unprotected condition of his mistress, and the strict regard with which her state of real or dissembled mourning would draw the eyes of the world upon her house-affairs, Malvolio might feel the honour of the family in some sort in his keeping; as it appears not that Olivia had any more brothers, or kinsmen, to look to it—for Sir Toby had dropped all such nice respects at the buttery-hatch. That Malvolio was meant to be represented as possessing estimable qualities, the expression of the Duke, in his anxiety to have him reconciled, almost infers: 'Pursue him, and entreat him to a peace.' Even in his abused state of chains and darkness, a sort of greatness seems never to desert him. He argues highly and well with the supposed Sir Topas, and philosophises gallantly upon his straw.* There must have been some shadow of worth about the man; he must have been something more than a mere vapour—a thing of straw, or Jack in office—before Fabian and Maria could have ventured sending him upon a courting-errand to Olivia. There was some consonancy (as he would say) in the undertaking, or the jest would have been too bold even for that house of misrule.

Bensley, accordingly, threw over the part an air of Spanish loftiness. He looked, spake, and moved like an old Castilian. He was starch, spruce, opinionated, but his superstructure of pride seemed bottomed upon a sense of worth. There was something in it beyond the coxcomb. It was big and swelling, but you could not be sure that it was hollow. You might wish to see it taken down, but you felt that it was upon an elevation. He was magnificent from the outset; but when the decent sobrieties of the character began to give way, and the poison of self-love, in his conceit of the Countess's affection, gradually to work, you would have thought that the hero of La Mancha in person stood before you. How he went smiling to himself! with what ineffable carelessness would he twirl his gold chain! what a dream it was! you were infected with the illusion, and did not wish that it should be removed! you had no room for laughter! if an unseasonable reflection of morality obtruded itself, it was a deep sense of the pitiable infirmity of man's nature, that can lay him open

---

* CLOWN. What is the opinion of Pythagoras concerning wild fowl?
MAL. That the soul of our grandam might haply inhabit a bird.
CLOWN. What thinkest thou of his opinion?
MAL. I think nobly of the soul, and no way approve of his opinion.

to such frenzies—but, in truth, you rather admired than pitied the lunacy while it lasted—you felt that an hour of such mistake was worth an age with the eyes open. Who would not wish to live but for a day in the conceit of such a lady's love as Olivia? Why, the Duke would have given his principality but for a quarter of a minute, sleeping or waking, to have been so deluded. The man seemed to tread upon air, to taste manna, to walk with his head in the clouds, to mate Hyperion. O! shake not the castles of his pride—endure yet for a season bright moments of confidence—'stand still, ye watches of the element,' that Malvolio may be still in fancy fair Olivia's lord!—but fate and retribution say no—I hear the mischievous titter of Maria—the witty taunts of Sir Toby—the still more insupportable triumph of the foolish knight—the counterfeit Sir Topas is unmasked—and 'thus the whirligig of time,' as the true clown hath it, 'brings in his revenges.' I confess that I never saw the catastrophe of this character, while Bensley played it, without a kind of tragic interest. There was good foolery too. Few now remember Dodd. What an Aguecheek the stage lost in him! Lovegrove, who came nearest to the old actors, revived the character some few seasons ago, and made it sufficiently grotesque; but Dodd was *it*, as it came out of nature's hands. It might be said to remain *in puris naturalibus*. In expressing slowness of apprehension, this actor surpassed all others. You could see the first dawn of an idea stealing over his countenance, climbing up by little and little, with a painful process, till it cleared up at last to the fulness of a twilight conception—its highest meridian. He seemed to keep back his intellect, as some have had the power to retard their pulsation. The balloon takes less time in filling than it took to cover the expansion of his broad moony face over all its quarters with expression. A glimmer of understanding would appear in a corner of his eye, and for lack of fuel go out again. A part of his forehead would catch a little intelligence, and be a long time in communicating it to the remainder.

I am ill at dates, but I think it is now better than five-and-twenty years ago, that walking in the gardens of Gray's Inn—they were then far finer than they are now—the accursed Verulam Buildings had not encroached upon all the east side of them, cutting out delicate green crankles, and shouldering away one of two of the stately alcoves of the terrace—the survivor stands gaping and relationless as if it remembered its brother—they are still the best gardens of any of the Inns of Court, my beloved Temple not forgotten —have the gravest character; their aspect being altogether reverend and law-breathing—Bacon has left the impress of his foot upon their gravel walks——taking my afternoon solace on a summer day upon the aforesaid terrace, a comely sad personage came towards me, whom, from his grave air and deportment, I judged to be one of the old Benchers of the Inn. He had a serious, thoughtful forehead, and seemed to be in meditations of mortality. As I have an instinctive awe of old Benchers. I was passing him with that sort of subindicative token of respect which one is apt to demonstrate towards a venerable stranger, and which rather denotes an inclination to greet him, than any positive motion of the body to that effect—a species of humility and will-worship which I observe, nine times out of ten, rather puzzles than pleases the person it is offered to—when the face turning full upon me, strangely identified itself with that of Dodd. Upon close inspection I was not mistaken. But could this sad thoughtful countenance be the same vacant face of folly which I had hailed so often under circumstances of gaiety; which I had never seen without a smile, or recognised but as the usher of mirth; that looked out so formally flat in Foppington, so frothily pert in Tattle, so impotently busy in Backbite; so blankly divested of all meaning, or resolutely expressive of none, in Acres, in Fribble, and a thousand agreeable impertinences? Was this the face—full of thought and carefulness—that had so often divested itself at will of every trace of either to give me diversion, to clear my cloudy face for two or three hours at least of its furrows? Was this the face—manly, sober, intelligent—which I had so often despised, made mocks at, made merry with? The re-membrance of the freedoms which I had taken with it came upon me with a reproach of insult. I could have asked it pardon. I thought it looked upon me with a sense of injury. There is something strange as well as sad in seeing actors— your pleasant fellows particularly—subjected to and suffering the common lot;—their fortunes, their casualties, their deaths, seem to belong to the scene, their actions to be amenable to poetic justice only. We can hardly connect them with more awful responsibilities. The death of this fine actor took place shortly after this meeting. He had quitted the stage some months; and, as I learned afterwards, had been in the habit of resorting daily to these gardens, almost to the day of his decease. In these serious walks, probably, he was divesting himself of many scenic and some real vanities—weaning himself from the frivolities of the lesser and the greater theatre—doing gentle penance for a life of no very reprehensible fooleries—taking off by degrees the buffoon mask, which he might feel he had worn too long—and rehearsing for a more solemn cast of part. Dying, he 'put on the weeds of Dominic.'*

If few can remember Dodd, many yet living will not easily forget the pleasant creature who in those days enacted the part of the Clown to Dodd's Sir Andrew.—Richard, or rather Dicky Suett—for so in his lifetime he delighted to be called, and time hath ratified the appellation—lieth buried on the north side of the cemetery of Holy Paul, to whose service his nonage and tender years were dedicated. There are who do yet remember him at that period—his pipe clear and harmonious. He would often speak of his chorister days, when he was 'cherub Dicky.'

What clipped his wings, or made it expedient that he should exchange the holy for the profane state; whether he had lost his good voice (his best recommendation to that office), like Sir John, 'with hallooing and singing of anthems'; or whether he was adjudged to lack something, even in those early years, of the gravity indispensable to an occupation which professeth to 'commerce with the skies,'—I could never rightly learn; but we find him, after the probation of a twelvemonth or so, reverting to a secular condition, and become one of us.

I think he was not altogether of that timber out of which cathedral seats and sounding-boards are hewed. But if a glad heart—kind, and therefore glad—be any part of sanctity, then might the robe of Motley, with which he invested

---

* Dodd was a man of reading, and left at his death a choice collection of old English literature. I should judge him to have been a man of wit. I know one instance of an impromptu which no length of study could have bettered. My merry friend, Jem White, had seen him one evening in Aguecheek, and recognising Dodd the next day in Fleet Street, was irresistibly impelled to take off his hat and salute him as the identical Knight of the preceding evening with a 'Save you, *Sir Andrew*.' Dodd, not at all disconcerted at this unusual address from a stranger, with a courteous half-rebuking wave of the hand, put him off with an 'Away, *Fool*.'

himself with so much humility after his deprivation, and which he wore so long with so much blameless satisfaction to himself and to the public, be accepted for a surplice—his white stole, and *albe*.

The first fruits of his secularisation was an engagement upon the boards of Old Drury, at which theatre he commenced, as I have been told, with adopting the manner of Parsons in old men's characters. At the period in which most of us knew him, he was no more an imitator than he was in any true sense himself imitable.

He was the Robin Goodfellow of the stage. He came in to trouble all things with a welcome perplexity, himself no whit troubled for the matter. He was known, like Puck, by his note—*Ha! Ha! Ha!* —sometimes deepening to *Ho! Ho! Ho!* with an irresistible accession, derived, perhaps, remotely from his ecclesiastical education, foreign to his prototype of—*O La!* Thousands of hearts yet respond to the chuckling *O La!* of Dicky Suett, brought back to their remembrance by the faithful transcript of his friend Matthews's mimicry. The 'force of nature could no further go.' He drolled upon the stock of these two syllables richer than the cuckoo.

Care, that troubles all the world, was forgotten in his composition. Had he had but two grains (nay, half a grain) of it, he could never have supported himself upon those two spider's strings, which served him (in the latter part of his unmixed existence) as legs. A doubt or a scruple must have made him totter, a sigh have puffed him down; the weight of a frown had staggered him, a wrinkle made him lose his balance. But on he went, scrambling upon those airy stilts of his, with Robin Goodfellow, 'thorough brake, thorough briar,' reckless of a scratched face or a torn doublet.

Shakspeare foresaw him, when he framed his fools and jesters. They have all the true Suett stamp, a loose and shambling gait, a slippery tongue, this last the ready midwife to a without-pain-delivered jest; in words, light as air, venting truths deep as the centre; with idlest rhymes tagging conceit when busiest, singing with Lear in the tempest, or Sir Toby at the buttery-hatch.

Jack Bannister and he had the fortune to be more of personal favourites with the town than any actors before or after. The difference, I take it, was this:—Jack was more *beloved* for his sweet, good-natured moral pretensions. Dicky was more *liked* for his sweet, good-natured, no pretensions at all. Your whole conscience stirred with Bannister's performance of Walter in the Children in the Wood—but Dicky seemed like a thing, as Shakspeare says of Love, too young to know what conscience is. He put us into Vesta's days. Evil fled before him—not as from Jack, as from an antagonist,—but because it could not touch him, any more than a cannon-ball a fly. He was delivered from the burthen of that death; and, when Death came himself, not in metaphor, to fetch Dicky, it is recorded of him by Robert Palmer, who kindly watched his exit, that he received the last stroke, neither varying his accustomed tranquillity, nor tune, with the simple exclamation, worthy to have been recorded in his epitaph—*O La! O La! Bobby!*

The elder Palmer (of stage-treading celebrity) commonly played Sir Toby in those days; but there is a solidity of wit in the jests of that half-Falstaff which he did not quite fill out. He was as much too showy as Moody (who sometimes took the part) was dry and sottish. In sock or buskin there was an air of swaggering gentility about Jack Palmer. He was a *gentleman* with a slight infusion of *the footman*. His brother Bob (of recenter memory), who was his shadow in everything while he lived, and dwindled into less than a shadow afterwards—was a *gentleman* with a little stronger infusion of the *latter ingredient;* that was all. It is amazing how a little of the more or less makes a difference in these things. When you saw Bobby in the Duke's Servant,* you said, 'What a pity such a pretty fellow was only a servant!' When you saw Jack figuring as Captain Absolute, you thought you could trace his promotion to some lady of quality who fancied the handsome fellow in his top-knot, and had bought him a commission. Therefore Jack in Dick Amlet was in-superable.

Jack had two voices, both plausible, hypocritical, and insinuating; but his secondary or supplemental voice still more decisively histrionic than his common one. It was reserved for the spectator; and the *dramatis personæ* were supposed to know nothing at all about it. The *lies* of Young Wilding, and the *sentiments* in Joseph Surface, were thus marked out in a sort of italics to the audience. This secret

* *High Life Below Stairs.*

correspondence with the company before the curtain (which is the bane and death of tragedy) has an extremely happy effect in some kinds of comedy, in the more highly artificial comedy of Congreve or of Sheridan especially, where the absolute sense of reality (so indispensable to scenes of interest) is not required, or would rather interfere to diminish your pleasure. The fact is, you do not believe in such characters as Surface—the villain of artificial comedy—even while you read or see them. If you did, they would shock and not divert you. When Ben, in Love for Love, returns from sea, the following exquisite dialogue occurs at his first meeting with his father:—

SIR SAMPSON. Thou hast been many a weary league, Ben, since I saw thee.

BEN. Ey, ey, been. Been far enough, an that be all.—Well, father how do all at home? how does brother Dick, and brother Val?

SIR SAMPSON. Dick! body o' me, Dick has been dead these two years. I writ you word when you were at Leghorn.

BEN. Mess, that's true; Marry, I had forgot. Dick's dead, as you say—well, and how?—I have a many questions to ask you——

Here is an instance of insensibility which in real life would be revolting, or rather in real life could not have co-existed with the warm-hearted temperament of the character. But when you read it in the spirit with which such playful selections and specious combinations rather than strict *metaphrases* of nature should be taken, or when you saw Bannister play it, it neither did, nor does, wound the moral sense at all. For what is Ben—the pleasant sailor which Bannister gives us—but a piece of satire—a creation of Congreve's fancy—a dreamy combination of all the accidents of a sailor's character—his contempt of money—his credulity to women —with that necessary estrangement from home which it is just within the verge of credibility to suppose *might* produce such an hallucination as is here described. We never think the worse of Ben for it, or feel it as a strain upon his character. But when an actor comes, and instead of the delightful phantom—the creature dear to half-belief—which Bannister exhibited—displays before our eyes a downright concretion of a Wapping sailor—a jolly warm-hearted Jack Tar—and nothing else—when instead of investing it with a delicious confusedness of the head, and a veering undirected goodness of purpose—he gives to it a downright daylight understanding, and a full consciousness of its actions; thrusting forward the sensibilities of the character with a pretence as if it stood upon nothing else, and was to be judged by them alone—we feel the discord of the thing; the scene is disturbed; a real man has got in among the *dramatis personæ*, and puts them out. We want the sailor turned out. We feel that his true place is not behind the curtain, but in the first or second gallery.

On the Artificial Comedy of the last Century

THE artificial Comedy, or Comedy of manners, is quite extinct on our stage. Congreve and Farquhar show their heads once in seven years only; to be exploded and put down instantly. The times cannot bear them. Is it for a few wild speeches, an occasional licence of dialogue? I think not altogether. The business of their dramatic characters will not stand the moral test. We screw everything up to that. Idle gallantry in a fiction, a dream, the passing pageant of an evening, startles us in the same way as the alarming indications of profligacy in a son or ward in real life should startle a parent or guardian. We have no such middle emotions as dramatic interests left. We see a stage libertine playing his loose pranks of two hours' duration, and of no after consequence, with the severe eyes which inspect real vices with their bearings upon two worlds. We are spectators to a plot or intrigue (not reducible in life to the point of strict morality), and take it all for truth. We substitute a real for a dramatic person, and judge him accordingly. We try him in our courts, from which there is no appeal to the *dramatis personæ*, his peers. We have been spoiled with—not sentimental comedy—but a tyrant far more pernicious to our pleasures which has succeeded to it, the exclusive and all-devouring drama of common life; where the moral point is everything; where, instead of the fictitious half-believed personages of the stage (the phantoms of old comedy), we recognize ourselves, our brothers, aunts, kinsfolk, allies, patrons, enemies,—the same as in life,—with an interest in what is going on so hearty and substantial, that we cannot afford our moral judgment, in its deepest and most vital results, to compromise or slumber for a moment. What is *there* transacting, by no modification is made to affect us in any other manner than the same events or characters would do in our relationships of life. We carry our fire-side concerns to the theatre with us. We do not go thither, like our ancestors, to escape from the pressure of reality, so much as to confirm our experience of it; to make assurance double, and take a bond of fate. We must live our toilsome lives twice over, as it was the mournful privilege of Ulysses to descend twice to the shades. All that neutral ground of character, which stood between vice and virtue; or which in fact was indifferent to neither, where neither properly was called in question; that happy breathing-place from the burthen of a perpetual moral questioning—the sanctuary and quiet Alsatia of hunted casuistry—is broken up and disfranchised, as injurious to the interests of society. The privileges of the place are taken away by law. We dare not dally with images, or names, of wrong. We bark like foolish dogs at shadows. We dread infection from the scenic representation of disorder, and fear a painted pustule. In our anxiety that our morality should not take cold, we wrap it up in a great blanket surtout of precaution against the breeze and sunshine.

I confess for myself that (with no great delinquencies to answer for) I am glad for a season to take an airing beyond the diocese of the strict conscience,—not to live always in the precincts of the law-courts,—but now and then, for a dream-while or so, to imagine a world with no meddling restrictions—to get into recesses, whither the hunter cannot follow me—

> ————Secret shades
> Of woody Ida's inmost grove,
> While yet there was no fear of Jove.

I come back to my cage and my restraint the fresher and more healthy for it. I wear my shackles more contentedly for having respired the breath of an imaginary freedom. I do not know how it is with others, but I feel the better always for the perusal of one of Congreve's—nay, why should I not add even of Wycherley's—comedies. I am the gayer at least for it; and I could never connect those sports of a witty fancy in any shape with any result to be drawn from them to imitation in real life. They are a world of themselves almost as much as fairyland. Take one of their characters, male or female (with few exceptions they are alike), and place it in a modern play, and my virtuous indignation shall rise against the profligate wretch as warmly as the Catos of the pit could desire; because in a modern play I am to judge of the right and the wrong. The standard of *police* is the measure of *political justice*. The atmosphere will blight it; it cannot live here. It has got into a moral world, where it has no business, from which it must needs fall headlong; as dizzy, and incapable of making a stand, as a Swedenborgian bad spirit that has wandered unawares into the sphere of one of his Good Men, or Angels. But in its own world do we feel the creature is so very bad?—The Fainalls and the Mirabels, the Dorimants and the Lady Touchwoods, in their own sphere, do not offend my moral sense; in fact they do not appeal to it at all. They seem engaged in their proper element. They break through no laws, or conscientious restraints. They know of none. They have got out of Christendom into the land—what shall I call it?—of cuckoldry—the Utopia of gallantry, where pleasure is duty, and the manners perfect freedom. It is altogether a speculative scene of things, which has no reference whatever to the world that is. No good person can be justly offended as a spectator, because no good person suffers on the stage. Judged morally, every character in these plays—the few exceptions only are *mistakes* —is alike essentially vain and worthless. The great art of Congreve is especially shown in this, that he has entirely excluded from his scenes—some little generosities in the part of Angelica perhaps excepted—not only anything like a faultless character, but any pretensions to goodness or good feelings whatsoever. Whether he did this designedly, or instinctively, the effect is as happy, as the design (if design) was bold. I used to wonder at the strange power which his Way of the World in particular possesses of interesting you all along in the pursuits of characters, for whom you absolutely care nothing—for you neither hate nor love his personages—and I think it is owing to this very indifference for any, that you endure the whole. He has spread a privation of moral light, I will call it, rather than by the ugly name of palpable darkness, over his creations; and his shadows flit before you without distinction or preference. Had he introduced a good character, a single gush of moral feeling, a revulsion of the judgment to actual life and actual duties, the impertinent Goshen would have only lighted to the discovery of deformities, which now are none, because we think them none.

Translated into real life, the characters of his, and his friend Wycherley's dramas, are profligates and strumpets,—the business of their brief existence, the undivided pursuit of lawless gallantry. No other spring of action, or possible motive of conduct, is recognised; principles which, universally acted upon, must reduce this frame of things to a chaos. But we do them wrong in so translating them. No such effects are produced, in *their* world. When we are among them, we are amongst a chaotic people. We are not to judge them by our usages. No reverend institutions are insulted by their proceedings—for they have none among them. No peace of families is violated—for no family ties exist among them. No purity of the marriage bed is stained—for none is supposed to have a being. No deep affections are disquieted, no holy wedlock bands are snapped asunder—for affection's depth and wedded faith are not of the growth of that soil. There is neither right nor wrong,—gratitude or its opposite,—claim or duty,—paternity or sonship. Of what consequence is it to Virtue, or how is she at all concerned about it, whether Sir Simon, or Dapperwit steal away Miss Martha; or who is the father of Lord Froth's or Sir Pliant's children?

The whole is a passing pageant, where we should sit as unconcerned at the issues, for life or death, as at a battle of the frogs and mice. But, like Don Quixote, we take part against the puppets, and quite as impertinently. We dare not contemplate an Atlantis, a scheme, out of which our coxcombical moral sense is for a little transitory ease excluded. We have not the courage to imagine a state of things for which there is neither reward nor punishment. We cling to the painful necessities of shame and blame. We would indict our very dreams.

Amidst the mortifying circumstances attendant upon growing old, it is something to have seen the School for Scandal in its glory. This comedy grew out of Congreve and Wycherley, but gathered some alloys of the sentimental comedy which followed theirs. It is impossible that it should be now *acted*, though it continues, at long intervals, to be announced in the bills. Its hero, when Palmer played it at least, was Joseph Surface. When I remember the gay boldness, the graceful solemn plausibility, the measured step, the insinuating voice—to express it in a word—the downright *acted* villainy of the part, so different from the pressure of conscious actual wickedness,—the hypocritical assumption of hypocrisy,—which made Jack so deservedly a favourite in that character, I must needs conclude the present generation of playgoers more virtuous than myself, or more dense. I freely confess that he divided the palm with me with his better brother; that, in fact, I liked him quite as well. Not but there are passages,—like that, for instance, where Joseph is made to refuse a pittance to a poor relation,—incongruities which Sheridan was forced upon by the attempt to join the artificial with the sentimental comedy, either of which must destroy the other—but over these obstructions Jack's manner floated him so lightly, that a refusal from him no more shocked you, than the easy compliance of Charles gave you in reality any pleasure; you got over the paltry question as quickly as you could, to get back into the regions of pure comedy, where no cold moral reigns. The highly artificial manner of Palmer in this character counteracted every disagreeable impression which you might have received from the contrast, supposing them real, between the two brothers. You did not believe in Joseph with the same faith with which you believed in Charles. The latter was a pleasant reality, the former a no less pleasant poetical foil to it. The comedy, I have said, is incongruous; a mixture of Congreve with sentimental incompatibilities; the gaiety upon the whole is buoyant; but it required the consummate art of Palmer to reconcile the discordant elements.

A player with Jack's talents, if we had one now, would not dare to do the part in the same manner. He would instinctively avoid every turn which might tend to unrealise, and so to make the character fascinating. He must take his cue from his spectators, who would expect a bad man and a good man as rigidly opposed to each other as the deathbeds of those geniuses are contrasted in the prints, which I am sorry to say have disappeared from the windows of my old friend Carrington Bowles, of St. Paul's Churchyard memory—(an exhibition as venerable as the adjacent cathedral, and almost coeval) of the bad and good man at the hour of death; where the ghastly apprehensions of the former, —and truly the grim phantom with his reality of a toasting-fork is not to be despised,—so finely contrast with the meek complacent kissing of the rod,—taking it in like honey and butter,—with which the latter submits to the scythe of the gentle bleeder, Time, who wields his lancet with the apprehensive finger of a popular young ladies' surgeon. What flesh, like loving grass, would not covet to meet half-way the stroke of such a delicate mower?—John Palmer was twice an actor in this exquisite part. He was playing to you all the while that he was playing upon Sir Peter and his lady. You had the first intimation of a sentiment before it was on his lips. His altered voice was meant to you, and you were to suppose that his fictitious co-flutterers on the stage perceived nothing at all of it. What was it to you if that half reality, the husband, was over-reached by the puppetry—or the thin thing (Lady Teazle's reputation) was persuaded it was dying of a plethory? The fortunes of Othello and Desdemona were not concerned in it. Poor Jack has passed from the stage in good time, that he did not live to this our age of seriousness. The pleasant old Teazle *King*, too, is gone in good time. His manner would scarce have passed current in our day. We must love or hate—acquit or condemn—censure or pity— exert our detestable coxcombry of moral judgment upon everything. Joseph Surface, to go down now must be a downright revolting villain—no compromise—his first appearance must shock and give horror—his specious plausibilities, which the pleasurable faculties of our fathers welcomed with such hearty greetings, knowing that no harm (dramatic harm even) could come, or was meant to come, of them, must inspire a cold and killing aversion. Charles (the real canting person of the scene—for the hypocrisy of Joseph has its ulterior legitimate ends, but his brother's professions of a good heart centre in downright self-satisfaction) must be *loved*, and Joseph *hated*. To balance one disagreeable reality with another, Sir Peter Teazle must be no longer the comic idea of a fretful old bachelor bridegroom, whose teasings (while King acted it) were evidently as much played off at you, as they were meant to concern anybody on the stage, —he must be a real person, capable in law of sustaining an

injury—a person towards whom duties are to be acknowledged—the genuine crim. con. antagonist of the
villainous seducer Joseph. To realise him more, his sufferings
under his unfortunate match must have the downright
pungency of life—must (or should) make you not mirthful
but uncomfortable, just as the same predicament would move
you in a neighbour or old friend. The delicious scenes which
give the play its name and zest, must affect you in the same
serious manner as if you heard the reputation of a dear
female friend attacked in your real presence. Crabtree and
Sir Benjamin—those poor snakes that live but in the sunshine
of your mirth—must be ripened by this hot-bed process of
realisation into asps or amphisbænas; and Mrs. Candour—O!
frightful!—become a hooded serpent. O! who that remembers
Parsons and Dodd—the wasp and butterfly of the School
for Scandal—in those two characters; and charming natural
Miss Pope, the perfect gentlewoman as distinguished from
the fine lady of comedy, in this latter part—would forego
the true scenic delight—the escape from life—the oblivion
of consequences—the holiday barring out of the pedant
Reflection—those Saturnalia of two or three brief hours,
well won from the world—to sit instead at one of our modern
plays—to have his coward conscience (that forsooth must
not be left for a moment) stimulated with perpetual appeals
—dulled rather, and blunted, as a faculty without repose
must be—and his moral vanity pampered with images of
notional justice, notional beneficence, lives saved without
the spectator's risk, and fortunes given away that cost the
author nothing?

No piece was, perhaps, ever so completely cast in all its
parts as this *manager's comedy*. Miss Farren had succeeded to
Mrs. Abington in Lady Teazle; and Smith, the original
Charles, had retired when I first saw it. The rest of the
characters, with very slight exceptions, remained. I remember it was then the fashion to cry down John Kemble,
who took the part of Charles after Smith; but, I thought,
very unjustly. Smith, I fancy was more airy, and took the
eye with a certain gaiety of person. He brought with him no
sombre recollections of tragedy. He had not to expiate the
fault of having pleased beforehand in lofty declamation. He
had no sins of Hamlet or of Richard to atone for. His failure
in these parts was a passport to success in one of so opposite

a tendency. But, as far as I could judge, the weighty sense of Kemble made up for more personal incapacity than he had to answer for. His harshest tones in this part came steeped and dulcified in good-humour. He made his defects a grace. His exact declamatory manner, as he managed it, only served to convey the points of his dialogue with more precision. It seemed to head the shafts to carry them deeper. Not one of his sparkling sentences was lost. I remember minutely how he delivered each in succession, and cannot by any effort imagine how any of them could be altered for the better. No man could deliver brilliant dialogue—the dialogue of Congreve or Wycherley—because none understood it—half so well as John Kemble. His Valentine, in Love for Love, was, to my recollection, faultless. He flagged sometimes in the intervals of tragic passion. He would slumber over the level parts of an heroic character. His Macbeth has been known to nod. But he always seemed to me to be particularly alive to pointed and witty dialogue. The relaxing levities of tragedy have not been touched by any since him—the playful court-bred spirit in which he condescended to the players in Hamlet—the sportive relief which he threw into the darker shades of Richard—disappeared with him. He had his sluggish moods, his torpors—but they were the halting-stones and resting-place of his tragedy—politic savings, and fetches of the breath—husbandry of the lungs, where nature pointed him to be an economist—rather, I think, than errors of the judgment. They were, at worst, less painful than the eternal tormenting unappeasable vigilance,—the 'lidless dragon eyes,' of present fashionable tragedy.

On the Acting of Munden

NOT many nights ago I had come home from seeing this extraordinary performer in Cockletop; and when I retired to my pillow, his whimsical image still stuck by me, in a manner as to threaten sleep. In vain I tried to divest myself of it, by conjuring up the most opposite associations. I resolved to be serious. I raised up the gravest topics of life; private misery, public calamity. All would not do:

——There the antic sate
Mocking our state——

his queer visnomy—his bewildering costume—all the strange
things which he had raked together—his serpentine rod,
swagging about in his pocket—Cleopatra's tear, and the rest
of his relics—O'Keefe's wild farce, and *his* wilder commentary
—till the passion of laughter, like grief in excess, relieved
itself by its own weight, inviting the sleep which in the first
instance it had driven away.

But I was not to escape so easily. No sooner did I fall into
slumbers, than the same image, only more perplexing, assailed
me in the shape of dreams. Not one Munden, but five
hundred, were dancing before me, like the faces which,
whether you will or no, come when you have been taking
opium—all the strange combinations, which this strangest
of all strange mortals ever shot his proper countenance into,
from the day he came commissioned to dry up the tears of
the town for the loss of the now almost forgotten Edwin. O
for the power of the pencil to have fixed them when I awoke!
A season or two since, there was exhibited a Hogarth gallery.
I do not see why there should not be a Munden gallery. In
richness and variety, the latter would not fall far short of
the former.

There is one face of Farley, one face of Knight, one (but
what a one it is!) of Liston; but Munden has none that you
can properly pin down, and call *his*. When you think he has
exhausted his battery of looks, in unaccountable warfare
with your gravity, suddenly he sprouts out an entirely new
set of features, like Hydra. He is not one, but legion; not
so much a comedian, as a company. If his name could be
multiplied like his countenance, it might fill a play-bill. He,
and he alone, literally *makes faces:* applied to any other
person, the phrase is a mere figure, denoting certain modi-
fications of the human countenance. Out of some invisible
wardrobe he dips for faces, as his friend Suett used for wigs,
and fetches them out as easily. I should not be surprised to
see him some day put out the head of a river-horse; or come
forth a pewitt, or lapwing, some feathered metamorphosis.

I have seen this gifted actor in Sir Christopher Curry—in
old Dornton—diffuse a glow of sentiment which has made
the pulse of a crowded theatre beat like that of one man;

when he has come in aid of the pulpit, doing good to the moral heart of a people. I have seen some faint approaches to this sort of excellence in other players. But in the grand grotesque of farce, Munden stands out as single and unaccompanied as Hogarth. Hogarth, strange to tell, had no followers. The school of Munden began, and must end, with himself.

Can any man *wonder*, like him? can any man *see ghosts*, like him? or *fight with his own shadow*—'SESSA'—as he does in that strangely-neglected thing, the Cobbler of Preston—where his alternations from the Cobbler to the Magnifico, and from the Magnifico to the Cobbler, keep the brain of the spectator in as wild a ferment, as if some Arabian Night were being acted before him. Who like him can throw, or ever attempted to throw, a preternatural interest over the commonest daily-life objects? A table or a joint-stool, in his conception, rises into a dignity equivalent to Cassiopeia's chair. It is invested with constellatory importance. You could not speak of it with more deference, if it were mounted into the firmament. A beggar in the hands of Michael Angelo, says Fuseli, rose the Patriarch of Poverty. So the gusto of Munden antiquates and ennobles what it touches. His pots and his ladles are as grand and primal as the seething-pots and hooks seen in old prophetic vision. A tub of butter, contemplated by him, amounts to a Platonic idea. He understands a leg of mutton in its quiddity. He stands wondering, amid the common-place materials of life, like primæval man with the sun and stars about him.

THE LAST ESSAYS OF ELIA

Preface

BY A FRIEND OF THE LATE ELIA

THIS poor gentleman, who for some months past had been in a declining way, hath at length paid his final tribute to nature.

To say truth, it is time he were gone. The humour of the thing, if ever there was much in it, was pretty well exhausted; and a two years' and a half existence has been a tolerable duration for a phantom.

I am now at liberty to confess, that much which I have heard objected to my late friend's writings was well-founded. Crude they are, I grant you—a sort of unlicked, incondite things—villainously pranked in an affected array of antique modes and phrases. They had not been *his*, if they had been other than such; and better it is, that a writer should be natural in a self-pleasing quaintness, than to affect a naturalness (so called) that should be strange to him. Egotistical they have been pronounced by some who did not know, that what he tells us, as of himself, was often true only (historically) of another; as in a former Essay (to save many instances)—where under the *first person* (his favourite figure) he shadows forth the forlorn estate of a country-boy placed at a London school, far from his friends and connections—in direct opposition to his own early history. If it be egotism to imply and twine with his own identity the griefs and affections of another—making himself many, or reducing many unto himself—then is the skilful novelist, who all along brings in his hero or heroine, speaking of themselves, the greatest egoist of all; who yet has never, therefore, been accused of that narrowness. And how shall the intenser dramatist escape being faulty, who, doubtless, under cover of passion uttered by another, oftentimes gives blameless vent to his most inward feelings, and expresses his own story modestly?

My late friend was in many respects a singular character. Those who did not like him, hated him; and some, who once liked him, afterwards became his bitterest haters. The truth is, he gave himself too little concern what he uttered, and in whose presence. He observed neither time nor place, and would e'en out with what came uppermost. With the severe religionist he would pass for a free-thinker; while the other faction set him down for a bigot, or persuaded themselves that he belied his sentiments. Few understood him; and I am not certain that at all times he quite understood himself. He too much affected that dangerous figure—irony. He sowed doubtful speeches, and reaped plain, unequivocal hatred. —He would interrupt the gravest discussion with some light jest; and yet, perhaps, not quite irrelevant in ears that could understand it. Your long and much talkers hated him. The informal habit of his mind, joined to an inveterate impediment of speech, forbade him to be an orator; and he seemed determined that no one else should play that part when he was present. He was *petit* and ordinary in his person and appearance. I have seen him sometimes in what is called good company, but where he has been a stranger, sit silent, and be suspected for an odd fellow; till some unlucky occasion provoking it, he would stutter out some senseless pun (not altogether senseless perhaps, if rightly taken), which has stamped his character for the evening. It was hit or miss with him; but nine times out of ten, he contrived by this device to send away a whole company his enemies. His conceptions rose kindlier than his utterance, and his happiest *impromptus* had the appearance of effort. He has been accused of trying to be witty, when in truth he was but struggling to give his poor thoughts articulation. He chose his companions for some individuality of character which they manifested.— Hence, not many persons of science, and few professed *literati*, were of his councils. They were, for the most part, persons of an uncertain fortune; and, as to such people commonly nothing is more obnoxious than a gentleman of settled (though moderate) income, he passed with most of them for a great miser. To my knowledge this was a mistake. His *intimados*, to confess a truth, were in the world's eye a ragged regiment. He found them floating on the surface of society; and the colour, or something else, in the weed pleased him. The burrs stuck to him—but they were good and loving burrs for all that. He never greatly cared for the society of what are called good people. If any of these were scandalised (and offences were sure to arise) he could not help it. When he has been remonstrated with for not making more concession to the feelings of good people, he would retort by asking, what one point did these good people ever concede to him? He was temperate in his meals and diversions, but always kept a little on this side of abstemiousness. Only in the use of the Indian weed he might be thought a little excessive. He took it, he would say, as a solvent of speech. Marry—as the friendly vapour ascended, how his prattle would curl up sometimes with it! the ligaments which tongue-tied him, were loosened, and the stammerer proceeded a statist!

I do not know whether I ought to bemoan or rejoice that my old friend is departed. His jests were beginning to grow obsolete, and his stories to be found out. He felt the approaches of age; and while he pretended to cling to life, you saw how slender were the ties left to bind him. Discoursing with him latterly on this subject, he expressed himself with a pettishness, which I thought unworthy of him. In our walks about his suburban retreat (as he called it) at Shacklewell, some children belonging to a school of industry had met us, and bowed and curtseyed, as he thought, in an especial manner to *him*. 'They take me for a visiting governor,' he muttered earnestly. He had a horror, which he carried to a foible, of looking like anything important and parochial. He thought that he approached nearer to that stamp daily. He had a general aversion from being treated like a grave or respectable character, and kept a wary eye upon the advances of age that should so entitle him. He herded always, while it was possible, with people younger than himself. He did not conform to the march of time, but was dragged along in the procession. His manners lagged behind his years. He was too much of the boy-man. The *toga virilis* never sate gracefully on his shoulders. The impressions of infancy had burnt into him, and he resented the impertinence of manhood. These were weaknesses; but such as they were, they are a key to explicate some of his writings.

I DO not know a pleasure more affecting than to range at will over the deserted apartments of some fine old family mansion. The traces of extinct grandeur admit of a better passion than envy: and contemplations on the great and good, whom we fancy in succession to have been its inhabitants, weave for us illusions, incompatible with the bustle of modern occupancy, and vanities of foolish present aristocracy. The same difference of feeling, I think, attends us between entering an empty and a crowded church. In the latter it is chance but some present human frailty—an act of inattention on the part of some of the auditory—or a trait of affectation, or worse, vainglory on that of the preacher—puts us by our best thoughts, disharmonising the place and the occasion. But wouldst thou know the beauty of holiness?—go alone on some week-day, borrowing the keys of good Master Sexton, traverse the cool aisles of some country church: think of the piety that has kneeled there—the congregations, old and young, that have found consolation there—the meek pastor— the docile parishioner. With no disturbing emotions, no cross conflicting comparisons, drink in the tranquillity of the place, till thou thyself become as fixed and motionless as the marble effigies that kneel and weep around thee.

Journeying northward lately, I could not resist going some few miles out of my road to look upon the remains of an old great house with which I had been impressed in this way in infancy. I was apprised that the owner of it had lately pulled it down; still I had a vague notion that it could not all have perished, that so much solidity with magnificence could not have been crushed all at once into the mere dust and rubbish which I found it.

The work of ruin had proceeded with a swift hand indeed, and the demolition of a few weeks had reduced it to—an antiquity.

I was astonished at the indistinction of everything. Where had stood the great gates? What bounded the court-yard? Whereabout did the out-houses commence? A few bricks only lay as representatives of that which was so stately and so spacious.

Death does not shrink up his human victim at this rate. The burnt ashes of a man weigh more in their proportion.

Had I seen these brick-and-mortar knaves at their process of destruction, at the plucking of every panel I should have felt the varlets at my heart. I should have cried out to them to spare a plank at least out of the cheerful store-room, in whose hot window-seat I used to sit and read Cowley, with the grass-plot before, and the hum and flappings of that one solitary wasp that ever haunted it about me—it is in mine ears now, as oft as summer returns; or a panel of the yellow-room.

Why, every plank and panel of that house for me had magic in it. The tapestried bedrooms—tapestry so much better than painting—not adorning merely, but peopling the wainscots—at which childhood ever and anon would steal a look, shifting its coverlid (replaced as quickly) to exercise its tender courage in a momentary eye-encounter with those stern bright visages, staring reciprocally—all Ovid on the walls, in colours vivider than his descriptions. Actæon in mid sprout, with the unappeasable prudery of Diana; and the still more provoking, and almost culinary coolness of Dan Phœbus, eel-fashion, deliberately divesting of Marsyas.

Then, that haunted room—in which old Mrs. Battle died —whereinto I have crept, but always in the day-time, with a passion of fear; and a sneaking curiosity, terror-tainted, to hold communication with the past.—*How shall they build it up again?*

It was an old deserted place, yet not so long deserted but that traces of the splendour of past inmates were everywhere apparent. Its furniture was still standing—even to the tarnished gilt leather battledores, and crumbling feathers of shuttlecocks in the nursery, which told that children had once played there. But I was a lonely child, and had the range at will of every apartment, knew every nook and corner, wondered and worshipped everywhere.

The solitude of childhood is not so much the mother of thought, as it is the feeder of love, and silence, and admiration. So strange a passion for the place possessed me in those years, that, though there lay—I shame to say how few roods distant from the mansion—half hid by trees what I judged some romantic lake, such was the spell which bound me to the house, and such my carefulness not to pass its strict and proper precincts, that the idle waters lay unexplored for me; and not till late in life, curiosity prevailing over elder devotion, I found, to my astonishment, a pretty brawling brook had been the Lacus Incognitus of my infancy. Variegated views, extensive prospects—and those at no great distance from the house—I was told of such—what were they to me, being out of the boundaries of my Eden?—So far from a wish to roam, I would have drawn, methought, still closer the fences of my chosen prison; and have been hemmed in by a yet securer cincture of those excluding garden walls. I could have exclaimed with that garden-loving poet—

> Bind me, ye woodbines, in your twines;
> Curl me about, ye gadding vines;
> And oh, so close your circles lace,
> That I may never leave this place;
> But, lest your fetters prove too weak,
> Ere I your silken bondage break,
> Do you, O brambles, chain me too,
> And, courteous briars, nail me through.

I was here as in a lonely temple. Snug fire-sides—the low-built roof—parlours ten feet by ten—frugal boards, and all the homeliness of home—these were the condition of my birth—the wholesome soil which I was planted in. Yet, without impeachment to their tenderest lessons, I am not sorry to have had glances at something beyond; and to have taken, if but a peep, in childhood, at the contrasting accidents of a great fortune.

To have the feeling of gentility, it is not necessary to have been born gentle. The pride of ancestry may be had on cheaper terms than to be obliged to an importunate race of ancestors; and the coatless antiquary in his unemblazoned cell, revolving the long line of a Mowbray's or De Clifford's pedigree, at those sounding names may warm himself into as gay a vanity as these who do inherit them. The claims of birth are ideal merely, and what herald shall go about to strip me of an idea? Is it trenchant to their swords? can it be hacked off as a spur can? or torn away like a tarnished garter? What else were the families of the great to us? what pleasure should we take in their tedious genealogies, or their capitulatory brass monuments? What to us the uninterrupted current of their bloods, if our own did not answer within us to a cognate and correspondent elevation.

Or wherefore else, O tattered and diminished 'Scutcheon that hung upon the time-worn walls of thy princely stairs, BLAKESMOOR! have I in childhood so oft stood poring upon the mystic characters—thy emblematic supporters, with their prophetic 'Resurgam'—till, every dreg of peasantry purging off, I received into myself Very Gentility? Thou wert first in my morning eyes; and of nights hast detained my steps from bedward, till it was but a step from gazing at thee to dreaming on thee.

This is the only true gentry by adoption; the veritable change of blood, and not, as empirics have fabled, by transfusion.

Who it was by dying that had earned the splendid trophy, I know not, I inquired not; but its fading rags, and colours cobweb-stained, told that its subject was of two centuries back.

And what if my ancestor at that date was some Damœtas —feeding flocks—not his own, upon the hills of Lincoln—did I in less earnest vindicate to myself the family trappings of this once proud Ægon? repaying by a backward triumph the insults he might possibly have heaped in his life-time upon my poor pastoral progenitor.

If it were presumption so to speculate, the present owners of the mansion had least reason to complain. They had long forsaken the old house of their fathers for a newer trifle; and I was left to appropriate to myself what images I could pick up, to raise my fancy, or to soothe my vanity.

I was the true descendant of those old W——s; and not the present family of that name, who had fled the old waste places.

Mine was that gallery of good old family portraits, which as I have gone over, giving them in fancy my own family name, one—and then another—would seem to smile, reaching forward from the canvas, to recognise the new relationship; while the rest looked grave, as it seemed, at the vacancy in their dwelling, and thoughts of fled posterity.

The Beauty with the cool blue pastoral drapery, and a lamb—that hung next the great bay window—with the bright yellow H——shire hair, and eye of watchet hue—so like my Alice!—I am persuaded she was a true Elia—Mildred Elia, I take it.

Mine, too, BLAKESMOOR, was thy noble Marble Hall, with its mosaic pavements, and its Twelve Cæsars—stately busts in marble—ranged round; of whose countenances, young reader of faces as I was, the frowning beauty of Nero, I remember, had most of my wonder: but the mild Galba had my love. There they stood in the coldness of death, yet freshness of immortality.

Mine, too, thy lofty Justice Hall, with its one chair of authority, high-backed and wickered, once the terror of luckless poacher, or self-forgetful maiden—so common since, that bats have roosted in it.

Mine, too,—whose else?—thy costly fruit-garden, with its sun-baked southern wall; the ampler pleasure-garden, rising backwards from the house in triple terraces, with flower-pots now of palest lead, save that a speck here and there, saved from the elements, bespake their pristine state to have been gilt and glittering; the verdant quarters backwarder still; and, stretching still beyond, in old formality, thy firry wilderness, the haunt of the squirrel, and the day-long murmuring wood-pigeon, with that antique image in the centre, God or Goddess I wist not; but child of Athens or old Rome paid never a sincerer worship to Pan or to Sylvanus in their native groves, than I to that fragmental mystery.

Was it for this, that I kissed my childish hands too fervently in your idol-worship, walks and windings of BLAKESMOOR! for this, or what sin of mine, has the plough passed over your pleasant places? I sometimes think that as men, when they die, do not die all, so of their extinguished habitations there may be a hope—a germ to be revivified.

Poor Relations

A POOR RELATION—is the most irrelevant thing in nature,—a piece of impertinent correspondency,—an odious approximation,—a haunting conscience,—a preposterous shadow, lengthening in the noon-tide of our prosperity,—an unwelcome remembrancer,—a perpetually recurring mortification, —a drain on your purse, a more intolerable dun upon your

pride,—a drawback upon success,—a rebuke to your rising,
—a stain in your blood,—a blot on your 'scutcheon,—a rent
in your garment,—a death's-head at your banquet,—
Agathocles' pot,—a Mordecai in your gate, a Lazarus at
your door,—a lion in your path,—a frog in your chamber,—a
fly in your ointment,—a mote in your eye,—a triumph to
your enemy, an apology to your friends,—the one thing not
needful,—the hail in harvest,—the ounce of sour in a pound
of sweet.

He is known by his knock. Your heart telleth you 'That
is Mr.——.' A rap, between familiarity and respect; that
demands, and at the same time seems to despair of, entertainment. He entereth smiling and—embarrassed. He holdeth
out his hand to you to shake, and—draweth it back again.
He casually looketh in about dinner-time—when the table
is full. He offereth to go away, seeing you have company—
but is induced to stay. He filleth a chair, and your visitor's
two children are accommodated at a side-table. He never
cometh upon open days, when your wife says, with some
complacency, 'My dear, perhaps Mr.——will drop in to-day.'
He remembereth birth-days—and professeth he is fortunate
to have stumbled upon one. He declareth against fish, the
turbot being small—yet suffereth himself to be importuned
into a slice, against his first resolution. He sticketh by the
port—yet will be prevailed upon to empty the remainder
glass of claret, if a stranger press it upon him. He is a puzzle
to the servants, who are fearful of being too obsequious, or
not civil enough, to him. The guests think 'they have seen
him before.' Every one speculateth upon his condition; and
the most part take him to be—a tide-waiter. He calleth you
by your Christian name, to imply that his other is the same
with your own. He is too familiar by half, yet you wish he
had less diffidence. With half the familiarity, he might pass
for a casual dependant; with more boldness, he would be in
no danger of being taken for what he is. He is too humble
for a friend; yet taketh on him more state than befits a client.
He is a worse guest than a country tenant, inasmuch as he
bringeth up no rent—yet 'tis odds, from his garb and demeanour, that your guests take him for one. He is asked to
make one at the whist table; refuseth on the score of poverty,
and—resents being left out. When the company break up,
he profereth to go for a coach—and lets the servant go. He

recollects your grandfather; and will thrust in some mean and quite unimportant anecdote of the family. He knew it when it was not quite so flourishing as 'he is blest in seeing it now.' He reviveth past situations, to institute what he calleth—favourable comparisons. With a reflecting sort of congratulation, he will inquire the price of your furniture; and insults you with a special commendation of your window-curtains. He is of opinion that the urn is the more elegant shape, but, after all, there was something more comfortable about the old tea-kettle—which you must remember. He dare say you must find a great convenience in having a carriage of your own, and appealeth to your lady if it is not so. Inquireth if you have had your arms done on vellum yet; and did not know, till lately, that such-and-such had been the crest of the family. His memory is unseasonable; his compliments perverse; his talk a trouble; his stay pertinacious; and when he goeth away, you dismiss his chair into a corner, as precipitately as possible, and feel fairly rid of two nuisances.

There is a worse evil under the sun, and that is—a female Poor Relation. You may do something with the other; you may pass him off tolerably well; but your indigent she-relative is hopeless. 'He is an old humorist,' you may say, 'and affects to go threadbare. His circumstances are better than folks would take them to be. You are fond of having a Character at your table, and truly he is one.' But in the indications of female poverty there can be no disguise. No woman dresses below herself from caprice. The truth must out without shuffling. 'She is plainly related to the L——s; or what does she at their house?' She is, in all probability, your wife's cousin. Nine times out of ten, at least, this is the case.—Her garb is something between a gentlewoman and a beggar, yet the former evidently predominates. She is most provokingly humble, and ostentatiously sensible to her inferiority. He may require to be repressed sometimes—*aliquando sufflaminandus erat*—but there is no raising her. You send her soup at dinner, and she begs to be helped—after the gentlemen. Mr.——request the honour of taking wine with her; she hesitates between Port and Madeira, and chooses the former—because he does. She calls the servant *Sir;* and insists on not troubling him to hold her plate. The housekeeper patronises her. The children's governess takes upon her to correct her, when she has mistaken the piano for harpsichord.

Richard Amlet, Esq., in the play, is a notable instance of the disadvantages to which this chimerical notion of *affinity constituting a claim to acquaintance*, may subject the spirit of a gentleman. A little foolish blood is all that is betwixt him and a lady with a great estate. His stars are perpetually crossed by the malignant maternity of an old woman, who persists in calling him 'her son Dick.' But she has wherewithal in the end to recompense his indignities, and float him again upon the brilliant surface, under which it has been her seeming business and pleasure all along to sink him. All men, besides, are not of Dick's temperament. I knew an Amlet in real life, who, wanting Dick's buoyancy, sank indeed. Poor W——was of my own standing at Christ's, a fine classic, and a youth of promise. If he had a blemish, it was too much pride; but its quality was inoffensive; it was not of that sort which hardens the heart, and serves to keep inferiors at a distance; it only sought to ward off derogation from itself. It was the principle of self-respect carried as far as it could go, without infringing upon that respect, which he would have every one else equally maintain for himself. He would have you to think alike with him on this topic. Many a quarrel have I had with him, when we were rather older boys, and our tallness made us more obnoxious to observation in the blue clothes, because I would not thread the alleys and blind ways of the town with him to elude notice, when we have been out together on a holiday in the streets of this sneering and prying metropolis. W——went, sore with these notions, to Oxford, where the dignity and sweetness of a scholar's life, meeting with the alloy of a humble introduction, wrought in him a passionate devotion to the place, with a profound aversion from the society. The servitor's gown (worse than his school array) clung to him with Nessian venom. He thought himself ridiculous in a garb, under which Latimer must have walked erect, and in which Hooker, in his young days, possibly flaunted in a vein of no discommendable vanity. In the depth of college shades, or in his lonely chamber, the poor student shrunk from observation. He found shelter among books, which insult not; and studies, that ask no questions of a youth's finances. He was lord of his library, and seldom cared for looking out beyond his domains. The healing influence of studious pursuits was upon him, to soothe and to abstract. He was almost a healthy man; when the waywardness of his fate broke out against him with a second and worse malignity. The father of W——had hitherto exercised the humble profession of house-painter at N——, near Oxford. A supposed interest with some of the heads of colleges had now induced him to take up his abode in that city, with the hope of being employed upon some public works which were talked of. From that moment I read in the countenance of the young man the determination which at length tore him from academical pursuits for ever. To a person unacquainted with our universities, the distance between the gownsmen and the townsmen, as they are called—the trading part of the latter especially—is carried to an excess that would appear harsh and incredible. The temperament of W——'s father was diametrically the reverse of his own. Old W——was a little, busy, cringing tradesman, who, with his son upon his arm, would stand bowing and scraping, cap in hand, to any thing that wore the semblance of a gown —insensible to the winks and opener remonstrances of the young man, to whose chamber-fellow, or equal in standing, perhaps, he was thus obsequiously and gratuitously ducking. Such a state of things could not last. W——must change the air of Oxford, or be suffocated. He chose the former; and let the sturdy moralist, who strains the point of the filial duties as high as they can bear, censure the dereliction; he cannot estimate the struggle. I stood with W——, the last afternoon I ever saw him, under the eaves of his paternal dwelling. It was in the fine lane leading from the High Street to the back of * * * * college, where W——kept his rooms. He seemed thoughtful and more reconciled. I ventured to rally him—finding him in a better mood—upon a representation of the Artist Evangelist, which the old man, whose affairs were beginning to flourish, had caused to be set up in a splendid sort of frame over his really handsome shop, either as a token of prosperity or badge of gratitude to his saint. W——looked up at the Luke, and, like Satan, 'knew his mounted sign—and fled.' A letter on his father's table, the next morning, announced that he had accepted a commission in a regiment about to embark for Portugal. He was among the first who perished before the walls of St. Sebastian.

I do not know how, upon a subject which I began with

treating half seriously, I should have fallen upon a recital so eminently painful; but this theme of poor relationship is replete with so much matter for tragic as well as comic associations, that it is difficult to keep the account distinct without blending. The earliest impressions which I received on this matter, are certainly not attended with anything painful, or very humiliating, in the recalling. At my father's table (no very splendid one) was to be found, every Saturday, the mysterious figure of an aged gentleman, clothed in neat black, of a sad yet comely appearance. His deportment was of the essence of gravity; his words few or none; and I was not to make a noise in his presence. I had little inclination to have done so—for my cue was to admire in silence. A particular elbow-chair was appropriated to him, which was in no case to be violated. A peculiar sort of sweet pudding, which appeared on no other occasion, distinguished the days of his coming. I used to think him a prodigiously rich man. All I could make out of him was, that he and my father had been schoolfellows, a world ago, at Lincoln, and that he came from the Mint. The Mint I knew to be a place where all the money was coined—and I thought he was the owner of all that money. Awful ideas of the Tower twined themselves about his presence. He seemed above human infirmities and passions. A sort of melancholy grandeur invested him. From some inexplicable doom I fancied him obliged to go about in an eternal suit of mourning; a captive—a stately being let out of the Tower on Saturdays. Often have I wondered at the temerity of my father, who, in spite of an habitual general respect which we all in common manifested towards him, would venture now and then to stand up against him in some argument, touching their youthful days. The houses of the ancient city of Lincoln are divided (as most of my readers know) between the dwellers on the hill and in the valley. This marked distinction formed an obvious division between the boys who lived above (however brought together in a common school) and the boys whose paternal residence was on the plain; a sufficient cause of hostility in the code of these young Grotiuses. My father had been a leading Mountaineer; and would still maintain the general superiority, in skill and hardihood, of the *Above Boys* (his own faction) over the *Below Boys* (so were they called), of which party his contemporary had been a chieftain. Many and hot were the skirmishes on this topic—the only one upon which the old gentleman was ever brought out—and bad blood bred; even sometimes almost to the recommencement (so I expected) of actual hostilities. But my father, who scorned to insist upon advantages, generally contrived to turn the conversation upon some adroit by-commendation of the old Minster; in the general preference of which, before all other cathedrals in the island, the dweller on the hill, and the plain-born, could meet on a conciliating level, and lay down their less important differences. Once only I saw the old gentleman really ruffled, and I remembered with anguish the thought that came over me: 'Perhaps he will never come here again.' He had been pressed to take another plate of the viand, which I have already mentioned as the indispensable concomitant of his visits. He had refused with a resistance amounting to rigour, when my aunt, an old Lincolnian, but who had something of this, in common with my cousin Bridget, that she would sometimes press civility out of season—uttered the following memorable application —'Do take another slice, Mr. Billet, for you do not get pudding every day.' The old gentleman said nothing at the time but he took occasion in the course of the evening, when some argument had intervened between them, to utter with an emphasis which chilled the company, and which chills me now as I write it—'Woman, you are superannuated!' John Billet did not survive long after the digesting of this affront; but he survived long enough to assure me that peace was actually restored! and, if I remember aright, another pudding was discreetly substituted in the place of that which had occasioned the offence. He died at the Mint (anno 1781), where he had long held, what he accounted, a comfortable independence; and with five pounds, fourteen shillings, and a penny, which were found in his escritoire after his decease, left the world, blessing God that he had enough to bury him, and that he had never been obliged to any man for a sixpence. This was—a Poor Relation.

Detached Thoughts on Books and Reading

To mind the inside of a book is to entertain one's self with the forced product of another man's brain. Now I think a man of quality and breeding may be much amused with the natural sprouts of his own. *Lord Foppington, in the Relapse.*

AN ingenious acquaintance of my own was so much struck with this bright sally of his Lordship, that he has left off reading altogether, to the great improvement of his originality. At the hazard of losing some credit on this head, I must confess that I dedicate no inconsiderable portion of my time to other people's thoughts. I dream away my life in others' speculations. I love to lose myself in other men's minds. When I am not walking, I am reading; I cannot sit and think. Books think for me.

I have no repugnances. Shaftesbury is not too genteel for me, nor Jonathan Wild too low. I can read anything which I call *a book*. There are things in that shape which I cannot allow for such.

In this catalogue of *books which are no books—biblia a-biblia* —I reckon Court Calendars, Directories, Pocket Books, Draught Boards, bound and lettered on the back, Scientific Treatises, Almanacs, Statutes at Large: the works of Hume, Gibbon, Robertson, Beattie, Soame Jenyns, and generally, all those volumes which 'no gentleman's library should be without': the Histories of Flavius Josephus (that learned Jew), and Paley's Moral Philosophy. With these exceptions, I can read almost anything. I bless my stars for a taste so catholic, so unexcluding.

I confess that it moves my spleen to see these *things in books' clothing* perched upon shelves, like false saints, usurpers of true shrines, intruders into the sanctuary, thrusting out the legitimate occupants. To reach down a well-bound semblance of a volume, and hope it some kind-hearted play-book, then, opening what 'seem its leaves,' to come bolt upon a withering Population Essay. To expect a Steele or a Farquhar, and find—Adam Smith. To view a well-arranged assortment of block-headed Encyclopædias (Anglicanas or Metropolitanas) set out in an array of russia, or morocco, when a tithe of that good leather would comfortably re-clothe my shivering folios—would renovate Paracelsus him-self, and enable old Raymund Lully to look like himself again in the world. I never see these impostors, but I long to strip them, to warm my ragged veterans in their spoils.

To be strong-backed and neat-bound is the desideratum of a volume. Magnificence comes after. This, when it can be afforded, is not to be lavished upon all kinds of books indiscriminately. I would not dress a set of Magazines, for instance, in full suit. The dishabille, or half-binding (with russia backs ever) is *our* costume. A Shakspeare or a Milton (unless the first editions), it were mere foppery to trick out in gay apparel. The possession of them confers no distinction. The exterior of them (the things themselves being so common), strange to say, raises no sweet emotions, no tickling sense of property in the owner. Thomson's Seasons, again, looks best (I maintain it) a little torn and dog's-eared. How beau-tiful to a genuine lover of reading are the sullied leaves, and worn-out appearance, nay, the very odour (beyond russia), if we would not forget kind feelings in fastidiousness, of an old 'Circulating Library' Tom Jones, or Vicar of Wakefield! How they speak of the thousand thumbs that have turned over their pages with delight!—of the lone sempstress, whom they may have cheered (milliner, or harder-working mantua-maker) after her long day's needle-toil, running far into mid-night, when she has snatched an hour, ill spared from sleep, to steep her cares, as in some Lethean cup, in spelling out their enchanting contents! Who would have them a whit less soiled? What better condition could we desire to see them in?

In some respects the better a book is, the less it demands from binding. Fielding, Smollett, Sterne, and all that class of perpetually self-reproductive volumes—Great Nature's Stereotypes—we see them individually perish with less regret, because we know the copies of them to be 'eterne.' But where a book is at once both good and rare—where the individual is almost the species, and when *that* perishes,

> We know not where is that Promethean torch
> That can its light relumine,—

such a book, for instance, as the Life of the Duke of Newcastle, by his Duchess—no casket is rich enough, no casing suf-ficiently durable, to honour and keep safe such a jewel.

Not only rare volumes of this description, which seem hopeless ever to be reprinted, but old editions of writers, such as Sir Philip Sydney, Bishop Taylor, Milton in his prose works, Fuller—of whom we *have* reprints, yet the books themselves, though they go about, and are talked of here and there, we know have not endenizened themselves (nor possibly ever will) in the national heart, so as to become stock books—it is good to possess these in durable and costly covers. I do not care for a First Folio of Shakspeare. I rather prefer the common editions of Rowe and Tonson, without notes, and with *plates*, which, being so execrably bad, serve as maps or modest remembrancers, to the text; and without pretending to any supposable emulation with it, are so much better than the Shakspeare gallery *engravings*, which *did*. I have a community of feeling with my countrymen about his Plays, and I like those editions of him best which have been oftenest tumbled about and handled.—On the contrary, I cannot read Beaumont and Fletcher but in Folio. The Octavo editions are painful to look at. I have no sympathy with them. If they were as much read as the current editions of the other poet, I should prefer them in that shape to the older one. I do not know a more heartless sight than the reprint of the Anatomy of Melancholy. What need was there of unearthing the bones of that fantastic old great man, to expose them in a winding-sheet of the newest fashion to modern censure? what hapless stationer could dream of Burton ever becoming popular?—The wretched Malone could not do worse, when he bribed the sexton of Stratford church to let him whitewash the painted effigy of old Shakspeare, which stood there, in rude but lively fashion depicted, to the very colour of the cheek, the eye, the eyebrow, hair, the very dress he used to wear—the only authentic testimony we had, however imperfect, of these curious parts and parcels of him. They covered him over with a coat of white paint. By——, if I had been a justice of peace for Warwickshire, I would have clapt both commentator and sexton fast in the stocks, for a pair of meddling sacrilegious varlets.

I think I see them at their work—these sapient trouble-tombs.

Shall I be thought fantastical if I confess that the names of some of our poets sound sweeter, and have a finer relish to the ear—to mine, at least—than that of Milton or of Shakespeare? It may be that the latter are more staled and rung upon in common discourse. The sweetest names, and which carry a perfume in the mention, are, Kit Marlowe, Drayton, Drummond of Hawthornden, and Cowley.

Much depends upon *when* and *where* you read a book. In the five or six impatient minutes, before the dinner is quite ready, who would think of taking up the Faëry Queen for a stop-gap, or a volume of Bishop Andrewes' sermons?

Milton almost requires a solemn service of music to be played before you enter upon him. But he brings his music, to which, who listens, had need bring docile thoughts, and purged ears.

Winter evenings—the world shut out—with less of ceremony the gentle Shakspeare enters. At such a season the Tempest, or his own Winter's Tale—

These two poets you cannot avoid reading aloud—to yourself, or (as it chances) to some single person listening. More than one—and it degenerates into an audience.

Books of quick interest, that hurry on for incidents, are for the eye to glide over only. It will not do to read them out. I could never listen to even the better kind of modern novels without extreme irksomeness.

A newspaper, read out, is intolerable. In some of the Bank offices it is the custom (to save so much individual time) for one of the clerks—who is the best scholar—to commence upon the 'Times,' or the 'Chronicle,' and recite its entire contents aloud, *pro bono publico*. With every advantage of lungs and elocution, the effect is singularly vapid. In barbers' shops and public-houses a fellow will get up and spell out a paragraph, which he communicates as some discovery. Another follows with *his* selection. So the entire journal transpires at length by piecemeal. Seldom-readers are slow readers, and, without this expedient, no one in the company would probably ever travel through the contents of a whole paper.

Newspapers always excite curiosity. No one ever lays one down without a feeling of disappointment.

What an eternal time that gentleman in black, at Nando's, keeps the paper! I am sick of hearing the waiter bawling out incessantly, 'The 'Chronicle' is in hand, Sir.'

Coming into an inn at night—having ordered your supper

—what can be more delightful than to find lying in the window-seat, left there time out of mind by the carelessness of some former guest—two or three numbers of the old Town and Country Magazine, with its amusing *tête-à-tête* pictures —'The Royal Lover and Lady G——'; 'The Melting Platonic and the old Beau,'—and such-like antiquated scandal? Would you exchange it—at that time, and in that place—for a better book?

Poor Tobin, who latterly fell blind, did not regret it so much for the weightier kinds of reading—the Paradise Lost, or Comus, he could have *read* to him—but he missed the pleasure of skimming over with his own eye a magazine, or a light pamphlet.

I should not care to be caught in the serious avenues of some cathedral alone, and reading *Candide*.

I do not remember a more whimsical surprise than having been once detected—by a familiar damsel—reclined at my ease upon the grass, on Primrose Hill (her Cythera), reading —*Pamela*. There was nothing in the book to make a man seriously ashamed at the exposure; but as she seated herself down by me, and seemed determined to read in company, I could have wished it had been—any other book. We read on very sociably for a few pages; and, not finding the author much to her taste, she got up, and—went away. Gentle casuist, I leave it to thee to conjecture, whether the blush (for there was one between us) was the property of the nymph or the swain in this dilemma. From me you shall never get the secret.

I am not much a friend to out-of-doors reading. I cannot settle my spirits to it. I knew a Unitarian minister, who was generally to be seen upon Snow Hill (as yet Skinner's Street *was not*), between the hours of ten and eleven in the morning, studying a volume of Lardner. I own this to have been a strain of abstraction beyond my reach. I used to admire how he sidled along, keeping clear of secular contacts. An illiterate encounter with a porter's knot, or a bread-basket, would have quickly put to flight all the theology I am master of, and have left me worse than indifferent to the five points.

There is a class of street-readers, whom I can never contemplate without affection—the poor gentry, who, not having wherewithal to buy or hire a book, filch a little learning at the open stalls—the owner, with his hard eye, casting envious looks at them all the while, and thinking when they will have done. Venturing tenderly, page after page, expecting every moment when he shall interpose his interdict, and yet unable to deny themselves the gratification, they 'snatch a fearful joy.' Martin B——, in this way, by daily fragments, got through two volumes of Clarissa, when the stall-keeper damped his laudable ambition, by asking him (it was in his younger days) whether he meant to purchase the work. M. declares, that under no circumstances in his life did he ever peruse a book with half the satisfaction which he took in those uneasy snatches. A quaint poetess of our day has moralised upon this subject in two very touching but homely stanzas.

> I saw a boy with eager eye
> Open a book upon a stall,
> And read, as he'd devour it all;
> Which, when the stall-man did espy,
> Soon to the boy I heard him call,
> 'You' Sir, you never buy a book,
> Therefore in one you shall not look.'
> The boy pass'd slowly on, and with a sigh
> He wish'd he never had been taught to read,
> Then of the old churl's books he should have had no need.
>
> Of sufferings the poor have many,
> Which never can the rich annoy:
> I soon perceived another boy,
> Who look'd as if he had not any
> Food, for that day at least—enjoy
> The sight of cold meat in a tavern larder.
> This boy's case, then thought I, is surely harder,
> Thus hungry, longing, thus without a penny,
> Beholding choice of dainty-dressed meat:
> No wonder if he wish he ne'er had learn'd to eat.

Stage Illusion

A PLAY is said to be well or ill acted, in proportion to the scenical illusion produced. Whether such illusion can in any case be perfect, is not the question. The nearest approach to it, we are told, is, when the actor appears wholly un-conscious of the presence of spectators. In tragedy—in all which is to affect the feelings—this undivided attention to his stage business seems indispensable. Yet it is, in fact, dispensed with every day by our cleverest tragedians; and while these references to an audience, in the shape of rant or sentiment, are not too frequent or palpable, a sufficient quantity of illusion for the purposes of dramatic interest may be said to be produced in spite of them. But, tragedy apart, it may be inquired whether, in certain characters in comedy, especially those which are a little extravagant, or which involve some notion repugnant to the moral sense, it is not a proof of the highest skill in the comedian when, without absolutely appealing to an audience, he keeps up a tacit understanding with them: and makes them, unconsciously to themselves, a party in the scene. The utmost nicety is required in the mode of doing this; but we speak only of the great artists in the profession.

The most mortifying infirmity in human nature, to feel in ourselves, or to contemplate in another, is, perhaps, cowardice. To see a coward *done to the life* upon a stage would produce anything but mirth. Yet we most of us remember Jack Bannister's cowards. Could anything be more agreeable, more pleasant? We loved the rogues. How was this effected but by the exquisite art of the actor in a perpetual subinsinu-ation to us, the spectators, even in the extremity of the shaking fit, that he was not half such a coward as we took him for? We saw all the common symptoms of the malady upon him; the quivering lip, the cowering knees, the teeth chattering; and could have sworn 'that man was frightened.' But we forgot all the while—or kept it almost a secret to ourselves—that he never once lost his self-possession; that he let out, by a thousand droll looks and gestures—meant at *us*, and not at all supposed to be visible to his fellows in the scene, that his confidence in his own resources had never once deserted him. Was this a genuine picture of a coward; or not rather a likeness, which the clever artist contrived to palm upon us instead of an original; while we secretly connived at the delusion for the purpose of greater pleasure, than a more genuine counterfeiting of the imbecility, helplessness, and utter self-desertion, which we know to be concomitants of cowardice in real life, could have given us?

Why are misers so hateful in the world, and so endurable on the stage, but because the skilful actor, by a sort of subreference, rather than direct appeal to us, disarms the character of a great deal of its odiousness, by seeming to engage *our* compassion for the insecure tenure by which he holds his money-bags and parchments? By this subtle vent half of the hatefulness of the character—the self-closeness with which in real life it coils itself up from the sympathies of men—evaporates. The miser becomes sympathetic; *i.e.*, is no genuine miser. Here again a diverting likeness is substituted for a very disagreeable reality.

Spleen, irritability—the pitiable infirmities of old men, which produce only pain to behold in the realities, counterfeited upon a stage, divert not altogether for the comic appendages to them, but in part from an inner conviction that they are *being acted* before us; that a likeness only is going on, and not the thing itself. They please by being done under the life, or beside it; not *to the life*. When Gattie acts an old man, is he angry indeed? or only a pleasant counterfeit, just enough of a likeness to recognise, without pressing upon us the uneasy sense of a reality?

Comedians, paradoxical as it may seem, may be too natural. It was the case with a late actor. Nothing could be more earnest or true than the manner of Mr. Emery; this told excellently in his Tyke, and characters of a tragic cast. But when he carried the same rigid exclusiveness of attention to the stage business, and wilful blindness and oblivion of everything before the curtain into his comedy, it produced a harsh and dissonant effect. He was out of keeping with the rest of the *Personæ Dramatis*. There was as little link between him and them, as betwixt himself and the audience. He was a third estate—dry, repulsive, and unsocial to all. Individually considered, his execution was masterly. But comedy is not this unbending thing; for this reason, that the same degree of credibility is not required of it as to serious scenes. The degrees of credibility demanded to the two things may be illustrated by the different sort of truth which we expect when a man tells us a mournful or a merry story. If we suspect the former of falsehood in any one tittle, we reject it altogether. Our tears refuse to flow at a suspected imposition. But the teller of a mirthful tale has latitude allowed him. We are content with less than absolute truth. 'Tis the same with dramatic illusion. We confess we love in comedy to see an audience naturalised behind the scenes—taken into the interest of the drama, welcomed as bystanders, however. There is something ungracious in a comic actor holding himself aloof from all participation or concern with those who are come to be diverted by him. Macbeth must see the dagger, and no ear but his own be told of it; but an old fool in farce may think he *sees something*, and by conscious words and looks express it, as plainly as he can speak, to pit, box, and gallery. When an impertinent in tragedy, an Osric, for instance, breaks in upon the serious passions of the scene, we approve of the contempt with which he is treated. But when the pleasant impertinent of comedy, in a piece purely meant to give delight, and raise mirth out of whimsical perplexities, worries the studious man with taking up his leisure, or making his house his home, the same sort of contempt expressed (however *natural*) would destroy the balance of delight in the spectators. To make the intrusion comic, the actor who plays the annoyed man must a little desert nature; he must, in short, be thinking of the audience, and express only so much dissatisfaction and peevishness as is consistent with the pleasure of comedy. In other words, his perplexity must seem half put on. If he repel the intruder with the sober set face of a man in earnest, and more especially if he deliver his expostulations in a tone which in the world must necessarily provoke a duel, his real-life manner will destroy the whimsical and purely dramatic existence of the other character (which to render it comic demands an antagonist comicality on the part of the character opposed to it), and convert what was meant for mirth, rather than belief, into a downright piece of impertinence indeed which would raise no diversion in us, but rather stir pain, to see inflicted in earnest upon any unworthy person. A very judicious actor (in most of his parts) seems to have fallen into an error of this sort in his playing with Mr. Wrench in the farce of Free and Easy.

Many instances would be tedious; these may suffice to show that comic acting at least does not always demand from the performer that strict abstraction from all reference to an audience which is exacted of it; but that in some cases a sort of compromise may take place, and all the purposes of dramatic delight be attained by a judicious understanding, not too openly announced, between the ladies and gentlemen —on both sides of the curtain.

To the Shade of Elliston

JOYOUSEST of once embodied spirits, whither at length hast thou flown? to what genial region are we permitted to conjecture that thou hast flitted?

Art thou sowing thy WILD OATS yet (the harvest time was still to come with thee) upon casual sands of Avernus? or art thou enacting ROVER (as we would gladlier think) by wandering Elysian streams?

This mortal frame, while thou didst play thy brief antics amongst us, was in truth anything but a prison to thee, as the vain Platonist dreams of this *body* to be no better than a county gaol, forsooth, or some house of durance vile, whereof the five senses are the fetters. Thou knewest better than to be in a hurry to cast off those gyves; and had notice to quit, I fear, before thou wert quite ready to abandon this fleshy tenement. It was thy Pleasure-House, thy Palace of Dainty Devices: thy Louvre, or thy White-Hall.

What new mysterious lodgings dost thou tenant now? or when may we expect thy aërial house-warming?

Tartarus we know, and we have read of the Blessed Shades; now cannot I intelligibly fancy thee in either.

Is it too much to hazard a conjecture, that (as the schoolmen admitted a receptacle apart for Patriarchs and unchrisom babes) there may exist—not far perchance from that store-house of all vanities, which Milton saw in vision —a LIMBO somewhere for PLAYERS? and that

Up thither like aerial vapours fly
Both all Stage things, and all that in Stage things
Built their fond hopes of glory, or lasting fame!
All the unaccomplished works of Authors' hands,
Abortive, monstrous, or unkindly mixed,
Damn'd upon earth, fleet thither—
Play, Opera, Farce, with all their trumpery.—

There, by the neighbouring moon (by some not improperly supposed thy Regent Planet upon earth), mayst thou not still be acting thy managerial pranks, great disembodied Lessee? but Lessee still, and still a manager.

In Green Rooms, impervious to mortal eye, the muse beholds thee wielding posthumous empire.

Thin ghosts of Figurantes (never plump on earth) circle thee in endlessly, and still their song is *Fie on sinful Phantasy!*

Magnificent were thy capriccios on this globe of earth, ROBERT WILLIAM ELLISTON! for as yet we know not thy new name in heaven.

It irks me to think, that, stript of thy regalities, thou shouldst ferry over, a poor forked shade, in crazy Stygian wherry. Methinks I hear the old boatman, paddling by the weedy wharf, with raucid voice, bawling 'SCULLS, SCULLS': to which, with waving hand, and majestic action, thou deignest no reply, other than in two curt monosyllables, 'No: Oars.'

But the laws of Pluto's kingdom know small difference between king and cobbler; manager and call-boy; and, if haply your dates of life were conterminant, you are quietly taking your passage, cheek by cheek (O ignoble levelling of Death) with the shade of some recently departed candle-snuffer.

But mercy! what strippings, what tearing off of histrionic robes, and private vanities! what denudations to the bone, before the surly Ferryman will admit you to set a foot within his battered lighter.

Crowns, sceptres; shield, sword, and truncheon; thy own coronation robes (for thou hast brought the whole property-man's wardrobe with thee, enough to sink a navy); the judge's ermine; the coxcomb's wig; the snuff-box *à la Foppington*—all must overboard, he positively swears—and that Ancient Mariner brooks no denial; for, since the tiresome monodrame of the old Thracian Harper, Charon, it is to be believed, hath shown small taste for theatricals.

Ay, now 'tis done. You are just boat-weight; *pura et puta anima.*

But, bless me, how *little* you look!

So shall we all look—kings and keysars—stripped for the last voyage.

But the murky rogue pushes off. Adieu, pleasant and thrice pleasant shade! with my parting thanks for many a heavy hour of life lightened by thy harmless extravaganzas, public or domestic.

Rhadamanthus, who tries the lighter causes below, leaving to his two brethren the heavy calendars—honest Rhadamanth, always partial to players, weighing their parti-coloured existence here upon earth,—making account of the few foibles, that may have shaded thy *real life*, as we call it (though substantially, scarcely less a vapour than thy idlest vagaries upon the boards of Drury), as but of so many echoes, natural repercussions, and results to be expected from the assumed extravagancies of thy *secondary* or *mock life*, nightly upon a stage—after a lenient castigation, with rods lighter than of those Medusean ringlets, but just enough to 'whip the offending Adam out of thee,' shall courteously dismiss thee at the right-hand gate—the O. P. side of Hades —that conducts to masques and merry-makings in the Theatre Royal of Proserpine.

PLAUDITO, ET VALETO.

Ellistoniana

My acquaintance with the pleasant creature, whose loss we all deplore, was but slight.

My first introduction to E., which afterwards ripened into an acquaintance a little on this side of intimacy, was over a counter in the Leamington Spa Library, then newly entered upon by a branch of his family. E., whom nothing misbecame—to auspicate, I suppose, the filial concern, and set it a-going with a lustre—was serving in person two damsels fair, who had come into the shop ostensibly to inquire for some new publication, but in reality to have a sight of the illustrious shopman, hoping some conference. With what an air did he reach down the volume, dispassionately giving his opinion of the worth of the work in question, and launching out into a dissertation on its comparative merits with those of certain publications of a similar stamp, its rivals! his enchanted customers fairly hanging on his lips, subdued to their authoritative sentence. So have I seen a gentleman in comedy *acting* the shopman. So Lovelace sold his gloves in King Street. I admired the histrionic art, by which he contrived to carry clean away every notion of disgrace, from the occupation he had so generously submitted to; and from that hour I judged him, with no after repentance, to be a person with whom it would be a felicity to be more acquainted.

To descant upon his merits as a Comedian would be superfluous. With his blended private and professional habits alone I have to do; that harmonious fusion of the manners of the player into those of everyday life, which brought the stage boards into streets, and dining-parlours, and kept up the play when the play was ended.—'I like Wrench,' a friend was saying to him one day, 'because he is the same, natural, easy creature, *on* the stage, that he is *off*.' 'My case exactly,' retorted Elliston—with a charming forgetfulness, that the converse of a proposition does not always lead to the same conclusion—'I am the same person *off* the stage that I am *on*.' The inference, at first sight, seems identical; but examine it a little, and it confesses only, that the one performer was never, and the other always, *acting*.

And in truth this was the charm of Elliston's private deportment. You had spirited performance always going on before your eyes, with nothing to pay. As where a monarch takes up his casual abode for a night, the poorest hovel which he honours by his sleeping in it, becomes *ipso facto* for that time a palace; so wherever Elliston walked, sate, or stood still, there was the theatre. He carried about with him his pit, boxes, and galleries, and set up his portable playhouse at corners of streets, and in the market-places. Upon flintiest pavements he trod the boards still; and if his theme chanced to be passionate, the green baize carpet of tragedy spontaneously rose beneath his feet. Now this was hearty, and showed a love for his art. So Apelles *always* painted—in thought. So G. D. *always* poetises. I hate a luke-warm artist. I have

known actors—and some of them of Elliston's own stamp—
who shall have agreeably been amusing you in the part of
a rake or a coxcomb, through the two or three hours of their
dramatic existence; but no sooner does the curtain fall with
its leaden clatter, but a spirit of lead seems to seize on all
their faculties. They emerge sour, morose persons, intolerable
to their families, servants, etc. Another shall have been
expanding your heart with generous deeds and sentiments,
till it even beats with yearnings of universal sympathy; you
absolutely long to go home and do some good action. The
play seems tedious, till you can get fairly out of the house,
and realise your laudable intentions. At length the final bell
rings, and this cordial representative of all that is amiable
in human breasts steps forth—a miser. Elliston was more of
a piece. Did he *play* Ranger? and did Ranger fill the general
bosom of the town with satisfaction? why should *he* not be
Ranger, and diffuse the same cordial satisfaction among his
private circles? with *his* temperament, *his* animal spirits, *his*
good-nature, *his* follies perchance, could he do better than
identify himself with his impersonation? Are we to like a
pleasant rake, or coxcomb, on the stage, and give ourselves
airs of aversion for the identical character, presented to us
in actual life? or what would the performer have gained by
divesting himself of the impersonation? Could the man
Elliston have been essentially different from his part, even
if he had avoided to reflect to us studiously, in private circles,
the airy briskness, the forwardness, and 'scape-goat trickeries
of his prototype?

'But there is something not natural in this everlasting
acting; we want the real man.'

Are you quite sure that it is not the man himself, whom you
cannot, or will not see, under some adventitious trappings,
which, nevertheless, sit not at all inconsistently upon him?
What if it is the nature of some men to be highly artificial?
The fault is least reprehensible in *players*. Cibber was his
own Foppington, with almost as much wit as Vanbrugh
could add to it.

'My conceit of his person,'—it is Ben Jonson speaking of
Lord Bacon,—'was never increased towards him by his *place*
or *honours*. But I have, and do reverence him for the *greatness*,
that was only proper to himself; in that he seemed to me
ever one of the *greatest* men, that had been in many ages. In

his adversity I ever prayed that Heaven would give him strength; for *greatness* he could not want.'

The quality here commended was scarcely less conspicuous in the subject of these idle reminiscences than in my Lord Verulam. Those who have imagined that an unexpected elevation to the direction of a great London Theatre affected the consequence of Elliston, or at all changed his nature, knew not the essential *greatness* of the man whom they disparage. It was my fortune to encounter him near St. Dunstan's Church (which, with its punctual giants, is now no more than dust and a shadow), on the morning of his election to that high office. Grasping my hand with a look of significance, he only uttered,—'Have you heard the news?'—then, with another look following up the blow, he subjoined, 'I am the future Manager of Drury Lane Theatre.'—Breathless as he saw me, he stayed not for congratulation or reply, but mutely stalked away, leaving me to chew upon his new-blown dignities at leisure. In fact, nothing could be said to it. Expressive silence alone could muse his praise. This was in his *great* style.

But was he less *great* (be witness, O ye Powers of Equanimity, that supported in the ruins of Carthage the consular exile, and more recently transmuted, for a more illustrious exile, the barren constableship of Elba into an image of Imperial France), when, in melancholy after-years, again, much near the same spot, I met him, when that sceptre had been wrested from his hand, and his dominion was curtailed to the petty managership, and part proprietorship, of the small Olympic, *his Elba?* He still played nightly upon the boards of Drury, but in parts, alas! allotted to him, not magnificently distributed by him. Waiving his great loss as nothing, and magnificently sinking the sense of fallen *material* grandeur in the more liberal resentment of depreciations done to his more lofty *intellectual* pretensions, 'Have you heard' (his customary exordium)—'have you heard,' said he, 'how they treat me? they put me in *comedy*.' Thought I —but his finger on his lips forbade any verbal interruption —'where could they have put you better?' Then, after a pause—'Where I formerly played Romeo, I now play Mercutio,'—and so again he stalked away, neither staying, nor caring for, responses.

O, it was a rich scene,—but Sir A—— C——, the best of

story-tellers and surgeons, who mends a lame narrative almost as well as he sets a fracture, alone could do justice to it,—that I was a witness to, in the tarnished room (that had once been green) of that same little Olympic. There, after his deposition from Imperial Drury, he substituted a throne. That Olympic Hill was his 'highest heaven'; himself 'Jove in his chair.' There he sat in state, while before him, on complaint of prompter, was brought for judgment—how shall I describe her?—one of those little tawdry things that flirt at the tails of choruses—a probationer for the town, in either of its senses—the pertest little drab—a dirty fringe and appendage of the lamp's smoke—who, it seems, on some disapprobation expressed by a 'highly respectable' audience,—had precipitately quitted her station on the boards, and withdrawn her small talents in disgust.

'And how dare you,' said her manager,—assuming a censorial severity, which would have crushed the confidence of a Vestris, and disarmed that beautiful Rebel herself of her professional caprices—I verily believe, he thought *her* standing before him—'how dare you, Madam, withdraw yourself, without a notice, from your theatrical duties?' 'I was hissed, Sir.' 'And you have the presumption to decide upon the taste of the town?' 'I don't know that, Sir, but I will never stand to be hissed,' was the subjoinder of young Confidence—when gathering up his features into one significant mass of wonder, pity, and expostulatory indignation—in a lesson never to have been lost upon a creature less forward than she who stood before him—his words were these: 'They have hissed *me*.'

'Twas the identical argument *a fortiori*, which the son of Peleus uses to Lycaon trembling under his lance, to persuade him to take his destiny with a good grace' 'I too am mortal.' And it is to be believed that in both cases the rhetoric missed of its application, for want of a proper understanding with the faculties of the respective recipients.

'Quite an Opera pit,' he said to me, as he was courteously conducting me over the benches of his Surrey Theatre, the last retreat, and recess, of his everyday waning grandeur.

Those who knew Elliston, will know the *manner* in which he pronounced the latter sentence of the few words I am about to record. One proud day to me he took his roast mutton with us in the Temple, to which I had superadded a preliminary haddock. After a rather plentiful partaking of the meagre banquet, not unrefreshed with the humbler sort of liquors, I made a sort of apology for the humility of the fare, observing that for my own part I never ate but one dish at dinner. 'I too never eat but one thing at dinner,'—was his reply—then after a pause—'reckoning fish as nothing.' The manner was all. It was as if by one peremptory sentence he had decreed the annihilation of all the savoury esculents, which the pleasant and nutritious-food-giving Ocean pours forth upon poor humans from her watery bosom. This was *greatness*, tempered with considerate *tenderness* to the feelings of his scanty but welcoming entertainer.

Great wert thou in thy life, Robert William Elliston! and *not lessened* in thy death, if report speak truly, which says that thou didst direct that thy mortal remains should repose under no inscription but one of pure *Latinity*. Classical was thy bringing up! and beautiful was the feeling on thy last bed, which, connecting the man with the boy, took thee back to thy latest exercise of imagination, to the days when, undreaming of Theatre and Managerships, thou wert a scholar, and an early ripe one, under the roofs builded by the munificent and pious Colet. For thee the Pauline Muses weep. In elegies, that shall silence this crude prose, they shall celebrate thy praise.

The Old Margate Hoy

I AM fond of passing my vacations (I believe I have said so before) at one or other of the Universities. Next to these my choice would fix me at some woody spot, such as the neighbourhood of Henley affords in abundance, on the banks of my beloved Thames. But somehow or other my cousin contrives to wheedle me, once in three or four seasons, to a watering-place. Old attachments cling to her in spite of experience. We have been dull at Worthing one summer, duller at Brighton another, dullest at Eastbourn a third, and are at this moment doing dreary penance at—Hastings!— and all because we were happy many years ago for a brief week at Margate. That was our first sea-side experiment, and many circumstances combined to make it the most agreeable holiday of my life. We had neither of us seen the sea, and we had never been from home so long together in company.

Can I forget thee, thou old Margate Hoy, with thy weather-beaten, sun-burnt captain, and his rough accommodations—ill exchanged for the foppery and fresh-water niceness of the modern steam-packet? To the winds and waves thou committedst thy goodly freightage, and didst ask no aid of magic fumes, and spells, and boiling cauldrons. With the gales of heaven thou wentest swimmingly; or, when it was their pleasure, stoodest still with sailor-like patience. Thy course was natural, not forced as in a hot-bed; nor didst thou go poisoning the breath of ocean with sulphureous smoke—a great sea chimera, chimneying and furnacing the deep; or liker to that fire-god parching up Scamander.

Can I forget thy honest, yet slender crew, with their coy reluctant responses (yet to the suppression of anything like contempt) to the raw questions, which we of the great city would be ever and anon putting to them, as to the uses of this or that strange naval implement? 'Specially can I forget thee, thou happy medium, thou shade of refuge between us and them, conciliating interpreter of their skill to our simplicity, comfortable ambassador between sea and land!—whose sailor-trousers did not more convincingly assure thee to be an adopted denizen of the former, than thy white cap, and whiter apron over them, with thy neat-figured practice in thy culinary vocation, bespoke thee to have been of inland nurture heretofore—a master cook of Eastcheap? How busily didst thou ply thy multifarious occupation, cook, mariner, attendant, chamberlain: here, there, like another Ariel, flaming at once about all parts of the deck, yet with kindlier ministrations—not to assist the tempest, but, as if touched with a kindred sense of our infirmities, to soothe the qualms which that untried motion might haply raise in our crude land-fancies. And when the o'erwashing billows drove us below deck (for it was far gone in October, and we had stiff and blowing weather), how did thy officious ministerings, still catering for our comfort, with cards, and cordials, and thy more cordial conversation, alleviate the closeness and the confinement of thy else (truth to say) not very savoury, nor very inviting, little cabin!

With these additaments to boot, we had on board a

fellow-passenger, whose discourse in verity might have be-
guiled a longer voyage than we meditated, and have made
mirth and wonder abound as far as the Azores. He was a
dark, Spanish-complexioned young man, remarkably handsome, with an officer-like assurance and an insuppressible
volubility of assertion. He was, in fact, the greatest liar I had
met with then, or since. He was none of your hesitating,
half-story-tellers (a most painful description of mortals) who
go on sounding your belief, and only giving you as much
as they see you can swallow at a time—the nibbling pickpockets of your patience—but one who committed downright,
daylight depredations upon his neighbour's faith. He did
not stand shivering upon the brink, but was a hearty,
thorough-paced liar, and plunged at once into the depths
of your credulity. I partly believe, he made pretty sure of
his company. Not many rich, not many wise, or learned,
composed at that time the common stowage of a Margate
packet. We were, I am afraid, a set of as unseasoned Londoners
(let our enemies give it a worse name) as Aldermanbury, or
Watling Street, at that time of day could have supplied.
There might be an exception or two among us, but I scorn
to make any invidious distinctions among such a jolly, companionable ship's company, as those were whom I sailed
with. Something too must be conceded to the *Genius Loci*.
Had the confident fellow told us half the legends on land
which he favoured us with on the other element, I flatter
myself the good sense of most of us would have revolted. But
we were in a new world, with everything unfamiliar about
us, and the time and place disposed us to the reception of
any prodigious marvel whatsoever. Time has obliterated
from my memory much of his wild fablings; and the rest
would appear but dull, as written, and to be read on shore.
He had been Aide-de-camp (among other rare accidents
and fortunes) to a Persian Prince and at one blow had
stricken off the head of the King of Carimania on horseback.
He, of course, married the Prince's daughter. I forget what
unlucky turn in the politics of that court, combining with
the loss of his consort, was the reason of his quitting Persia;
but, with the rapidity of a magician, he transported himself,
along with his hearers, back to England, where we still
found him in the confidence of great ladies. There was some
story of a princess—Elizabeth, if I remember—having

intrusted to his care an extraordinary casket of jewels, upon some extraordinary occasion—but, as I am not certain of the name or circumstance at this distance of time, I must leave it to the Royal daughters of England to settle the honour among themselves in private. I cannot call to mind half his pleasant wonders; but I perfectly remember, that in the course of his travels he had seen a phœnix; and he obligingly undeceived us of the vulgar error, that there is but one of that species at a time, assuring us that they were not uncommon in some parts of Upper Egypt. Hitherto he had found the most implicit listeners. His dreaming fancies had transported us beyond the 'ignorant present.' But when (still hardying more and more in his triumphs over our simplicity) he went on to affirm that he had actually sailed through the legs of the Colossus at Rhodes, it really became necessary to make a stand. And here I must do justice to the good sense and intrepidity of one of our party, a youth, that had hitherto been one of his most deferential auditors, who, from his recent reading, made bold to assure the gentleman, that there must be some mistake, as 'the Colossus in question had been destroyed long since'; to whose opinion, delivered with all modesty, our hero was obliging enough to concede thus much, that 'the figure was indeed a little damaged.' This was the only opposition he met with, and it did not at all seem to stagger him, for he proceeded with his fables, which the same youth appeared to swallow with still more complacency than ever,—confirmed, as it were, by the extreme candour of that concession. With these prodigies he wheedled us on till we came in sight of the Reculvers, which one of our own company (having been the voyage before) immediately recognising, and pointing out to us, was considered by us as no ordinary seaman.

All this time sat upon the edge of the deck quite a different character. It was a lad, apparently very poor, very infirm, and very patient. His eye was ever on the sea, with a smile; and, if he caught now and then some snatches of these wild legends, it was by accident, and they seemed not to concern him. The waves to him whispered more pleasant stories. He was as one, being with us, but not of us. He heard the bell of dinner ring without stirring; and when some of us pulled out our private stores—our cold meat and our salads—he produced none, and seemed to want none. Only a solitary biscuit he had laid in; provision for the one or two days and nights, to which these vessels then were oftentimes obliged to prolong their voyage. Upon a nearer acquaintance with him, which he seemed neither to court nor decline, we learned that he was going to Margate, with the hope of being admitted into the Infirmary there for sea-bathing. His disease was a scrofula, which appeared to have eaten all over him. He expressed great hopes of a cure; and when we asked him, whether he had any friends where he was going, he replied 'he *had* no friends.'

These pleasant, and some mournful passages, with the first of the sea, co-operating with youth, and a sense of holidays, and out-of-door adventure, to me that had been pent up in populous cities for many months before,—have left upon my mind the fragrance as of summer days gone by, bequeathing nothing but their remembrance for cold and wintry hours to chew upon.

Will it be thought a digression (it may spare some un-welcome comparisons), if I endeavour to account for the *dissatisfaction* which I have heard so many persons confess to have felt (as I did myself feel in part on this occasion), *at the sight of the sea for the first time?* I think the reason usually given—referring to the incapacity of actual objects for satisfying our preconceptions of them—scarcely goes deep enough into the question. Let the same person see a lion, an elephant, a mountain for the first time in his life, and he shall perhaps feel himself a little mortified. The things do not fill up that space which the idea of them seemed to take up in his mind. But they have still a correspondency to his first notion, and in time grow up to it, so as to produce a very similar impression: enlarging themselves (if I may say so) upon familiarity. But the sea remains a disappointment. —Is it not, that in *the latter* we had expected to behold (absurdly, I grant, but, I am afraid, by the law of imagination, unavoidably) not a definite object, as those wild beasts, or that mountain compassable by the eye, but *all the sea at once*, THE COMMENSURATE ANTAGONIST OF THE EARTH? I do not say we tell ourselves so much, but the craving of the mind is to be satisfied with nothing less. I will suppose the case of a young person of fifteen (as I then was) knowing nothing of the sea, but from description. He comes to it for the first time—all that he has been reading of it all his life, and *that* the most enthusiastic part of life,—all he has gathered from narratives of wandering seamen,—what he has gained from true voyages, and what he cherishes as credulously from romance and poetry,—crowding their images, and exacting strange tributes from expectation.—He thinks of the great deep, and of those who go down unto it; of its thousand isles, and of the vast continents it washes; of its receiving the mighty Plate, or Orellana, into its bosom, without disturbance, or sense of augmentation; of Biscay swells, and the mariner

> For many a day, and many a dreadful night,
> Incessant labouring round the stormy Cape;

of fatal rocks, and the 'still-vexed Bermoothes'; of great whirlpools, and the water-spout; of sunken ships, and sumless treasures swallowed up in the unrestoring depths; of fishes and quaint monsters, to which all that is terrible on earth—

> Be but as buggs to frighten babes withal,
> Compared with the creatures in the sea's entral;

of naked savages, and Juan Fernandez; of pearls, and shells; of coral beds, and of enchanted isles; of mermaids' grots—

I do not assert that in sober earnest he expects to be shown all these wonders at once, but he is under the tyranny of a mighty faculty, which haunts him with confused hints and shadows of all these; and when the actual object opens first upon him, seen (in tame weather, too, most likely) from our unromantic coasts—a speck, a slip of sea-water, as it shows to him—what can it prove but a very unsatisfying and even diminutive entertainment? Or if he has come to it from the mouth of a river, was it much more than the river widening? and, even out of sight of land, what had he but a flat watery horizon about him, nothing comparable to the vast o'er-curtaining sky, his familiar object, seen daily without dread or amazement?—Who, in similar circumstances, has not been tempted to exclaim with Charoba, in the poem of Gebir,

> Is this the mighty ocean? is this *all*?

I love town or country; but this detestable Cinque Port is neither. I hate these scrubbed shoots, thrusting out their starved foliage from between the horrid fissures of dusty innutritious rocks; which the amateur calls 'verdure to the edge of the sea.' I require woods, and they show me stunted coppices. I cry out for the water-brooks, and pant for fresh streams, and inland murmurs. I cannot stand all day on the naked beach, watching the capricious hues of the sea, shifting like the colours of a dying mullet. I am tired of looking out at the windows of this island-prison. I would fain retire into the interior of my cage. While I gaze upon the sea, I want to be on it, over it, across it. It binds me in with chains, as of iron. My thoughts are abroad. I should not so feel in Staffordshire. There is no home for me here. There is no sense of home at Hastings. It is a place of fugitive resort, an heterogeneous assemblage of sea-mews and stock-brokers, Amphitrites of the town, and misses that coquet with the Ocean. If it were what it was in its primitive shape, and what it ought to have remained, a fair, honest fishing-town, and no more, it were something—with a few straggling fishermen's huts scattered about, artless as its cliffs, and with their materials filched from them, it were something. I could abide to dwell with Meshech; to assort with fisher-swains, and smugglers. There are, or I dream there are, many of this latter occupation here. Their faces become the place. I like a smuggler. He is the only honest thief. He robs nothing but the revenue,—an abstraction I never greatly cared about. I could go out with them in their mackerel boats, or about their less ostensible business, with some satisfaction. I can even tolerate those poor victims to monotony, who from day to day pace along the beach, in endless progress and recurrence, to watch their illicit countrymen—townsfolk or brethren perchance—whistling to the sheathing and unsheathing of their cutlasses (their only solace), who, under the mild name of preventive service, keep up a legitimated civil warfare in the deplorable absence of a foreign one, to show their detestation of run hollands, and zeal for Old England. But it is the visitants from town, that come here to *say* that they have been here, with no more relish of the sea than a pond-perch or a dace might be supposed to have, that are my aversion. I feel like a foolish dace in these regions, and have as little toleration for myself here as for them. What can they want here? if they had a true relish of the ocean, why have they brought all this land luggage with them? or why pitch their civilised tents in the desert? What mean these scanty book-rooms—marine libraries as they entitle them—

if the sea were, as they would have us believe, a book 'to read strange matter in'? what are their foolish concert-rooms, if they come, as they would fain be thought to do, to listen to the music of the waves? All is false and hollow pretension. They come, because it is the fashion, and to spoil the nature of the place. They are, mostly, as I have said, stock-brokers; but I have watched the better sort of them—now and then, an honest citizen (of the old stamp), in the simplicity of his heart, shall bring down his wife and daughters, to taste the sea breezes. I always know the date of their arrival. It is easy to see it in their countenance. A day or two they go wandering on the shingles, picking up cockle-shells, and thinking them great things; but, in a poor week, imagination slackens: they begin to discover that cockles produce no pearls, and then—O then!—if I could interpret for the pretty creatures (I know they have not the courage to confess it themselves) how gladly would they exchange their sea-side rambles for a Sunday walk on the green-sward of their accustomed Twickenham meadows!

I would ask of one of these sea-charmed emigrants, who think they truly love the sea, with its wild usages, what would their feelings be, if some of the unsophisticated aborigines of this place, encouraged by their courteous questionings here, should venture, on the faith of such assured sympathy between them, to return the visit, and come up to see—London. I must imagine them with their fishing-tackle on their back, as we carry our town necessaries. What a sensation would it cause in Lothbury? What vehement laughter would it not excite among

The daughters of Cheapside, and wives of Lombard Street!

I am sure that no town-bred or inland-born subjects can feel their true and natural nourishment at these sea-places. Nature, where she does not mean us for mariners and vagabonds, bids us stay at home. The salt foam seems to nourish a spleen. I am not half so good-natured as by the milder waters of my natural river. I would exchange these sea-gulls for swans, and scud a swallow for ever about the banks of Thamesis.

The Convalescent

A PRETTY severe fit of indisposition which, under the name of a nervous fever, has made a prisoner of me for some weeks past, and is but slowly leaving me, has reduced me to an incapacity of reflectiong upon any topic foreign to itself. Expect no healthy conclusions from me this month, reader; I can offer you only sick men's dreams.

And truly the whole state of sickness is such; for what else is it but a magnificent dream for a man to lie a-bed, and draw daylight curtains about him; and, shutting out the sun, to induce a total oblivion of all the works which are going on under it? To become insensible to all the operations of life, except the beatings of one feeble pulse?

If there be a regal solitude, it is a sick bed. How the patient lords it there; what caprices he acts without control! how king-like he sways his pillow—tumbling, and tossing, and shifting, and lowering, and thumping, and flatting, and moulding it, to the ever-varying requisitions of his throbbing temples.

He changes sides oftener than a politician. Now he lies full length, then half-length, obliquely, transversely, head and feet quite across the bed; and none accuses him of tergiversation. Within the four curtains he is absolute. They are his Mare Clausum.

How sickness enlarges the dimensions of a man's self to himself! he is his own exclusive object. Supreme selfishness is inculcated upon him as his only duty. 'Tis the Two Tables of the Law to him. He has nothing to think of but how to get well. What passes out of doors, or within them, so he hear not the jarring of them, affects him not.

A little while ago he was greatly concerned in the event of a lawsuit, which was to be the making or the marring of his dearest friend. He was to be seen trudging about upon this man's errand to fifty quarters of the town at once, jogging this witness, refreshing that solicitor. The cause was to come on yesterday. He is absolutely as indifferent to the decision as if it were a question to be tried at Pekin. Perad-

231

venture from some whispering, going on about the house, not intended for his hearing, he picks up enough to make him understand that things went cross-grained in the court yesterday, and his friend is ruined. But the word 'friend,' and the word 'ruin,' disturb him no more than so much jargon. He is not to think of anything but how to get better.

What a world of foreign cares are merged in that absorbing consideration!

He has put on the strong armour of sickness; he is wrapped in the callous hide of suffering; he keeps his sympathy, like some curious vintage, under trustly lock and key, for his own use only.

He lies pitying himself, honing and moaning to himself; he yearneth over himself; his bowels are even melted within him, to think what he suffers; he is not ashamed to weep over himself.

He is for ever plotting how to do some good to himself; studying little stratagems and artificial alleviations.

He makes the most of himself; dividing himself, by an allowable fiction, into as many distinct individuals, as he hath sore and sorrowing members. Sometimes he meditates —as of a thing apart from him—upon his poor aching head, and that dull pain which, dozing or waking, lay in it all the past night like a log, or palpable substance of pain, not to be removed without opening the very skull, as it seemed, to take it thence. Or he pities his long, clammy, attenuated fingers. He compassionates himself all over; and his bed is a very discipline of humanity, and tender heart.

He is his own sympathiser; and instinctively feels that none can so well perform that office for him. He cares for few spectators to his tragedy. Only that punctual face of the old nurse pleases him, that announces his broths and his cordials. He likes it because it is so unmoved, and because he can pour forth his feverish ejaculations before it as unreservedly as to his bed-post.

To the world's business he is dead. He understands not what the callings and occupations of mortals are; only he has a glimmering conceit of some such thing, when the doctor makes his daily call: and even in the lines on that busy face he reads no multiplicity of patients, but solely conceives of himself as *the sick man*. To what other uneasy couch the good man is hastening, when he slips out of his chamber, folding up his thin douceur so carefully, for fear of rustling—is no speculation which he can at present entertain. He thinks only of the regular return of the same phenomenon at the same hour to-morrow.

Household rumours touch him not. Some faint murmur, indicative of life going on within the house, soothes him, while he knows not distinctly what it is. He is not to know anything, not to think of anything. Servants gliding up or down the distant staircase, treading as upon velvet, gently keep his ear awake, so long as he troubles not himself further than with some feeble guess at their errands. Exacter knowledge would be a burthen to him: he can just endure the pressure of conjecture. He opens his eye faintly at the dull stroke of the muffled knocker, and closes it again without asking 'Who was it?' He is flattered by a general notion that inquiries are making after him, but he cares not to know the name of the inquirer. In the general stillness, and awful hush of the house, he lies in state, and feels his sovereignty.

To be sick is to enjoy monarchal prerogatives. Compare the silent tread, and quiet ministry, almost by the eye only, with which he is served—with the careless demeanour, the unceremonious goings in and out (slapping of doors, or leaving them open) of the very same attendants, when he is getting a little better—and you will confess, that from the bed of sickness (throne let me rather call it) to the elbow-chair of convalescence, is a fall from dignity, amounting to a deposition.

How convalescence shrinks a man back to his pristine stature! where is now the space, which he occupied so lately, in his own, in the family's eye?

The scene of his regalities, his sick room, which was his presence chamber, where he lay and acted his despotic fancies—how is it reduced to a common bedroom! The trimness of the very bed has something petty and unmeaning about it. It is *made* every day. How unlike to that wavy, many-furrowed, oceanic surface, which it presented so short a time since, when to *make* it was a service not to be thought of at oftener than three or four day revolutions, when the patient was with pain and grief to be lifted for a little while out of it, to submit to the encroachments of unwelcome neatness, and decencies which his shaken frame deprecated; then to be lifted into it again, for another three or four days' respite, to flounder it out of shape again, while every fresh furrow was an historical record of some shifting posture, some uneasy turning, some seeking for a little ease; and the shrunken skin scarce told a truer story than the crumpled coverlid.

Hushed are those mysterious sighs—those groans—so much more awful, while we knew not from what caverns of vast hidden suffering they proceeded. The Lernean pangs are quenched. The riddle of sickness is solved; and Philoctetes is become an ordinary personage.

Perhaps some relic of the sick man's dream of greatness survives in the still lingering visitations of the medical attendant. But how is he, too, changed with everything else! Can this be he—this man of news—of chat—of anecdote—of everything but physic—can this be he, who so lately came between the patient and his cruel enemy, as on some solemn embassy from Nature, erecting herself into a high mediating party?—Pshaw! 'tis some old woman.

Farewell with him all that made sickness pompous—the spell that hushed the household—the desert-like stillness, felt throughout its inmost chambers—the mute attendance—the inquiry by looks—the still softer delicacies of self-attention— the sole and single eye of distemper alonely fixed upon itself —world-thoughts excluded—the man a world unto himself —his own theatre—

What a speck is he dwindled into!

In this flat swamp of convalescence, left by the ebb of sickness, yet far enough from the terra firma of established health, your note, dear Editor, reached me, requesting—an article. In Articulo Mortis, thought I; but it is something hard—and the quibble, wretched as it was, relieved me. The summons, unseasonable as it appeared, seemed to link me on again to the petty businesses of life, which I had lost sight of; a gentle call to activity, however trivial; a wholesome weaning from that preposterous dream of self-absorption— the puffy state of sickness—in which I confess to have lain so long, insensible to the magazines and monarchies of the world alike; to its laws, and to its literature. The hypochondriac flatus is subsiding; the acres, which in imagination I had spread over—for the sick man swells in the sole contemplation of his single sufferings, till he becomes a

Tityus to himself—are wasting to a span; and for the giant of self-importance, which I was so lately, you have me once again in my natural pretensions—the lean and meagre figure of your insignificant Essayist.

Sanity of True Genius

So far from the position holding true, that great wit (or genius, in our modern way of speaking) has a necessary alliance with insanity, the greatest wits, on the contrary, will ever be found to be the sanest writers. It is impossible for the mind to conceive of a mad Shakspeare. The greatness of wit, by which the poetic talent is here chiefly to be understood, manifests itself in the admirable balance of all the faculties. Madness is the disproportionate straining or excess of any one of them. 'So strong a wit,' says Cowley, speaking of a poetical friend,

> '——did Nature to him frame,
> As all things but his judgment overcame;
> His judgment like the heavenly moon did show,
> Tempering that mighty sea below.'

The ground of the mistake is, that men, finding in the raptures of the higher poetry a condition of exaltation, to which they have no parallel in their own experience, besides the spurious resemblance of it in dreams and fevers, impute a state of dreaminess and fever to the poet. But the true poet dreams being awake. He is not possessed by his subject, but has dominion over it. In the groves of Eden he walks familiar as in his native paths. He ascends the empyrean heaven, and is not intoxicated. He treads the burning marl without dismay; he wins his flight without self-loss through realms of chaos 'and old night.' Or if, abandoning himself to that severer chaos of a 'human mind untuned,' he is content awhile to be mad with Lear, or to hate mankind (a sort of madness) with Timon, neither is that madness, nor this misanthropy, so unchecked, but that,—never letting the reins of reason wholly go, while most he seems to do so,—he has his better genius still whispering at his ear, with the good servant Kent suggesting saner counsels, or with the honest steward Flavius recommending kindlier resolutions. Where he seems most to recede from humanity, he will be found the truest to it. From beyond the scope of Nature if he summon possible existences, he subjugates them to the law of her consistency. He is beautifully loyal to that sovereign directress, even when he appears most to betray and desert her. His ideal tribes submit to policy; his very monsters are tamed to his hand, even as that wild sea-brood, shepherded by Proteus. He tames, and he clothes them with attributes of flesh and blood, till they wonder at themselves, like Indian Islanders forced to submit to European vesture. Caliban, the Witches, are as true to the laws of their own nature (ours with a difference), as Othello, Hamlet, and Macbeth. Herein the great and the little wits are differenced; that if the latter wander ever so little from nature or actual existence, they lose themselves and their readers. Their phantoms are lawless; their visions nightmares. They do not create, which implies shaping and consistency. Their imaginations are not active —for to be active is to call something into act and form—but passive, as men in sick dreams. For the super-natural, or something super-added to what we know of nature, they give you the plainly non-natural. And if this were all, and that these mental hallucinations were discoverable only in the treatment of subjects out of nature, or transcending it, the judgment might with some plea be pardoned if it ran riot, and a little wantonised: but even in the describing of real and every-day life, that which is before their eyes, one of these lesser wits shall more deviate from nature,—show more of that inconsequence, which has a natural alliance with frenzy, —than a great genius in his 'maddest fits,' as Withers some-where calls them. We appeal to any one that is acquainted with the common run of Lane's novels,—as they existed some twenty or thirty years back,—those scanty intellectual viands of the whole female reading public, till a happier genius arose, and expelled for ever the innutritious phantoms, —whether he has not found his brain more 'betossed,' his memory more puzzled, his sense of when and where more confounded, among the improbable events, the incoherent incidents, the inconsistent characters, or no-characters, of some third-rate love-intrigue—where the persons shall be a Lord Glendamour and a Miss Rivers, and the scene only alternate between Bath and Bond Street—a more bewildering dreaminess induced upon him, than he has felt wandering over all the fairy-grounds of Spenser. In the productions we refer to, nothing but names and places is familiar: the persons are neither of this world nor of any other conceivable one: an endless stream of activities without purpose, or purposes destitute of motive:—we meet phantoms in our known walks; *fantasques* only christened. In the poet we have names which announce fiction; and we have absolutely no place at all for the things and persons of the Faëry Queen; prate not of their 'whereabout.' But in their inner nature, and the law of their speech and actions, we are at home, and upon acquainted ground. The one turns life into a dream; the other to the wildest dreams gives the sobrieties of everyday occurrences. By what subtle art of tracing the mental processes it is effected, we are not philosophers enough to explain, but in that wonderful episode of the cave of Mammon, in which the Money God appears first in the lowest form of a miser, is then a worker of metals, and becomes the god of all the treasures of the world; and has a daughter, Ambition, before whom all the world kneels for favours—with the Hesperian fruit, the waters of Tantalus, with Pilate washing his hands vainly, but not impertinently, in the same stream—that we should be at one moment in the cave of an old hoarder of treasures, at the next at the forge of the Cyclops, in a palace and yet in hell, all at once, with the shifting mutations of the most rambling dream, and our judgment yet all the time awake, and neither able nor willing to detect the fallacy,—is a proof of that hidden sanity which still guides the poet in the wildest—seeming aberrations.

It is not enough to say that the whole episode is a copy of the mind's conceptions in sleep; it is, in some sort—but what a copy! Let the most romantic of us, that has been entertained all night with the spectacle of some wild and magnificent vision, recombine it in the morning, and try it by his waking judgment. That which appeared so shifting, and yet so coherent, while that faculty was passive, when it comes under cool examination shall appear so reasonless and so unlinked, that we are ashamed to have been so deluded; and to have taken, though but in sleep, a monster for a god. But the transitions in this episode are every whit as violent as in the most extravagant dream, and yet the waking judgment ratifies them.

237

Captain Jackson

AMONG the deaths in our obituary for this month, I observe with concern 'At his cottage on the Bath Road, Captain Jackson.' The name and attribution are common enough; but a feeling like reproach persuades me, that this could have been no other in fact than my dear old friend, who some five-and-twenty years ago rented a tenement, which he was pleased to dignify with the appellation here used, about a mile from Westbourn Green. Alack, how good men, and the good turns they do us, slide out of memory, and are recalled but by the surprise of some such sad memento as that which now lies before us!

He whom I mean was a retired half-pay officer, with a wife and two grown-up daughters, whom he maintained with the port and notions of gentlewomen upon that slender professional allowance. Comely girls they were too.

And was I in danger of forgetting this man?—his cheerful suppers—the noble tone of hospitality, when first you set your foot in *the cottage*—the anxious ministerings about you, where little or nothing (God knows) was to be ministered. —Althea's horn in a poor platter—the power of self-enchantment, by which, in his magnificent wishes to entertain you, he multiplied his means to bounties.

You saw with your bodily eyes indeed what seemed a bare scrag, cold savings from the foregone meal—remnant hardly sufficient to send a mendicant from the door contented. But in the copious will—the revelling imagination of your host—the 'mind, the mind, Master Shallow,' whole beeves were spread before you—hecatombs—no end appeared to the profusion.

It was the widow's cruse—the loaves and fishes; carving could not lessen, nor helping diminish it—the stamina were left—the elemental bone still flourished, divested of its accidents.

'Let us live while we can,' methinks I hear the open-handed creature exclaim; 'while we have, let us not want,' 'here is plenty left'; 'want for nothing'—with many more

such hospitable sayings, the spurs of appetite, and old concomitants of smoking boards, and feast-oppressed chargers.
Then sliding a slender ratio of Single Gloucester upon his
wife's plate, or the daughters', he would convey the remnant
rind into his own, with a merry quirk of 'the nearer the bone,'
etc., and declaring that he universally preferred the outside.
For we had our table distinctions, you are to know, and
some of us in a manner sate above the salt. None but his
guest or guests dreamed of tasting flesh luxuries at night;
the fragments were *verè hospitibus sacra*. But of one thing or
another there was always enough, and leavings: only he
would sometimes finish the remainder crust, to show that
he wished no savings.

Wine we had none; nor, except on very rare occasions,
spirits; but the sensation of wine was there. Some thin kind
of ale I remember—'British beverage,' he would say! 'Push
about, my boys'; 'Drink to your sweethearts, girls.' At every
meagre draught a toast must ensue, or a song. All the forms
of good liquor were there, with none of the effects wanting.
Shut your eyes, and you would swear a capacious bowl of
punch was foaming in the centre, with beams of generous
Port or Madeira radiating to it from each of the table
corners. You got flustered, without knowing whence; tipsy
upon words; and reeled under the potency of his unper-
forming Bacchanalian encouragements.

We had our songs—'Why, Soldiers, why,'—and the 'British
Grenadiers'—in which last we were all obliged to bear chorus.
Both the daughters sang. Their proficiency was a nightly
theme—the masters he had given them—the 'no-expense'
which he spared to accomplish them in a science 'so necessary
to young women.' But then—they could not sing 'without
the instrument.'

Sacred, and, by me, never-to-be-violated, secrets of
Poverty! Should I disclose your honest aims at grandeur,
your makeshift efforts of magnificence? Sleep, sleep, with
all thy broken keys, if one of the bunch be extant; thrummed
by a thousand ancestral thumbs; dear, cracked spinnet of
dearer Louisa! Without mention of mine, be dumb, thou
thin accompanier of her thinner warble! A veil be spread
over the dear delighted face of the well-deluded father,
who now haply listening to cherubic notes, scarce feels
sincerer pleasure than when she awakened thy time-shaken

chords responsive to the twitterings of that slender image of a voice.

We were not without our literary talk either. It did not extend far, but as far as it went, it was good. It was bottomed well; had good grounds to go upon. In *the cottage* was a room, which tradition authenticated to have been the same in which Glover, in his occasional retirements, had penned the greater part of his Leonidas. This circumstance was nightly quoted, though none of the present inmates, that I could discover, appeared ever to have met with the poem in question. But that was no matter. Glover had written there, and the anecdote was pressed into the account of the family importance. It diffused a learned air through the apartment, the little side casement of which (the poet's study window), opening upon a superb view as far as the pretty spire of Harrow, over domains and patrimonial acres, not a rood nor square yard whereof our host could call his own, yet gave occasion to an immoderate expansion of—vanity shall I call it?—in his bosom, as he showed them in a glowing summer evening. It was all his, he took it all in, and communicated rich portions of it to his guests. It was a part of his largess, his hospitality; it was going over his grounds; he was lord for the time of showing them, and you the implicit lookers-up to his magnificence.

He was a juggler, who threw mists before your eyes—you had no time to detect his fallacies. He would say, 'Hand me the *silver* sugar tongs'; and before you could discover it was a single spoon, and that *plated*, he would disturb and captivate your imagination by a misnomer of 'the urn' for a tea-kettle; or by calling a homely bench a sofa. Rich men direct you to their furniture, poor ones divert you from it; he neither did one nor the other, but by simply assuming that everything was handsome about him, you were positively at a demur what you did, or did not see, at *the cottage*. With nothing to live on, he seemed to live on everything. He had a stock of wealth in his mind; not that which is properly termed *Content*, for in truth he was not to be *contained* at all, but overflowed all bounds by the force of a magnificent self-delusion.

Enthusiasm is catching; and even his wife, a sober native of North Britain, who generally saw things more as they were, was not proof against the continual collision of his credulity. Her daughters were rational and discreet young women; in the main, perhaps, not insensible to their true circumstances. I have seen them assume a thoughtful air at times. But such was the preponderating opulence of his fancy, that I am persuaded, not for any half-hour together did they ever look their own prospects fairly in the face. There was no resisting the vortex of his temperament. His riotous imagination conjured up handsome settlements before their eyes, which kept them up in the eye of the world too, and seem at last to have realised themselves; for they both have married since, I am told, more than respectably.

It is long since, and my memory waxes dim on some subjects, or I should wish to convey some notion of the manner in which the pleasant creature described the circumstances of his own wedding-day. I faintly remember something of a chaise-and-four, in which he made his entry into Glasgow on that morning to fetch the bride home, or carry her thither, I forget which. It so completely made out the stanza of the old ballad—

> When we came down through Glasgow town,
> We were a comely sight to see;
> My love was clad in black velvet,
> And I myself in cramasie.

I suppose it was the only occasion upon which his own actual splendour at all corresponded with the world's notions on that subject. In homely cart, or travelling caravan, by whatever humble vehicle they chanced to be transported in less prosperous days, the ride through Glasgow came back upon his fancy, not as a humiliating contrast, but as a fair occasion for reverting to that one day's state. It seemed an 'equipage etern' from which no power of fate or fortune, once mounted, had power thereafter to dislodge him.

There is some merit in putting a handsome face upon indigent circumstances. To bully and swagger away the sense of them before strangers, may not be always discommendable. Tibbs, and Bobadil, even when detected, have more of our admiration than contempt. But for a man to put the cheat upon himself; to play the Bobadil at home; and, steeped in poverty up to the lips, to fancy himself all the while chin-deep in riches, is a strain of constitutional philosophy, and a mastery over fortune, which was reserved for my old friend Captain Jackson.

The Superannuated Man

Sera tamen respexit
Libertas.   Virgil.
A Clerk I was in London gay.—O'Keefe.

If peradventure, Reader, it has been thy lot to waste the golden years of thy life—thy shining youth—in the irksome confinement of an office; to have thy prison days prolonged through middle age down to decrepitude and silver hairs, without hope of release or respite; to have lived to forget that there are such things as holidays, or to remember them but as the prerogatives of childhood; then, and then only, will you be able to appreciate my deliverance.

It is now six-and-thirty years since I took my seat at the desk in Mincing Lane. Melancholy was the transition at fourteen from the abundant playtime, and the frequently-intervening vacations of school days, to the eight, nine, and sometimes ten hours' a day attendance at the counting-house. But time partially reconciles us to anything. I gradually became content—doggedly contented, as wild animals in cages.

It is true I had my Sundays to myself; but Sundays, admirable as the institution of them is for purposes of worship, are for that very reason the very worst adapted for days of unbending and recreation. In particular, there is a gloom for me attendant upon a city Sunday, a weight in the air. I miss the cheerful cries of London, the music, and the ballad-singers—the buzz and stirring murmur of the streets. Those eternal bells depress me. The closed shops repel me. Prints, pictures, all the glittering and endless succession of knacks and gewgaws, and ostentatiously displayed wares of tradesmen, which make a week-day saunter through the less busy parts of the metropolis so delightful—are shut out. No bookstalls deliciously to idle over—No busy faces to recreate the idle man who contemplates them ever passing by—the very face of business a charm by contrast to his temporary relaxation from it. Nothing to be seen but unhappy countenances—or half-happy at best—of emancipated 'prentices and little tradesfolks, with here and there a servant-maid that has got leave to go out, who, slaving all the week, with the habit has lost almost the capacity of enjoying a free hour; and livelily expressing the hollowness of a day's pleasuring. The very strollers in the fields on that day look anything but comfortable.

But besides Sundays, I had a day at Easter, and a day at Christmas, with a full week in the summer to go and air myself in my native fields of Hertfordshire. This last was a great indulgence; and the prospect of its recurrence, I believe, alone kept me up through the year, and made my durance tolerable. But when the week came round, did the glittering phantom of the distance keep touch with me? or rather was it not a series of seven uneasy days, spent in restless pursuit of pleasure, and a wearisome anxiety to find out how to make the most of them? Where was the quiet, where the promised rest? Before I had a taste of it, it was vanished. I was at the desk again, counting upon the fifty-one tedious weeks that must intervene before such another snatch would come. Still the prospect of its coming threw something of an illumination upon the darker side of my captivity. Without it, as I have said, I could scarcely have sustained my thraldom.

Independently of the rigours of attendance, I have ever been haunted with a sense (perhaps a mere caprice) of incapacity for business. This, during my latter years, had increased to such a degree, that it was visible in all the lines of my countenance. My health and my good spirits flagged. I had perpetually a dread of some crisis, to which I should be found unequal. Besides my daylight servitude, I served over again all night in my sleep, and would awake with terrors of imaginary false entries, errors in my accounts, and the like. I was fifty years of age, and no prospect of emancipation presented itself. I had grown to my desk, as it were; and the wood had entered into my soul.

My fellows in the office would sometimes rally me upon the trouble legible in my countenance; but I did not know that it had raised the suspicions of any of my employers, when, on the fifth of last month, a day ever to be remembered by me, L——, the junior partner in the firm, calling me on one side, directly taxed me with my bad looks, and frankly inquired the cause of them. So taxed, I honestly made confession of my infirmity, and added that I was afraid I should eventually be obliged to resign his service. He spoke some words of course to hearten me, and there the matter rested. A whole week I remained labouring under the impression that I had acted imprudently in my disclosure; that I had foolishly given a handle against myself, and had been anticipating my own dismissal. A week passed in this manner, the most anxious one, I verily believe, in my whole life, when on the evening of the 12th of April, just as I was about quitting my desk to go home (it might be about eight o'clock) I received an awful summons to attend the presence of the whole assembled firm in the formidable back parlour. I thought now my time is surely come, I have done for myself, I am going to be told that they have no longer occasion for me. L——, I could see, smiled at the terror I was in, which was a little relief to me,—when to my utter astonishment B——, the eldest partner, began a formal harangue to me on the length of my services, my very meritorious conduct during the whole of the time (the deuce, thought I, how did he find out that? I protest I never had the confidence to think as much). He went on to descant on the expediency of retiring at a certain time of life (how my heart panted!), and asking me a few questions as to the amount of my own property, of which I have a little, ended with a proposal, to which his three partners nodded a grave assent, that I should accept from the house, which I had served so well, a pension for life to the amount of two-thirds of my accustomed salary—a magnificent offer! I do not know what I answered between surprise and gratitude, but it was understood that I accepted their proposal, and I was told that I was free from that hour to leave their service. I stammered out a bow, and at just ten minutes after eight I went home—for ever. This noble benefit—gratitude forbids me to conceal their names—I owe to the kindness of the most munificent firm in the world—the house of Boldero, Merryweather, Bosanquet, and Lacy.

Esto perpetua!

For the first day or two I felt stunned, overwhelmed. I could only apprehend my felicity; I was too confused to taste it sincerely. I wandered about, thinking I was happy, and knowing that I was not. I was in the condition of a prisoner in the old Bastile, suddenly let loose after a forty years' confinement. I could scarce trust myself with myself. It was like passing out of Time into Eternity—for it is a sort of Eternity for a man to have his Time all to himself. It seemed to me that I had more time on my hands than I could ever manage. From a poor man, poor in Time, I was suddenly lifted up into a vast revenue; I could see no end of my possessions; I wanted some steward, or judicious bailiff, to manage my estates in Time for me. And here let me caution persons grown old in active business, not lightly, nor without weighing their own resources, to forego their customary employment all at once, for there may be danger in it. I feel it by myself, but I know that my resources are sufficient; and now that those first giddy raptures have subsided, I have a quiet home-feeling of the blessedness of my condition. I am in no hurry. Having all holidays, I am as though I had none. If Time hung heavy upon me, I could walk it away; but I do *not* walk all day long, as I used to do in those old transient holidays, thirty miles a day, to make the most of them. If Time were troublesome, I could read it away; but I do *not* read in that violent measure, with which, having no Time in my own but candlelight Time, I used to weary out my head and eyesight in bygone winters. I walk, read, or scribble (as now), just when the fit seizes me. I no longer hunt after pleasure; I let it come to me. I am like the man

———— that's born, and has his years come to him,
In some green desert.

'Years!' you will say; 'what is this superannuated simpleton calculating upon? He has already told us he is past fifty.'

I have indeed lived nominally fifty years, but deduct out of them the hours which I have lived to other people, and not to myself, and you will find me still a young fellow. For *that* is the only true Time, which a man can properly call his own, that which he has all to himself; the rest, though in some sense he may be said to live it, is other people's Time, not his. The remnant of my poor days, long or short, is at least multiplied for me threefold. My ten next years, if I stretch so far, will be as long as any preceding thirty. 'Tis a fair rule-of-three sum.

Among the strange fantasies which beset me at the commencement of my freedom, and of which all traces are not yet gone, one was, that a vast tract of time had intervened since I quitted the Counting House. I could not conceive of it as an affair of yesterday. The partners, and the clerks with whom I had for so many years, and for so many hours in each day of the year, been closely associated—being suddenly removed from them—they seemed as dead to me. There is a fine passage, which may serve to illustrate this fancy, in a Tragedy by Sir Robert Howard, speaking of a friend's death:—

> ———— 'Twas but just now he went away;
> I have not since had time to shed a tear;
> And yet the distance does the same appear
> As if he had been a thousand years from me.
> Time takes no measure in Eternity.

To dissipate this awkward feeling, I have been fain to go among them once or twice since; to visit my old desk-fellows—my co-brethren of the quill—that I had left below in the state militant. Not all the kindness with which they received me could quite restore to me that pleasant familiarity, which I had heretofore enjoyed among them. We cracked some of our old jokes, but methought they went off but faintly. My old desk; the peg where I hung my hat, were appropriated to another. I knew it must be, but I could not take it kindly. D——l take me, if I did not feel some remorse —beast, if I had not—at quitting my old compeers, the faithful partners of my toils for six-and-thirty years, that smoothed for me with their jokes and conundrums the rugged-ness of my professional road. Had it been so rugged then, after all? or was I a coward simply? Well, it is too late to repent; and I also know that these suggestions are a common fallacy of the mind on such occasions. But my heart smote me. I had violently broken the bands betwixt us. It was at least not courteous. I shall be some time before I get quite reconciled to the separation. Farewell, old cronies, yet not for long, for again and again I will come among ye, if I shall have your leave. Farewell, Ch——, dry, sarcastic, and friendly! Do——, mild, slow to move, and gentlemanly! Pl——, officious to do, and to volunteer, good services!— and thou, thou dreary pile, fit mansion for a Gresham or a Whittington of old, stately house of Merchants; with thy labyrinthine passages, and light-excluding, pent-up offices, where candles for one-half the year supplied the place of the sun's light; unhealthy contributor to my weal, stern fosterer of my living, farewell! In thee remain, and not in the obscure collection of some wandering bookseller, my 'works'! There let them rest, as I do from my labours, piled on thy massy shelves, more MSS. in folio than ever Aquinas left, and full as useful! My mantle I bequeath among ye.

A fortnight has passed since the date of my first communication. At that period I was approaching to tranquillity, but had not reached it. I boasted of a calm indeed, but it was comparative only. Something of the first flutter was left; an unsettling sense of novelty; the dazzle to weak eyes of unaccustomed light. I missed my old chains, forsooth, as if they had been some necessary part of my apparel. I was a poor Carthusian, from strict cellular discipline suddenly by some revolution returned upon the world. I am now as if I had never been other than my own master. It is natural to me to go where I please, to do what I please. I find myself at eleven o'clock in the day in Bond Street, and it seems to me that I have been sauntering there at that very hour for years past. I digress into Soho, to explore a book-stall. Methinks I have been thirty years a collector. There is nothing strange nor new in it. I find myself before a fine picture in the morning. Was it ever otherwise? What is become of Fish Street Hill? Where is Fenchurch Street? Stones of old Mincing Lane, which I have worn with my daily pilgrimage for six-and-thirty years, to the footsteps of what toil-worn clerk are your everlasting flints now vocal? I indent the gayer flags of Pall Mall. It is 'Change time, and I am strangely among the Elgin marbles. It was no hyperbole when I ventured to compare the change in my condition to a passing into another world. Time stands still in a manner to me. I have lost all distinction of season. I do not know the day of the week or of the month. Each day used to be individually felt by me in its reference to the foreign post days; in its distance from, or propinquity to, the next Sunday. I had my Wednesday feelings, my Saturday nights' sensations. The genius of each day was upon me distinctly during the whole of it, affecting my appetite, spirits, etc. The phantom of the next day, with the dreary five to follow, sate as a load upon my poor Sabbath recreations. What charm has washed that Ethiop white? What is gone of Black Monday? All days are the same. Sunday itself—that unfortunate failure of a holiday, as it too often proved, what with my sense of its fugitiveness, and over-care to get the greatest quantity of pleasure out of it—is melted down into a week day. I can spare to go to church now, without grudging the huge cantle which it used to seem to cut out of the holiday. I have Time for everything. I can visit a sick friend. I can interrupt the man of much occupation when he is busiest. I can insult over him with an invitation to take a day's pleasure with me to Windsor this fine May-morning. It is Lucretian pleasure to behold the poor drudges, whom I have left behind in the world, carking and caring; like horses in a mill, drudging on in the same eternal round—and what is it all for? A man can never have too much Time to himself, nor too little to do. Had I a little son, I would christen him NOTHING-TO-DO; he should do nothing. Man, I verily believe, is out of his element as long as he is operative. I am altogether for the life contemplative. Will no kindly earthquake come and swallow up those accursed cotton mills? Take me that lumber of a desk there, and bowl it down

As low as to the fiends.

I am not longer *****, clerk to the Firm of, etc. I am Retired Leisure. I am to be met with in trim gardens. I am already come to be known by my vacant face and careless gesture, perambulating at no fixed pace, nor with any settled purpose. I walk about; not to and from. They tell me, a certain *cum dignitate* air, that has been buried so long with my other good parts, has begun to shoot forth in my person. I grow into gentility perceptibly. When I take up a newspaper, it is to read the state of the opera. *Opus operatum est.* I have done all that I came into this world to do. I have worked task-work, and have the rest of the day to myself.

The Genteel Style in Writing

IT is an ordinary criticism, that my Lord Shaftesbury, and Sir William Temple, are models of the genteel style in writing. We should prefer saying—of the lordly, and the gentlemanly. Nothing can be more unlike, than the inflated finical rhapsodies of Shaftesbury and the plain natural chit-chat of Temple. The man of rank is discernible in both writers; but in the one it is only insinuated gracefully, in the other it stands out offensively. The peer seems to have written with his coronet on, and his Earl's mantle before him; the commoner in his elbow-chair and undress.—What can be more pleasant than the way in which the retired statesman peeps out in his essays, penned by the latter in his delightful retreat at Shene? They scent of Nimeguen and the Hague. Scarce an authority is quoted under an ambassa-dor. Don Francisco de Melo, a 'Portugal Envoy in England,' tells him it was frequent in his country for men, spent with age and other decays, so as they could not hope for above a year or two of life, to ship themselves away in a Brazil fleet, and after their arrival there to go on a great length, some-times of twenty or thirty years, or more, by the force of that vigour they recovered with that remove. 'Whether such an effect (Temple beautifully adds) might grow from the air, or the fruits of that climate, or by approaching nearer the sun, which is the fountain of light and heat, when their natural heat was so far decayed: or whether the piecing out of an old man's life were worth the pains; I cannot tell: perhaps the play is not worth the candle.' Monsieur Pompone, 'French Ambassador in his (Sir William's) time at the Hague,' certifies him, that in his life he had never heard of any man in France that arrived at a hundred years of age; a limitation of life which the old gentleman imputes to the excellence of their climate, giving them such a liveliness of temper and humour, as disposes them to more pleasures of all kinds than in other countries; and moralises upon the matter very sensibly. The 'late Robert Earl of Leicester' furnishes him with a story of a Countess of Desmond, married out of

England in Edward the Fourth's time, and who lived far in King James's reign. The 'same noble person' gives him an account, how such a year, in the same reign, there went about the country a set of morrice-dancers, composed of ten men who danced, a Maid Marian, and a tabor and pipe; and how these twelve, one with another, made up twelve hundred years. 'It was not so much (says Temple) that so many in one small county (Hertfordshire) should live to that age, as that they should be in vigour and in humour to travel and to dance.' Monsieur Zulichem, one of his 'colleagues at the Hague,' informs him of a cure for the gout; which is confirmed by another 'Envoy,' Monsieur Serinchamps, in that town, who had tried it.—Old Prince Maurice of Nassau recommends to him the use of hammocks in that complaint; having been allured to sleep, while suffering under it himself, by the 'constant motion or swinging of those airy beds.' Count Egmont, and the Rhinegrave who 'was killed last summer before Maestricht,' impart to him their experiences.

But the rank of the writer is never more innocently disclosed, than where he takes for granted the compliments paid by foreigners to his fruit-trees. For the taste and perfection of what we esteem the best, he can truly say, that the French, who have eaten his peaches and grapes at Shene in no very ill year, have generally concluded that the last are as good as any they have eaten in France on this side Fontainebleau; and the first as good as any they have eat in Gascony. Italians have agreed his white figs to be as good as any of that sort in Italy, which is the earlier kind of white fig there; for in the later kind and the blue, we cannot come near the warm climates, no more than in the Frontignac or Muscat grape. His orange-trees, too, are as large as any he saw when he was young in France, except those of Fontainebleau; or what he has seen since in the Low Countries, except some very old ones of the Prince of Orange's. Of grapes he had the honour of bringing over four sorts into England, which he enumerates, and supposes that they are all by this time pretty common among some gardeners in his neighbourhood, as well as several persons of quality; for he ever thought all things of this kind 'the commoner they are made the better.' The garden pedantry with which he asserts that 'tis to little purpose to plant any of the best fruits, as peaches or grapes, hardly, he doubts, beyond Northamptonshire at the furthest northwards; and praises the 'Bishop of Munster at Cosevelt,' for attempting nothing beyond cherries in that cold climate; is equally pleasant and in character. 'I may perhaps' (he thus ends his sweet Garden Essay with a passage worthy of Cowley) 'be allowed to know something of this trade, since I have so long allowed myself to be good for nothing else, which few men will do, or enjoy their gardens, without often looking abroad to see how other matters play, what motions in the state, and what invitations they may hope for into other scenes. For my own part, as the country life, and this part of it more particularly, were the inclination of my youth itself, so they are the pleasure of my age; and I can truly say that, among many great employments that have fallen to my share, I have never asked or sought for any of them, but have often endeavoured to escape from them, into the ease and freedom of a private scene, where a man may go his own way and his own pace, in the common paths and circles of life. The measure of choosing well is whether a man likes what he has chosen, which, I thank God, has befallen me; and though among the follies of my life, building and planting have not been the least, and have cost me more than I have the confidence to own; yet they have been fully recompensed by the sweetness and satisfaction of this retreat, where, since my resolution taken of never entering again into any public employments, I have passed five years without ever once going to town, though I am almost in sight of it, and have a house there always ready to receive me. Nor has this been any sort of affectation, as some have thought it, but a mere want of desire or humour to make so small a remove; for when I am in this corner, I can truly say with Horace, *Me quoties reficit, etc.*'

> Me, when the cold Digentian stream revives,
> What does my friend believe I think or ask?
> Let me yet less possess, so I may live,
> Whate'er of life remains, unto myself.
> May I have books enough; and one year's store,
> Not to depend upon each doubtful hour:
> This is enough of mighty Jove to pray,
> Who, as he pleases, gives and takes away.

The writings of Temple are, in general, after this easy copy. On one occasion, indeed, his wit, which was mostly subordinate to nature and tenderness, has seduced him into a string of felicitous antitheses; which, it is obvious to remark, have been a model to Addison and succeeding essayists. 'Who would not be covetous, and with reason,' he says, 'if health could be purchased with gold? who not ambitious, if it were at the command of power, or restored by honour? but, alas! a white staff will not help gouty feet to walk better than a common cane; nor a blue riband bind up a wound so well as a fillet. The glitter of gold, or of diamonds, will but hurt sore eyes instead of curing them; and an aching head will be no more eased by wearing a crown than a common night-cap.' In a far better style, and more accordant with his own humour of plainness, are the concluding sentences of his 'Discourse upon Poetry.' Temple took a part in the controversy about the ancient and the modern learning; and, with that partiality so natural and so graceful in an old man, whose state engagements had left him little leisure to look into modern productions, while his retirement gave him occasion to look back upon the classic studies of his youth—decided in favour of the latter. 'Certain it is,' he says, 'that, whether the fierceness of the Gothic humours, or noise of their perpetual wars, frighted it away, or that the unequal mixture of the modern languages would not bear it—the great heights and excellency both of poetry and music fell with the Roman learning and empire, and have never since recovered the admiration and applauses that before attended them. Yet, such as they are amongst us, they must be confessed to be the softest and the sweetest, the most general and most innocent amusements of common time and life. They still find room in the courts of princes, and the cottages of shepherds. They serve to revive and animate the dead calm of poor and idle lives, and to allay or divert the violent passions and perturbations of the greatest and the busiest men. And both these effects are of equal use to human life; for the mind of man is like the sea, which is neither agreeable to the beholder nor the voyager, in a calm or in a storm, but is so to both when a little agitated by gentle gales; and so the mind, when moved by soft and easy passions or affections. I know very well that many who pretend to be wise by the forms of being grave, are apt to despise both poetry and music, as toys and trifles too light for the use or entertainment of serious men. But whoever find themselves wholly insensible to their charms, would, I think, do well to keep their own counsel, for fear of reproaching their own temper, and bringing the goodness of their natures, if not of their understandings, into question, While this world lasts, I doubt not but the pleasure and request of these two entertainments will do so too; and happy those that content themselves with these, or any other so easy and so innocent, and do not trouble the world or other men, because they cannot be quiet themselves, though nobody hurts them.' 'When all is done (he concludes), human life is at the greatest and the best but like a froward child, that must be played with, and humoured a little, to keep it quiet, till it falls asleep, and then the care is over.'

Barbara S——

On the noon of the 14th of November, 1743 or 4, I forget which it was, just as the clock had struck one, Barbara S——, with her accustomed punctuality, ascended the long rambling staircase, with awkward interposed landing-places, which led to the office, or rather a sort of box with a desk in it, whereat sat the then Treasurer of (what few of our readers may remember) the Old Bath Theatre. All over the island it was the custom, and remains so I believe to this day, for the players to receive their weekly stipend on the Saturday. It was not much that Barbara had to claim.

This little maid had just entered her eleventh year; but her important station at the theatre, as it seemed to her, with the benefits which she felt to accrue from her pious application of her small earnings, had given an air of womanhood to her steps and to her behaviour. You would have taken her to have been at least five years older.

Till latterly she had merely been employed in choruses, or where children were wanted to fill up the scene. But the manager, observing a diligence and adroitness in her above her age, had for some few months past intrusted to her the performance of whole parts. You may guess the self-consequence of the promoted Barbara. She had already drawn tears in young Arthur; had rallied Richard with infantine petulance in the Duke of York; and in her turn had rebuked

253

that petulance when she was Prince of Wales. She would have done the elder child in Morton's pathetic after—piece to the life; but as yet the 'Children in the Wood' was not.

Long after this little girl was grown an aged woman, I have seen some of these small parts, each making two or three pages at most, copied out in the rudest hand of the then prompter, who doubtless transcribed a little more carefully and fairly for the grown-up tragedy ladies of the establishment. But such as they were, blotted and scrawled, as for a child's use, she kept them all; and in the zenith of her after reputation it was a delightful sight to behold them bound up in costliest morocco, each single—each small part making a *book*—with fine clasps, gilt-splashed, etc. She had conscientiously kept them as they had been delivered to her; not a blot had been effaced or tampered with. They were precious to her for their affecting remembrancings. They were her principia, her rudiments; the elementary atoms; the little steps by which she pressed forward to perfection. 'What,' she would say, 'could India-rubber, or a pumice-stone, have done for these darlings?'

I am in no hurry to begin my story—indeed I have little or none to tell—so I will just mention an observation of hers connected with that interesting time.

Not long before she died I had been discoursing with her on the quantity of real present emotion which a great tragic performer experiences during acting. I ventured to think, that though in the first instance such players must have possessed the feelings which they so powerfully called up in others, yet by frequent repetition those feelings must become deadened in great measure, and the performer trust to the memory of past emotion, rather than express a present one. She indignantly repelled the notion, that with a truly great tragedian the operation, by which such effects were produced upon an audience, could ever degrade itself into what was purely mechanical. With much delicacy, avoiding to instance in her *self*-experience, she told me, that so long ago as when she used to play the part of the Little Son to Mrs. Porter's Isabella (I think it was), when that impressive actress has been bending over her in some heart-rending colloquy, she has felt real hot tears come trickling from her, which (to use her powerful expression) have perfectly scalded her back.

I am not quite so sure that it was Mrs. Porter; but it was

some great actress of that day. The name is indifferent; but the fact of the scalding tears I most distinctly remember.

I was always fond of the society of players, and am not sure that an impediment in my speech (which certainly kept me out of the pulpit) even more than certain personal disqualifications, which are often got over in that profession, did not prevent me at one time of life from adopting it. I have had the honour (I must ever call it) once to have been admitted to the tea-table of Miss Kelly. I have played at serious whist with Mr. Liston. I have chatted with ever good-humoured Mrs. Charles Kemble. I have conversed as friend to friend with her accomplished husband. I have been indulged with a classical conference with Macready; and with a sight of the Player-picture gallery, at Mr. Mathews's, when the kind owner, to remunerate me for my love of the old actors (whom he loves so much), went over it with me, supplying to his capital collection, what alone the artist could not give them—voice; and their living motion. Old tones, half-faded, of Dodd, and Parsons, and Baddeley, have lived again for me at his bidding. Only Edwin he could not restore to me. I have supped with——; but I am growing a coxcomb.

As I was about to say—at the desk of the then treasurer of the old Bath theatre—not Diamond's—presented herself the little Barbara S——.

The parents of Barbara had been in reputable circumstances. The father had practised, I believe, as an apothecary in the town. But his practice, from causes which I feel my own infirmity too sensibly that way to arraign—or perhaps from that pure infelicity which accompanies some people in their walk through life, and which it is impossible to lay at the door of imprudence—was now reduced to nothing. They were in fact in the very teeth of starvation, when the manager, who knew and respected them in better days, took the little Barbara into his company.

At the period I commenced with, her slender earnings were the sole support of the family, including two younger sisters. I must throw a veil over some mortifying circumstances. Enough to say, that her Saturday's pittance was the only chance of a Sunday's (generally their only) meal of meat.

One thing I will only mention, that in some child's part, where in her theatrical character she was to sup off a roast fowl (O joy to Barbara!) some comic actor, who was for the night caterer for this dainty—in the misguided humour of his part, threw over the dish such a quantity of salt (O grief and pain of heart to Barbara!) that when she crammed a portion of it into her mouth, she was obliged sputteringly to reject it; and what with shame of her ill-acted part, and pain of real appetite at missing such a dainty, her little heart sobbed almost to breaking, till a flood of tears, which the well-fed spectators were totally unable to comprehend, mercifully relieved her.

This was the little starved, meritorious maid, who stood before old Ravenscroft, the treasurer, for her Saturday's payment.

Ravenscroft was a man, I have heard many old theatrical people besides herself say, of all men least calculated for a treasurer. He had no head for accounts, paid away at random, kept scarce any books, and summing up at the week's end, if he found himself a pound or so deficient, blest himself that it was no worse.

Now Barbara's weekly stipend was a bare half guinea.— By mistake he popped into her hand—a whole one.

Barbara tripped away.

She was entirely unconscious at first of the mistake: God knows, Ravenscroft would never have discovered it.

But when she had got down to the first of those uncouth landing-places, she became sensible of an unusual weight of metal pressing her little hand.

Now mark the dilemma.

She was by nature a good child. From her parents and those about her she had imbibed no contrary influence. But then they had taught her nothing. Poor men's smoky cabins are not always porticoes of moral philosophy. This little maid had no instinct to evil, but then she might be said to have no fixed principle. She had heard honesty commended, but never dreamed of its application to herself. She thought of it as something which concerned grown-up people, men and women. She had never known temptation, or thought of preparing resistance against it.

Her first impulse was to go back to the old treasurer, and explain to him his blunder. He was already so confused with age, besides a natural want of punctuality, that she would have had some difficulty in making him understand it. She saw *that* in an instant. And then it was such a bit of money! and then the image of a larger allowance of butcher's-meat on their table next day came across her, till her little eyes glistened, and her mouth moistened. But then Mr. Ravenscroft had always been so good-natured, had stood her friend behind the scenes, and even recommended her promotion to some of her little parts. But again the old man was reputed to be worth a world of money. He was supposed to have fifty pounds a year clear of the theatre. And then came staring upon her the figures of her little stockingless and shoeless sisters. And when she looked at her own neat white cotton stockings, which her situation at the theatre had made it indispensable for her mother to provide for her, with hard straining and pinching from the family stock, and thought how glad she should be to cover their poor feet with the same—and how then they could accompany her to rehearsals, which they had hitherto been precluded from doing, by reason of their unfashionable attire,—in these thoughts she reached the second landing-place—the second, I mean, from the top—for there was still another left to traverse.

Now virtue support Barbara!

And that never-failing friend did step in—for at that moment a strength not her own, I have heard her say, was revealed to her—a reason above reasoning—and without her own agency, as it seemed (for she never felt her feet to move), she found herself transported back to the individual desk she had just quitted, and her hand in the old hand of Ravenscroft, who in silence took back the refunded treasure, and who had been sitting (good man) insensible to the lapse of minutes, which to her were anxious ages, and from that moment a deep peace fell upon her heart, and she knew the quality of honesty.

A year or two's unrepining application to her profession brightened up the feet and the prospects of her little sisters, set the whole family upon their legs again, and released her from the difficulty of discussing moral dogmas upon a landing-place.

I have heard her say that it was a surprise, not much short of mortification to her, to see the coolness with which the old man pocketed the difference, which had caused her such mortal throes.

This anecdote of herself I had in the year 1800, from the

mouth of the late Mrs. Crawford,* then sixty-seven years of age (she died soon after); and to her struggles upon this childish occasion I have sometimes ventured to think her indebted for that power of rending the heart in the representation of conflicting emotions, for which in after years she was considered as little inferior (if at all so in the part of Lady Randolph) even to Mrs. Siddons.

The Tombs in the Abbey

IN A LETTER TO R——S——, ESQ.

THOUGH in some points of doctrine, and perhaps of discipline, I am diffident of lending a perfect assent to that church which you have so worthily *historified*, yet may the ill time never come to me, when with a chilled heart or a portion of irreverent sentiment, I shall enter her beautiful and time-hallowed Edifices. Judge, then, of my mortification when, after attending the choral anthems of last Wednesday at Westminster, and being desirous of renewing my acquaintance, after lapsed years, with the tombs and antiquities there, I found myself excluded; turned out, like a dog, or some profane person, into the common street, with feelings not very congenial to the place, or to the solemn service which I had been listening to. It was a jar after that music.

You had your education at Westminster; and doubtless among those dim aisles and cloisters, you must have gathered much of that devotional feeling in those young years, on which your purest mind feeds still—and may it feed! The antiquarian spirit, strong in you, and gracefully blending ever with the religious, may have been sown in you among those wrecks of splendid mortality. You owe it to the place of your education; you owe it to your learned fondness for the architecture of your ancestors; you owe it to the venerableness of your ecclesiastical establishment, which is daily lessened and called in question through these practices—to speak aloud your sense of them; never to desist raising your voice against them, till they be totally done away with and

* The maiden name of this lady was Street, which she changed, by successive marriages, for those of Dancer, Barry, and Crawford. She was Mrs. Crawford, a third time a widow, when I knew her.

abolished; till the doors of Westminster Abbey be no longer closed against the decent, though low-in-purse, enthusiast, or blameless devotee, who must commit an injury against his family economy, if he would be indulged with a bare admission within its walls. You owe it to the decencies, which you wish to see maintained, in its impressive services, that our Cathedral be no longer an object of inspection to the poor at those times only, in which they must rob from their attendance on the worship every minute which they can bestow upon the fabric. In vain the public prints have taken up this subject,—in vain such poor, nameless writers as myself express their indignation. A word from you, sir,—a hint in your Journal—would be sufficient to fling open the doors of the Beautiful Temple again, as we can remember them when we were boys. At that time of life, what would the imaginative faculty (such as it is) in both of us, have suffered, if the entrance to so much reflection had been obstructed by the demand of so much silver!—If we had scraped it up to gain an occasional admission (as we certainly should have done) would the sight of those tombs have been as impressive to us (while we have been weighing anxiously prudence against sentiment) as when the gates stood open as those of the adjacent Park; when we could walk in at any time, as the mood brought us, for a shorter or longer time, as that lasted? Is the being shown over a place the same as silently for ourselves detecting the genius of it? In no part of our beloved Abbey now can a person find entrance (out of service time) under the sum of *two shillings*. The rich and the great will smile at the anti-climax, presumed to lie in these two short words. But you can tell them, sir, how much quiet worth, how much capacity for enlarged feeling, how much taste and genius, may coexist, especially in youth, with a purse incompetent to this demand. A respected friend of ours, during his late visit to the metropolis, presented himself for admission to St. Paul's. At the same time a decently clothed man, with as decent a wife and child, were bargaining for the same indulgence. The price was only twopence each person. The poor but decent man hesitated, desirous to go in; but there were three of them, and he turned away reluctantly. Perhaps he wished to have seen the tomb of Nelson. Perhaps the Interior of the Cathedral was his object. But in the state of his finances, even sixpence might reasonably seem too much. Tell the Aristocracy of the country (no man can do it more impressively); instruct them of what value these insignificant pieces of money, these minims to their sight, may be to their humbler brethren. Shame these Sellers out of the Temple. Stifle not the suggestions of your better nature with the pretext, that an indiscriminate admission would expose the Tombs to violation. Remember your boy-days. Did you ever see, or hear, of a mob in the Abbey, while it was free to all? Do the rabble come there, or trouble their heads about such speculations? It is all that you can do to drive them into your churches; they do not voluntarily offer themselves. They have, alas! no passion for antiquities; for tomb of king or prelate, sage or poet. If they had, they would be no longer the rabble.

For forty years that I have known the Fabric, the only well-attested charge of violation adduced has been—a ridiculous dismemberment committed upon the effigy of that amiable spy, Major André. And is it for this—the wanton mischief of some schoolboy, fired perhaps with raw notions of Transatlantic Freedom—or the remote possibility of such a mischief occurring again, so easily to be prevented by stationing a constable within the walls, if the vergers are incompetent to the duty—is it upon such wretched pretences that the people of England are made to pay a new Peter's Pence, so long abrogated; or must content themselves with contemplating the ragged Exterior of their Cathedral? The mischief was done about the time that you were a scholar there. Do you know anything about the unfortunate relic?—

Amicus Redivivus

Where were ye, Nymphs, when the remorseless deep
Closed o'er the head of your loved Lycidas?

I DO not know when I have experienced a stranger sensation, than on seeing my old friend, G. D., who had been paying me a morning visit, a few Sundays back, at my cottage at Islington, upon taking leave, instead of turning down the right-hand path by which he had entered—with staff in hand, and at noonday, deliberately march right forwards into the midst of the stream that runs by us, and totally disappear.

A spectacle like this at dusk would have been appalling enough; but in the broad, open daylight, to witness such an unreserved motion towards self-destruction in a valued friend, took from me all power of speculation.

How I found my feet I know not. Consciousness was quite gone. Some spirit, not my own, whirled me to the spot. I remember nothing but the silvery apparition of a good white head emerging; nigh which a staff (the hand unseen that wielded it) pointed upwards, as feeling for the skies. In a moment (if time was in that time) he was on my shoulders; and I—freighted with a load more precious than his who bore Anchises.

And here I cannot but do justice to the officious zeal of sundry passers-by, who, albeit arriving a little too late to participate in the honours of the rescue, in philanthropic shoals came thronging to communicate their advice as to the recovery; prescribing variously the application, or non-application, of salt, etc., to the person of the patient. Life, meantime, was ebbing fast away, amidst the stifle of conflicting judgments, when one, more sagacious than the rest, by a bright thought, proposed sending for the Doctor. Trite as the counsel was, and impossible, as one should think, to be missed on,—shall I confess?—in this emergency it was to me as if an Angel had spoken. Great previous exertions— and mine had not been inconsiderable—are commonly followed by a debility of purpose. This was a moment of irresolution.

MONOCULUS—for so, in default of catching his true name, I choose to designate the medical gentleman who now appeared—is a grave, middle-aged person, who, without having studied at the college, or truckled to the pedantry of a diploma, hath employed a great portion of his valuable time in experimental processes upon the bodies of unfortunate fellow-creatures, in whom the vital spark, to mere vulgar thinking, would seem extinct and lost for ever. He omitteth no occasion of obtruding his services, from a case of common surfeit suffocation to the ignobler obstructions, sometimes induced by a too-wilful application of the plant *cannabis* outwardly. But though he declineth not altogether these drier extinctions, his occupation tendeth, for the most part, to water-practice; for the convenience of which, he hath judiciously fixed his quarter near the grand repository of the stream mentioned, where day and night, from his little watch-tower, at the Myddelton Head, he listeneth to detect the wrecks of drowned mortality—partly, as he saith, to be upon the spot—and partly, because the liquids which he useth to prescribe to himself and his patients, on these distressing occasions, are ordinarily more conveniently to be found at these common hostelries than in the shops and phials of the apothecaries. His ear hath arrived to such finesse by practice, that it is reported he can distinguish a plunge, at half a furlong distance; and can tell if it be casual or deliberate. He weareth a medal, suspended over a suit, originally of a sad brown, but which, by time and frequency of nightly divings, has been dinged into a true professional sable. He passeth by the name of Doctor, and is remarkable for wanting his left eye. His remedy—after a sufficient application of warm blankets, friction, etc., is a simple tumbler or more, of the purest Cognac, with water, made as hot as the convalescent can bear it. Where he findeth, as in the case of my friend, a squeamish subject, he condescendeth to be the taster; and showeth, by his own example, the innocuous nature of the prescription. Nothing can be more kind or encouraging than this procedure. It addeth confidence to the patient, to see his medical adviser go hand in hand with himself in the remedy. When the doctor swalloweth his own draught, what peevish invalid can refuse to pledge him in the potion? In fine, MONOCULUS is a humane, sensible man, who, for a slender pittance, scarce enough to sustain life, is content to wear it out in the endeavour to save the lives of others—his pretensions so moderate that with difficulty I could press a crown upon him, for the price of restoring the existence of such an invaluable creature to society as G. D.

It was pleasant to observe the effect of the subsiding alarm upon the nerves of the dear absentee. It seemed to have given a shake to memory, calling up notice after notice, of all the providential deliverances he had experienced in the course of his long and innocent life. Sitting up in my couch—my couch which, naked and void of furniture hitherto, for the salutary repose which it administered, shall be honoured with costly valance, at some price, and henceforth be a state-bed at Colebrook,—he discoursed of marvellous escapes—by carelessness of nurses—by pails of gelid, and kettles of the boiling element, in infancy—by orchard pranks, and snapping twigs, in schoolboy frolics—by descent of tiles at Trumpington, and of heavier tomes at Pembroke—by studious watchings, inducing frightful vigilance—by want, and the fear of want, and all the sore throbbings of the learned head.— Anon, he would burst out into little fragments of chanting —of songs long ago—ends of deliverance hymns, not remembered before since childhood, but coming up now, when his heart was made tender as a child's—for the *tremor cordis*, in the retrospect of a recent deliverance, as in the case of impending danger, acting upon an innocent heart, will produce a self-tenderness, which we should do ill to christen cowardice; and Shakspeare, in the latter crisis, has made his good Sir Hugh to remember the sitting by Babylon, and to mutter of shallow rivers.

Waters of Sir Hugh Myddelton—what a spark you were like to have extinguished for ever! Your salubrious streams to this City, for now near two centuries, would hardly have atoned for what you were in a moment washing away. Mockery of a river—liquid artifice—wretched conduit! henceforth rank with canals and sluggish aqueducts. Was it for this that, smit in boyhood with the explorations of that Abyssinian traveller, I paced the vales of Amwell to explore your tributary springs, to trace your salutary waters sparkling through green Hertfordshire, and cultured Enfield parks?— —Ye have no swans—no Naiads—no river God—or did the benevolent hoary aspect of my friend tempt ye to suck him in, that ye also might have the tutelary genius of your waters?

Had he been drowned in Cam, there would have been some consonancy in it; but what willows had ye to wave and rustle over his moist sepulture?—or, having no *name*, besides that unmeaning assumption of *eternal novity*, did ye think to get one by the noble prize, and henceforth to be termed the STREAM DYERIAN?

> And could such spacious virtue find a grave
> Beneath the imposthumed bubble of a wave?

I protest, George, you shall not venture out again—no, not by daylight—without a sufficient pair of spectacles—in your musing moods especially. Your absence of mind we have borne, till your presence of body came to be called in question by it. You shall not go wandering into Euripus with Aristotle, if we can help it. Fie, man, to turn dipper at your years, after your many tracts in favour of sprinkling only!

I have nothing but water in my head o'nights since this frightful accident. Sometimes I am with Clarence in his dream. At others, I behold Christian beginning to sink, and crying out to his good brother Hopeful (that is, to me), 'I sink in deep waters; the billows go over my head, all the waves go over me. Selah.' Then I have before me Palinurus, just letting go the steerage. I cry out too late to save. Next follow—a mournful procession—*suicidal faces*, saved against their will from drowning; dolefully trailing a length of reluctant gratefulness, with ropy weeds pendent from locks of watchet hue—constrained Lazari—Pluto's half-subjects—stolen fees from the grave—bilking Charon of his fare. At their head Arion—or is it G. D.?—in his singing garments marcheth singly, with harp in hand, and votive garland, which Machaon (or Dr. Hawes) snatcheth straight, intending to suspend it to the stern God of Sea. Then follow dismal streams of Lethe, in which the half-drenched on earth are constrained to drown downright, by wharfs where Ophelia twice acts her muddy death.

And, doubtless, there is some notice in that invisible world when one of us approacheth (as my friend did so lately) to their inexorable precincts. When a soul knocks once, twice, at Death's door, the sensation aroused within the palace must be considerable; and the grim Feature, by modern science so often dispossessed of his prey, must have learned by this time to pity Tantalus.

A pulse assuredly was felt along the line of the Elysian shades, when the near arrival of G. D. was announced by no equivocal indications. From their seats of Asphodel arose the gentler and the graver ghosts—poet, or historian—of Grecian or of Roman lore—to crown with unfading chaplets the half-finished love-labours of their unwearied scholiast. Him Markland expected—him Tyrwhitt hoped to encounter —him the sweet lyrist of Peter House, whom he had barely seen upon earth,* with newest airs prepared to greet——; and patron of the gentle Christ's boy—who should have been his patron through life—the mild Askew, with longing

* Graium *tantum vidit.*

aspirations leaned foremost from his venerable Æsculapian chair, to welcome into that happy company the matured virtues of the man, whose tender scions in the boy he himself upon earth had so prophetically fed and watered.

Some Sonnets of Sir Philip Sydney

SYDNEY's Sonnets—I speak of the best of them—are among the very best of their sort. They fall below the plain moral dignity, the sanctity, and high yet modest spirit of self-approval, of Milton, in his compositions of a similar structure. They are in truth what Milton, censuring the Arcadia, says of that work (to which they are a sort of after-tune or application), 'vain and amatorious' enough, yet the things in their kind (as he confesses to be true of the romance) may be 'full of worth and wit.' They savour of the Courtier, it must be allowed, and not of the Commonwealthsman. But Milton was a Courtier when he wrote the Masque at Ludlow Castle, and still more a Courtier when he composed the Arcades. When the national struggle was to begin, he becomingly cast these vanities behind him; and if the order of time had thrown Sir Philip upon the crisis which preceded the revolution, there is no reason why he should not have acted the same part in that emergency, which has glorified the name of a later Sydney. He did not want for plainness or boldness of spirit. His letter on the French match may testify he could speak his mind freely to Princes. The times did not call him to the scaffold.

The Sonnets which we oftenest call to mind of Milton were the compositions of his maturest years. Those of Sydney, which I am about to produce, were written in the very heyday of his blood. They are stuck full of amorous fancies—far-fetched conceits, befitting his occupation; for True Love thinks no labour to send out Thoughts upon the vast and more than Indian voyages, to bring home rich pearls, outlandish wealth, gums, jewels, spicery, to sacrifice in self-depreciating similitudes, as shadows of true amiabilities in the Beloved. We must be Lovers—or at least the cooling touch of time, the *circum præcordia frigus*, must not have so damped our faculties, as to take away our recollection that we were once so—before we can duly appreciate the glorious vanities, and graceful hyperboles, of the passion. The images which lie before our feet (though by some accounted the only natural) are least natural for the high Sydnean love to express its fancies by. They may serve for the loves of Tibullus, or the dear Author of the Schoolmistress; for passions that creep and whine in Elegies and Pastoral Ballads. I am sure Milton never loved at this rate. I am afraid some of his addresses (*ad Leonoram*, I mean) have rather erred on the farther side; and that the poet came not much short of a religious inde-corum, when he could thus apostrophise a singing-girl:—

> Angelus unicuique suus (sic credite gentes)
>   Obtigit æthereis ales ab ordinibus.
> Quid mirum, Leonora, tibi si gloria major,
>   Nam tua præsentem vox sonat ipsa Deum?
> Aut Deus, aut vacui certè mens tertia cœli,
>   Per tua secreto guttura serpit agens;
> Serpit agens, facilisque docet mortalia corda
>   Sensim immortali assuescere posse sono.
> QUOD SI CUNCTA QUIDEM DEUS EST, PER CUNCTAQUE FUSUS,
> IN TE UNA LOQUITUR, CÆTERA MUTUS HABET.

This is loving in a strange fashion; and it requires some candour of construction (besides the slight darkening of a dead language) to cast a veil over the ugly appearance of something very like blasphemy in the last two verses. I think the Lover would have been staggered if he had gone about to express the same thought in English. I am sure Sydney has no flights like this. His extravaganzas do not strike at the sky, though he takes leave to adopt the pale Dian into a fellowship with his mortal passions.

1

> With how sad steps, O Moon, thou climb'st the skies;
> How silently; and with how wan a face!
> What! may it be, that even in heavenly place
> That busy Archer his sharp arrow tries?
> Sure, if that long-with-love-acquainted eyes
> Can judge of love, thou feel'st a lover's case;
> I read it in thy looks; thy languisht grace
> To me, that feel the like, thy state descries.
> Then, even of fellowship, O Moon, tell me,
> Is constant love deem'd there but want of wit?

Are beauties there as proud as here they be?
Do they above love to be loved, and yet
Those lovers scorn, whom that love doth possess?
Do they call *virtue* there—*ungratefulness?*

The last line of this poem is a little obscured by transposition. He means, Do they call ungratefulness there a virtue?

2

Come, Sleep, O Sleep, the certain knot of peace,
The baiting-place of wit, the balm of woe,
The poor man's wealth, the prisoner's release,
The indifferent judge between the high and low;
With shield of proof shield me from out the prease*
Of those fierce darts despair at me doth throw;
O make in me those civil wars to cease:
I will good tribute pay if thou do so.
Take thou of me sweet pillows, sweetest bed;
A chamber deaf to noise, and blind to light;
A rosy garland, and a weary head.
And if these things, as being thine by right,
Move not thy heavy grace, thou shalt in me,
Livelier than elsewhere, STELLA's image see.

3

The curious wits, seeing dull pensiveness
Bewray itself in my long-settled eyes,
Whence those same fumes of melancholy rise,
With idle pains, and missing aim, do guess.
Some, that know how my spring I did address,
Deem that my Muse some fruit of knowledge plies;
Others, because the Prince my service tries,
Think, that I think state errors to redress;
But harder judges judge, ambition's rage,
Scourge of itself, still climbing slippery place,
Holds my young brain captived in golden cage.
O fools, or over-wise! alas, the race
Of all my thoughts hath neither stop nor start,
But only STELLA's eyes, and STELLA's heart.

4

Because I oft in dark abstracted guise
Seem most alone in greatest company,
With dearth of words, or answers quite awry,

* Press.

267

To them that would make speech of speech arise;
They deem, and of their doom the rumour flies,
That poison foul of bubbling *Pride* doth lie
So in my swelling breast, that only I
Fawn on myself, and others do despise;
Yet *Pride*, I think, doth not my soul possess,
Which looks too oft in his unflattering glass;
But one worse fault—*Ambition*—I confess,
That makes me oft my best friends overpass,
Unseen, unheard—while Thought to highest place
Bends all his powers, even unto STELLA's grace.

5

Having this day, my horse, my hand, my lance,
Guided so well that I obtained the prize,
Both by the judgment of the English eyes,
And of some sent from that *sweet enemy*,—France;
Horsemen my skill in horsemanship advance;
Townsfolk my strength; a daintier judge applies
His praise to sleight, which from good use doth rise;
Some lucky wits impute it but to chance;
Others, because of both sides I do take
My blood from them, who did excel in this,
Think Nature me a man of arms did make.
How far they shot awry! the true cause is,
STELLA looked on, and from her heavenly face
Sent forth the beams which made so fair my race.

6

In martial sports I had my cunning tried,
And yet to break more staves did me address,
While with the people's shouts (I must confess)
Youth, luck, and praise, even fill'd my veins with pride—
When Cupid having me (his slave) descried
In Mars' livery, prancing in the press,
'What now, Sir Fool!' said he: 'I would no less:
Look here, I say.' I look'd, and STELLA spied,
Who hard by made a window send forth light.
My heart then quaked, then dazzled were mine eyes;
One hand forgot to rule, th' other to fight;
Nor trumpet's sound I heard, nor friendly cries.
My foe came on, and beat the air for me—
Till that her blush made me my shame to see.

7

No more, my dear, no more these counsels try;
O give my passions leave to run their race;
Let Fortune lay on me her worst disgrace;
Let folk o'ercharged with brain against me cry;
Let clouds bedim my face, break in mine eye;
Let me no steps, but of lost labour, trace;
Let all the earth with scorn recount my case—
But do not will me from my love to fly.
I do not envy Aristotle's wit,
Nor do aspire to Cæsar's bleeding fame;
Nor aught do care, though some above me sit;
Nor hope, nor wish, another course to frame,
But that which once may win thy cruel heart:
Thou art my wit, and thou my virtue art.

8

Love still a boy, and oft a wanton, is,
School'd only by his mother's tender eye;
What wonder, then, if he his lesson miss,
When for so soft a rod dear play he try?
And yet my STAR, because a sugar'd kiss
In sport I suck'd, while she asleep did lie,
Doth lour, nay chide, nay threat, for only this.
Sweet, it was saucy LOVE, not humble I.
But no 'scuse serves; she makes her wrath appear
In Beauty's throne—see now who dares comes near
Those scarlet judges, threat'ning bloody pain?
O heav'nly Fool, thy most kiss-worthy face
Anger invests with such a lovely grace,
That anger's self I needs must kiss again.

9

I never drank of Aganippe well,
Nor ever did in shade of Tempe sit,
And Muses scorn with vulgar brains to dwell;
Poor layman I, for sacred rites unfit.
Some do I hear of Poet's fury tell,
But (God wot) wot not what they mean by it;
And this I swear by blackest brook of hell,
I am no pick-purse of another's wit.
How falls it then, that with so smooth an ease
My thoughts I speak, and what I speak doth flow

In verse, and that my verse best wits doth please?
Guess me the cause—what, is it thus?—fye, no.
Or so?—much less. How then? sure thus it is,
My lips are sweet, inspired with STELLA's kiss.

10

Of all the kings that ever here did reign,
Edward, named Fourth, as first in praise I name,
Not for his fair outside, nor well-lined brain—
Although less gifts imp feathers oft on Fame.
Nor that he could, young-wise, wise-valiant, frame
His sire's revenge, join'd with a kingdom's gain;
And, gain'd by Mars could yet mad Mars so tame,
That Balance weigh'd what Sword did late obtain.
Nor that he made the Floure-de-luce so 'fraid,
Though strongly hedged of bloody Lions' paws,
That witty Lewis to him a tribute paid.
Nor this, nor that, nor any such small cause—
But only, for this worthy knight durst prove
To lose his crown rather than fail his love.

11

O happy Thames, that didst my STELLA bear,
I saw thyself, with many a smiling line
Upon thy cheerful face, Joy's livery wear,
While those fair planets on thy streams did shine;
The boat for joy could not to dance forbear,
While wanton winds, with beauty so divine
Ravish'd, stay'd not, till in her golden hair
They did themselves (O sweetest prison) twine.
And fain those Æol's youth there would their stay
Have made; but, forced by nature still to fly,
First did with puffing kiss those locks display.
She, so dishevell'd, blush'd; from window I
With sight thereof cried out, O fair disgrace,
Let honour's self to thee grant highest place!

12

Highway, since you my chief Parnassus be;
And that my Muse, to some ears not unsweet,
Tempers her words to trampling horses' feet,
More soft than to a chamber melody;
Now blessed You bear onward blessed Me
To Her, where I my heart safe left shall meet,

My Muse and I must you of duty greet
With thanks and wishes, wishing thankfully,
Be you still fair, honour'd by public heed,
By no encroachment wrong'd, nor time forgot;
Nor blamed for blood, nor shamed for sinful deed.
And that you know, I envy you no lot
Of highest wish, I wish you so much bliss,
Hundreds of years you STELLA's feet may kiss.

Of the foregoing, the first, the second, and the last sonnet, are my favourites. But the general beauty of them all is, that they are so perfectly characteristical. The spirit of 'learning and of chivalry,'—of which union, Spenser has entitled Sydney to have been the 'president,'—shines through them. I confess I can see nothing of the 'jejune' or 'frigid' in them; much less of the 'stiff' and 'cumbrous'—which I have some-times heard objected to the Arcadia. The verse runs off swiftly and gallantly. It might have been tuned to the trumpet; or tempered (as himself expresses it) to 'trampling horses' feet.' They abound in felicitous phrases—

O heav'nly Fool, thy most kiss-worthy face—
8th Sonnet.

————— Sweet pillows, sweetest bed;
A chamber deaf to noise, and blind to light;
A rosy garland, and a weary head.
2nd Sonnet.

————— That sweet enemy,—France—
5th Sonnet.

But they are not rich in words only, in vague and unlocalised feelings—the failing too much of some poetry of the present day—they are full, material and circumstantiated. Time and place appropriates every one of them. It is not a fever of passion wasting itself upon a thin diet of dainty words, but a transcendent passion pervading and illuminating action, pursuits, studies, feats of arms, the opinions of contemporaries and his judgment of them. An historical thread runs through them, which almost affixes a date to them; marks the *when* and *where* they were written.

I have dwelt the longer upon what I conceive the merit of these poems, because I have been hurt by the wantonness

(I wish I could treat it by a gentler name) with which W. H.
takes every occasion of insulting the memory of Sir Philip
Sydney. But the decisions of the Author of Table Talk, etc.
(most profound and subtle where they are, as for the most
part, just) are more safely to be relied upon, on subjects and
authors he has a partiality for, than on such as he has conceived an accidental prejudice against. Milton wrote sonnets,
and was a king-hater; and it was congenial perhaps to
sacrifice a courtier to a patriot. But I was unwilling to lose
a *fine idea* from my mind. The noble images, passions,
sentiments, and poetical delicacies of character, scattered all
over the Arcadia (spite of some stiffness and encumberment),
justify to me the character which his contemporaries have
left us of the writer. I cannot think with the 'Critic,' that
Sir Philip Sydney was that *opprobrious thing* which a foolish
nobleman in his insolent hostility chose to term him. I call
to mind the epitaph made on him, to guide me to juster
thoughts of him; and I repose upon the beautiful lines in
the 'Friend's Passion for his Astrophel,' printed with the
Elegies of Spenser and others.

> You knew—who knew not Astrophel?
> (That I should live to say I knew,
> And have not in possession still!)—
> Things known permit me to renew—
>   Of him you know his merit such,
>   I cannot say—you hear—too much.
>
> Within these woods of Arcady
> He chief delight and pleasure took;
> And on the mountain Partheny,
> Upon the crystal liquid brook,
> The Muses met him every day,
>   That taught him sing, to write, and say.
>
> When he descended down the mount,
> His personage seemed most divine:
> A thousand graces one might count
> Upon his lovely cheerful eyne.
>   To hear him speak, and sweetly smile,
>   You were in Paradise the while.
>
> *A sweet attractive kind of grace;*
> *A full assurance given by looks;*

Continual comfort in a face,
The lineaments of Gospel books—
I trow that count'nance cannot lye,
Whose thoughts are legible in the eye.

Above all others this is he,
Which erst approvèd in his song,
That love and honour might agree,
And that pure love will do no wrong.
  Sweet saints, it is no sin or blame
  To love a man of virtuous name.

Did never love so sweetly breathe
In any mortal breast before :
Did never Muse inspire beneath
A Poet's brain with finer store.
  He wrote of Love with high conceit,
  And Beauty rear'd above her height.

Or let any one read the deeper sorrows (grief running
into rage) in the Poem,—the last in the collection accompanying the above,—which from internal testimony I believe
to be Lord Brooke's—beginning with 'Silence augmenteth
grief,' and then seriously ask himself, whether the subject
of such absorbing and confounding regrets could have been
that thing which Lord Oxford termed him.

Newspapers Thirty-five Years Ago

DAN STUART once told us, that he did not remember that
he ever deliberately walked into the Exhibition at Somerset
House in his life. He might occasionally have escorted a
party of ladies across the way that were going in; but he
never went in of his own head. Yet the office of the Morning
Post newspaper stood then just where it does now—we are
carrying you back, Reader, some thirty years or more—with
its gilt-globe-topt front facing that emporium of our artists'
grand Annual Exposure. We sometimes wish that we had
observed the same abstinence with Daniel.

A word or two of D. S. He ever appeared to us one of the finest-tempered of Editors. Perry, of the Morning Chronicle, was equally pleasant, with a dash, no slight one either, of the courtier. S. was frank, plain, and English all over. We have worked for both these gentlemen.

It is soothing to contemplate the head of the Ganges; to trace the first little bubblings of a mighty river,

> With holy reverence to approach the rocks,
> Whence glide the streams renowned in ancient song.

Fired with a perusal of the Abyssinian Pilgrim's exploratory ramblings after the cradle of the infant Nilus, we well remember on one fine summer holiday (a 'whole day's leave' we called it at Christ's hospital) sallying forth at rise of sun, not very well provisioned either for such an undertaking, to trace the current of the New River—Myddeltonian stream! —to its scaturient source, as we had read, in meadows by fair Amwell. Gallantly did we commence our solitary quest —for it was essential to the dignity of a DISCOVERY, that no eye of schoolboy, save our own, should beam on the detection. By flowery spots, and verdant lanes skirting Hornsey, Hope trained us on in many a baffling turn; endless, hopeless meanders, as it seemed; or as if the jealous waters had *dodged* us, reluctant to have the humble spot of their nativity revealed; till spent, and nigh famished, before set of the same sun, we sate down somewhere by Bowes Farm near Tottenham, with a tithe of our proposed labours only yet accomplished; sorely convinced in spirit, that that Brucian enterprise was as yet too arduous for our young shoulders.

Not more refreshing to the thirsty curiosity of the traveller is the tracing of some mighty waters up to their shallow fontlet, than it is to a pleased and candid reader to go back to the inexperienced essays, the first callow flights in authorship, of some established name in literature; from the Gnat which preluded to the Æneid, to the Duck which Samuel Johnson trod on.

In those days every Morning Paper, as an essential retainer to its establishment, kept an author, who was bound to furnish daily a quantum of witty paragraphs. Sixpence a joke—and it was thought pretty high too—was Dan Stuart's settled remuneration in these cases. The chat of the day, scandal, but, above all, *dress*, furnished the material. The length of no paragraph was to exceed seven lines. Shorter they might be, but they must be poignant.

A fashion of *flesh*, or rather *pink*-coloured hose for the ladies, luckily coming up at the juncture when we were on our probation for the place of Chief Jester to S.'s Paper, established our reputation in that line. We were pronounced a 'capital hand.' O the conceits which we varied upon *red* in all its prismatic differences! from the trite and obvious flower of Cytherea, to the flaming costume of the lady that has her sitting upon 'many waters.' Then there was the collateral topic of ankles. What an occasion to a truly chaste writer, like ourself, of touching that nice brink, and yet never tumbling over it, of a seemingly ever approximating something 'not quite proper'; while, like a skilful posture-master balancing betwixt decorums and their opposites, he keeps the line, from which a hair's-breadth deviation is destruction; hovering in the confines of light and darkness, or where 'both seem either'; a hazy uncertain delicacy; Autolycus-like in the Play, still putting off his expectant auditory with 'Whoop, do me no harm, good man!' But, above all, that conceit arrided us most at that time, and still tickles our midriff to remember, where, allusively to the flight of Astræa —*ultima Cœlestum terras reliquit*—we pronounced—in reference to the stockings still—that MODESTY, TAKING HER FINAL LEAVE OF MORTALS, HER LAST BLUSH WAS VISIBLE IN HER ASCENT TO THE HEAVENS BY THE TRACT OF THE GLOWING INSTEP. This might be called the crowning conceit: and was esteemed tolerable writing in those days.

But the fashion of jokes, with all other things, passes away; as did the transient mode which had so favoured us. The ankles of our fair friends in a few weeks began to reassume their whiteness, and left us scarce a leg to stand upon. Other female whims followed, but none methought so pregnant, so invitatory of shrewd conceits, and more than single meanings.

Somebody has said, that to swallow six cross-buns daily, consecutively for a fortnight, would surfeit the stoutest digestion. But to have to furnish as many jokes daily, and that not for a fortnight, but for a long twelvemonth, as we were constrained to do, was a little harder exaction. 'Man goeth forth to his work until the evening'—from a reasonable hour in the morning, we presume it was meant. Now, as our main occupation took us up from eight till five every day in the

City; and as our evening hours, at that time of life, had generally to do with anything rather than business, it follows, that the only time we could spare for this manufactory of jokes—our supplementary livelihood, that supplied us in every want beyond mere bread and cheese—was exactly that part of the day which (as we have heard of No Man's Land) may be fitly denominated No Man's Time; that is, no time in which a man ought to be up, and awake, in. To speak more plainly, it is that time of an hour, or an hour and a half's duration, in which a man, whose occasions call him up so preposterously, has to wait for his breakfast.

O those headaches at dawn of day, when at five, or half-past five in summer, and not much later in the dark seasons, we were compelled to rise, having been perhaps not above four hours in bed—(for we were no go-to-beds with the lamb, though we anticipated the lark ofttimes in her rising—we like a parting cup at midnight, as all young men did before these effeminate times, and to have our friends about us—we were not constellated under Aquarius, that watery sign, and therefore incapable of Bacchus, cold, washy, bloodless—we were none of your Basilian water-sponges, nor had taken our degrees at Mount Ague—we were right toping Capulets, jolly companions, we and they)—but to have to get up, as we said before, curtailed of half our fair sleep, fasting, with only a dim vista of refreshing bohea, in the distance—to be necessitated to rouse ourselves at the detestable rap of an old hag of a domestic, who seemed to take a diabolical pleasure in her announcement that it was 'time to rise'; and whose chappy knuckles we have often yearned to amputate, and string them up at our chamber door, to be a terror to all such unseasonable rest-breakers in future——

'Facil' and sweet, as Virgil sings, had been the 'descending' of the over-night, balmy the first sinking of the heavy head upon the pillow; but to get up, as he goes on to say,

—revocare gradus, superasque evadere ad auras—

and to get up, moreover, to make jokes with malice prepended —there was the 'labour,' there the 'work.'

No Egyptian taskmaster ever devised a slavery like to that, our slavery. No fractious operants ever turned out for half the tyranny which this necessity exercised upon us. Half a dozen jests in a day (bating Sundays too), why, it seems nothing! We make twice the number every day in our lives as a matter of course, and claim no Sabbatical exemptions. But then they come into our head. But when the head has to go out to them—when the mountain must go to Mahomet—

Reader, try it for once, only for one short twelvemonth.

It was not every week that a fashion of pink stockings came up; but mostly, instead of it, some rugged untractable subject; some topic impossible to be contorted into the risible; some feature, upon which no smile could play; some flint, from which no process of ingenuity could procure a scintillation. There they lay; there your appointed tale of brick-making was set before you, which you must finish, with or without straw, as it happened. The craving Dragon—*the Public*—like him in Bel's temple—must be fed; it expected its daily rations; and Daniel, and ourselves, to do us justice, did the best we could on this side bursting him.

While we were wringing out coy sprightlinesses for the Post, and writhing under the toil of what is called 'easy writing,' Bob Allen, our *quondam* schoolfellow, was tapping his impracticable brains in a like service for the Oracle. Not that Robert troubled himself much about wit. If his paragraphs had a sprightly air about them, it was sufficient. He carried this nonchalance so far at last, that a matter of intelligence, and that no very important one, was not seldom palmed upon his employers for a good jest; for example sake—'*Walking yesterday morning casually down Snow Hill, who should we meet but Mr. Deputy Humphreys! we rejoice to add, that the worthy Deputy appeared to enjoy a good state of health. We do not remember ever to have seen him look better.*' This gentleman so surprisingly met upon Snow Hill, from some peculiarities in gait or gesture, was a constant butt for mirth to the small paragraph mongers of the day; and our friend thought that he might have his fling at him with the rest. We met A. in Holborn shortly after this extraordinary rencounter, which he told with tears of satisfaction in his eyes, and chuckling at the anticipated effects of its announcement next day in the paper. We did not quite comprehend where the wit of it lay at the time; nor was it easy to be detected, when the thing came out advantaged by type and letter-press. He had better have met anything that morning than a Common Council Man. His services were shortly after dispensed with, on the plea that his paragraphs of late had been deficient in point.

The one in question, it must be owned, had an air, in the opening especially, proper to awaken curiosity; and the sentiment, or moral, wears the aspect of humanity and good neighbourly feeling. But somehow the conclusion was not judged altogether to answer to the magnificent promise of the premises. We traced our friend's pen afterwards in the True Briton, the Star, the Traveller,—from all which he was successively dismissed, the Proprietors having 'no further occasion for his services.' Nothing was easier than to detect him. When wit failed, or topics ran low, there constantly appeared the following:—'*It is not generally known that the three Blue Balls at the Pawnbrokers' shops are the ancient arms of Lombardy. The Lombards were the first money-brokers in Europe.*' Bob has done more to set the public right on this important point of blazonry, than the whole College of Heralds.

The appointment of a regular wit has long ceased to be a part of the economy of a Morning Paper. Editors find their own jokes, or do as well without them. Parson Este, and Topham, brought up the set custom of 'witty paragraphs' first in the World. Boaden was a reigning paragraphist in his day, and succeeded poor Allen in the Oracle. But, as we said, the fashion of jokes passes away; and it would be difficult to discover in the biographer of Mrs. Siddons, any traces of that vivacity and fancy which charmed the whole town at the commencement of the present century. Even the prelusive delicacies of the present writer—the curt 'Astræan allusion' —would be thought pedantic and out of date, in these days.

From the office of the Morning Post (for we may as well exhaust our Newspaper Reminiscences at once) by change of property in the paper, we were transferred, mortifying exchange! to the office of the Albion Newspaper, late Rackstrow's Museum, in Fleet Street. What a transition —from a handsome apartment, from rose-wood desks, and silver inkstands, to an office—no office, but a *den* rather, but just redeemed from the occupation of dead monsters, of which it seemed redolent—from the centre of loyalty and fashion, to a focus of vulgarity and sedition! Here in murky closet, inadequate from its square contents to the receipt of the two bodies of Editor and humble paragraph-maker, together at one time, sat in the discharge of his new editorial functions (the 'Bigod' of Elia) the redoubted John Fenwick.

F., without a guinea in his pocket, and having left not

many in the pockets of his friends whom he might command, had purchased (on tick doubtless) the whole and sole Editorship, Proprietorship, with all the rights and titles (such as they were worth) of the Albion from one Lovell; of whom we know nothing, save that he had stood in the pillory for a libel on the Prince of Wales. With this hopeless concern— for it had been sinking ever since its commencement, and could now reckon upon not more than a hundred subscribers —F. resolutely determined upon pulling down the Government in the first instance, and making both our fortunes by way of corollary. For seven weeks and more did this infatuated democrat go about borrowing seven-shilling pieces, and lesser coin, to meet the daily demands of the Stamp office, which allowed no credit to publications of that side in politics. An outcast from politer bread, we attached our small talents to the forlorn fortunes of our friend. Our occupation now was to write treason.

Recollections of feelings—which were all that now remained from our first boyish heats kindled by the French Revolution, when, if we were misled, we erred in the company of some who are accounted very good men now—rather than any tendency at this time to Republican doctrines— assisted us in assuming a style of writing, while the paper lasted, consonant in no very under tone to the right earnest fanaticism of F. Our cue was now to insinuate, rather than recommend, possible abdications. Blocks, axes, Whitehall tribunals, were covered with flowers of so cunning a periphrasis as Mr. Bayes says, never naming the *thing* directly —that the keen eye of an Attorney General was insufficient to detect the lurking snake among them. There were times, indeed, when we sighed for our more gentleman-like occupation under Stuart. But with change of masters it is ever change of service. Already one paragraph, and another, as we learned afterwards from a gentleman at the Treasury, had begun to be marked at that office, with a view of its being submitted at least to the attention of the proper Law Officers —when an unlucky, or rather lucky epigram from our pen, aimed at Sir J——s M——h, who was on the eve of departing for India to reap the fruits of his apostasy, as F. pronounced it (it is hardly worth particularising), happening to offend the nice sense of Lord, or, as he then delighted to be called, Citizen Stanhope, deprived F. at once of the last hopes of a guinea from the last patron that had stuck by us; and breaking up our establishment, left us to the safe, but somewhat mortifying, neglect of the Crown Lawyers. It was about this time, or a little earlier, that Dan Stuart made that curious confession to us, that he had 'never deliberately walked into an Exhibition at Somerset House in his life.'

Barrenness of the Imaginative Faculty in the Productions of Modern Art

HOGARTH excepted, can we produce any one painter within the last fifty years, or since the humour of exhibiting began, that has treated a story *imaginatively?* By this we mean, upon whom his subject has so acted, that it has seemed to direct *him*—not to be arranged by him? Any upon whom its leading or collateral points have impressed themselves so tyrannically, that he dared not treat it otherwise, lest he should falsify a revelation? Any that has imparted to his compositions, not merely so much truth as is enough to convey a story with clearness, but that individualising property, which should keep the subject so treated distinct in feature from every other subject, however similar, and to common apprehensions almost identical; so as that we might say, this and this part could have found an appropriate place in no other picture in the world but this? Is there anything in modern art—we will not demand that it should be equal—but in any way analogous to what Titian has effected, in that wonderful bringing together of two times in the Ariadne, in the National Gallery? Precipitous, with his reeling satyr rout about him, re-peopling and re-illuming suddenly the waste places, drunk with a new fury beyond the grape, Bacchus, born in fire, fire-like flings himself at the Cretan. This is the time present. With this telling of the story—an artist, and no ordinary one, might remain richly proud. Guido, in his harmonious version of it, saw no further. But from the depths of the imaginative spirit Titian has recalled past time, and laid it contributory with the present to one simultaneous effect. With the desert all ringing with the mad cymbals of his followers, made lucid with the presence and new offers of a god,—as if unconscious of Bacchus, or but idly casting her eyes as upon some unconcerning pageant—her soul undistracted from Theseus —Ariadne is still pacing the solitary shore in as much heart-silence, and in almost the same local solitude, with which she awoke at daybreak to catch the forlorn last glances of the sail that bore away the Athenian.

Here are two points miraculously co-uniting; fierce society, with the feeling of solitude still absolute; noonday revelations, with the accidents of the dull grey dawn unquenched and lingering; the *present* Bacchus, with the *past* Ariadne; two stories, with double Time; separate, and harmonising. Had the artist made the woman one shade less indifferent to the God; still more, had she expressed a rapture at his advent, where would have been the story of the mighty desolation of the heart previous? merged in the insipid accident of a flattering offer met with a welcome acceptance. The broken heart for Theseus was not lightly to be pieced up by a God.

We have before us a fine rough print, from a picture by Raphael in the Vatican. It is the Presentation of the new-born Eve to Adam by the Almighty. A fairer mother of mankind we might imagine, and a goodlier sire perhaps of men since born. But these are matters subordinate to the conception of the *situation*, displayed in this extraordinary production. A tolerably modern artist would have been satisfied with tempering certain raptures of connubial antici-pation, with a suitable acknowledgment to the Giver of the blessing, in the countenance of the first bridegroom; some-thing like the divided attention of the child (Adam was here a child-man) between the given toy, and the mother who had just blest it with the bauble. This is the obvious, the first-sight view, the superficial. An artist of a higher grade, considering the awful presence they were in, would have taken care to subtract something from the expression of the more human passion, and to heighten the more spiritual one. This would be as much as an exhibition-goer, from the opening of Somerset House to last year's show, has been encouraged to look for. It is obvious to hint at a lower expression yet, in a picture that, for respects of drawing and colouring, might be deemed not wholly inadmissible within these art-fostering walls, in which the raptures should be as ninety-nine, the gratitude as one, or perhaps zero! By neither the one passion nor the other has Raphael expounded the situation of Adam. Singly upon his brow sits the absorbing sense of wonder at the created miracle. The *moment* is seized by the intuitive artist, perhaps not self-conscious of his art, in which neither of the conflicting emotions—a moment how abstracted!—have had time to spring up, or to battle for indecorous mastery.—We have seen a landscape of a justly admired neoteric, in which he aimed at delineating a fiction, one of the most severely beautiful in antiquity—the gardens of the Hesperides. To do Mr.——justice, he had painted a laudable orchard, with fitting seclusion, and a veritable dragon (of which a Polypheme, by Poussin, is somehow a fac-simile for the situation), looking over into the world shut out backwards, so that none but a 'still-climbing Hercules' could hope to catch a peep at the admired Ternary of Recluses. No conventual porter could keep his eyes better than this custos with the 'lidless eyes.' He not only sees that none *do* intrude into that privacy, but, as clear as daylight, that none but *Hercules aut Diabolus* by any manner of means *can*. So far all is well. We have absolute solitude here or nowhere. *Ab extra* the damsels are snug enough. But here the artist's courage seems to have failed him. He began to pity his pretty charge, and, to comfort the irksomeness, has peopled their solitude with a bevy of fair attendants, maids of honour, or ladies of the bed-chamber, according to the approved etiquette at a court of the nineteenth century; giving to the whole scene the air of a *fête-champêtre*, if we will but excuse the absence of the gentlemen. This is well, and Watteauish. But what is become of the solitary mystery—the

> Daughters three
> That sing around the golden tree?

This is not the way in which Poussin would have treated this subject.

The paintings, or rather the stupendous architectural designs, of a modern artist, have been urged as objections to the theory of our motto. They are of a character, we confess, to stagger it. His towered structures are of the highest order of the material sublime. Whether they were dreams, or transcripts of some elder workmanship—Assyrian ruins old —restored by this mighty artist, they satisfy our most stretched and craving conceptions of the glories of the antique world. It is a pity that they were ever peopled. On that side, the imagination of the artist halts, and appears defective. Let us examine the point of the story in the Belshazzar's Feast. We will introduce it by an apposite anecdote.

The court historians of the day record, that at the first dinner given by the late King (then Prince Regent) at the Pavilion, the following characteristic frolic was played off. The guests were select and admiring; the banquet profuse and admirable; the lights lustrous and oriental; the eye was perfectly dazzled with the display of plate, among which the great gold salt-cellar, brought from the regalia in the Tower for this especial purpose, itself a tower! stood conspicuous for its magnitude. And now the Rev. * * * *, the then admired court Chaplain, was proceeding with the grace, when, at a signal given, the lights were suddenly overcast, and a huge transparency was discovered, in which glittered in gold letters—

'BRIGHTON—EARTHQUAKE—SWALLOW-UP-ALIVE!'

Imagine the confusion of the guests; the Georges and garters, jewels, bracelets, moulted upon the occasion! The fans dropped, and picked up the next morning by the sly court-pages! Mrs. Fitz-what's-her-name fainting, and the Countess of * * * holding the smelling-bottle, till the good-humoured Prince caused harmony to be restored, by calling in fresh candles, and declaring that the whole was nothing but a pantomime *hoax*, got up by the ingenious Mr. Farley, of Covent Garden, from hints which his Royal Highness himself had furnished! Then imagine the infinite applause that followed, the mutual rallyings, the declarations that 'they were not much frightened,' of the assembled galaxy.

The point of time in the picture exactly answers to the appearance of the transparency in the anecdote. The huddle, the flutter, the bustle, the escape, the alarm, and the mock alarm; the prettinesses heightened by consternation; the courtier's fear which was flattery; and the lady's which was affectation; all that we may conceive to have taken place in a mob of Brighton courtiers, sympathising with the well-acted surprise of their sovereign; all this, and no more, is exhibited by the well-dressed lords and ladies in the Hall of Belus. Just this sort of consternation we have seen among a flock of disquieted wild geese at the report only of a gun having gone off!

But is this vulgar fright, this mere animal anxiety for the preservation of their persons,—such as we have witnessed at a theatre, when a slight alarm of fire has been given—an adequate exponent of a supernatural terror? the way in which the finger of God, writing judgments, would have been met by the withered conscience? There is a human fear, and a divine fear. The one is disturbed, restless, and bent upon escape. The other is bowed down, effortless, passive. When the spirit appeared before Eliphaz in the visions of the night, and the hair of his flesh stood up, was it in the thoughts of the Temanite to ring the bell of his chamber, or to call up the servants? But let us see in the text what there is to justify all this huddle of vulgar consternation.

From the words of Daniel it appears that Belshazzar had made a great feast to a thousand of his lords, and drank wine before the thousand. The golden and silver vessels are gorgeously enumerated, with the princes, the king's concubines, and his wives. Then follows—

'In the same hour came forth fingers of a man's hand, and wrote over against the candlestick upon the plaster of the wall of the king's palace; and the *king* saw the part of the hand that wrote. Then the *king's* countenance was changed and his thoughts troubled him, so that the joints of his loins were loosened, and his knees smote one against another.'

This is the plain text. By no hint can it be otherwise inferred, but that the appearance was solely confined to the fancy of Belshazzar, that his single brain was troubled. Not a word is spoken of its being seen by any one else there present, not even by the queen herself, who merely undertakes for the interpretation of the phenomenon, as related to her, doubtless, by her husband. The lords are simply said to be astonished; *i.e.*, at the trouble and the change of countenance in their sovereign. Even the prophet does not appear to have seen the scroll, which the king saw. He recalls it only, as Joseph did the Dream to the King of Egypt. 'Then was the part of the hand sent from him [the Lord], and this writing was written.' He speaks of the phantasm as past.

Then what becomes of this needless multiplication of the miracle? this message to a royal conscience, singly expressed

—for it was said, 'Thy kingdom is divided,'—simultaneously impressed upon the fancies of a thousand courtiers, who were implied in it neither directly nor grammatically?

But admitting the artist's own version of the story, and that the sight was seen also by the thousand courtiers—let it have been visible to all Babylon—as the knees of Belshazzar were shaken, and his countenance troubled, even so would the knees of every man in Babylon, and their countenances, as of an individual man, have been troubled; bowed, bent down, so would they have remained, stupor-fixed, with no thought of struggling with that inevitable judgment.

Not all that is optically possible to be seen, is to be shown in every picture. The eye delightedly dwells upon the brilliant individualities in a Marriage at Cana, by Veronese, or Titian, to the very texture and colour of the wedding garments, the ring glittering upon the bride's fingers, the metal and fashion of the wine-pots; for at such seasons there is leisure and luxury to be curious. But in a 'day of judgment,' or in a 'day of lesser horrors, yet divine,' as at the impious feast of Belshazzar, the eye should see, as the actual eye of an agent or patient in the immediate scene would see, only in masses and indistinction. Not only the female attire and jewelry exposed to the critical eye of fashion, as minutely as the dresses in a Lady's Magazine, in the criticised picture,—but perhaps the curiosities of anatomical science, and studied diversities of posture, in the falling angels and sinners of Michael Angelo,—have no business in their great subjects. There was no leisure for them.

By a wise falsification, the great masters of painting got at their true conclusions; by not showing the actual appearances, that is, all that was to be seen at any given moment by an indifferent eye, but only what the eye might be supposed to see in the doing or suffering of some portentous action. Suppose the moment of the swallowing up of Pompeii. There they were to be seen—houses, coulumns, architectural proportions, differences of public and private buildings, men and women at their standing occupations, the diversified thousand postures, attitudes, dresses, in some confusion truly, but physically they were visible. But what eye saw them at that eclipsing moment, which reduces confusion to a kind of unity, and when the senses are upturned from their proprieties, when sight and hearing are a feeling only?

A thousand years have passed, and we are at leisure to contemplate the weaver fixed standing at his shuttle, the baker at his oven, and turn over with antiquarian coolness the pots and pans of Pompeii.

'Sun, stand thou still upon Gibeon, and thou, Moon, in the valley of Ajalon.' Who, in reading this magnificent Hebraism, in his conception, sees aught but the heroic son of Nun, with the outstretched arm, and the greater and lesser light obsequious? Doubtless there were to be seen hill and dale, and chariots and horsemen, on open plain, or winding by secret defiles, and all the circumstances and stratagems of war. But whose eyes would have been conscious of this array at the interposition of the synchronic miracle? Yet in the picture of this subject by the artist of the Belshazzar's Feast—no ignoble work either—the marshalling and landscape of the war is everything, the miracle sinks into an anecdote of the day; and the eye may 'dart through rank and file traverse' for some minutes, before it shall discover, among his armed followers, *which is Joshua!* Not modern art alone, but ancient, where only it is to be found if anywhere, can be detected erring, from defect of this imaginative faculty. The world has nothing to show of the preternatural in painting, transcending the figure of Lazarus bursting his grave-clothes, in the great picture at Angerstein's. It seems a thing between two beings. A ghastly horror at itself struggles with newly-apprehending gratitude at second life bestowed. It cannot forget that it was a ghost. It has hardly felt that it is a body. It has to tell of the world of spirits.—Was it from a feeling, that the crowd of half-impassioned bystanders, and the still more irrelevant herd of passers-by at a distance, who have not heard, or but faintly have been told of the passing miracle, admirable as they are in design and hue— for it is a glorified work—do not respond adequately to the action—that the single figure of the Lazarus has been attributed to Michael Angelo, and the mighty Sebastian unfairly robbed of the fame of the greater half of the interest? Now that there were not indifferent passers-by within actual scope of the eyes of those present at the miracle, to whom the sound of it had but faintly, or not at all, reached, it would be hardihood to deny; but would they see them? or can the mind in the conception of it admit of such unconcerning objects; can it think of them at all? or what associating league to the imagination can there be between the seers, and the seers not, of a presential miracle?

Were an artist to paint upon demand a picture of a Dryad, we will ask whether, in the present low state of expectation, the patron would not, or ought not to be fully satisfied with a beautiful naked figure recumbent under wide-stretched oaks? Dis-seat those woods, and place the same figure among fountains, and fall of pellucid water, and you have a—Naiad! Not so in a rough print we have seen after Julio Romano, we think—for it is long since—*there*, by no process, with mere change of scene, could the figure have reciprocated characters. Long, grotesque, fantastic, yet with a grace of her own, beautiful in convolution and distortion, linked to her connatural tree, co-twisting with its limbs her own, till both seemed either—these, animated branches; those, disanimated members—yet the animal and vegetable lives sufficiently kept distinct—*his* Dryad lay—an approximation of two natures, which to conceive, it must be seen; analogous to, not the same with, the delicacies of Ovidian transformations.

To the lowest subjects, and, to a superficial comprehension, the most barren, the Great Masters gave loftiness and fruitfulness. The large eye of genius saw in the meanness of present objects their capabilities of treatment from their relations to some grand Past or Future. How has Raphael —we must still linger about the Vatican—treated the humble craft of the shipbuilder, in *his* Building of the Ark? It is in that scriptural series, to which we have referred, and which, judging from some fine rough old graphic sketches of them which we possess, seem to be of a higher and more poetic grade than even the Cartoons. The dim of sight are the timid and the shrinking. There is a cowardice in modern art. As the Frenchman, of whom Coleridge's friend made the prophetic guess at Rome, from the beard and horns of the Moses of Michael Angelo collected no inferences beyond that of a He Goat and a Cornuto; so from this subject, of mere mechanic promise, it would instinctively turn away, as from one incapable of investiture with any grandeur. The dock-yards at Woolwich would object derogatory associations. The depôt at Chatham would be the mote and the beam in its intellectual eye. But not to the nautical preparations in the ship-yards of Civita Vecchia did Raphael look for instructions, when he imagined the building of the Vessel that was to be conservatory of the wrecks of the species of drowned mankind. In the intensity of the action, he keeps ever out of sight the meanness of the operation. There is the Patriarch, in calm forethought, and with holy prescience, giving directions. And there are his agents—the solitary but sufficient Three— hewing, sawing, every one with the might and earnestness of a Demiurgus; under some instinctive rather than technical guidance! giant-muscled; every one a Hercules, or liker to those Vulcanian Three, that in sounding caverns under Mongibello wrought in fire—Brontes, and black Steropes, and Pyracmon. So work the workmen that should repair a world!

Artists again err in the confounding of *poetic* with *pictorial subjects*. In the latter, the exterior accidents are nearly everything, the unseen qualities as nothing. Othello's colour—the infirmities and corpulence of a Sir John Falstaff—do they haunt us perpetually in the reading? or are they obtruded upon our conceptions one time for ninety-nine that we are lost in admiration of the respective moral or intellectual attributes of the character? But in a picture Othello is *always* a Blackamoor; and the other only Plump Jack. Deeply corporealised, and enchained hopelessly in the grovelling fetters of externality, must be the mind, to which, in its better moments, the image of the high-souled, high-intelligenced Quixote—the errant Star of Knighthood, made more tender by eclipse—has never presented itself divested from the unhallowed accompaniment of a Sancho, or a rabblement at the heels of Rosinante. That man has read his book by halves; he has laughed, mistaking his author's purport, which was—tears. The artist that pictures Quixote (and it is in this degrading point that he is every season held up at our Exhibitions) in the shallow hope of exciting mirth, would have joined the rabble at the heels of his starved steed. We wish not to see *that* counterfeited, which we would not have wished to see in the reality. Conscious of the heroic inside of the noble Quixote, who, on hearing that his withered person was passing, would have stepped over his threshold to gaze upon his forlorn habiliments, and the 'strange bed-fellows which misery brings a man acquainted with'? Shade of Cervantes! who in thy Second Part could put into the mouth of thy Quixote those high aspirations of a super-chivalrous gallantry, where he replies to one of the shepherdesses, apprehensive that he would spoil their pretty net-works, and inviting him to be a guest with them, in accents like these: 'Truly, fairest Lady, Actæon was not more astonished when he saw Diana bathing herself at the fountain, than I have been in beholding your beauty: I commend the manner of your pastime, and thank you for your kind offers; and, if I may serve you, so I may be sure you will be obeyed, you may command me: for my profession is this, To show myself thankful, and a doer of good to all sorts of people, especially of the rank that your person shows you to be; and if those nets, as they take up but a little piece of ground, should take up the whole world, I would seek out new worlds to pass through, rather than break them: and (he adds) that you may give credit to this my exaggeration, behold at least he that promiseth you this, is Don Quixote de la Mancha, if haply this name hath come to your hearing.' Illustrious Romancer! were the 'fine frenzies,' which possessed the brain of thy own Quixote, a fit subject, as in this Second Part, to be exposed to the jeers of Duennas and Serving-men? to be monstered, and shown up at the heartless banquets of great men? Was that pitiable infirmity, which in thy First Part misleads him, *always from within*, into half-ludicrous, but more than half-compassionable and admirable errors, not infliction enough from heaven, that men by studied artifices must devise and practise upon the humour, to inflame where they should soothe it? Why, Goneril would have blushed to practise upon the abdicated king at this rate, and the she-wolf Regan not have endured to play the pranks upon his fled wits, which thou hast made thy Quixote suffer in Duchesses' halls, and at the hands of that unworthy nobleman.*

In the First Adventures, even, it needed all the art of the most consummate artist in the Book way that the world hath yet seen, to keep up in the mind of the reader the heroic attributes of the character without relaxing; so as absolutely that they shall suffer no alloy from the debasing fellowship of the clown. If it ever obtrudes itself as a disharmony, are we inclined to laugh; or not, rather, to indulge a contrary emotion?—Cervantes, stung, perchance, by the relish with which *his* Reading Public had received the fooleries of the

---

* Yet from this Second Part, our cried-up pictures are mostly selected; the waiting-women with beards, etc.

man, more to their palates than the generosities of the master, in the sequel let his pen run riot, lost the harmony and the balance, and sacrificed a great idea to the taste of his contemporaries. We know that in the present day the Knight has fewer admirers than the Squire. Anticipating, what did actually happen to him—as afterwards it did to his scarce inferior follower, the Author of 'Guzman de Alfarache'—that some less knowing hand would prevent him by a spurious Second Part; and judging that it would be easier for his competitor to outbid him in the comicalities, than in the *romance*, of his work, he abandoned his Knight, and has fairly set up the Squire for his Hero. For what else has he unsealed the eyes of Sancho? and instead of that twilight state of semi-insanity—the madness at second-hand—the contagion, caught from a stronger mind infected—that war between native cunning, and hereditary deference, with which he has hitherto accompanied his master—two for a pair almost —does he substitute a downright Knave, with open eyes, for his own ends only following a confessed Madman; and offering at one time to lay, if not actually laying, hands upon him! From the moment that Sancho loses his reverence, Don Quixote is become—a treatable lunatic. Our artists handle him accordingly.

The Wedding

I DO not know when I have been better pleased than at being invited last week to be present at the wedding of a friend's daughter. I like to make one at these ceremonies, which to us old people give back our youth in a manner, and restore our gayest season, in the remembrance of our own success, or the regrets, scarcely less tender, of our own youthful disappointments, in this point of a settlement. On these occasions I am sure to be in good-humour for a week or two after, and enjoy a reflected honeymoon. Being without a family, I am flattered with these temporary adoptions into a friend's family; I feel a sort of cousinhood, or uncleship, for the season; I am inducted into degrees of affinity; and, in the participated socialities of the little community, I lay down for a brief while my solitary bachelorship. I carry this humour so far,

that I take it unkindly to be left out, even when a funeral is
going on in the house of a dear friend. But to my subject.——

The union itself had been long settled, but its celebration
had been hitherto deferred, to an almost unreasonable state
of suspense in the lovers by some invincible prejudices which
the bride's father had unhappily contracted upon the subject
of the too early marriages of females. He has been lecturing
any time these five years—for to that length the courtship
has been protracted—upon the propriety of putting off the
solemnity, till the lady should have completed her five-and-
twentieth year. We all began to be afraid that a suit, which
as yet had abated of none of its ardours, might at last be
lingered on, till passion had time to cool, and love go out in
the experiment. But a little wheedling on the part of his
wife, who was by no means a party to these overstrained
notions, joined to some serious expostulations on that of his
friends, who, from the growing infirmities of the old gentleman, could not promise ourselves many years' enjoyment of
his company, and were anxious to bring matters to a conclusion during his lifetime, at length prevailed; and on
Monday last the daughter of my old friend, Admiral——,
having attained the *womanly* age of nineteen, was conducted
to the church by her pleasant cousin J——, who told some
few years older.

Before the youthful part of my female readers express their
indignation at the abominable loss of time occasioned to
the lovers by the preposterous notions of my old friend, they
will do well to consider the reluctance which a fond parent
naturally feels at parting with his child. To this unwillingness,
I believe, in most cases may be traced the difference of opinion
on this point between child and parent, whatever pretences
of interest or prudence may be held out to cover it. The
hard-heartedness of fathers is a fine theme for romance
writers, a sure and moving topic; but is there not something
untender, to say no more of it, in the hurry which a beloved
child is sometimes in to tear herself from the paternal stock,
and commit herself to strange graftings? The case is heightened where the lady, as in the present instance, happens to
be an only child. I do not understand these matters experi-
mentally, but I can make a shrewd guess at the wounded
pride of a parent upon these occasions. It is no new observation, I believe, that a lover in most cases has no rival so

much to be feared as the father. Certainly there is a jealousy in *unparalleled subjects*,which is little less heart-rending than the passion which we more strictly christen by that name. Mothers' scruples are more easily got over; for this reason, I suppose, that the protection transferred to a husband is less a derogation and a loss to their authority than to the paternal. Mothers, besides, have a trembling foresight, which paints the inconveniences (impossible to be conceived in the same degree by the other parent) of a life of forlorn celibacy, which the refusal of a tolerable match may entail upon their child. Mothers' instinct is a surer guide here, than the cold reasonings of a father on such a topic. To this instinct may be imputed, and by it alone may be excused the unbeseeming artifices, by which some wives push on the matrimonial projects of their daughters, which the husband, however approving, shall entertain with comparative indifference. A little shamelessness on this head is pardonable. With this explanation, forwardness becomes a grace, and maternal importunity receives the name of a virtue.—But the parson stays, while I preposterously assume his office; I am preaching, while the bride is on the threshold.

Nor let any of my female readers suppose that the sage reflections which have just escaped me have the obliquest tendency of application to the young lady, who, it will be seen, is about to venture upon a change in her condition, at a *mature and competent age*, and not without the fullest approbation of all parties. I only deprecate *very hasty marriages*.

It had been fixed that the ceremony should be gone through at an early hour, to give time for a little *déjeuné* afterwards, to which a select party of friends had been invited. We were in church a little before the clock struck eight.

Nothing could be more judicious or graceful than the dress of the bride-maids—the three charming Miss Foresters —on this morning. To give the bride an opportunity of shining singly, they had come habited all in green. I am ill at describing female apparel; but while *she* stood at the altar in vestments white and candid as her thoughts, a sacrificial whiteness, *they* assisted in robes, such as might become Diana's nymphs—Foresters indeed—as such who had not yet come to the resolution of putting off cold virginity. These young maids, not being so blest as to have a mother living, I am told, keep single for their father's sake, and live altogether so happy with their remaining parent, that the hearts of their lovers are ever broken with the prospect (so inauspicious to their hopes) of such uninterrupted and provoking home-comfort. Gallant girls! each a victim worthy of Iphigenia!

I do not know what business I have to be present in solemn places. I cannot divest me of an unseasonable disposition to levity upon the most awful occasions. I was never cut out for a public functionary. Ceremony and I have long shaken hands; but I could not resist the importunities of the young lady's father, whose gout unhappily confined him at home, to act as parent on this occasion, and *give away the bride*. Something ludicrous occurred to me at this most serious of all moments—a sense of my unfitness to have the disposal, even in imagination, of the sweet young creature beside me. I fear I was betrayed to some lightness, for the awful eye of the parson—and the rector's eye of Saint Mildred's in the Poultry is no trifle of a rebuke—was upon me in an instant, souring my incipient jest to the tristful severities of a funeral.

This was the only misbehaviour which I can plead to upon this solemn occasion, unless what was objected to me after the ceremony, by one of the handsome Miss T——s, to be accounted a solecism. She was pleased to say that she had never seen a gentleman before me give away a bride, in black. Now black has been my ordinary apparel so long —indeed I take it to be the proper costume of an author— the stage sanctions it—that to have appeared in some lighter colour would have raised more mirth at my expense than the anomaly had created censure. But I could perceive that the bride's mother, and some elderly ladies present (God bless them!) would have been well content, if I had come in any other colour than that. But I got over the omen by a lucky apologue, which I remembered out of Pilpay, or some Indian author, of all the birds being invited to the linnet's wedding, at which, when all the rest came in their gayest feathers, the raven alone apologised for his cloak because 'he had no other.' This tolerably reconciled the elders. But with the young people all was merriment, and shaking of hands, and congratulations, and kissing away the bride's tears, and kissing from her in return, till a young lady, who assumed some experience in these matters, having worn the nuptial bands some four or five weeks longer than her friend, rescued her, archly observing, with half an eye upon the bridegroom, that at this rate she would have 'none left.'

My friend the Admiral was in fine wig and buckle on this occasion—a striking contrast to his usual neglect of personal appearance. He did not once shove up his borrowed locks (his custom ever at his morning studies) to betray the few grey stragglers of his own beneath them. He wore an aspect of thoughtful satisfaction. I trembled for the hour, which at length approached, when after a protracted *breakfast* of three hours—if stores of cold fowls, tongues, hams, botargoes, dried fruits, wines, cordials, etc., can deserve so meagre an appellation—the coach was announced, which was come to carry off the bride and bridegroom for a season, as custom has sensibly ordained, into the country; upon which design, wishing them a felicitous journey, let us return to the assembled guests.

> As when a well-graced actor leaves the stage,
> The eyes of men
> Are idly bent on him that enters next,

so idly did we bend our eyes upon one another, when the chief performers in the morning's pageant had vanished. None told his tale. None sipped her glass. The poor Admiral made an effort—it was not much. I had anticipated so far. Even the infinity of full satisfaction, that had betrayed itself through the prim looks and quiet deportment of his lady, began to wane into something of misgiving. No one knew whether to take their leaves or stay. We seemed assembled upon a silly occasion. In this crisis, betwixt tarrying and departure, I must do justice to a foolish talent of mine, which had otherwise like to have brought me into disgrace in the fore-part of the day; I mean a power, in any emergency, of thinking and giving vent to all manner of strange nonsense. In this awkward dilemma I found it sovereign. I rattled off some of my most excellent absurdities. All were willing to be relieved, at any expense of reason, from the pressure of the intolerable vacuum which had succeeded to the morning bustle. By this means I was fortunate in keeping together the better part of the company to a late hour; and a rubber of whist (the Admiral's favourite game) with some rare strokes of chance as well as skill, which came opportunely on his side—lengthened out till midnight—dismissed the old gentleman at last to his bed with comparatively easy spirits.

I have been at my old friend's various times since. I do not know a visiting place where every guest is so perfectly at his ease; nowhere, where harmony is so strangely the result of confusion. Everybody is at cross purposes, yet the effect is so much better than uniformity. Contradictory orders; servants pulling one way; master and mistress driving some other, yet both diverse; visitors huddled up in corners; chairs unsymmetrised; candles disposed by chance; meals at odd hours, tea and supper at once, or the latter preceding the former; the host and the guest conferring, yet each upon a different topic, each understanding himself, neither trying to understand or hear the other; draughts and politics, chess and political economy, cards and conversation on nautical matters, going on at once, without the hope, or indeed the wish, of distinguishing them, make it altogether the most perfect *concordia discors* you shall meet with. Yet somehow the old house is not quite what it should be. The Admiral still enjoys his pipe, but he has no Miss Emily to fill it for him. The instrument stands where it stood, but she is gone, whose delicate touch could sometimes for a short minute appease the warring elements. He has learnt, as Marvel expresses it, to 'make his destiny his choice.' He bears bravely up, but he does not come out with his flashes of wild wit so thick as formerly. His sea-songs seldomer escape him. His wife, too, looks as if she wanted some younger body to scold and set to rights. We all miss a junior presence. It is wonderful how one young maiden freshens up, and keeps green, the paternal roof. Old and young seem to have an interest in her, so long as she is not absolutely disposed of. The youthfulness of the house is flown. Emily is married.

Rejoicings upon the New Year's Coming of Age

THE *Old Year* being dead, and the *New Year* coming of age, which he does, by Calendar Law, as soon as the breath is out of the old gentleman's body, nothing would serve the young spark but he must give a dinner upon the occasion, to which all the *Days* in the year were invited. The *Festivals*, whom he deputed as his stewards, were mightily taken with the notion. They had been engaged time out of mind, they said, in providing mirth and good cheer for mortals below; and it was time they should have a taste of their own bounty. It was stiffly debated among them whether the *Fasts* should be admitted. Some said the appearance of such lean, starved guests, with their mortified faces, would pervert the ends of the meeting. But the objection was overruled by *Christmas Day*, who had a design upon *Ash Wednesday* (as you shall hear), and a mighty desire to see how the old Dominie would behave himself in his cups. Only the *Vigils* were requested to come with their lanterns, to light the gentlefolks home at night.

All the *Days* came to their day. Covers were provided for three hundred and sixty-five guests at the principal table; with an occasional knife and fork at the side-board for the *Twenty-Ninth of February*.

I should have told you that cards of invitation had been issued. The carriers were the *Hours;* twelve little, merry, whirligig foot-pages, as you should desire to see, that went all round, and found out the persons invited well enough, with the exception of *Easter Day*, *Shrove Tuesday*, and a few such *Moveables*, who had lately shifted their quarters.

Well, they all met at last, foul *Days*, fine *Days*, all sorts of *Days*, and a rare din they made of it. There was nothing but, Hail! fellow *Day*, well met—brother *Day*—sister *Day*— only *Lady Day* kept a little on the aloof, and seemed somewhat scornful. Yet some said *Twelfth Day* cut her out and out, for she came in a tiffany suit, white and gold, like a queen on a frost-cake, all royal, glittering, and *Epiphanous*. The rest came, some in green, some in white—but old *Lent and his family* were not yet out of mourning. Rainy *Days* came in, dripping; and sunshiny *Days* helped them to change their stockings. *Wedding Day* was there in his marriage finery, a little the worse for wear. *Pay Day* came late, as he always does; and *Doomsday* sent word—he might be expected.

April Fool (as my young lord's jester) took upon himself to marshal the guests, and wild work he made with it. It would have posed old Erra Pater to have found out any given *Day* in the year, to erect a scheme upon—good *Days*, bad *Days*, were so shuffled together, to the confounding of all sober horoscopy.

He had stuck the *Twenty-First of June* next to the *Twenty-Second of December*, and the former looked like a Maypole siding a marrow-bone. *Ash Wednesday* got wedged in (as was concerted) betwixt *Christmas* and *Lord Mayor's Days*. Lord! how he laid about him! Nothing but barons of beef and turkeys would go down with him—to the great greasing and detriment of his new sackcloth bib and tucker. And still *Christmas Day* was at his elbow, plying him with the wassail-bowl, till he roared, and hiccupp'd, and protested there was no faith in dried ling, but commended it to the devil for a sour, windy, acrimonious, censorious, hy-po-crit-crit-critical mess, and no dish for a gentleman. Then he dipt his fist into the middle of the great custard that stood before his *left-hand neighbour*, and daubed his hungry beard all over with it, till you would have taken him for the *Last Day in December*, it so hung in icicles.

At another part of the table, *Shrove Tuesday* was helping the *Second of September* to some cock broth,—which courtesy the latter returned with the delicate thigh of a hen pheasant —so there was no love lost for that matter. The *Last of Lent* was spunging upon *Shrovetide's* pancakes; which *April Fool* perceiving, told him he did well, for pancakes were proper to a *Good Fry-day*.

In another part, a hubbub arose about the *Thirtieth of January*, who, it seems, being a sour, puritanic character, that thought nobody's meat good or sanctified enough for him, had smuggled into the room a calf's head, which he had had cooked at home for that purpose, thinking to feast thereon incontinently; but as it lay in the dish, *March Many-weathers*, who is a very fine lady, and subject to the megrims, screamed out there was a 'human head in the platter,' and raved about Herodias' daughter to that degree, that the obnoxious viand was obliged to be removed; nor did she recover her stomach till she had gulped down a *Restorative*, confected of *Oak Apple*, which the merry *Twenty-Ninth of May* always carries about with him for that purpose.

The King's health * being called for after this, a notable dispute arose between the *Twelfth of August* (a zealous old Whig gentlewoman) and the *Twenty-Third of April* (a new-fangled lady of the Tory stamp), as to which of them should have the honour to propose it. *August* grew hot upon the matter, affirming time out of mind the prescriptive right to have lain with her, till her rival had basely supplanted her; whom she represented as little better than a *kept* mistress, who went about in *fine clothes*, while she (the legitimate BIRTHDAY) had scarcely a rag, etc.

April Fool, being made mediator, confirmed the right, in the strongest form of words, to the appellant, but decided for peace' sake that the exercise of it should remain with the present possessor. At the same time, he slyly rounded the first lady in the ear, that an action might lie against the Crown for *bigeny*.

It beginning to grow a little duskish, *Candlemas* lustily bawled out for lights, which was opposed by all the *Days*, who protested against burning daylight. Then fair water was handed round in silver ewers, and the *same lady* was observed to take an unusaul time in *Washing* herself.

May Day, with that sweetness which is peculiar to her, in a neat speech proposing the health of the founder, crowned her goblet (and by her example the rest of the company) with garlands. This being done, the lordly *New Year*, from the upper end of the table, in a cordial but somewhat lofty tone, returned thanks. He felt proud on that occasion of meeting so many of his worthy father's late tenants, promised to improve their farms, and at the same time to abate (if anything was found unreasonable) in their rents.

At the mention of this, the four *Quarter Days* involuntarily looked at each other, and smiled; *April Fool* whistled to an old tune of 'New Brooms'; and a surly old rebel at the further end of the table (who was discovered to be no other than the *Fifth of November*) muttered out, distinctly enough to be heard by the whole company, words to this effect, that 'when the

* King George IV.

298

old one is gone, he is a fool that looks for a better.' Which rudeness of his, the guests resenting, unanimously voted his expulsion; and the malcontent was thrust out neck and heels into the cellar, as the properest place for such a *boutefeu* and firebrand as he had shown himself to be.

Order being restored—the young lord (who, to say truth, had been a little ruffled, and put beside his oratory) in as few, and yet as obliging words as possible, assured them of entire welcome; and, with a graceful turn, singling out poor *Twenty-Ninth of February*, that had sate all this while mumchance at the side-board, begged to couple his health with that of the good company before him—which he drank accordingly; observing that he had not seen his honest face any time these four years—with a number of endearing expressions besides. At the same time, removing the solitary *Day* from the forlorn seat which had been assigned him, he stationed him at his own board, somewhere between the *Greek Calends* and *Latter Lammas*.

Ash Wednesday, being now called upon for a song, with his eyes fast stuck in his head, and as well as the Canary he had swallowed would give him leave, struck up a Carol, which *Christmas Day* had taught him for the nonce; and was followed by the latter, who gave 'Miserere,' in fine style, hitting off the mumping notes and lengthened drawl of *Old Mortification* with infinite humour. *April Fool* swore they had exchanged conditions; but *Good Friday* was observed to look extremely grave; and *Sunday* held her fan before her face that she might not be seen to smile.

Shrove-tide, *Lord Mayor's Day*, and *April Fool*, next joined in a glee—

Which is the properest day to drink?

in which all the *Days* chiming in, made a merry burden.

They next fell to quibbles and conundrums. The question being proposed, who had the greatest number of followers —the *Quarter Days* said, there could be no question as to that; for they had all the creditors in the world dogging their heels. But *April Fool* gave it in favour of the *Forty Days before Easter;* because the debtors in all cases outnumbered the creditors, and they kept *lent* all the year.

All this while *Valentine's Day* kept courting pretty *May*, who sate next him, slipping amorous *billets-doux* under the table, till the *Dog Days* (who are naturally of a warm constitution) began to be jealous, and to bark and rage exceedingly. *April Fool*, who likes a bit of sport above measure, and had some pretensions to the lady besides, as being but a cousin once removed,—clapped and halloo'd them on; and as fast as their indignation cooled, those mad wags, the *Ember Days*, were at it with their bellows, to blow it into a flame; and all was in a ferment; till old Madam *Septuagesima* (who boasts herself the *Mother of the Days*) wisely diverted the conversation with a tedious tale of the lovers which she could reckon when she was young; and of one Master *Rogation Day* in particular, who was for ever putting the *question* to her; but she kept him at a distance, as the chronicle would tell—by which I apprehend she meant the Almanack. Then she rambled on to the *Days that were gone*, the *good old Days*, and so to the *Days before the Flood*—which plainly showed her old head to be little better than crazed and doited.

Day being ended, the *Days* called for their cloaks and great-coats, and took their leaves. *Lord Mayor's Day* went off in a Mist, as usual; *Shortest Day* in a deep black Fog, that wrapt the little gentleman all round like a hedge-hog. Two *Vigils*—so watchmen are called in heaven—saw *Christmas Day* safe home—they had been used to the business before. Another *Vigil*—a stout, sturdy patrole, called the *Eve of St. Christopher*—seeing *Ash Wednesday* in a condition little better than he should be—e'en whipt him over his shoulders, pick-a-back fashion, and *Old Mortification* went floating home singing—

On the bat's back do I fly,

and a number of old snatches besides, between drunk and sober; but very few Aves or Penitentiaries (you may believe me) were among them. *Longest Day* set off westward in beautiful crimson and gold—the rest, some in one fashion, some in another; but *Valentine* and pretty *May* took their departure together in one of the prettiest silvery twilights a Lover's Day could wish to set in.

Old China

I HAVE an almost feminine partiality for old china. When I go to see any great house, I inquire for the china-closet, and next for the picture gallery. I cannot defend the order of preference, but by saying, that we have all some taste or other, of too ancient a date to admit of our remembering distinctly that it was an acquired one. I call to mind the first play, and the first exhibition, that I was taken to; but I am not conscious of a time when china jars and saucers were introduced into my imagination.

I had no repugnance then—why should I now have?—to those little, lawless, azure-tinctured grotesques, that under the notion of men and women, float about, uncircumscribed by any element, in that world before perspective—a china tea-cup.

I like to see my old friends—whom distance cannot diminish—figuring up in the air (so they appear to our optics), yet on *terra firma* still—for so we must in courtesy interpret that speck of deeper blue,—which the decorous artist, to prevent absurdity, had made to spring up beneath their sandals.

I love the men with women's faces, and the women, if possible, with still more womanish expressions.

Here is a young and courtly Mandarin, handing tea to a lady from a salver—two miles off. See how distance seems to set off respect! And here the same lady, or another—for likeness is identity on tea-cups—is stepping into a little fairy boat, moored on the hither side of this calm garden river, with a dainty mincing foot, which in a right angle of incidence (as angles go in our world) must infallibly land her in the midst of a flowery mead—a furlong off on the other side of the same strange stream!

Farther on—if far or near can be predicated of their world—see horses, trees, pagodas, dancing the hays.

Here—a cow and rabbit couchant, and co-extensive—so objects show, seen through the lucid atmosphere of fine Cathay.

I was pointing out to my cousin last evening, over our Hyson (which we are old-fashioned enough to drink unmixed still of an afternoon), some of these *speciosa miracula* upon a set of extraordinary old blue china (a recent purchase) which we were now for the first time using; and could not help remarking, how favourable circumstances had been to us of late years, that we could afford to please the eye sometimes with trifles of this sort—when a passing sentiment seemed to overshade the brows of my companion. I am quick at detecting these summer clouds in Bridget.

'I wish the good old times would come again,' she said, 'when we were not quite so rich. I do not mean, that I want to be poor; but there was a middle state'—so she was pleased to ramble on,—'in which I am sure we were a great deal happier. A purchase is but a purchase, now that you have money enough and to spare. Formerly it used to be a triumph. When we coveted a cheap luxury (and, O! how much ado I had to get you to consent in those times!)—we were used to have a debate two or three days before, and to weigh the *for* and *against*, and think what we might spare it out of, and what saving we could hit upon, that should be an equivalent. A thing was worth buying then, when we felt the money that we paid for it.

'Do you remember the brown suit, which you made to hang upon you, till all your friends cried shame upon you, it grew so threadbare—and all because of that folio Beaumont and Fletcher, which you dragged home late at night from Barker's in Covent Garden? Do you remember how we eyed it for weeks before we could make up our minds to the purchase, and had not come to a determination till it was near ten o'clock of the Saturday night, when you set off from Islington, fearing you should be too late—and when the old bookseller with some grumbling opened his shop, and by the twinkling taper (for he was setting bedwards) lighted out the relic from his dusty treasures—and when you lugged it home, wishing it were twice as cumbersome—and when you presented it to me—and when we were exploring the perfectness of it (*collating*, you called it)—and while I was repairing some of the loose leaves with paste, which your impatience would not suffer to be left till daybreak—was there no pleasure in being a poor man? or can those neat black clothes which you wear now, and are so careful to

keep brushed, since we have become rich and finical, give
you half the honest vanity with which you flaunted it about
in that overworn suit—your old corbeau—for four or five
weeks longer than you should have done, to pacify your
conscience for the mighty sum of fifteen—or sixteen shillings
was it?—a great affair we thought it then—which you had
lavished on the old folio. Now you can afford to buy any
book that pleases you, but I do not see that you ever bring
me home any nice old purchases now.

'When you came home with twenty apologies for laying
out a less number of shillings upon that print after Lionardo,
which we christened the "Lady Blanch"; when you looked
at the purchase, and thought of the money—and thought of
the money, and looked again at the picture—was there no
pleasure in being a poor man? Now, you have nothing to
do but to walk into Colnaghi's, and buy a wilderness of
Lionardos. Yet do you?

'Then, do you remember our pleasant walks to Enfield,
and Potter's Bar, and Waltham, when we had a holiday—
holidays, and all other fun, are gone now we are rich—and
the little hand-basket in which I used to deposit our day's
fare of savoury cold lamb and salad—and how you would
pry about at noon-tide for some decent house, where we
might go in and produce our store—only paying for the ale
that you must call for—and speculate upon the looks of the
landlady, and whether she was likely to allow us a table-
cloth and wish for such another honest hostess as Izaak
Walton has described many a one on the pleasant banks of
the Lea, when he went a-fishing—and sometimes they would
prove obliging enough, and sometimes they would look
grudgingly upon us—but we had cheerful looks still for one
another, and would eat our plain food savourily, scarcely
grudging Piscator his Trout Hall? Now—when we go out a
day's pleasuring, which is seldom, moreover, we *ride* part
of the way—and go into a fine inn, and order the best of
dinners, never debating the expense—which, after all, never
has half the relish of those chance country snaps, when we
were at the mercy of uncertain usage, and a precarious
welcome.

'You are too proud to see a play anywhere now but in
the pit. Do you remember where it was we used to sit, when
we saw the Battle of Hexham, and the Surrender of Calais,

and Bannister and Mrs. Bland in the Children in the Wood —when we squeezed out our shillings apiece to sit three or four times in a season in the one-shilling gallery—where you felt all the time that you ought not to have brought me—and more strongly I felt obligation to you for having brought me —and the pleasure was the better for a little shame—and when the curtain drew up, what cared we for our place in the house, or what mattered it where we were sitting, when our thoughts were with Rosalind in Arden, or with Viola at the Court of Illyria. You used to say that the Gallery was the best place of all for enjoying a play socially—that the relish of such exhibitions must be in proportion to the infrequency of going—that the company we met there, not being in general readers of plays, were obliged to attend the more, and did attend, to what was going on, on the stage —because a word lost would have been a chasm, which it was impossible for them to fill up. With such reflections we consoled our pride then—and I appeal to you whether, as a woman, I met generally with less attention and accommodation than I have done since in more expensive situations in the house? The getting in indeed, and the crowding up those inconvenient staircases, was bad enough,—but there was still a law of civility to woman recognised to quite as great an extent as we ever found in the other passages—and how a little difficulty overcome heightened the snug seat and the play, afterwards! Now we can only pay our money and walk in. You cannot see, you say, in the galleries now. I am sure we saw, and heard too, well enough then—but sight, and all, I think, is gone with our poverty.

'There was pleasure in eating strawberries, before they became quite common—in the first dish of peas, while they were yet dear—to have them for a nice supper, a treat. What treat can we have now? If we were to treat ourselves now— that is, to have dainties a little above our means, it would be selfish and wicked. It is the very little more that we allow ourselves beyond what the actual poor can get at, that makes what I call a treat—when two people living together, as we have done, now and then indulge themselves in a cheap luxury, which both like; while each apologises, and is willing to take both halves of the blame to his single share. I see no harm in people making much of themselves, in that sense of the word. It may give them a hint how to make much of others. But now—what I mean by the word—we never do make much of ourselves. None but the poor can do it. I do not mean the veriest poor of all, but persons as we were, just above poverty.

'I know what you were going to say, that it is mighty pleasant at the end of the year to make all meet,—and much ado we used to have every Thirty-first Night of December to account for our exceedings—many a long face did you make over your puzzled accounts, and in contriving to make it out how we had spent so much—or that we had not spent so much—or that it was impossible we should spend so much next year—and still we found our slender capital decreasing —but then, betwixt ways, and projects, and compromises of one sort or another, and talk of curtailing this charge, and doing without that for the future—and the hope that youth brings, and laughing spirits (in which you were never poor till now), we pocketed up our loss, and in conclusion, with "lusty brimmers" (as you used to quote it out of *hearty cheerful Mr. Cotton*, as you called him), we used to welcome in "the coming guest." Now we have no reckoning at all at the end of the old year—no flattering promises about the new year doing better for us.'

Bridget is so sparing of her speech on most occasions, that when she gets into a rhetorical vein, I am careful how I interrupt it. I could not help, however, smiling at the phantom of wealth which her dear imagination had conjured up out of a clear income of poor——hundred pounds a year. 'It is true we were happier when we were poor but we were also younger, my cousin. I am afraid we must put up with the excess, for if we were to shake the superflux into the sea, we should not much mend ourselves. That we had much to struggle with, as we grew up together, we have reason to be most thankful. It strengthened and knit our compact closer. We could never have been what we have been to each other, if we had always had the sufficiency which you now complain of. The resisting power—those natural dilations of the youthful spirit, which circumstances cannot straiten —with us are long since passed away. Competence to age is supplementary youth, a sorry supplement indeed, but I fear the best that is to be had. We must ride where we formerly walked: live better and lie softer—and shall be wise to do so —than we had means to do in those good old days you speak of. Yet could those days return—could you and I once more walk our thirty miles a day—could Bannister and Mrs. Bland again be young, and you and I be young to see them—could the good old one-shilling gallery days return—they are dreams, my cousin, now—but could you and I at this moment, instead of this quiet argument, by our well-carpeted fireside, sitting on this luxurious sofa—be once more struggling up those inconvenient staircases, pushed about, and squeezed, and elbowed by the poorest rabble of poor gallery scramblers —could I once more hear those anxious shrieks of yours— and the delicious *Thank God, we are safe*, which always followed when the topmost stair, conquered, let in the first light of the whole cheerful theatre down beneath us—I know not the fathom line that ever touched a descent so deep as I would be willing to bury more wealth in than Crœsus had, or the great Jew R—— is supposed to have, to purchase it. And now do just look at that merry little Chinese waiter holding an umbrella, big enough for a bed-tester, over the head of that pretty insipid half Madonna-ish chit of a lady in that very blue summer-house.'

The Child Angel : A Dream

I CHANCED upon the prettiest, oddest, fantastical thing of a dream the other night, that you shall hear of. I had been reading the 'Loves of the Angels,' and went to bed with my head full of speculations, suggested by that extraordinary legend. It had given birth to innumerable conjectures; and, I remember the last waking thought, which I gave expression to on my pillow, was a sort of wonder, 'what could come of it.'

I was suddenly transported, how or whither I could scarcely make out—but to some celestial region. It was not the real heavens neither—nor the downright Bible heaven— but a kind of fairy-land heaven, about which a poor human fancy may have leave to sport and air itself, I will hope, without presumption.

Methought—what wild things dreams are!—I was present —at what would you imagine?—at an angel's gossiping.

Whence it came, or how it came, or who bid it come, or whether it came purely of its own head, neither you nor I know—but there lay, sure enough, wrapt in its little cloudy swaddling-bands—a Child Angel.

Sun-threads—filmy beams—ran through the celestial napery of what seemed its princely cradle. All the winged orders hovered round, watching when the new-born should open its yet closed eyes; which, when it did, first one, and then the other—with a solicitude and apprehension, yet not such as, stained with fear, dim the expanding eyelids of mortal infants, but as if to explore its path in those its unhereditary palaces—what an inextinguishable titter that time spared not celestial visages! Nor wanted there to my seeming—O, the inexplicable simpleness of dreams!—bowls of that cheering nectar,

—which mortals *caudle* call below.

Nor were wanting faces of female ministrants,—stricken in years, as it might seem,—so dexterous were those heavenly attendants to counterfeit kindly similitudes of earth, to greet with terrestrial child-rites the young *present*, which earth had made to heaven.

Then were celestial harpings heard, not in full symphony, as those by which the spheres are tutored; but, as loudest instruments on earth speak oftentimes, muffled; so to accommodate their sound the better to the weak ears of the imperfect-born. And, with the noise of those subdued soundings, the Angelet sprang forth, fluttering its rudiments of pinions—but forthwith flagged and was recovered into the arms of those full-winged angels. And a wonder it was to see how, as years went round in heaven—a year in dreams is as a day—continually its white shoulders put forth buds of wings, but wanting the perfect angelic nutriment, anon was shorn of its aspiring, and fell fluttering—still caught by angel handsem, for ever to put forth shoots, and to fall fluttering, because its birth was not of the unmixed vigour of heaven.

And a name was given to the Babe Angel, and it was to be called *Ge-Urania*, because its production was of earth and heaven.

And it could not taste of death, by reason of its adoption into immortal palaces: but it was to know weakness, and reliance, and the shadow of human imbecility; and it went with a lame gait; but in its goings it exceeded all mortal children in grace and swiftness. Then pity first sprang up in angelic bosoms; and yearnings (like the human) touched them at the sight of the immortal lame one.

And with pain did then first those Intuitive Essences, with pain and strife to their natures (not grief), put back their bright intelligences, and reduce their ethereal minds, schooling them to degrees and slower processes, so to adapt their lessons to the gradual illumination (as must needs be) of the half-earth-born; and what intuitive notices they could not repel (by reason that their nature is, to know all things at once) the half-heavenly novice, by the better part of its nature, aspired to receive into its understanding; so that Humility and Aspiration went on even-paced in the instruction of the glorious Amphibium.

But, by reason that Mature Humanity is too gross to breathe the air of that super-subtile region, its portion was, and is, to be a child for ever.

And because the human part of it might not press into the heart and inwards of the palace of its adoption, those full-natured angels tended it by turns in the purlieus of the palace, where were shady groves and rivulets, like this green earth from which it came; so Love, with Voluntary Humility, waited upon the entertainment of the new-adopted.

And myriads of years rolled round (in dreams Time is nothing), and still it kept, and is to keep, perpetual childhood, and is the Tutelar Genius of Childhood upon earth, and still goes lame and lovely.

By the banks of the river Pison is seen, lone sitting by the grave of the terrestrial Adah, whom the angel Nadir loved, a Child; but not the same which I saw in heaven. A mournful hue overcasts its lineaments; nevertheless, a correspondency is between the child by the grave, and that celestial orphan, whom I saw above: and the dimness of the grief upon the heavenly, is a shadow or emblem of that which stains the beauty of the terrestrial. And this correspondency is not to be understood but by dreams.

And in the archives of heaven I had grace to read, how that once the angel Nadir, being exiled from his place for mortal passion, upspringing on the wings of parental love (such power had parental love for a moment to suspend the else-irrevocable law) appeared for a brief instant in this station, and, depositing a wondrous Birth, straightway disappeared, and the palaces knew him no more. And this charge was the self-same Babe, who goeth lame and lovely—but Adah sleepeth by the river Pison.

Confessions of a Drunkard

DEHORTATIONS from the use of strong liquors have been the favourite topic of sober declaimers in all ages, and have been received with abundance of applause by water-drinking critics. But with the patient himself, the man that is to be cured, unfortunately their sound has seldom prevailed. Yet the evil is acknowledged, the remedy simple. Abstain. No force can oblige a man to raise the glass to his head against his will. 'Tis as easy as not to steal, not to tell lies.

Alas! the hand to pilfer, and the tongue to bear false witness, have no constitutional tendency. These are actions indifferent to them. At the first instance of the reformed will, they can be brought off without a murmur. The itching finger is but a figure in speech, and the tongue of the liar can with the same natural delight give forth useful truths with which it has been accustomed to scatter their pernicious contraries. But when a man has commenced sot——

O pause, thou sturdy moralist, thou person of stout nerves and a strong head, whose liver is happily untouched, and ere thy gorge riseth at the *name* which I have written, first learn what the *thing* is; how much of compassion, how much of human allowance, thou mayest virtuously mingle with thy disapprobation. Trample not on the ruins of a man. Exact not, under so terrible a penalty as infamy, a resuscitation from a state of death almost as real as that from which Lazarus rose not but by a miracle.

Begin a reformation, and custom will make it easy. But what if the beginning be dreadful, the first steps not like climbing a mountain but going through fire? what if the whole system must undergo a change violent as that which we conceive of the mutation of form in some insects? what if a process comparable to flaying alive be to be gone through? is the weakness that sinks under such struggles to be confounded with the pertinacity which clings to other vices, which have induced no constitutional necessity, no engagement of the whole victim, body and soul?

I have known one in that state, when he has tried to abstain but for one evening,—though the poisonous potion had long ceased to bring back its first enchantments, though he was sure it would rather deepen his gloom than brighten it,—in the violence of the struggle, and the necessity he has felt of getting rid of the present sensation at any rate, I have known him to scream out, to cry aloud, for the anguish and pain of the strife within him.

Why should I hesitate to declare, that the man of whom I speak is myself? I have no puling apology to make to mankind. I see them all in one way or another deviating from the pure reason. It is to my own nature alone I am accountable for the woe that I have brought upon it.

I believe that there are constitutions, robust heads and iron insides, whom scarce any excesses can hurt; whom brandy (I have seen them drink it like wine), at all events whom wine, taken in ever so plentiful a measure, can do no worse injury to than just to muddle their faculties, perhaps never very pellucid. On them this discourse is wasted. They would but laugh at a weak brother, who, trying his strength with them, and coming off foiled from the contest, would fain persuade them that such agonistic exercises are dangerous. It is to a very different description of persons I speak. It is to the weak, the nervous; to those who feel the want of some artificial aid to raise their spirits in society to what is no more than the ordinary pitch of all around them without it. This is the secret of our drinking. Such must fly the convivial board in the first instance, if they do not mean to sell themselves for term of life.

Twelve years ago I had completed my six-and-twentieth year. I had lived from the period of leaving school to that time pretty much in solitude. My companions were chiefly books, or at most one or two living ones of my own book-loving and sober stamp. I rose early, went to bed betimes, and the faculties which God had given me, I have reason to think, did not rust in me unused.

About that time I fell in with some companions of a different order. They were men of boisterous spirits, sitters up a-nights, disputants, drunken; yet seemed to have something noble about them. We dealt about the wit, or what passes for it after midnight, jovially. Of the quality called fancy I certainly possessed a larger share than my companions. Encouraged by their applause, I set up for a professed joker! I, who of all men am least fitted for such an occupation, having, in addition to the greatest difficulty which I experience at all times of finding words to express my meaning, a natural nervous impediment in my speech!

Reader, if you are gifted with nerves like mine, aspire to any character but that of a wit. When you find a tickling relish upon your tongue disposing you to that sort of conversation, especially if you find a preternatural flow of ideas setting in upon you at the sight of a bottle and fresh glasses, avoid giving way to it as you would fly your greatest destruction. If you cannot crush the power of fancy, or that within you which you mistake for such, divert it, give it some other play. Write an essay, pen a character or description,—but not as I do now, with tears trickling down your cheeks.

To be an object of compassion to friends, of derision to foes; to be suspected by strangers, stared at by fools; to be esteemed dull when you cannot be witty, to be applauded for witty when you know that you have been dull; to be called upon for the extemporaneous exercise of that faculty which no premeditation can give; to be spurred on to efforts which end in contempt; to be set on to provoke mirth which procures the procurer hatred; to give pleasure and be paid with squinting malice; to swallow draughts of life-destroying wine which are to be distilled into airy breath to tickle vain auditors; to mortgage miserable morrows for nights of madness; to waste whole seas of time upon those who pay it back in little inconsiderable drops of grudging applause, —are the wages of buffoonery and death.

Time, which has a sure stroke at dissolving all connexions which have no solider fastening than this liquid cement, more kind to me than my own taste or penetration, at length opened my eyes to the supposed qualities of my first friends. No trace of them is left but in the vices which they introduced, and the habits they infixed. In them my friends survive still, and exercise ample retribution for any supposed infidelity that I may have been guilty of towards them.

My next more immediate companions were and are persons of such intrinsic and felt worth, that though accidentally their acquaintance has proved pernicious to me, I do not know that if the thing were to do over again, I should have the courage to eschew the mischief at the price of forfeiting the benefit. I came to them reeking from the steams of my late over-heated notions of companionship; and the slightest fuel which they unconsciously afforded, was sufficient to feed my old fires into a propensity.

They were no drinkers, but, one from professional habits, and another from a custom derived from his father, smoked tobacco. The devil could not have devised a more subtle trap to re-take a backsliding penitent. The transition, from gulping down draughts of liquid fire to puffing out innocuous blasts of dry smoke, was so like cheating him. But he is too hard for us when we hope to commute. He beats us at barter; and when we think to set off a new failing against an old infirmity, 'tis odds but he puts the trick upon us of two for one. That (comparatively) white devil of tobacco brought with him in the end seven worse than himself.

It were impertinent to carry the reader through all the processes by which, from smoking at first with malt liquor, I took my degrees through thin wines, through stronger wine and water, through small punch, to those juggling compositions, which, under the name of mixed liquors, slur a great deal of brandy or other poison under less and less water continually, until they come next to none, and so to none at all. But it is hateful to disclose the secrets of my Tartarus.

I should repel my readers, from a mere incapacity of believing me, were I to tell them what tobacco has been to me, the drudging service which I have paid, the slavery which I have vowed to it. How, when I have resolved to quit it, a feeling as of ingratitude has started up; how it has put on personal claims and made the demands of a friend upon me. How the reading of it casually in a book, as where Adams takes his whiff in the chimney-corner of some inn in Joseph Andrews, or Piscator in the Compleat Angler breaks his fast upon a morning pipe in that delicate room *Piscatoribus Sacrum*, has in a moment broken down the resistance of weeks. How a pipe was ever in my midnight path before me, till the vision forced me to realise it,—how then its ascending vapours curled, its fragrance lulled, and the thousand delicious ministerings conversant about it, employing every faculty, extracted the sense of pain. How from illuminating it came to darken, from quick solace it turned to a negative relief, thence to a restlessness and dissatisfaction, thence to a positive misery. How, even now, when the whole secret stands confessed in all its dreadful truth before me, I feel myself linked to it beyond the power of revocation. Bone of my bone——

Persons not accustomed to examine the motives of their actions, to reckon up the countless nails that rivet the chains of habit, or perhaps being bound by none so obdurate as those I have confessed to, may recoil from this as from an overcharged picture. But what short of such a bondage is it, which in spite of protesting friends, a weeping wife, and a reprobating world, chains down many a poor fellow, of no original indisposition to goodness, to his pipe and his pot?

I have seen a print after Correggio, in which three female figures are ministering to a man who sits fast bound at the root of a tree. Sensuality is soothing him, Evil Habit is nailing him to a branch, and Repugnance at the same instant of time is applying a snake to his side. In his face is feeble delight, the recollection of past rather than perception of present pleasures, languid enjoyment of evil with utter imbecility to good, a Sybaritic effeminacy, a submission to bondage, the springs of the will gone down like a broken clock, the sin and the suffering co-instantaneous, or the latter forerunning the former, remorse preceding action—all this represented in one point of time.—When I saw this, I admired the wonderful skill of the painter. But when I went away, I wept, because I thought of my own condition.

Of *that* there is no hope that it should ever change. The waters have gone over me. But out of the black depths, could I be heard, I would cry out to all those who have but set a foot in the perilous flood. Could the youth, to whom the flavour of his first wine is delicious as the opening scenes of life or the entering upon some newly discovered paradise, look into my desolation, and be made to understand what a dreary thing it is when a man shall feel himself going down a precipice with open eyes and a passive will,—to see his destruction and have no power to stop it, and yet to feel it all the way emanating from himself; to perceive all goodness emptied out of him, and yet not to be able to forget a time when it was otherwise; to bear about the piteous spectacle of his own self-ruins:—could he see my fevered eye, feverish with last night's drinking, and feverishly looking for this night's repetition of the folly; could he feel the body of the death out of which I cry hourly with feebler and feebler outcry to be delivered,—it were enough to make him dash the sparkling beverage to the earth in all the pride of its mantling temptation; to make him clasp his teeth,

and not undo 'em
To suffer WET DAMNATION to run thro' 'em.

Yea, but (methinks I hear somebody object) if sobriety be that fine thing you would have us to understand, if the comforts of a cool brain are to be preferred to that state of heated excitement which you describe and deplore, what hinders in your instance that you do not return to those habits from which you would induce others never to swerve? if the blessing be worth preserving, is it not worth recovering?

Recovering!—O if a wish could transport me back to those days of youth, when a draught from the next clear spring could slake any heats which summer suns and youthful exercise had power to stir up in the blood, how gladly would I return to thee, pure element, the drink of children, and of child-like holy hermit! In my dreams I can sometimes fancy thy cool refreshment purling over my burning tongue. But my waking stomach rejects it. That which refreshes innocence only makes me sick and faint.

But is there no middle way betwixt total abstinence and the excess which kills you?—For your sake, reader, and that you may never attain to my experience, with pain I must utter the dreadful truth, that there is none, none that I can find. In my stage of habit (I speak not of habits less confirmed—for some of them I believe the advice to be most prudential), in the stage which I have reached, to stop short of that measure which is sufficient to draw on torpor and sleep, the benumbing apoplectic sleep of the drunkard, is to have taken none at all. The pain of the self-denial is all one. And what that is, I had rather the reader should believe on my credit, than know from his own trial. He will come to know it, whenever he shall arrive in that state, in which, paradoxical as it may appear, *reason shall only visit him through intoxication:* for it is a fearful truth, that the intellectual faculties by repeated acts of intemperance may be driven from their orderly sphere of action, their clear daylight ministeries, until they shall be brought at last to depend, for the faint manifestation of their departing energies, upon the returning periods of the fatal madness to which they owe their devastation. The drinking man is never less himself than during his sober intervals. Evil is so far his good. *

Behold me then, in the robust period of life, reduced to imbecility and decay. Hear me count my gains, and the profits which I have derived from the midnight cup.

Twelve years ago, I was possessed of a healthy frame of mind and body. I was never strong, but I think my constitution (for a weak one) was as happily exempt from the tendency to any malady as it was possible to be. I scarce knew what it was to ail anything. Now, except when I am losing myself in a sea of drink, I am never free from those uneasy sensations in head and stomach, which are so much worse to bear than any definite pains or aches.

At that time I was seldom in bed after six in the morning, summer and winter. I awoke refreshed, and seldom without some merry thoughts in my head, or some piece of a song to welcome the new-born day. Now, the first feeling which besets me, after stretching out the hours of recumbence to their last possible extent, is a forecast of the wearisome day that lies before me, with a secret wish that I could have lain on still, or never awaked.

Life itself, my waking life, has much of the confusion, the trouble, and obscure perplexity, of an ill dream. In the day time I stumble upon dark fountains.

Business, which, though never very particularly adapted to my nature, yet as something of necessity to be gone through, and therefore best undertaken with cheerfulness, I used to enter upon with some degree of alacrity, now wearies, affrights, perplexes me. I fancy all sorts of discouragements, and am ready to give up an occupation which gives me bread, from a harassing conceit of incapacity. The slightest commission given me by a friend, or any small duty which I have to perform for myself, as giving orders to a tradesman, etc.,

---

* When poor M—— painted his last picture, with a pencil in one trembling hand, and a glass of brandy and water in the other, his fingers owed the comparative steadiness with which they were enabled to go through their task in an imperfect manner to a temporary firmness derived from a repetition of practices, the general effect of which had shaken both them and him so terribly.

haunts me as a labour impossible to be got through. So much the springs of action are broken.

The same cowardice attends me in all my intercourse with mankind. I dare not promise that a friend's honour, or his cause, would be safe in my keeping, if I were put to the expense of any manly resolution in defending it. So much the springs of moral action are deadened within me.

My favourite occupations in times past now cease to entertain. I can do nothing readily. Application for ever so short a time kills me. This poor abstract of my condition was penned at long intervals, with scarcely any attempt at connexion of thought, which is now difficult to me.

The noble passages which formerly delighted me in history or poetic fiction, now only draw a few weak tears, allied to dotage. My broken and dispirited nature seems to sink before anything great and admirable.

I perpetually catch myself in tears, for any cause, or none. It is inexpressible how much this infirmity adds to a sense of shame, and a general feeling of deterioration.

These are some of the instances, concerning which I can say with truth, that it was not always so with me.

Shall I lift up the veil of my weakness any further?—or is this disclosure sufficient?

I am a poor nameless egotist, who have no vanity to consult by these Confessions. I know not whether I shall be laughed at, or heard seriously. Such as they are, I commend them to the reader's attention, if he find his own case any way touched. I have told him what I am come to. Let him stop in time.

Popular Fallacies

I.—THAT A BULLY IS ALWAYS A COWARD

THIS axiom contains a principle of compensation, which disposes us to admit the truth of it. But there is no safe trusting to dictionaries and definitions. We should more willingly fall in with this popular language, if we did not find *brutality* sometimes awkwardly coupled with *valour* in the same vocabulary. The comic writers, with their poetical justice, have contributed not a little to mislead us upon this point. To see a hectoring fellow exposed and beaten upon the stage, has something in it wonderfully diverting. Some people's share of animal spirits is notoriously low and defective. It has not strength to raise a vapour, or furnish out the wind of a tolerable bluster. These love to be told that huffing is no part of valour. The truest courage with them is that which is the least noisy and obtrusive. But confront one of these silent heroes with the swaggerer of real life, and his confidence in the theory quickly vanishes. Pretensions do not uniformly bespeak non-performance. A modest, inoffensive deportment does not necessarily imply valour; neither does the absence of it justify us in denying that quality. Hickman wanted modesty—we do not mean *him* of Clarissa—but who ever doubted his courage? Even the poets—upon whom this equitable distribution of qualities should be most binding—have thought it agreeable to nature to depart from the rule upon occasion. Harapha, in the Agonistes, is indeed a bully upon the received notions. Milton has made him at once a blusterer, a giant, and a dastard. But Almanzor, in Dryden, talks of driving armies singly before him—and does it. Tom Brown had a shrewder insight into this kind of character than either of his predecessors. He divides the palm more equably, and allows his hero a sort of dimidiate pre-eminence:—'Bully Dawson kicked by half the town, and half the town kicked by Bully Dawson.' This was true distributive justice.

II.—THAT ILL-GOTTEN GAIN NEVER PROSPERS

The weakest part of mankind have this saying commonest in their mouth. It is the trite consolation administered to the easy dupe, when he has been tricked out of his money or estate, that the acquisition of it will do the owner *no good.* But the rogues of this world—the prudenter part of them, at least,—know better; and if the observation had been as true as it is old, would not have failed by this time to have discovered it. They have pretty sharp distinctions of the fluctuating and the permanent. 'Lightly come, lightly go,' is a proverb, which they can very well afford to leave, when they leave little else, to the losers. They do not always find manors, got by rapine or chicanery, insensibly to melt away, as the poets will have it; or that all gold glides, like thawing snow, from the thief's hand that grasps it. Church land, alienated to lay uses, was formerly denounced to have this slippery quality. But some portions of it somehow always stuck so fast, that the denunciators have been fain to postpone the prophecy of refundment to a late posterity.

III.—THAT A MAN MUST NOT LAUGH AT HIS OWN JEST

The severest exaction surely ever invented upon the self-denial of poor human nature! This is to expect a gentleman to give a treat without partaking of it; to sit esurient at his own table, and commend the flavour of his venison upon the absurd strength of his never touching it himself. On the contrary, we love to see a wag *taste* his own joke to his party; to watch a quirk or a merry conceit flickering upon the lip some seconds before the tongue is delivered of it. If it be good, fresh, and racy—begotten of the occasion; if he that utters it never thought it before, he is naturally the first to be tickled with it; and any suppression of such complacence we hold to be churlish and insulting. What does it seem to imply but that your company is weak or foolish enough to be moved by an image or a fancy, that shall stir you not at all, or but faintly? This is exactly the humour of the fine gentleman in Mandeville, who, while he dazzles his guests with the display of some costly toy, affects himself to 'see nothing considerable in it.'

IV.—THAT SUCH A ONE SHOWS HIS BREEDING—THAT IT IS EASY TO PERCEIVE HE IS NO GENTLEMAN

A speech from the poorest sort of people, which always indicates that the party vituperated is a gentleman. The very fact which they deny is that which galls and exasperates them to use this language. The forbearance with which it is usually received is a proof what interpretation the bystander sets upon it. Of a kin to this, and still less politic, are the phrases with which, in their street rhetoric, they ply one another more grossly;—*He is a poor creature.—He has not a rag to cover ——etc.;* though this last, we confess, is more frequently applied by females to females. They do not perceive that the satire glances upon themselves. A poor man, of all things in the world, should not upbraid an antagonist with poverty. Are there no other topics—as, to tell him his father was hanged—his sister, etc.——, without exposing a secret which should be kept snug between them; and doing an affront to the order to which they have the honour equally to belong? All this while they do not see how the wealthier man stands by and laughs in his sleeve at both.

V.—THAT THE POOR COPY THE VICES OF THE RICH

A smooth text to the letter: and, preached from the pulpit, is sure of a docile audience from the pews lined with satin. It is twice sitting upon velvet to a foolish squire to be told, that *he*—and not *perverse nature*, as the homilies would make us imagine, is the true cause of all the irregularities in his parish. This is striking at the root of free-will indeed, and denying the originality of sin in any sense. But men are not such implicit sheep as this comes to. If the abstinence from evil on the part of the upper classes is to derive itself from no higher principle than the apprehension of setting ill patterns to the lower, we beg leave to discharge them from all squeamishness on that score: they may even take their fill of pleasures, where they can find them. The Genius of Poverty, hampered and straitened as it is, is not so barren of invention, but it can trade upon the staple of its own vice, without drawing upon their capital. The poor are not quite such servile imitators as they take them for. Some of them are very clever artists in their way. Here and there we find an original. Who taught the poor to steal, to pilfer? They did not go to the great for schoolmasters in these faculties, surely. It is well if in some vices they allow us to be—no copyists. In no other sense is it true that the poor copy them, than as servants may be said to *take after* their masters and mistresses, when they succeed to their reversionary cold meats. If the master, from indisposition, or some other cause, neglect his food, the servant dines notwithstanding.

'O, but (some will say) the force of example is great.' We knew a lady who was so scrupulous on this head, that she would put up with the calls of the most impertinent visitor, rather than let her servant say she was not at home, for fear of teaching her maid to tell an untruth; and this in the very face of the fact, which she knew well enough, that the wench was one of the greatest liars upon the earth without teaching; so much so, that her mistress possibly never heard two words of consecutive truth from her in her life. But nature must go for nothing: example must be everything. This liar in grain, who never opened her mouth without a lie, must be guarded against a remote inference, which she (pretty casuist!) might possibly draw from a form of words—literally false, but essentially deceiving no one—that under some circumstances a fib might not be so exceedingly sinful—a fiction, too, not at all in her own way, or one that she could be suspected of adopting, for few servant-wenches care to be denied to visitors.

This word *example* reminds us of another fine word which is in use upon these occasions—*encouragement*. 'People in our sphere must not be thought to give encouragement to such proceedings.' To such a frantic height is this principle capable of being carried, that we have known individuals who have thought it within the scope of their influence to sanction despair, and give *éclat* to—suicide. A domestic in the family of a county member lately deceased, from love, or some unknown cause, cut his throat, but not successfully. The poor fellow was otherwise much loved and respected; and great interest was used in his behalf, upon his recovery, that he might be permitted to retain his place; his word being first pledged, not without some substantial sponsors to promise for him, that the like should never happen again. His master was inclinable to keep him, but his mistress thought otherwise; and John in the end was dismissed, her ladyship declaring that she 'could not think of encouraging any such doings in the county.'

VI.—THAT ENOUGH IS AS GOOD AS A FEAST

Not a man, woman, or child, in ten miles round Guildhall, who really believes this saying. The inventor of it did not believe it himself. It was made in revenge by somebody, who was disappointed of a regale. It is a vile cold-scrag-of-mutton sophism; a lie palmed upon the palate, which knows better things. If nothing else could be said for a feast, this is sufficient, that from the superflux there is usually something left for the next day. Morally interpreted, it belongs to a class of proverbs which have a tendency to make us undervalue *money*. Of this cast are those notable observations, that money is not health; riches cannot purchase everything: the metaphor which makes gold to be mere muck, with the morality which traces fine clothing to the sheep's back, and denounces pearl as the unhandsome excretion of an oyster. Hence, too, the phrase which imputes dirt to acres—a sophistry so barefaced, that even the literal sense of it is true only in a wet season. This, and abundance of similar sage saws assuming to inculcate *content*, we verily believe to have been the invention of some cunning borrower, who had designs upon the purse of his wealthier neighbour, which he could only hope to carry by force of these verbal jugglings. Translate any one of these sayings out of the artful metonymy which envelops it, and the trick is apparent. Goodly legs and shoulders of mutton, exhilarating cordials, books, pictures, the opportunities of seeing foreign countries, independence, heart's ease, a man's own time to himself, are not *muck*—however we may be pleased to scandalise with that appellation the faithful metal that provides them for us.

VII.—OF TWO DISPUTANTS THE WARMEST IS GENERALLY IN THE WRONG

Our experience would lead us to quite an opposite conclusion. Temper, indeed, is no test of truth; but warmth and earnestness are a proof at least of a man's own conviction of the rectitude of that which he maintains. Coolness is as often the result of an unprincipled indifference to truth or falsehood, as of a sober confidence in a man's own side in a dispute. Nothing is more insulting sometimes than the appearance of this philosophic temper. There is little Titubus, the stammering law-stationer in Lincoln's Inn—we have seldom known this shrewd little fellow engaged in an argument where we were not convinced he had the best of it, if his tongue would but fairly have seconded him. When he has been spluttering excellent broken sense for an hour together, writhing and labouring to be delivered of the point of dispute—the very gist of the controversy knocking at his teeth, which like some obstinate iron-grating still obstructed its deliverance—his puny frame convulsed, and face reddening all over at an unfairness in the logic which he wanted articulation to expose, it has moved our gall to see a smooth portly fellow of an adversary, that cared not a button for the merits of the question, by merely laying his hand upon the head of the stationer, and desiring him to be *calm* (your tall disputants have always the advantage), with a provoking sneer carry the argument clean from him in the opinion of all the bystanders, who have gone away clearly convinced that Titubus must have been in the wrong, because he was in a passion; and that Mr.——, meaning his opponent, is one of the fairest and at the same time one of the most dispassionate arguers breathing.

VIII.—THAT VERBAL ALLUSIONS ARE NOT WIT, BECAUSE THEY WILL NOT BEAR A TRANSLATION

The same might be said of the wittiest local allusions. A custom is sometimes as difficult to explain to a foreigner as a pun. What would become of a great part of the wit of the last age, if it were tried by this test? How would certain topics, as aldermanity, cuckoldry, have sounded to a Terentian auditory, though Terence himself had been alive to translate them? *Senator urbanus* with *Curruca* to boot for a synonym, would but faintly have done the business. Words, involving notions, are hard enough to render; it is too much to expect us to translate a sound, and give an elegant version to a jingle. The Virgilian harmony is not translatable, but by substituting harmonious sounds in another language for it. To Latinise a pun, we must seek a pun in Latin that will answer to it; as, to give an idea of the double endings in Hudibras, we must have recourse to a similar practice in the old monkish doggerel. Dennis, the fiercest oppugner of puns in ancient or modern times, professes himself highly tickled with the 'a stick,' chiming to 'ecclesiastic.' Yet what is this but a species of pun, a verbal consonance?

IX.—THAT THE WORST PUNS ARE THE BEST

If by worst be only meant the most far-fetched and startling, we agree to it. A pun is not bound by the laws which limit nicer wit. It is a pistol let off at the ear; not a feather to tickle the intellect. It is an antic which does not stand upon manners, but comes bounding into the presence, and does not show the less comic for being dragged in sometimes by the head and shoulders. What though it limp a little, or prove defective in one leg?—all the better. A pun may easily be too curious and artificial. Who has not at one time or other been at a party of professors (himself perhaps an old offender in that line), where, after ringing a round of the most ingenious conceits, every man contributing his shot, and some there the most expert shooters of the day; after making a poor *word* run the gauntlet till it is ready to drop; after hunting and winding it through all the possible ambages of similar sounds; after squeezing, and hauling, and tugging at it, till the very milk of it will not yield a drop further,— suddenly some obscure, unthought-of fellow in a corner, who was never 'prentice to the trade, whom the company for very pity passed over, as we do by a known poor man when a money-subscription is going round, no one calling upon him for his quota—has all at once come out with something so whimsical, yet so pertinent; so brazen in its pretensions, yet so impossible to be denied; so exquisitely good, and so deplorably bad, at the same time,—that it has proved a Robin Hood's shot; anything ulterior to that is despaired of; and the party breaks up, unanimously voting it to be the very worst (that is, best) pun of the evening. This species of wit is the better for not being perfect in all its parts. What it gains in completeness, it loses in naturalness. The more exactly it satisfies the critical, the less hold it has upon some other faculties. The puns which are most entertaining are those which will least bear an analysis. Of this kind is the following, recorded with a sort of stigma, in one of Swift's Miscellanies.

An Oxford scholar, meeting a porter who was carrying a hare through the streets, accosts him with this extraordinary question: 'Prithee, friend, is that thy own hare, or a wig?'

There is no excusing this, and no resisting it. A man might blur ten sides of paper in attempting a defence of it against a critic who should be laughter-proof. The quibble in itself is not considerable. It is only a new turn given by a little false pronunciation, to a very common, though not very courteous inquiry. Put by one gentleman to another at a dinner-party, it would have been vapid; to the mistress of the house it would have shown much less wit than rudeness. We must take in the totality of time, place, and person; the pert look of the inquiring scholar, the desponding looks of the puzzled porter: the one stopping at leisure, the other hurrying on with his burden; the innocent though rather abrupt tendency of the first member of the question, with the utter and inextricable irrelevancy of the second; the place—a public street, not favourable to frivolous investigations; the affrontive quality of the primitive inquiry (the common question) invidiously transferred to the derivative (the new turn given to it) in the implied satire; namely, that few of that tribe are expected to eat of the good things which they carry, they being in most countries considered rather as the temporary trustees than owners of such dainties,—which the fellow was beginning to understand; but then the *wig* again comes in, and he can make nothing of it; all put together constitute a picture: Hogarth could have made it intelligible on canvas.

Yet nine out of ten critics will pronounce this a very bad pun, because of the defectiveness in the concluding member, which is its very beauty, and constitutes the surprise. The same person shall cry up for admirable the cold quibble from Virgil about the broken Cremona *; because it is made out in all its parts, and leaves nothing to the imagination. We venture to call it cold; because, of thousands who have admired it, it would be difficult to find one who has heartily chuckled at it. As appealing to the judgment merely (setting the risible faculty aside), we must pronounce it a monument of curious felicity. But as some stories are said to be too good to be true, it may with equal truth be asserted of this biverbal allusion, that it is too good to be natural. One cannot help suspecting that the incident was invented to fit the line. It would have been better had it been less perfect. Like some Virgilian hemistichs, it has suffered by filling up. The *nimium Vicina* was enough in conscience; the *Cremonæ* afterwards loads it. It is, in fact, a double pun; and we have always observed that a superfœtation in this sort of wit is dangerous. When a man has said a good thing, it is seldom politic to follow it up. We do not care to be cheated a second time; or, perhaps the mind of man (with reverence be it spoken) is not capacious enough to lodge two puns at a time. The impression, to be forcible, must be simultaneous and undivided.

* Swift.

X.—THAT HANDSOME IS THAT HANDSOME DOES

Those who use this proverb can never have seen Mrs. Conrady.

The soul, if we may believe Plotinus, is a ray from the celestial beauty. As she partakes more or less of this heavenly light, she informs, with corresponding characters, the fleshly tenement which she chooses, and frames to herself a suitable mansion.

All which only proves that the soul of Mrs. Conrady, in her pre-existent state, was no great judge of architecture.

To the same effect, in a Hymn in honour of Beauty, divine Spenser *platonising*, sings:—

> ———Every spirit as it is more pure,
> And hath in it the more of heavenly light,
> So it the fairer body doth procure
> To habit in, and it more fairly dight
> With cheerful grace and amiable sight.
> For of the soul the body form doth take:
> For soul is form and doth the body make.

But Spenser, it is clear, never saw Mrs. Conrady.

These poets, we find, are no safe guides in philosophy; for here, in his very next stanza but one, is a saving clause, which throws us all out again, and leaves us as much to seek as ever:—

> Yet oft it falls, that many a gentle mind
> Dwells in deformed tabernacle drown'd,
> Either by chance, against the course of kind,
> Or through unaptness in the substance found,
> Which it assumed of some stubborn ground,
> That will not yield unto her form's direction,
> But is performed with some foul imperfection.

From which it would follow, that Spenser had seen somebody like Mrs. Conrady.

The spirit of this good lady—her previous *anima*—must have stumbled upon one of these untoward tabernacles which he speaks of. A more rebellious commodity of clay for a ground, as the poet calls it, no gentle mind—and sure hers is one of the gentlest—ever had to deal with.

Pondering upon her inexplicable visage—inexplicable, we

mean, but by this modification of the theory—we have come to a conclusion that, if one must be plain, it is better to be plain all over, than amidst a tolerable residue of features, to hang out one that shall be exceptionable. No one can say of Mrs. Conrady's countenance that it would be better if she had but a nose. It is impossible to pull her to pieces in this manner. We have seen the most malicious beauties of her own sex baffled in the attempt at a selection. The *tout-ensemble* defies particularising. It is too complete—too consistent, as we may say—to admit of these invidious reservations. It is not as if some Apelles had picked out here a lip—and there a chin—out of the collected ugliness of Greece, to frame a model by. It is a symmetrical whole. We challenge the minutest connoisseur to cavil at any part or parcel of the countenance in question; to say that this, or that, is improperly placed. We are convinced that true ugliness, no less than is affirmed of true beauty, is the result of harmony. Like that, too, it reigns without a competitor. No one ever saw Mrs. Conrady, without pronouncing her to be the plainest woman that he ever met with in the course of his life. The first time that you are indulged with a sight of her face, is an era in your existence ever after. You are glad to have seen it—like Stonehenge. No one can pretend to forget it. No one ever apologised to her for meeting her in the street on such a day and not knowing her: the pretext would be too bare. Nobody can mistake her for another. Nobody can say of her, 'I think I have seen that face somewhere, but I cannot call to mind where.' You must remember that in such a parlour it first struck you—like a bust. You wondered where the owner of the house had picked it up. You wondered more when it began to move its lips—so mildly too! No one ever thought of asking her to sit for her picture. Lockets are for remembrance; and it would be clearly superfluous to hang an image at your heart, which, once seen, can never be out of it. It is not a mean face either; its entire originality precludes that. Neither is it of that order of plain faces which improve upon acquaintance. Some very good but ordinary people, by an unwearied perseverance in good offices, put a cheat upon our eyes; juggle our senses out of their natural impressions; and set us upon discovering good indications in a countenance, which had escaped us, lurking about an under lip. But when Mrs.

Conrady has done you a service, her face remains the same; when she has done you a thousand, and you know that she is ready to double the number, still it is that individual face. Neither can you say of it, that it would be a good face if it were not marked by the small-pox—a compliment which is always more admissive than excusatory—for either Mrs. Conrady never had the small-pox; or, as we say, took it kindly. No, it stands upon its own merits fairly. There it is. It is her mark, her token; that which she is known by.

XI.—THAT WE MUST NOT LOOK A GIFT HORSE
IN THE MOUTH

Nor a lady's age in the parish register. We hope we have more delicacy than to do either; but some faces spare us the trouble of these *dental* inquiries. And what if the beast, which my friend would force upon my acceptance, prove, upon the face of it, a sorry Rosinante, a lean, ill-favoured jade, whom no gentleman could think of setting up in his stables? Must I, rather than not be obliged to my friend, make her a companion to Eclipse or Lightfoot? A horse-giver, no more than a horse-seller, has a right to palm his spavined article upon us for good ware. An equivalent is expected in either case; and, with my own good-will, I would no more be cheated out of my thanks than out of my money. Some people have a knack of putting upon you gifts of no real value, to engage you to substantial gratitude. We thank them for nothing. Our friend Mitis carries this humour of never refusing a present, to the very point of absurdity—if it were possible to couple the ridiculous with so much mistaken delicacy, and real good-nature. Not an apartment in his fine house (and he has a true taste in household decorations), but is stuffed up with some preposterous print or mirror—the worst adapted to his panels that may be—the presents of his friends that know his weakness; while his noble Vandykes are displaced, to make room for a set of daubs, the work of some wretched artist of his acquaintance, who, having had them returned upon his hands for bad likenesses, finds his account in bestowing them here gratis. The good creature has not the heart to mortify the painter at the expense of an honest refusal. It is pleasant (if it did not vex one at the same time) to see him sitting in his dining parlour, surrounded with obscure aunts and cousins to God knows whom, while the true Lady Marys and Lady Bettys of his own honourable family, in favour to these adopted frights, are consigned to the staircase and the lumber-room. In like manner his goodly shelves are one by one stripped of his favourite old authors, to give place to a collection of presentation copies—the flour and bran of modern poetry. A presentation copy, reader— if haply you are yet innocent of such favours—is a copy of a book which does not sell, sent you by the author, with his foolish autograph at the beginning of it; for which, if a stranger, he only demands your friendship; if a brother author, he expects from you a book of yours, which does sell, in return. We can speak to experience, having by us a tolerable assortment of these gift-horses. Not to ride a metaphor to death—we are willing to acknowledge, that in some gifts there is sense. A duplicate out of a friend's library (where he has more than one copy of a rare author) is intelligible. There are favours, short of the pecuniary—a thing not fit to be hinted at among gentlemen—which confer as much grace upon the acceptor as the offerer; the kind, we confess, which is most to our palate, is of those little con- ciliatory missives, which for their vehicle generally choose a hamper—little odd presents of game, fruit, perhaps wine— though it is essential to the delicacy of the latter, that it be home-made. We love to have our friend in the country sitting thus at our table by proxy; to apprehend his presence (though a hundred miles may be between us) by a turkey, whose goodly aspect reflects to us his 'plump corpusculum'; to taste him in grouse or woodcock; to feel him gliding down in the toast peculiar to the latter; to concorporate him in a slice of Canterbury brawn. This is indeed to have him within ourselves; to know him intimately; such participation is methinks unitive, as the old theologians phrase it. For these considerations we should be sorry if certain restrictive regu- lations, which are thought to bear hard upon the peasantry of this country, were entirely done away with. A hare, as the law now stands, makes many friends. Caius conciliates Titius (knowing his *goût*) with a leash of partridges. Titius (sus- pecting his partiality for them) passes them to Lucius; who, in his turn, preferring his friend's relish to his own, makes them over to Marcius; till in their ever-widening progress, and round of unconscious circum-migration, they distribute the seeds of harmony over half a parish. We are well-disposed

to this kind of sensible remembrances; and are the less apt
to be taken by those little airy tokens—impalpable to the
palate—which, under the names of rings, lockets, keep-sakes,
amuse some people's fancy mightily. We could never away
with these indigestible trifles. They are the very kick-shaws
and foppery of friendship.

XII.—THAT HOME IS HOME THOUGH IT IS NEVER SO HOMELY

Homes there are, we are sure, that are no homes; the home
of the very poor man, and another which we shall speak to
presently. Crowded places of cheap entertainment, and the
benches of alehouses, if they could speak, might bear mournful
testimony to the first. To them the very poor man resorts for
an image of the home, which he cannot find at home. For a
starved grate, and a scanty firing, that is not enough to keep
alive the natural heat in the fingers of so many shivering
children with their mother, he finds in the depths of winter
always a blazing hearth, and a hob to warm his pittance of
beer by. Instead of the clamours of a wife, made gaunt by
famishing, he meets with a cheerful attendance beyond the
merits of the trifle which he can afford to spend. He has
companions which his home denies him, for the very poor
man has no visitors. He can look into the goings on of the
world, and speak a little to politics. At home there are no
politics stirring, but the domestic. All interests, real or
imaginary, all topics that should expand the mind of man,
and connect him to a sympathy with general existence, are
crushed in the absorbing consideration of food to be obtained
for the family. Beyond the price of bread, news is senseless
and impertinent. At home there is no larder. Here there is at
least a show of plenty; and while he cooks his lean scrap of
butcher's meat before the common bars, or munches his
humbler cold viands, his relishing bread and cheese with an
onion, in a corner, where no one reflects upon his poverty,
he has a sight of the substantial joint providing for the land-
lord and his family. He takes an interest in the dressing of it;
and while he assists in removing the trivet from the fire, he
feels that there is such a thing as beef and cabbage, which
he was beginning to forget at home. All this while he deserts
his wife and children. But what wife, and what children?
Prosperous men, who object to this desertion, image to them-

selves some clean contented family like that which they go home to. But look at the countenance of the poor wives who follow and persecute their good-man to the door of the public-house, which he is about to enter, when something like shame would restrain him, if stronger misery did not induce him to pass the threshold. That face, ground by want, in which every cheerful, every conversable lineament has been long effaced by misery,—is that a face to stay at home with? is it more a woman, or a wild cat? alas! it is the face of the wife of his youth, that once smiled upon him. It can smile no longer. What comforts can it share? what burthens can it lighten? Oh, 'tis a fine thing to talk of the humble meal shared together! But what if there be no bread in the cupboard? The innocent prattle of his children takes out the sting of a man's poverty. But the children of the very poor do not prattle. It is none of the least frightful features in that condition, that there is no childishness in its dwellings. Poor people, said a sensible old nurse to us once, do not bring up their children; they drag them up.

The little careless darling of the wealthier nursery, in their hovel is transformed betimes into a premature reflecting person. No one has time to dandle it, no one thinks it worth while to coax it, to soothe it, to toss it up and down, to humour it. There is none to kiss away its tears. If it cries, it can only be beaten. It has been prettily said, that 'a babe is fed with milk and praise.' But the aliment of this poor babe was thin, unnourishing; the return to its little baby-tricks, and efforts to engage attention, bitter ceaseless objurgation. It never had a toy, or knew what a coral meant. It grew up without the lullaby of nurses, it was a stranger to the patient fondle, the hushing caress, the attracting novelty, the costlier plaything, or the cheaper off-hand contrivance to divert the child; the prattled nonsense (best sense to it), the wise impertinences, the wholesome lies, the apt story interposed that puts a stop to present sufferings, and awakens the passions of young wonder. It was never sung to—no one ever told to it a tale of the nursery. It was dragged up, to live or to die as it happened. It had no young dreams. It broke at once into the iron realities of life. A child exists not for the very poor as any object of dalliance; it is only another mouth to be fed, a pair of little hands to be betimes inured to labour. It is the rival, till it can be the co-operator, for food with the parent. It is never his mirth, his diversion, his solace: it never makes him young again, with recalling his young times. The children of the very poor have no young times. It makes the very heart to bleed to overhear the casual street-talk between a poor woman and her little girl, a woman of the better sort of poor, in a condition rather above the squalid beings which we have been contemplating. It is not of toys, of nursery books, of summer holidays (fitting that age); of the promised sight, of play; of praised sufficiency at school. It is of mangling and clear-starching, of the price of coals, or of potatoes. The questions of the child, that should be the very outpourings of curiosity in idleness, are marked with forecast and melancholy providence. It has come to be a woman,—before it was a child. It has learned to go to market; it chaffers, it haggles, it envies, it murmurs; it is knowing, acute, sharpened; it never prattles. Had we not reason to say that the home of the very poor is no home?

There is yet another home, which we are constrained to deny to be one. It has a larder, which the home of the poor man wants; its fireside conveniences, of which the poor dream not. But with all this, it is no home. It is—the house of a man that is infested with many visitors. May we be branded for the veriest churl, if we deny our heart to the many noble-hearted friends that at times exchange their dwelling for our poor roof! It is not of guests that we complain, but of endless, purposeless visitants; droppers-in, as they are called. We sometimes wonder from what sky they fall. It is the very error of the position of our lodging; its horoscopy was ill calculated, being just situate in a medium —a plaguy suburban mid-space—fitted to catch idlers from town or country. We are older than we were, and age is easily put out of its way. We have fewer sands in our glass to reckon upon, and we cannot brook to see them drop in endlessly succeeding impertinences. At our time of life, to be alone sometimes is as needful as sleep. It is the refreshing sleep of the day. The growing infirmities of age manifest themselves in nothing more strongly, than in an inveterate dislike of interruption. The thing which we are doing, we wish to be permitted to do. We have neither much knowledge nor devices; but there are fewer in the place to which we hasten. We are not willingly put out of our way, even at a game of nine-pins. While youth was, we had vast reversions in time future; we are reduced to a present pittance, and obliged to economise in that article. We bleed away our moments now as hardly as our ducats. We cannot bear to have our thin wardrobe eaten and fretted into by moths. We are willing to barter our good time with a friend, who gives us in exchange his own. Herein is the distinction between the genuine guest and the visitant. This latter takes your good time, and gives you his bad in exchange. The guest is domestic to you as your good cat, or household bird; the visitant is your fly, that flaps in at your window, and out again, leaving nothing but a sense of disturbance, and victuals spoiled. The inferior functions of life begin to move heavily. We cannot concoct our food with interruptions. Our chief meal, to be nutritive, must be solitary. With difficulty we can eat before a guest; and never understood what the relish of public feasting meant. Meats have no sapor, nor digestion fair play, in a crowd. The unexpected coming in of a visitant stops the machine. There is a punctual generation who time their calls to the precise commencement of your dining-hour —not to eat—but to see you eat. Our knife and fork drop instinctively, and we feel that we have swallowed our latest morsel. Others again show their genius, as we have said, in knocking the moment you have just sat down to a book. They have a peculiar compassionate sneer, with which they 'hope that they do not interrupt your studies.' Though they flutter off the next moment, to carry their impertinences to the nearest student that they can call their friend, the tone of the book is spoiled; we shut the leaves, and with Dante's lovers, read no more that day. It were well if the effect of intrusion were simply co-extensive with its presence, but it mars all the good hours afterwards. These scratches in appearance leave an orifice that closes not hastily. 'It is a prostitution of the bravery of friendship,' says worthy Bishop Taylor, 'to spend it upon impertinent people, who are, it may be, loads to their families, but can never ease my loads.' This is the secret of their gaddings, their visits, and morning calls. They too have homes, which are—no homes.

XIII.—THAT YOU MUST LOVE ME AND LOVE MY DOG

'Good sir, or madam—as it may be—we most willingly embrace the offer of your friendship. We have long known your excellent qualities. We have wished to have you nearer to us; to hold you within the very innermost fold of our heart. We can have no reserve towards a person of your open and noble nature. The frankness of your humour suits us exactly. We have been long looking for such a friend. Quick—let us disburthen our troubles into each other's bosom—let us make our single joys shine by reduplication—But *yap, yap, yap!* what is this confounded cur? he has fastened his tooth, which is none of the bluntest, just in the fleshy part of my leg.'

'It is my dog, sir. You must love him for my sake. Here, Test—Test—Test!'

'But he has bitten me.'

'Ay, that he is apt to do, till you are better acquainted with him. I have had him three years. He never bites me.'

Yap, yap, yap!—'He is at it again.'

'Oh, sir, you must not kick him. He does not like to be kicked. I expect my dog to be treated with all the respect due to myself.'

'But do you always take him out with you, when you go a friendship-hunting?'

'Invariably. 'Tis the sweetest, prettiest, best-conditioned animal. I call him my *test*—the touchstone by which to try a friend. No one can properly be said to love me, who does not love him.'

'Excuse us, dear sir—or madam, aforesaid—if upon further consideration we are obliged to decline the otherwise invaluable offer of your friendship. We do not like dogs.'

'Mighty well, sir,—you know the conditions—you may have worse offers. Come along, Test.'

The above dialogue is not so imaginary, but that, in the intercourse of life, we have had frequent occasions of breaking off an agreeable intimacy by reason of these canine appendages. They do not always come in the shape of dogs; they sometimes wear the more plausible and human character of kinsfolk, near acquaintances, my friend's friend, his partner, his wife, or his children. We could never yet form a friendship—not to speak of more delicate correspondence—however much to our taste, without the intervention of some third anomaly, some impertinent clog affixed to the relation—the understood *dog* in the proverb. The good things of life are not to be had singly, but come to us with a mixture; like a schoolboy's holiday, with a task affixed to the tail of it. What a delightful companion * * * *, if he did not always bring his tall cousin with him! He seems to grow with him; like some of those double births which we remember to have read of with such wonder and delight in the old 'Athenian Oracle,' where Swift commenced author by writing Pindaric Odes (what a beginning for him!) upon Sir William Temple. There is the picture of the brother, with the little brother peeping out at his shoulder; a species of fraternity, which we have no name of kin close enough to comprehend. When **** comes, poking in his head and shoulder into your room, as if to feel his entry, you think, surely you have now got him to yourself—what a three hours' chat we shall have!— but ever in the haunch of him, and before his diffident body is well disclosed in your apartment, appears the haunting shadow of the cousin, overpeering his modest kinsman, and sure to overlay the expected good talk with his insufferable procerity of stature, and uncorresponding dwarfishness of observation. Misfortunes seldom come alone. 'Tis hard when a blessing comes accompanied. Cannot we like Sempronia, without sitting down to chess with her eternal brother; or know Sulpicia, without knowing all the round of her card-playing relations?—must my friend's brethren of necessity be mine also? must we be hand and glove with Dick Selby the parson, or Jack Selby the calico-printer, because W. S., who is neither, but a ripe wit and a critic, has the misfortune to claim a common parentage with them? Let him lay down his brothers; and 'tis odds that we will cast him in a pair of ours (we have a superflux) to balance the concession. Let F. H. lay down his garrulous uncle; and Honorius dismiss his vapid wife, and superfluous establishment of six boys: things between boy and manhood—too ripe for play, too raw for conversation—that come in, impudently staring their father's old friend out of countenance; and will neither aid nor let alone, the conference; that we may once more meet upon equal terms, as we were wont to do in the disengaged state of bachelorhood.

It is well if your friend, or mistress, be content with these canicular probations. Few young ladies but in this sense keep a dog. But while Rutilia hounds at you her tiger aunt; or Ruspina expects you to cherish and fondle her viper sister, whom she has preposterously taken into her bosom, to try stinging conclusions upon your constancy; they must not complain if the house be rather thin of suitors. Scylla must have broken off many excellent matches in her time, if she insisted upon all that loved her, loving her dogs also.

An excellent story to this moral is told of Merry, of Della Cruscan memory. In tender youth he loved and courted a modest appanage to the Opera—in truth a dancer,—who had won him by the artless contrast between her manners and situation. She seemed to him a native violet, that had been transplanted by some rude accident, into that exotic and artificial hotbed. Nor, in truth, was she less genuine and sincere than she appeared to him. He wooed and won this flower. Only for appearance' sake, and for due honour to the bride's relations, she craved that she might have the attendance of her friends and kindred at the approaching solemnity. The request was too amiable not to be conceded: and in this solicitude for conciliating the good-will of mere relations, he found a presage of her superior attentions to himself, when the golden shaft should have 'killed the flock of all affections else.' The morning came: and at the Star and Garter, Richmond—the place appointed for the break-fasting—accompanied with one English friend, he impatiently awaited what reinforcements the bride should bring to grace the ceremony. A rich muster she had made. They came in six coaches—the whole corps du ballet—French, Italian, men and women. Monsieur de B., the famous *pirouetter* of the day, led his fair spouse, but craggy, from the banks of the Seine. The Prima Donna had sent her excuse. But the first and second Buffa were there; and Signor Sc—, and Signora Ch—, and Madame V—, with a countless cavalcade besides of chorusers, figurantes! at the sight of whom Merry after-wards declared, that 'then for the first time it struck him seriously, that he was about to marry—a dancer.' But there was no help for it. Besides, it was her day; these were, in fact, her friends and kinsfolk. The assemblage, though whim-sical, was all very natural. But when the bride—handing out of the last coach a still more extraordinary figure than the rest—presented to him as her *father*—the gentleman that was to *give her away*—no less a person than Signor Delpini himself —with a sort of pride, as much as to say, See what I have brought to do us honour!—the thought of so extraordinary a paternity quite overcame him; and slipping away under some pretence from the bride and her motley adherents, poor Merry took horse from the back yard to the nearest sea-coast, from which, shipping himself to America, he shortly after consoled himself with a more congenial match in the person of Miss Brunton; relieved from his intended clown father, and a bevy of painted buffas for bridesmaids.

XIV.—THAT WE SHOULD RISE WITH THE LARK

At what precise minute that little airy musician doffs his night-gear, and prepares to tune up his unseasonable matins, we are not naturalists enough to determine. But for a mere human gentleman—that has no orchestra business to call him from his warm bed to such preposterous exercises—we take ten, or half after ten (eleven, of course, during this Christmas solstice), to be the very earliest hour at which he can begin to think of abandoning his pillow. To think of it, we say; for to do it in earnest requires another half hour's good consideration. Not but there are pretty sun-risings, as we are told, and such like gawds, abroad in the world, in summer-time especially, some hours before what we have assigned; which a gentleman may see, as they say, only for getting up. But having been tempted once or twice, in earlier life, to assist at those ceremonies, we confess our curiosity abated. We are no longer ambitious of being the sun's courtiers, to attend at his morning levees. We hold the good hours of the dawn too sacred to waste them upon such observances; which have in them, besides, something Pagan and Persic. To say truth, we never anticipated our usual hour, or got up with the sun (as 'tis called), to go a journey, or upon a foolish whole day's pleasuring, but we suffered for it all the long hours after in listlessness and headaches; Nature herself sufficiently declaring her sense of our presumption in aspiring to regulate our frail waking courses by the measures of that celestial and sleepless traveller. We deny not that there is something sprightly and vigorous, at the outset especially, in these break-of-day excursions. It is flattering to get the start of a lazy world; to conquer death by proxy in his image. But the seeds of sleep and mortality are in us; and we pay usually, in strange qualms before night falls, the penalty of the unnatural inversion. Therefore, while the busy part of mankind are fast huddling on their clothes, are already up and about their occupations, content to have swallowed their sleep by wholesale; we choose to linger a-bed, and digest our dreams. It is the very time to recombine the wandering images, which night in a confused mass presented; to snatch them from forgetfulness; to shape, and mould them. Some people have no good of their dreams. Like fast feeders, they gulp them too grossly, to taste them curiously. We love to chew the cud of a foregone vision: to collect the scattered rays of a brighter phantasm, or act over again, with firmer nerves, the sadder nocturnal tragedies; to drag into day-light a struggling and half-vanishing night-mare; to handle and examine the terrors, or the airy solaces. We have too much respect for these spiritual communications, to let them go so lightly. We are not so stupid, or so careless as that Imperial forgetter of his dreams, that we should need a seer to remind us of the form of them. They seem to us to have as much significance as our waking concerns: or rather to import us more nearly, as more nearly we approach by years to the shadowy world, whither we are hastening. We have shaken hands with the world's business; we have done with it; we have discharged ourself of it. Why should we get up? we have neither suit to solicit, nor affairs to manage. The drama has shut in upon us at the fourth act. We have nothing here to expect, but in a short time a sick bed, and a dismissal. We delight to anticipate death by such shadows as night affords. We are already half acquainted with ghosts. We were never much in the world. Disappointment early struck a dark veil between us and its dazzling illusions. Our spirits showed grey before our hairs. The mighty changes of the world already appear as but the vain stuff out of which dramas are composed. We have asked no more of life than what the mimic images in play-houses present us with. Even those types have waxed fainter. Our clock appears to have struck. We are SUPERANNUATED. In this dearth of mundane satisfaction, we contract politic alliances with shadows. It is good to have friends at court. The abstracted media of dreams seem no ill introduction to that spiritual presence, upon which, in no long time, we expect to be thrown. We are trying to know a little of the usages of that colony; to learn the language, and the faces we shall meet with there, that we may be the less awkward at our first coming among them. We willingly call a phantom our fellow, as knowing we shall soon be of their dark companionship. Therefore, we cherish dreams. We try to spell in them the alphabet of the invisible world; and think we know already, how it shall be with us. Those uncouth shapes, which, while we clung to flesh and blood, affrighted us, have become familiar. We feel attenuated into their meagre essences, and have given the hand of half-way approach to incorporeal being. We once thought life to be something; but it has unaccountably fallen from us before its time. Therefore we choose to dally with visions. The sun has no purposes of ours to light us to. Why should we get up?

XV.—THAT WE SHOULD LIE DOWN WITH THE LAMB

We could never quite understand the philosophy of this arrangement, or the wisdom of our ancestors in sending us for instruction to these woolly bedfellows. A sheep, when it is dark, has nothing to do but to shut his silly eyes, and sleep if he can. Man found out long sixes,—Hail, candle-light! without disparagement to sun and moon, the kindliest luminary of the three—if we may not rather style thee their radiant deputy, mild viceroy of the moon!—We love to read, talk, sit silent, eat, drink, sleep, by candle-light. They are everybody's sun and moon. This is our peculiar and household planet. Wanting it, what savage unsocial nights must our ancestors have spent, wintering in caves and unillumined fastnesses! They must have lain about and grumbled at one another in the dark. What repartees could have passed, when you must have felt about for a smile, and handled a neighbour's cheek to be sure that he understood it? This accounts for the seriousness of the elder poetry. It has a sombre cast (try Hesiod or Ossian), derived from the tradition of those unlantern'd nights. Jokes came in with candles. We wonder how they saw to pick up a pin, if they had any. How did they sup? what a mélange of chance carving they must have made of it!—here one had got a leg of a goat, when he wanted a horse's shoulder—there another had dipped his scooped palm in a kid-skin of wild honey, when he meditated right mare's milk. There is neither good eating nor drinking in fresco. Who, even in these civilised times, has never experienced this, when at some economic table he has commenced dining after dusk, and waited for the flavour till the lights came? The senses absolutely give and take reciprocally. Can you tell pork from veal in the dark? or distinguish Sherris from pure

Malaga? Take away the candle from the smoking man; by the glimmering of the left ashes, he knows that he is still smoking, but he knows it only by an inference; till the restored light, coming in aid of the olfactories, reveals to both senses the full aroma. Then how he redoubles his puffs! how he burnishes!—There is absolutely no such thing as reading but by a candle. We have tried the affectation of a book at noon-day in gardens, and in sultry arbours; but it was labour thrown away. Those gay motes in the beam come about you, hovering and teasing, like so many coquettes, that will have you all to their self, and are jealous of your abstractions. By the midnight taper, the writer digests his meditations. By the same light we must approach to their perusal, if we would catch the flame, the odour. It is a mockery, all that is reported of the influential Phœbus. No true poem ever owed its birth to the sun's light. They are abstracted works—

> Things that were born, when none but the still night,
> And his dumb candle, saw his pinching throes.

Marry, daylight—daylight might furnish the images, the crude material; but for the fine shapings, the true turning and filing (as mine author hath it), they must be content to hold their inspiration of the candle. The mild internal light, that reveals them, like fires on the domestic hearth, goes out in the sunshine. Night and silence call out the starry fancies. Milton's Morning Hymn in Paradise, we would hold a good wager, was penned at midnight; and Taylor's rich description of a sun-rise smells decidedly of the taper. Even ourself, in these our humbler lucubrations, tune our best-measured cadences (Prose has her cadences) not unfrequently to the charm of the drowsier watchman, 'blessing the doors'; or the wild sweep of winds at midnight. Even now a loftier speculation than we have yet attempted, courts our endeavours. We would indite something about the Solar System.— *Betty, bring the candles.*

XVI.—THAT A SULKY TEMPER IS A MISFORTUNE

We grant that it is, and a very serious one—to a man's friends, and to all that have to do with him; but whether the condition of the man himself is so much to be deplored may admit of a question. We can speak a little to it, being ourselves but lately recovered—we whisper it in confidence, reader,—out of a long and desperate fit of the sullens. Was the cure a blessing? The conviction which wrought it, came too clearly to leave a scruple of the fanciful injuries—for they were mere fancies—which had provoked the humour. But the humour itself was too self-pleasing, while it lasted—we know how bare we lay ourself in the confession—to be abandoned all at once with the grounds of it. We still brood over wrongs which we know to have been imaginary; and for our old acquaintance N——, whom we find to have been a truer friend than we took him for, we substitute some phantom—a Caius or a Titius—as like him as we dare to form it, to wreak our yet unsatisfied resentments on. It is mortifying to fall at once from the pinnacle of neglect; to forego the idea of having been ill-used and contumaciously treated by an old friend. The first thing to aggrandise a man in his own conceit, is to conceive of himself as neglected. There let him fix if he can. To undeceive him is to deprive him of the most tickling morsel within the range of self-complacency. No flattery can come near it. Happy is he who suspects his friend of an injustice; but supremely blest, who thinks all his friends in a conspiracy to depress and under-value him. There is a pleasure (we sing not to the profane) far beyond the reach of all that the world calls joy—a deep, enduring satisfaction in the depths, where the superficial seek it not, of discontent. Were we to recite one half of this mystery,—which we were let into by our late dissatisfaction, all the world would be in love with disrespect; we should wear a slight for a bracelet, and neglects and contumacies would be the only matter for courtship. Unlike to that mysterious book in the Apocalypse, the study of this mystery is unpalatable only in the commencement. The first sting of a suspicion is grievous; but wait—out of that wound, which to flesh and blood seemed so difficult, there is balm and honey to be extracted. Your friend passed you on such or such a day,—having in his company one that you conceived worse than ambiguously disposed towards you,— passed you in the street without notice. To be sure, he is something short-sighted; and it was in your power to have accosted *him*. But facts and sane inferences are trifles to a true adept in the science of dissatisfaction. He must have seen you; and S——, who was with him, must have been the cause of the contempt.

It galls you, and well it may. But have patience. Go home, and make the worst of it, and you are a made man from this time. Shut yourself up, and—rejecting, as an enemy to your peace, every whispering suggestion that but insinuates there may be a mistake—reflect seriously upon the many lesser instances which you had begun to perceive, in proof of your friend's disaffection towards you. None of them singly was much to the purpose, but the aggregate weight is positive; and you have this last affront to clench them. Thus far the process is anything but agreeable. But now to your relief comes in the comparative faculty. You conjure up all the kind feelings you have had for your friend; what you have been to him, and what you would have been to him, if he would have suffered you; how you defended him in this or that place; and his good name—his literary reputation, and so forth, was always dearer to you than your own! Your heart, spite of itself, yearns towards him. You could weep tears of blood but for a restraining pride. How say you! do you not yet begin to apprehend a comfort?—some allay of sweetness in the bitter waters? Stop not here, nor penuriously cheat yourself of your reversions. You are on vantage ground. Enlarge your speculations, and take in the rest of your friends, as a spark kindles more sparks. Was there one among them who has not to you proved hollow, false, slippery as water? Begin to think that the relation itself is inconsistent with mortality. That the very idea of friendship, with its component parts, as honour, fidelity, steadiness, exists but in your single bosom. Image yourself to yourself, as the only possible friend in a world incapable of that communion. Now the gloom thickens. The little star of self-love twinkles, that is to encourage you through deeper glooms than this. You are not yet at the half point of your elevation. You are not yet, believe me, half sulky enough. Adverting to the world in general (as these circles in the mind will spread to infinity), reflect with what strange injustice you have been treated in quarters where (setting gratitude and the expectation of friendly returns aside as chimeras) you pretended no claim beyond justice, the naked due of all men. Think the very idea of right and fit fled from the earth, or your breast the solitary receptacle of it, till you have swelled yourself into at least one hemisphere; the other being the vast Arabia Stony of your friends and the world aforesaid. To grow bigger every

moment in your own conceit, and the world to lessen; to
deify yourself at the expense of your species; to judge the
world—this is the acme and supreme point of your mystery—
these the true PLEASURES of SULKINESS. We profess no more
of this grand secret than what ourself experimented on one
rainy afternoon in the last week, sulking in our study. We
had proceeded to the penultimate point, at which the true
adept seldom stops, where the consideration of benefit forgot
is about to merge in the meditation of general injustice—
when a knock at the door was followed by the entrance of the
very friend whose not seeing of us in the morning (for we will
now confess the case our own), an accidental oversight, had
given rise to so much agreeable generalisation! To mortify
us still more, and take down the whole flattering superstructure which pride had piled upon neglect, he had brought
in his hand the identical S——, in whose favour we had
suspected him of the contumacy. Asseverations were needless,
where the frank manner of them both was convictive of the
injurious nature of the suspicion. We fancied that they perceived our embarrassment; but were too proud or something
else, to confess to the secret of it. We had been but too lately
in the condition of the noble patient in Argos:—

> Qui se credebat miros audire tragœdos,
> In vacuo lætus sessor plausorque theatro—

and could have exclaimed with equal reason against the
friendly hands that cured us—

> Pol, me occidistis, amici,
> Non servastis, ait; cui sic extorta voluptas,
> Et demptus per vim mentis gratissimus error.

MISCELLANEOUS ESSAYS

To comfort the desponding parent with the thought that, without diminishing the stock which is imperiously demanded to furnish the more pressing and homely wants of our nature, he has disposed of one or more perhaps out of a numerous offspring, under the shelter of a care scarce less tender than the paternal, where not only their bodily cravings shall be supplied, but that mental *pabulum* is also dispensed, which HE hath declared to be no less necessary to our sustenance, who said, that, 'not by bread alone man can live': for this Christ's Hospital unfolds her bounty. Here neither, on the one hand, are the youth lifted up above their family, which we must suppose liberal, though reduced; nor on the other hand, are they liable to be depressed below its level by the mean habits and sentiments which a common charity-school generates. It is, in a word, an Institution to keep those who have yet held up their heads in the world from sinking; to keep alive the spirit of a decent household, when poverty was in danger of crushing it; to assist those who are the most willing, but not always the most able, to assist themselves; to separate a child from his family for a season, in order to render him back hereafter, with feelings and habits more congenial to it, than he could even have attained by remaining at home in the bosom of it. It is a preserving and renovating principle, an antidote for the *res angusta domi*, when it presses, as it always does, most heavily upon the most ingenuous natures.

This is Christ's Hospital; and whether its character would be improved by confining its advantages to the very lowest of the people, let those judge who have witnessed the looks, the gestures, the behaviour, the manner of their play with one another, their deportment towards strangers, the whole aspect and physiognomy of that vast assemblage of boys on the London foundation, who freshen and make alive again with their sports the else mouldering cloisters of the old Grey Friars—which strangers who have never witnessed, if they pass through Newgate Street, or by Smithfield, would do well to go a little out of their way to see.

For the Christ's Hospital boy feels that he is no charity-boy; he feels it in the antiquity and regality of the foundation to which he belongs; in the usage which he meets with at school, and the treatment he is accustomed to out of its bounds; in the respect and even kindness, which his well-known garb never fails to procure him in the streets of the metropolis; he feels it in his education, in that measure of classical attainments, which every individual at that school, though not destined to a learned profession, has it in his power to procure, attainments which it would be worse than folly to put in the reach of the labouring classes to acquire; he feels it in the numberless comforts, and even magnificences, which surround him; in his old and awful cloisters, with their traditions; in his spacious schoolrooms, and in the well-ordered, airy, and lofty rooms where he sleeps; in his stately dining-hall, hung round with pictures, by Verrio, Lely, and others, one of them surpassing in size and grandeur almost any other in the kingdom*; above all, in the very extent and magnitude of the body to which he belongs, and the consequent spirit, the intelligence, and public conscience, which is the result of so many various yet wonderfully combining members. Compared with this last-named advantage, what is the stock of information (I do not here speak of book-learning, but of that knowledge which boy receives from boy), the mass of collected opinions, the intelligence in common, among the few and narrow members of an ordinary boarding-school?

The Christ's Hospital or Blue-coat boy has a distinctive character of his own, as far removed from the abject qualities of a common charity-boy as it is from the disgusting forwardness of a lad brought up at some other of the public schools. There is *pride* in it, accumulated from the circumstances which I have described, as differencing him from the former; and there is *a restraining modesty* from a sense of obligation and dependence, which must ever keep his deportment from assimilating to that of the latter. His very garb, as it is antique and venerable, feeds his self-respect; as it is a badge of dependence, it restrains the natural petulance of that age from breaking out into overt acts of insolence. This produces

---

* By Verrio, representing James the Second on his throne, surrounded by his courtiers (all curious portraits), receiving the mathematical pupils at their presentation: a custom still kept up on New-year's-day at Court.

silence and a reserve before strangers, yet not that cowardly shyness which boys mewed up at home will feel; he will speak up when spoken to, but the stranger must begin the conversation with him. Within his bounds he is all fire and play; but in the streets he steals along with all the self-concentration of a young monk. He is never known to mix with other boys, they are a sort of laity to him. All this proceeds, I have no doubt, from the continual consciousness which he carries about him of the difference of his dress from that of the rest of the world; with a modest jealousy over himself, lest, by over-hastily mixing with common and secular playfellows, he should commit the dignity of his cloth. Nor let any one laugh at this; for, considering the propensity of the multitude, and especially of the small multitude, to ridicule anything unusual in dress—above all, where such peculiarity may be construed by malice into a mark of disparagement—this reserve will appear to be nothing more than a wise instinct in the Blue-coat boy. That it is neither pride nor rusticity, at least that it has none of the offensive qualities of either, a stranger may soon satisfy himself by putting a question to any of these boys: he may be sure of an answer couched in terms of plain civility, neither loquacious nor embarrassed. Let him put the same question to a parish-boy, or to one of the trencher-caps in the —— cloisters, and the impudent reply of the one shall not fail to exasperate any more than the certain servility, and mercenary eye to reward, which he will meet with in the other, can fail to depress and sadden him.

The Christ's Hospital boy is a religious character. His school is eminently a religious foundation; it has its peculiar prayers, its services at set times, its graces, hymns, and anthems, following each other in an almost monastic closeness of succession. This religious character in him is not always untinged with superstition. That is not wonderful, when we consider the thousand tales and traditions which must circulate, with undisturbed credulity, amongst so many boys, that have so few checks to their belief from any intercourse with the world at large; upon whom their equals in age must work so much, their elders so little. With this leaning towards an over-belief in matters of religion, which will soon correct itself when he comes out into society, may be classed a turn for romance above most other boys. This is to be traced in the same manner to their excess of society with each other, and defect of mingling with the world. Hence the peculiar avidity with which such books as the Arabian Nights' Entertainments, and others of a still wilder cast, are, or at least were in my time, sought for by the boys. I remember when some half-dozen of them set off from school, without map, card, or compass, on a serious expedition to find out *Philip Quarll's Island*.

The Christ's Hospital boy's sense of right and wrong is peculiarly tender and apprehensive. It is even apt to run out into ceremonial observances, and to impose a yoke upon itself beyond the strict obligations of the moral law. Those who were contemporaries with me at that school thirty years ago, will remember with what more than Judaic rigour the eating of the fat of certain boiled meats* was interdicted. A boy would have blushed as at the exposure of some heinous immorality, to have been detected eating that forbidden portion of his allowance of animal food, the whole of which, while he was in health, was little more than sufficient to allay his hunger. The same, or even greater, refinement was shown in the rejection of certain kinds of sweet-cake. What gave rise to these supererogatory penances, these self-denying ordinances, I could never learn†; they certainly argue no defect of the conscientious principle. A little excess in that article is not undesirable in youth, to make allowance for the inevitable waste which comes in maturer years. But in the less ambiguous line of duty, in those directions of the moral feelings which cannot be mistaken or depreciated, I will relate what took place in the year 1785, when Mr. Perry, the steward, died. I must be pardoned for taking my instances from my own times. Indeed, the vividness of my recollections, while I am upon this subject, almost bring back those times; they are present to me still. But I believe that in the years which have elapsed since the period which I speak of, the character of the Christ's Hospital boy is very little changed. Their situation in point of many comforts is improved; but that which I ventured before to term the *public conscience* of

* Under the denomination of *gags*.

† I am told that the late steward [Mr. Hathaway] who evinced on many occasions a most praiseworthy anxiety to promote the comfort of the boys, had occasion for all his address and perseverance to eradicate the first of these unfortunate prejudices, in which he at length happily succeeded, and thereby restored to one-half of the animal nutrition of the school those honours which painful superstition and blind zeal had so long conspired to withhold from it.

the school, the pervading moral sense, of which every mind partakes and to which so many individual minds contribute, remains, I believe, pretty much the same as when I left it. I have seen, within this twelvemonth almost, the change which has been produced upon a boy of eight or nine years of age, upon being admitted into that school; how, from a pert young coxcomb, who thought that all knowledge was comprehended within his shallow brains, because a smattering of two or three languages and one or two sciences were stuffed into him by injudicious treatment at home, by a mixture with the wholesome society of so many schoolfellows, in less time than I have spoken of, he has sunk to his own level, and is contented to be carried on in the quiet orbit of modest self-knowledge in which the common mass of that unpresumptuous assemblage of boys seem to move: from being a little unfeeling mortal, he has got to feel and reflect. Nor would it be a difficult matter to show how, at a school like this, where the boy is neither entirely separated from home, nor yet exclusively under its influence, the best feelings, the filial for instance, are brought to a maturity which they could not have attained under a completely domestic education; how the relation of a parent is rendered less tender by unremitted association, and the very awfulness of age is best apprehended by some sojourning amidst the comparative levity of youth; how absence, not drawn out by too great extension into alienation or forgetfulness, puts an edge upon the relish of occasional intercourse, and the boy is made the better *child* by that which keeps the force of that relation from being felt as perpetually pressing on him; how the substituted paternity, into the care of which he is adopted, while in everything substantial it makes up for the natural, in the necessary omission of individual fondnesses and partialities, directs the mind only the more strongly to appreciate that natural and first tie, in which such weaknesses are the bond of strength, and the appetite which craves after them betrays no perverse palate. But these speculations rather belong to the question of the comparative advantages of a public over a private education in general. I must get back to my favourite school; and to that which took place when our old and good steward died.

And I will say, that when I think of the frequent instances which I have met with in children, of a hard-heartedness, a callousness, and insensibility to the loss of relations, even of those who have begot and nourished them, I cannot but consider it as a proof of something in the peculiar conformation of that school, favourable to the expansion of the best feelings of our nature, that, at the period which I am noticing, out of five hundred boys there was not a dry eye to be found among them, nor a heart that did not beat with genuine emotion. Every impulse to play, until the funeral day was past, seemed suspended throughout the school; and the boys, lately so mirthful and sprightly, were seen pacing their cloisters alone, or in sad groups standing about, few of them without some token, such as their slender means could provide, a black riband or something, to denote respect and a sense of their loss. The time itself was a time of anarchy, a time in which all authority (out of school hours) was abandoned. The ordinary restraints were for those days superseded; and the gates, which at other times kept us in, were left without watchers. Yet, with the exception of one or two graceless boys at most, who took advantage of that suspension of authorities to *skulk out*, as it was called, the whole body of that great school kept rigorously within their bounds, by a voluntary self-imprisonment; and they who broke bounds, though they escaped punishment from any master, fell into a general disrepute among us, and, for that which at any other time would have been applauded and admired as a mark of spirit, were consigned to infamy and reprobation; so much *natural government* have gratitude and the principles of reverence and love, and so much did a respect to their dead friend prevail with these Christ's Hospital boys, above any fear which his presence among them when living could ever produce. And if the impressions which were made on my mind so long ago are to be trusted, very richly did their steward deserve this tribute. It is a pleasure to me even now to call to mind his portly form, the regal awe which he always contrived to inspire, in spite of a tenderness and even weakness of nature that would have enfeebled the reins of discipline in any other master; a yearning of tenderness towards those under his protection, which could make five hundred boys at once feel towards him each as to their individual father. He had faults, with which we had nothing to do; but, with all his faults, indeed, Mr. Perry was a most extraordinary creature. Contemporary with him and still living, though he has long since resigned his occupation, will it be impertinent to mention the name of our excellent upper grammar-master, the Rev. James Boyer? He was a disciplinarian, indeed, of a different stamp from him whom I have just described; but, now the terrors of the rod, and of a temper a little too hasty to leave the more nervous of us quite at our ease to do justice to his merits in those days, are long since over, ungrateful were we if we should refuse our testimony to that unwearied assiduity with which he attended to the particular improvement of each of us. Had we been the offspring of the first gentry in the land, he could not have been instigated by the strongest views of recompense and reward to have made himself a greater slave to the most laborious of all occupations than he did for us sons of charity, from whom, or from our parents, he could expect nothing. He has had his reward in the satisfaction of having discharged his duty, in the pleasurable consciousness of having advanced the respectability of that institution to which, both man and boy, he was attached; in the honours to which so many of his pupils have successfully aspired at both our Universities; and in the staff with which the Governors of the Hospital, at the close of his hard labours, with the highest expressions of the obligations the school lay under to him, unanimously voted to present him.

I have often considered it among the felicities of the constitution of this school, that the offices of steward and schoolmaster are kept distinct; the strict business of education alone devolving upon the latter, while the former has the charge of all things out of school, the control of the provisions, the regulation of meals, of dress, of play, and the ordinary intercourse of the boys. By this division of management, a superior respectability must attach to the teacher while his office is unmixed with any of these lower concerns. A still greater advantage over the construction of common boarding-schools is to be found in the settled salaries of the masters, rendering them totally free of obligation to any individual pupil or his parents. This never fails to have its effect at schools where each boy can reckon up to a hair what profit the master derives from him, where he views him every day in the light of a caterer, a provider for the family, who is to get so much by him in each of his meals. Boys will see and consider these things; and how much must the sacred character of preceptor suffer in their minds by these degrading associations! The very bill which the pupil carries home with him at Christmas, eked out, perhaps, with elaborate though necessary minuteness, instructs him that his teachers have other ends than the mere love to learning, in the lessons which they give him; and though they put into his hands the fine sayings of Seneca or Epictetus, yet they themselves are none of those disinterested pedagogues to teach philosophy *gratis*. The master, too, is sensible that he is seen in this light; and how much this must lessen that affectionate regard to the learners which alone can sweeten the bitter labour of instruction, and convert the whole business into unwelcome and uninteresting task-work, many preceptors that I have conversed with on the subject are ready, with a sad heart, to acknowledge. From this inconvenience the settled salaries of the masters of this school in great measure exempt them; while the happy custom of choosing masters (indeed every officer of the establishment) from those who have received their education there, gives them an interest in advancing the character of the school, and binds them to observe a tenderness and a respect to the children, in which a stranger, feeling that dependence which I have spoken of, might well be expected to fail.

In affectionate recollections of the place where he was bred up, in hearty recognitions of old schoolfellows met with again after the lapse of years, or in foreign countries, the Christ's Hospital boy yields to none; I might almost say, he goes beyond most other boys. The very compass and magnitude of the school, its thousand bearings, the space it takes up in the imagination beyond the ordinary schools, impresses a remembrance, accompanied with an elevation of mind, that attends him through life. It is too big, too affecting an object, to pass away quickly from his mind. The Christ's Hospital boy's friends at school are commonly his intimates through life. For me, I do not know whether a constitutional imbecility does not incline me too obstinately to cling to the remembrances of childhood; in an inverted ratio to the usual sentiments of mankind, nothing that I have been engaged in since seems of any value or importance, compared to the colours which imagination gave to everything then. I belong to no *body corporate* such as I then made a part of. —And here, before I close, taking leave of the general reader, and addressing myself solely to my old schoolfellows, that were contemporaries with me from the year 1782 to 1789, let me have leave to remember some of those circumstances of our school, which they will not be unwilling to have brought back to their minds.

And first, let us remember, as first in importance in our childish eyes, the young men (as they almost were) who, under the denomination of *Grecians*, were waiting the expiration of the period when they should be sent, at the charges of the Hospital, to one or other of our universities, but more frequently to Cambridge. These youths, from their superior acquirements, their superior age and stature, and the fewness of their numbers (for seldom above two or three at a time were inaugurated into that high order), drew the eyes of all, and especially of the younger boys, into a reverent observance and admiration. How tall they used to seem to us! how stately would they pace along the cloisters! while the play of the lesser boys was absolutely suspended, or its boisterousness at least allayed, at their presence! Not that they ever beat or struck the boys—that would have been to have demeaned themselves—the dignity of their persons alone insured them all respect. The task of blows, of corporal chastisement, they left to the common monitors, or heads of wards, who, it must be confessed, in our time had rather too much licence allowed them to oppress and misuse their inferiors; and the interference of the Grecian, who may be considered as the spiritual power, was not unfrequently called for, to mitigate by its mediation the heavy unrelenting arm of this temporal power, or monitor. In fine, the Grecians were the solemn Muftis of the school. Æras were computed from their time;—it used to be said, such or such a thing was done when S—— or T—— was Grecian.

As I ventured to call the Grecians, the Muftis of the school, the King's boys, * as their character then was, may well pass for the Janissaries. They were the terror of all the other boys; bred up under that hardy sailor, as well as excellent mathematician, and co-navigator with Captain Cook, William Wales. All his systems were adapted to fit them for the rough element which they were destined to encounter. Frequent and severe punishments, which were expected to be borne

---

* The mathematical pupils, bred up to the sea, on the foundation of Charles the Second.

with more than Spartan fortitude, came to be considered less as inflictions of disgrace than as trials of obstinate endurance. To make his boys hardy, and to give them early sailor-habits, seemed to be his only aim; to this everything was subordinate. Moral obliquities, indeed, were sure of receiving their full recompense, for no occasion of laying on the lash was ever let slip; but the effects expected to be produced from it were something very different from contrition or mortification. There was in William Wales a perpetual fund of humour, a constant glee about him, which, heightened by an inveterate provincialism of north-country dialect, absolutely took away the sting from his severities. His punishments were a game at patience, in which the master was not always worst contented when he found himself at times overcome by his pupil. What success this discipline had, or how the effects of it operated upon the after-lives of these King's boys, I cannot say: but I am sure that, for the time, they were absolute nuisances to the rest of the school. Hardy, brutal, and often wicked, they were the most graceless lump in the whole mass; older and bigger than the other boys (for, by the system of their education they were kept longer at school by two or three years than any of the rest, except the Grecians), they were a constant terror to the younger part of the school; and some who may read this, I doubt not, will remember the consternation into which the juvenile fry of us were thrown, when the cry was raised in the cloisters, that *the First Order was coming*—for so they termed the first form or class of those boys. Still these sea-boys answered some good purposes in the school. They were the military class among the boys, foremost in athletic exercises, who extended the fame of the prowess of the school far and near; and the apprentices in the vicinage, and sometimes the butchers' boys in the neighbouring market, had sad occasion to attest their valour.

The time would fail me if I were to attempt to enumerate all those circumstances, some pleasant, some attended with some pain, which, seen through the mist of distance, come sweetly softened to the memory. But I must crave leave to remember our transcending superiority in those invigorating sports, leap-frog, and basting the bear; our delightful excursions in the summer holidays to the New River, near Newington, where, like otters, we would live the long day in the water, never caring for dressing ourselves, when we had once stripped; our savoury meals afterwards, when we came home almost famished with staying out all day without our dinners; our visits at other times to the Tower, where, by ancient privilege, we had free access to all the curiosities; our solemn processions through the City at Easter, with the Lord Mayor's largess of buns, wine, and a shilling, with the festive questions and civic pleasantries of the dispensing Aldermen, which were more to us than all the rest of the banquet; our stately suppings in public, where the well-lighted hall, and the confluence of well-dressed company who came to see us, made the whole look more like a concert or assembly, than a scene of a plain bread and cheese collation; the annual orations upon St. Matthew's day, in which the senior scholar, before he had done, seldom failed to reckon up, among those who had done honour to our school by being educated in it, the names of those accomplished critics and Greek scholars, Joshua Barnes and Jeremiah Markland (I marvel they left out Camden while they were about it). Let me have leave to remember our hymns and anthems, and well-toned organ; the doleful tune of the burial anthem chaunted in the solemn cloisters, upon the seldom-occurring funeral of some schoolfellow; the festivities at Christmas, when the richest of us would club our stock to have a gaudy day, sitting round the fire, replenished to the height with logs, and the pennyless, and he that could contribute nothing, partook in all the mirth, and in some of the substantialities of the feasting; the carol sung by night at that time of the year, which, when a young boy, I have so often lain awake to hear from seven (the hour of going to bed) till ten, when it was sung by the older boys and monitors, and have listened to it, in their rude chaunting, till I have been transported in fancy to the fields of Bethlehem, and the song which was sung at that season, by angels' voices to the shepherds.

Nor would I willingly forget any of those things which administered to our vanity. The hem-stitched bands and town-made shirts, which some of the most fashionable among us wore; the town-girdles, with buckles of silver, or shining stone; the badges of the sea-boys; the cots, or superior shoe-strings, of the monitors; the medals of the markers (those who were appointed to hear the Bible read in the wards on Sunday morning and evening), which bore on their obverse in silver, as certain parts of our garments carried, in meaner metal, the countenance of our Founder, that godly and royal child, King Edward the Sixth, the flower of the Tudor name—the young flower that was untimely cropt, as it began to fill our land with its early odours—the boy-patron of boys—the serious and holy child who walked with Cranmer and Ridley—fit associate, in those tender years, for the bishops, and future martyrs of our Church, to receive, or (as occasion sometimes proved), to give instruction.

> But, ah! what means the silent tear?
>   Why, e'en 'mid joy, my bosom heave?
> Ye long-lost scenes, enchantments dear!
>   Lo! now I linger o'er your grave.
>
> —Fly, then, ye hours of rosy hue,
>   And bear away the bloom of years!
> And quick succeed, ye sickly crew
>   Of doubts and sorrows, pains and fears!
>
> Still will I ponder Fate's unaltered plan,
> Nor, tracing back the child, forget that I am man. *

On the Tragedies of Shakspeare

CONSIDERED WITH REFERENCE TO THEIR FITNESS FOR STAGE-REPRESENTATION

TAKING a turn the other day in the Abbey, I was struck with the affected attitude of a figure, which I do not remember to have seen before, and which upon examination proved to be a whole-length of the celebrated Mr. Garrick. Though I would not go so far with some good Catholics abroad as to shut players altogether out of consecrated ground, yet I own I was not a little scandalised at the introduction of theatrical airs and gestures into a place set apart to remind us of the saddest realities. Going nearer, I found inscribed under this harlequin figure the following lines:—

* Lines meditated in the cloisters of Christ's Hospital, in the *Poetics* of Mr. George Dyer.

To paint fair Nature, by divine command
Her magic pencil in his glowing hand,
A Shakspeare rose; then, to expand his fame
Wide o'er this breathing world, a Garrick came.
Though sunk in death the forms the Poet drew,
The Actor's genius bade them breathe anew;
Though, like the bard himself, in night they lay,
Immortal Garrick called them back to day:
And till Eternity with power sublime
Shall mark the mortal hour of hoary Time,
Shakspeare and Garrick like twin-stars shall shine,
And earth irradiate with a beam divine.

It would be an insult to my readers' understanding to attempt anything like a criticism on this farrago of false thoughts and nonsense. But the reflection it led me into was a kind of wonder, how, from the days of the actor here celebrated to our own, it should have been the fashion to compliment every performer in his turn, that has had the luck to please the Town in any of the great characters of Shakspeare, with the notion of possessing a *mind congenial with the poet's:* how people should come thus unaccountably to confound the power of originating poetical images and conceptions with the faculty of being able to read or recite the same when put into words*; or what connection that absolute mastery over the heart and soul of man, which a great dramatic poet possesses, has with those low tricks upon the eye and ear, which a player by observing a few general effects, which some common passion, as grief, anger, etc., usually has upon the gestures and exterior, can so easily compass. To know the internal workings and movements of a great mind, of an Othello or a Hamlet for instance, the *when* and the *why* and the *how far* they should be moved; to what pitch a passion is becoming; to give the reins and to pull in the curb exactly at the moment when the drawing in or the slackening is most graceful; seems to demand a reach of intellect of a vastly different extent from that which is employed upon the bare imitation of the signs of these passions in the countenance or gesture, which signs are

* It is observable that we fall into this confusion only in *dramatic* recitations. We never dream that the gentleman who reads Lucretius in public with great applause, is therefore a great poet and philosopher; nor do we find that Tom Davis, the bookseller, who is recorded to have recited the Paradise Lost better than any man in England in his day (though I cannot help thinking there must be some mistake in this tradition) was therefore, by his intimate friends, set upon a level with Milton.

usually observed to be most lively and emphatic in the weaker sort of minds, and which signs can after all but indicate some passion, as I said before, anger, or grief, generally; but of the motives and grounds of the passion, wherein it differs from the same passion in low and vulgar natures, of these the actor can give no more idea by his face or gesture than the eye (without a metaphor) can speak, or the muscles utter intelligible sounds. But such is the instantaneous nature of the impressions which we take in at the eye and ear at a play-house, compared with the slow apprehension oftentimes of the understanding in reading, that we are apt not only to sink the play-writer in the consideration which we pay to the actor, but even to identify in our minds, in a perverse manner, the actor with the character which he represents. It is difficult for a frequent play-goer to disembarrass the idea of Hamlet from the person and voice of Mr. K. We speak of Lady Macbeth, while we are in reality thinking of Mrs. S. Nor is this confusion incidental alone to unlettered persons, who, not possessing the advantage of reading, are necessarily dependent upon the stage-player for all the pleasure which they can receive from the drama, and to whom the very idea of *what an author is* cannot be made comprehensible without some pain and perplexity of mind: the error is one from which persons otherwise not meanly lettered, find it almost impossible to extricate themselves.

Never let me be so ungrateful as to forget the very high degree of satisfaction which I received some years back from seeing for the first time a tragedy of Shakspeare performed, in which those two great performers sustained the principal parts. It seemed to embody and realise conceptions which had hitherto assumed no distinct shape. But dearly do we pay all our life after for this juvenile pleasure, this sense of distinctness. When the novelty is past, we find to our cost that instead of realising an idea, we have only materialised and brought down a fine vision to the standard of flesh and blood. We have let go a dream, in quest of an unattainable substance.

How cruelly this operates upon the mind, to have its free conceptions thus cramped and pressed down to the measure of a strait-lacing actuality, may be judged from that delightful sensation of freshness, with which we turn to those plays of Shakspeare which have escaped being performed, and to those passages in the acting plays of the same writer which have happily been left out in the performance. How far the very custom of hearing anything *spouted*, withers and blows upon a fine passage, may be seen in those speeches from Henry the Fifth, etc., which are current in the mouths of schoolboys, from their being to be found in *Enfield's Speaker*, and such kind of books! I confess myself utterly unable to appreciate that celebrated soliloquy in Hamlet, beginning 'To be or not to be,' or to tell whether it be good, bad or indifferent, it has been so handled and pawed about by declamatory boys and men, and torn so inhumanly from its living place and principle of continuity in the play, till it is become to me a perfect dead member.

It may seem a paradox, but I cannot help being of opinion that the plays of Shakspeare are less calculated for performance on a stage, than those of almost any other dramatist whatever. Their distinguishing excellence is a reason that they should be so. There is so much in them, which comes not under the province of acting, with which eye, and tone, and gesture, have nothing to do.

The glory of the scenic art is to personate passion, and the turns of passion; and the more coarse and palpable the passion is, the more hold upon the eyes and ears of the spectators the performer obviously possesses. For this reason, scolding scenes, scenes where two persons talk themselves into a fit of fury, and then in a surprising manner talk themselves out of it again, have always been the most popular upon our stage. And the reason is plain, because the spectators are here most palpably appealed to, they are the proper judges in this war of words, they are the legitimate ring that should be formed round such 'intellectual prize-fighters.' Talking is the direct object of the imitation here. But in all the best dramas, and in Shakspeare above all, how obvious it is, that the form of *speaking*, whether it be in soliloquy or dialogue, is only a medium, and often a highly artificial one, for putting the reader or spectator into possession of that knowledge of the inner structure and workings of mind in a character, which he could otherwise never have arrived at *in that form of composition* by any gift short of intuition. We do here as we do with novels written in the *epistolary form*. How many improprieties, perfect solecisms in letter-writing, do we put up with in Clarissa and other books, for the sake of the delight which that form upon the whole gives us!

But the practice of stage representation reduces everything to a controversy of elocution. Every character, from the boisterous blasphemings of Bajazet to the shrinking timidity of womanhood, must play the orator. The love dialogues of Romeo and Juliet, those silver-sweet sounds of lovers' tongues by night! the more intimate and sacred sweetness of nuptial colloquy between an Othello or a Posthumus with their married wives, all those delicacies which are so delightful in the reading, as when we read of those youthful dalliances in Paradise—

> As beseem'd
> Fair couple link'd in happy nuptial league,
> Alone;

by the inherent fault of stage representation, how are these things sullied and turned from their very nature by being exposed to a large assembly; when such speeches as Imogen addresses to her lord, come drawling out of the mouth of a hired actress, whose courtship, though nominally addressed to the personated Posthumus, is manifestly aimed at the spectators, who are to judge of her endearments and her returns of love!

The character of Hamlet is perhaps that by which, since the days of Betterton, a succession of popular performers have had the greatest ambition to distinguish themselves. The length of the part may be one of their reasons. But for the character itself, we find it in a play, and therefore we judge it a fit subject of dramatic representation. The play itself abounds in maxims and reflections beyond any other, and therefore we consider it as a proper vehicle for conveying moral instruction. But Hamlet himself—what does he suffer meanwhile by being dragged forth as the public schoolmaster, to give lectures to the crowd! Why, nine parts in ten of what Hamlet does, are transactions between himself and his moral sense; they are the effusions of his solitary musings, which he retires to holes and corners and the most sequestered parts of the palace to pour forth; or rather, they are the silent meditations with which his bosom is bursting, reduced to *words* for the sake of the reader, who must else remain ignorant of what is passing there. These profound sorrows, these light-and-noise-abhorring ruminations, which the tongue scarce dares utter to deaf walls and chambers, how can they be represented by a gesticulating actor, who comes and mouths them out before an audience, making four hundred people his confidants at once! I say not that it is the fault of the actor so to do; he must pronounce them *ore rotundo;* he must accompany them with his eye; he must insinuate them into his auditory by some trick of eye, tone or gesture, or he fails. *He must be thinking all the while of his appearance, because he knows that all the while the spectators are judging of it.* And this is the way to represent the shy, negligent, retiring Hamlet!

It is true that there is no other mode of conveying a vast quantity of thought and feeling to a great portion of the audience, who otherwise would never earn it for themselves by reading, and the intellectual acquisition gained this way may, for aught I know, be inestimable; but I am not arguing that Hamlet should not be acted, but how much Hamlet is made another thing by being acted. I have heard much of the wonders which Garrick performed in this part; but as I never saw him, I must have leave to doubt whether the representation of such a character came within the province of his art. Those who tell me of him, speak of his eye, of the magic of his eye, and of his commanding voice: physical properties, vastly desirable in an actor, and without which he can never insinuate meaning into an auditory,—but what have they to do with Hamlet; what have they to do with intellect? In fact, the things aimed at in theatrical representation, are to arrest the spectator's eye upon the form and the gesture, and so to gain a more favourable hearing to what is spoken: it is not what the character is, but how he looks; not what he says, but how he speaks it. I see no reason to think that if the play of Hamlet were written over again by some such writer as Banks or Lillo, retaining the process of the story, but totally omitting all the poetry of it, all the divine features of Shakspeare, his stupendous intellect; and only taking care to give us enough of passionate dialogue, which Banks or Lillo were never at a loss to furnish; I see not how the effect could be much different upon an audience, nor how the actor has it in his power to represent Shakspeare to us differently from his representation of Banks or Lillo. Hamlet would still be a youthful accomplished prince, and must be gracefully personated; he might be puzzled in his mind, wavering in his conduct, seemingly cruel to Ophelia; he might see a ghost, and start at it, and address it kindly when he found it to be his father; all this in the poorest and most homely language of the servilest creeper after nature that ever consulted the palate of an audience; without troubling Shakspeare for the matter: and I see not but there would be room for all the power which an actor has, to display itself. All the passions and changes of passion might remain: for those are much less difficult to write or act than is thought; it is a trick easy to be attained, it is but rising or falling a note or two in the voice, a whisper with a significant foreboding look to announce its approach, and so contagious the counterfeit appearance of any emotion is, that let the words be what they will, the look and tone shall carry it off and make it pass for deep skill in the passions.

It is common for people to talk of Shakspeare's plays being *so natural;* that everybody can understand him. They are natural indeed, they are grounded deep in nature, so deep that the depth of them lies out of the reach of most of us. You shall hear the same persons say that George Barnwell is very natural, and Othello is very natural, that they are both very deep; and to them they are the same kind of thing. At the one they sit and shed tears, because a good sort of young man is tempted by a naughty woman to commit a *trifling peccadillo,* the murder of an uncle or so,* that is all, and so comes to an untimely end, which is *so moving;* and at the other, because a blackamoor in a fit of jealousy kills his innocent white wife; and the odds are that ninety-nine out of a hundred would willingly behold the same catastrophe happen to both the heroes, and have thought the rope more due to Othello than to Barnwell. For of the texture of

* If this note could hope to meet the eye of any of the Managers, I would entreat and beg of them, in the name of both the Galleries, that this insult upon the morality of the common people of London should cease to be eternally repeated in the holiday weeks. Why are the 'Prentices of this famous and well-governed city, instead of an amusement, to be treated over and over again with a nauseous sermon of George Barnwell? Why *at the end of their vistas* are we to place the *gallows?* Were I an uncle, I should not much like a nephew of mine to have such an example placed before his eyes. It is really making uncle-murder too trivial to exhibit it as done upon such slight motives;—it is attributing too much to such characters as Millwood:—it is putting things into the heads of good young men, which they would never otherwise have dreamed of. Uncles that think anything of their lives, should fairly petition the Chamberlain against it.

Othello's mind, the inward construction marvellously laid open with all its strengths and weaknesses, its heroic confidences and its human misgivings, its agonies of hate springing from the depths of love, they see no more than the spectators at a cheaper rate, who pay their pennies a-piece to look through the man's telescope in Leicester Fields, see into the inward plot and topography of the moon. Some dim thing or other they see; they see an actor personating a passion, of grief, or anger, for instance, and they recognise it as a copy of the usual external effects of such passions; or at least as being true to *that symbol of the emotion which passes current at the theatre for it*, for it is often no more than that: but of the grounds of the passion, its correspondence to a great or heroic nature, which is the only worthy object of tragedy,—that common auditors know anything of this, or can have any such notions dinned into them by the mere strength of an actor's lungs,—that apprehensions foreign to them should be thus infused into them by storm, I can neither believe, nor understand how it can be possible.

We talk of Shakspeare's admirable observation of life, when we should feel, that not from a petty inquisition into those cheap and everyday characters which surrounded him, as they surround us, but from his own mind, which was, to borrow a phrase of Ben Jonson's, the very 'sphere of humanity,' he fetched those images of virtue and of knowledge, of which every one of us recognising a part, think we comprehend in our natures the whole; and oftentimes mistake the powers which he positively creates in us, for nothing more than indigenous faculties of our own minds, which only waited the application of corresponding virtues in him to return a full and clear echo of the same.

To return to Hamlet.—Among the distinguishing features of that wonderful character, one of the most interesting (yet painful) is that soreness of mind which makes him treat the intrusions of Polonius with harshness, and that asperity which he puts on in his interviews with Ophelia. These tokens of an unhinged mind (if they be not mixed in the latter case with a profound artifice of love, to alienate Ophelia by affected discourtesies, so to prepare her mind for the breaking off of that loving intercourse, which can no longer find a place amidst business so serious as that which he has to do) are parts of his character, which to reconcile with our admiration of Hamlet, the most patient consideration of his situation is no more than necessary; they are what we *forgive afterwards*, and explain by the whole of his character, but *at the time* they are harsh and unpleasant. Yet such is the actor's necessity of giving strong blows to the audience, that I have never seen a player in this character, who did not exaggerate and strain to the utmost these ambiguous features,—these temporary deformities in the character. They make him express a vulgar scorn at Polonius which utterly degrades his gentility, and which no explanation can render palatable; they make him show contempt, and curl up the nose at Ophelia's father,—contempt in its very grossest and most hateful form; but they get applause by it: it is natural, people say; that is, the words are scornful, and the actor expresses scorn, and that they can judge of: but why so much scorn, and of that sort, they never think of asking.

So to Ophelia.—All the Hamlets that I have ever seen, rant and rave at her as if she had committed some great crime, and the audience are highly pleased, because the words of the part are satirical, and they are enforced by the strongest expression of satirical indignation of which the face and voice are capable. But then, whether Hamlet is likely to have put on such brutal appearances to a lady whom he loved so dearly, is never thought on. The truth is, that in all such deep affections as had subsisted between Hamlet and Ophelia, there is a stock of *supererogatory love* (if I may venture to use the expression), which in any great grief of heart, especially where that which preys upon the mind cannot be communicated, confers a kind of indulgence upon the grieved party to express itself, even to its heart's dearest object, in the language of a temporary alienation; but it is not alienation, it is a distraction purely, and so it always makes itself to be felt by that object: it is not anger, but grief assuming the appearance of anger,—love awkwardly counterfeiting hate, as sweet countenances when they try to frown: but such sternness and fierce disgust as Hamlet is made to show, is no counterfeit, but the real face of absolute aversion,—of irreconcileable alienation. It may be said he puts on the madman; but then he should only so far put on this counterfeit lunacy as his own real distraction will give him leave; that is, incompletely, imperfectly; not in that confirmed, practised way, like a master of his art, or as Dame Quickly would say, 'like one of those harlotry players.'

I mean no disrespect to any actor, but the sort of pleasure which Shakspeare's plays give in the acting seems to me not at all to differ from that which the audience receive from those of other writers; and, *they being in themselves essentially so different from all others*, I must conclude that there is something in the nature of acting which levels all distinctions. And, in fact, who does not speak indifferently of the Gamester and of Macbeth as fine stage performances, and praise the Mrs. Beverley in the same way as the Lady Macbeth of Mrs. S.? Belvidera, and Calista, and Isabella, and Euphrasia, are they less liked than Imogen, or than Juliet, or than Desdemona? Are they not spoken of and remembered in the same way? Is not the female performer as great (as they call it) in one as in the other? Did not Garrick shine, and was he not ambitious of shining, in every drawling tragedy that his wretched day produced,—the productions of the Hills, and the Murphys, and the Browns,—and shall he have that honour to dwell in our minds for ever as an inseparable concomitant with Shakspeare? A kindred mind! O who can read that affecting sonnet of Shakspeare which alludes to his profession as a player—:

> Oh for my sake do you with Fortune chide,
> The guilty goddess of my harmless deeds,
> That did not better for my life provide
> Than public means which public custom breeds—
> Thence comes it that my name receives a brand;
> And almost thence my nature is subdued
> To what it works in, like the dyer's hand.—

Or that other confession:—

> Alas! 'tis true, I have gone here and there,
> And made myself a motley to thy view,
> Gored mine own thoughts, sold cheap what is most dear—

Who can read these instances of jealous self-watchfulness in our sweet Shakspeare, and dream of any congeniality between him and one that, by every tradition of him, appears to have been as mere a player as ever existed; to have had his mind tainted with the lowest players' vices,—envy and jealousy, and miserable cravings after applause; one who in

365

the exercise of his profession was jealous even of the women-performers that stood in his way; a manager full of managerial tricks and stratagems and finesse; that any resemblance should be dreamed of between him and Shakspeare,—Shakspeare who, in the plenitude and consciousness of his own powers, could with that noble modesty, which we can neither imitate nor appreciate, express himself thus of his own sense of his own defects:—

> Wishing me like to one more rich in hope,
> Featured like him, like him with friends possest;
> Desiring *this man's art, and that man's scope.*

I am almost disposed to deny to Garrick the merit of being an admirer of Shakspeare! A true lover of his excellences he certainly was not; for would any true lover of them have admitted into his matchless scenes such ribald trash as Tate and Cibber, and the rest of them, that

> With their darkness durst affront his light,

have foisted into the acting plays of Shakspeare? I believe it impossible that he could have had a proper reverence for Shakspeare, and have condescended to go through that interpolated scene in Richard the Third, in which Richard tries to break his wife's heart by telling her he loves another woman, and says, 'if she survives this she is immortal.' Yet I doubt not he delivered this vulgar stuff with as much anxiety of emphasis as any of the genuine parts: and for acting, it is as well calculated as any. But we have seen the part of Richard lately produce great fame to an actor by his manner of playing it, and it lets us into the secret of acting, and of popular judgments of Shakspeare derived from acting. Not one of the spectators who have witnessed Mr. C.'s exertions in that part, but has come away with a proper conviction that Richard is a very wicked man, and kills little children in their beds, with something like the pleasure which the giants and ogres in children's books are represented to have taken in that practice; moreover, that he is very close and shrewd, and devilish cunning, for you could see that by his eye.

But is, in fact, this the impression we have in reading the Richard of Shakspeare? Do we feel anything like disgust, as we do at that butcher-like representation of him that passes for him on the stage? A horror at his crimes blends with the effect which we feel, but how is it qualified, how is it carried off, by the rich intellect which he displays, his resources, his wit, his buoyant spirits, his vast knowledge and insight into characters, the poetry of his part,—not an atom of all which is made perceivable in Mr. C.'s way of acting it. Nothing but his crimes, his actions, is visible; they are prominent and staring; the murderer stands out, but where is the lofty genius, the man of vast capacity,—the profound, the witty, accomplished Richard?

The truth is, the characters of Shakspeare are so much the objects of meditation rather than of interest or curiosity as to their actions, that while we are reading any of his great criminal characters,—Macbeth, Richard, even Iago,—we think not so much of the crimes which they commit, as of the ambition, the aspiring spirit, the intellectual activity, which prompts them to overleap these moral fences. Barnwell is a wretched murderer; there is a certain fitness between his neck and the rope; he is the legitimate heir to the gallows; nobody who thinks at all can think of any alleviating circumstances in his case to make him a fit object of mercy. Or to take an instance from the higher tragedy, what else but a mere assassin is Glenalvon? Do we think of anything but of the crime which he commits, and the rack which he deserves? That is all which we really think about him. Whereas in corresponding characters in Shakspeare, so little do the actions comparatively affect us, that while the impulses, the inner mind in all its perverted greatness, solely seems real and is exclusively attended to, the crime is comparatively nothing. But when we see these things represented, the acts which they do are comparatively everything, their impulses nothing. The state of sublime emotion into which we are elevated by those images of night and horror which Macbeth is made to utter, that solemn prelude with which he entertains the time till the bell shall strike which is to call him to murder Duncan,—when we no longer read it in a book, when we have given up that vantage ground of abstraction which reading possesses over seeing, and come to see a man in his bodily shape before our eyes actually preparing to commit a murder, if the acting be true and impressive, as I have witnessed it in Mr. K.'s performance of that part, the painful anxiety about the act, the natural longing to prevent it while it yet seems unperpetrated, the too close pressing semblance of reality, give a pain and an uneasiness which totally destroy all the delight which the words in the book convey, where the deed doing never presses upon us with the painful sense of presence: it rather seems to belong to history,—to something past and inevitable, if it has anything to do with time at all. The sublime images, the poetry alone, is that which is present to our minds in the reading.

So to see Lear acted,—to see an old man tottering about the stage with a walking-stick, turned out of doors by his daughters in a rainy night, has nothing in it but what is painful and disgusting. We want to take him into shelter and relieve him. That is all the feeling which the acting of Lear ever produced in me. But the Lear of Shakspeare cannot be acted. The contemptible machinery by which they mimic the storm which he goes out in, is not more inadequate to represent the horrors of the real elements, than any actor can be to represent Lear; they might more easily propose to personate the Satan of Milton upon a stage, or one of Michael Angelo's terrible figures. The greatness of Lear is not in corporal dimension, but in intellectual: the explosions of his passion are terrible as a volcano; they are storms turning up and disclosing to the bottom that sea, his mind, with all its vast riches. It is his mind which is laid bare. This case of flesh and blood seems too insignificant to be thought on; even as he himself neglects it. On the stage we see nothing but corporal infirmities and weakness, the impotence of rage; while we read it, we see not Lear, but we are Lear,—we are in his mind, we are sustained by a grandeur which baffles the malice of daughters and storms; in the aberrations of his reason, we discover a mighty irregular power of reasoning, immethodised from the ordinary purposes of life, but exerting its powers, as the wind blows where it listeth, at will upon the corruptions and abuses of mankind. What have looks, or tones, to do with that sublime identification of his age with that of the *heavens themselves*, when, in his reproaches to them for conniving at the injustice of his children, he reminds them that 'they themselves are old'? What gesture shall we appropriate to this? What has the voice or the eye to do with such things? But the play is beyond all art, as the tamperings with it show: it is too hard and stony; it must have love-scenes, and a happy ending.

It is not enough that Cordelia is a daughter, she must shine as a lover too. Tate has put his hook in the nostrils of this Leviathan, for Garrick and his followers, the show-men of the scene, to draw the mighty beast about more easily. A happy ending!—as if the living martyrdom that Lear had gone through,—the flaying of his feelings alive, did not make a fair dismissal from the stage of life the only decorous thing for him. If he is to live and be happy after, if he could sustain this world's burden after, why all this pudder and preparation,—why torment us with all this unnecessary sympathy? As if the childish pleasure of getting his gilt robes and sceptre again could tempt him to act over again his misused station—as if, at his years and with his experience, anything was left but to die.

Lear is essentially impossible to be represented on a stage. But how many dramatic personages are there in Shakspeare, which though more tractable and feasible (if I may so speak) than Lear, yet from some circumstance, some adjunct to their character, are improper to be shown to our bodily eye! Othello for instance. Nothing can be more soothing, more flattering to the nobler parts of our natures, than to read of a young Venetian lady of the highest extraction, through the force of love and from a sense of merit in him whom she loved, laying aside every consideration of kindred, and country, and colour, and wedding with a *coal-black Moor*— (for such he is represented, in the imperfect state of knowledge respecting foreign countries in those days, compared with our own, or in compliance with popular notions, though the Moors are now well enough known to be by many shades less unworthy of a white woman's fancy)—it is the perfect triumph of virtue over accidents, of the imagination over the senses. She sees Othello's colour in his mind. But upon the stage, when the imagination is no longer the ruling faculty, but we are left to our poor unassisted senses, I appeal to every one that has seen Othello played, whether he did not, on the contrary, sink Othello's mind in his colour; whether he did not find something extremely revolting in the court-ship and wedded caresses of Othello and Desdemona; and whether the actual sight of the thing did not over-weigh all that beautiful compromise which we make in reading;— and the reason it should do so is obvious, because there is just so much reality presented to our senses as to give a perception of disagreement, with not enough of belief in the internal motives,—all that which is unseen,—to overpower and reconcile the first and obvious prejudices.* What we see upon a stage is body and bodily action; what we are conscious of in reading is almost exclusively the mind, and its movements; and this I think may sufficiently account for the very different sort of delight with which the same play so often affects us in the reading and the seeing.

It requires little reflection to perceive, that if those characters in Shakspeare which are within the precincts of nature, have yet something in them which appeals too exclusively to the imagination, to admit of their being made objects to the senses without suffering a change and a diminution,—that still stronger the objection must lie against representing another line of characters, which Shakspeare has introduced to give a wildness and a supernatural elevation to his scenes, as if to remove them still farther from that assimilation to common life in which their excellence is vulgarly supposed to consist. When we read the incantations of those terrible beings the Witches in Macbeth, though some of the ingredients of their hellish composition savour of the grotesque, yet is the effect upon us other than the most serious and appalling that can be imagined? Do we not feel spellbound as Macbeth was? Can any mirth accompany a sense of their presence? We might as well laugh under a consciousness of the principle of Evil himself being truly and really present with us. But attempt to bring these things on to a stage, and you turn them instantly into so many old women, that men and children are to laugh at. Contrary to the old saying, that 'seeing is believing,' the sight actually destroys the faith; and the mirth in which we indulge at their expense, when we see these creatures upon a stage, seems to be a sort of indemnification which we make to ourselves for the terror which they put us in when reading made them an object of

* The error of supposing that because Othello's colour does not offend us in the reading, it should also not offend us in the seeing, is just such a fallacy as supposing that an Adam and Eve in a picture shall affect us just as they do in the poem. But in the poem we for a while have Paradisaical senses given us, which vanish when we see a man and his wife without clothes in the picture. The painters themselves feel this, as is apparent by the awkward shifts they have recourse to, to make them look not quite naked; by a sort of prophetic anachronism, antedating the invention of fig-leaves. So in the reading of the play, we see with Desdemona's eyes: in the seeing of it, we are forced to look with our own.

belief,—when we surrendered up our reason to the poet, as children to their nurses and their elders; and we laugh at our fears as children, who thought they saw something in the dark, triumph when the bringing in of a candle discovers the vanity of their fears. For this exposure of supernatural agents upon a stage is truly bringing in a candle to expose their own delusiveness. It is the solitary taper and the book that generates a faith in these terrors; a ghost by chandelier light, and in good company, deceives no spectators,—a ghost that can be measured by the eye, and his human dimensions made out at leisure. The sight of a well-lighted house, and a well-dressed audience, shall arm the most nervous child against any apprehensions: as Tom Brown says of the impenetrable skin of Achilles with his impenetrable armour over it, 'Bully Dawson would have fought the devil with such advantages.'

Much has been said, and deservedly, in reprobation of the vile mixture which Dryden has thrown into the Tempest: doubtless without some such vicious alloy, the impure ears of that age would never have sate out to hear so much innocence of love as is contained in the sweet courtship of Ferdinand and Miranda. But is the Tempest of Shakspeare at all a subject for stage representation? It is one thing to read of an enchanter, and to believe the wondrous tale while we are reading it; but to have a conjurer brought before us in his conjuring-gown, with his spirits about him, which none but himself and some hundred of favoured spectators before the curtain are supposed to see, involves such a quantity of the *hateful incredible*, that all our reverence for the author cannot hinder us from perceiving such gross attempts upon the senses to be in the highest degree childish and inefficient. Spirits and fairies cannot be represented, they cannot even be painted,—they can only be believed. But the elaborate and anxious provision of scenery, which the luxury of the age demands, in these cases works a quite contrary effect to what is intended. That which in comedy, or plays of familiar life, adds so much to the life of the imitation, in plays which appeal to the higher faculties positively destroys the illusion which it is introduced to aid. A parlour or a drawing-room, —a library opening into a garden—a garden with an alcove in it,—a street, or the piazza of Covent Garden, does well enough in a scene; we are content to give as much credit to it as it demands; or rather, we think little about it,—it is little more than reading at the top of a page, 'Scene, a garden'; we do not imagine ourselves there, but we readily admit the imitation of familiar objects. But to think by the help of painted trees and caverns, which we know to be painted, to transport our minds to Prospero, and his island and his lonely cell*; or by the aid of a fiddle dexterously thrown in, in an interval of speaking, to make us believe that we hear those super-natural noises of which the isle was full: the Orrery Lecturer at the Haymarket might as well hope, by his musical glasses cleverly stationed out of sight behind his apparatus, to make us believe that we do indeed hear the crystal spheres ring out that chime, which if it were to enwrap our fancy long, Milton thinks,

> Time would run back and fetch the age of gold,
> And speckled Vanity
> Would sicken soon and die,
> And leprous Sin would melt from earthly mould;
> Yea, Hell itself woud pass away,
> And leave its dolorous mansions to the peering day.

The garden of Eden, with our first parents in it, is not more impossible to be shown on a stage, than the Enchanted Isle, with its no less interesting and innocent first settlers.

The subject of Scenery is closely connected with that of the Dresses, which are so anxiously attended to on our stage. I remember the last time I saw Macbeth played, the discrepancy I felt at the changes of garment which he varied, the shiftings and re-shiftings, like a Romish priest at mass. The luxury of stage-improvements, and the importunity of the public eye, require this. The coronation robe of the Scottish monarch was fairly a counterpart to that which our King wears when he goes to the Parliament House, just so full and cumbersome, and set out with ermine and pearls. And if things must be represented, I see not what to find fault with in this. But in reading, what robe are we conscious of? Some dim images of royalty—a crown and sceptre may float before our eyes, but who shall describe the fashion of it? Do we see in our mind's eye what Webb or any other

---

* It will be said these things are done in pictures. But pictures and scenes are very different things. Painting is a world of itself, but in scene-painting there is the attempt to deceive: and there is the discordancy, never to be got over, between painted scenes and real people.

robe-maker could pattern? This is the inevitable consequence of imitating everything, to make all things natural. Whereas the reading of a tragedy is a fine abstraction. It presents to the fancy just so much of external appearances as to make us feel that we are among flesh and blood, while by far the greater and better part of our imagination is employed upon the thoughts and internal machinery of the character. But in acting, scenery, dress, the most contemptible things, call upon us to judge of their naturalness.

Perhaps it would be no bad similitude, to liken the pleasure which we take in seeing one of these fine plays acted, compared with that quiet delight which we find in the reading of it, to the different feelings with which a reviewer, and a man that is not a reviewer, reads a fine poem. The accursed critical habit—the being called upon to judge and pronounce, must make it quite a different thing to the former. In seeing these plays acted, we are affected just as judges. When Hamlct compares the two pictures of Gertrude's first and second husband, who wants to see the pictures? But in the acting, a miniature must be lugged out; which we know not to be the picture, but only to show how finely a miniature may be represented. This showing of everything levels all things: it makes tricks, bows, and curtseys, of importance. Mrs. S. never got more fame by anything than by the manner in which she dismisses the guests in the banquet-scene in Macbeth: it is as much remembered as any of her thrilling tones or impressive looks. But does such a trifle as this enter into the imaginations of the readers of that wild and wonderful scene? Does not the mind dismiss the feasters as rapidly as it can? Does it care about the gracefulness of the doing it? But by acting, and judging of acting, all these non-essentials are raised into an importance, injurious to the main interest of the play.

I have confined my observations to the tragic parts of Shakspeare. It would be no very difficult task to extend the inquiry to his comedies; and to show why Falstaff, Shallow, Sir Hugh Evans, and the rest, are equally incompatible with stage representation. The length to which this Essay has run will make it, I am afraid, sufficiently distasteful to the Amateurs of the Theatre, without going any deeper into the subject at present.

On the Genius and Character of Hogarth

WITH SOME REMARKS ON A PASSAGE IN THE WRITING
OF THE LATE MR. BARRY

ONE of the earliest and noblest enjoyments I had when a boy, was in the contemplation of those capital prints by Hogarth, the Harlot's and Rake's Progresses, which, along with some others, hung upon the walls of a great hall in an old-fashioned house in ——shire, and seemed the solitary tenants (with myself) of that antiquated and life-deserted apartment.

Recollection of the manner in which those prints used to affect me has often made me wonder, when I have heard Hogarth described as a mere comic painter, as one of those whose chief ambition was to *raise a laugh*. To deny that there are throughout the prints which I have mentioned circumstances introduced of a laughable tendency, would be to run counter to the common notions of mankind; but to suppose that in their *ruling character* they appeal chiefly to the risible faculty, and not first and foremost to the very heart of man, its best and most serious feelings, would be to mistake no less grossly their aim and purpose. A set of severer Satires (for they are not so much Comedies, which they have been likened to, as they are strong and masculine Satires) less mingled with anything of mere fun, were never written upon paper, or graven upon copper. They resemble Juvenal, or the satiric touches in Timon of Athens.

I was pleased with the reply of a gentleman, who being asked which book he esteemed most in his library, answered, —'Shakspeare': being asked which he esteemed next best, replied, 'Hogarth.' His graphic representations are indeed books: they have the teeming, fruitful, suggestive meaning of *words*. Other pictures we look at,—his prints we read.

In pursuance of this parallel, I have sometimes entertained myself with comparing the Timon of Athens of Shakspeare (which I have just mentioned) and Hogarth's Rake's Progress together. The story, the moral, in both is nearly the same. The wild course of riot and extravagance, ending in the one with driving the Prodigal from the society of men into the solitude of the deserts, and in the other with conducting the

Rake through his several stages of dissipation into the still more complete desolations of the mad-house, in the play and in the picture, are described with almost equal force and nature. The levee of the Rake, which forms the subject of the second plate in the series, is almost a transcript of Timon's levee in the opening scene of that play. We find a dedicating poet, and other similar characters, in both.

The concluding scene in the Rake's Progress is perhaps superior to the last scenes of Timon. If we seek for something of kindred excellence in poetry, it must be in the scenes of Lear's beginning madness, where the King and the Fool and the Tom-o'-Bedlam conspire to produce such a medley of mirth checked by misery, and misery rebuked by mirth; where the society of those 'strange bed-fellows' which misfortunes have brought Lear acquainted with, so finely sets forth the destitute state of the monarch; while the lunatic bans of the one, and the disjointed sayings and wild but pregnant allusions of the other, so wonderfully sympathise with that confusion, which they seem to assist in the production of, in the senses of that 'child-changed father.'

In the scene in Bedlam, which terminates the Rake's Progress, we find the same assortment of the ludicrous with the terrible. Here is desperate madness, the overturning of originally strong thinking faculties, at which we shudder, as we contemplate the duration and pressure of affliction which it must have asked to destroy such a building;—and here is the gradual hurtless lapse into idiocy, of faculties, which at their best of times never having been strong, we look upon the consummation of their decay with no more of pity than is consistent with a smile. The mad tailor, the poor driveller that has gone out of his wits (and truly he appears to have had no great journey to go to get past their confines) for the love of Charming Betty Careless,—these half-laughable, scarce-pitiable objects, take off from the horror which the principal figure would of itself raise, at the same time that they assist the feeling of the scene by contributing to the general notion of its subject:—

> Madness, thou chaos of the brain,
> What art, that pleasure giv'st and pain?
> Tyranny of Fancy's reign!
> Mechanic Fancy, that can build

Vast labyrinths and mazes wild,
With rule disjointed, shapeless measure,
Fill'd with horror, fill'd with pleasure!
Shapes of horror, that would even
Cast doubts of mercy upon heaven;
Shapes of pleasure, that but seen,
Would split the shaking sides of Spleen.*

Is it carrying the spirit of comparison to excess to remark, that in the poor kneeling weeping female who accompanies her seducer in his sad decay, there is something analogous to Kent, or Caius, as he delights rather to be called, in Lear,—the noblest pattern of virtue which even Shakspeare has conceived,—who follows his royal master in banishment, that had pronounced *his* banishment, and, forgetful at once of his wrongs and dignities, taking on himself the disguise of a menial, retains his fidelity to the figure, his loyalty to the carcass, the shadow, the shell and empty husk of Lear?

In the perusal of a book, or of a picture, much of the impression which we receive depends upon the habit of mind which we bring with us to such perusal. The same circumstance may make one person laugh, which shall render another very serious; or in the same person the first impression may be corrected by after-thought. The mis-employed incongruous characters at the Harlot's Funeral, on a superficial inspection, provoke to laughter; but when we have sacrificed the first emotion to levity a very different frame of mind succeeds, or the painter has lost half his purpose. I never look at that wonderful assemblage of depraved beings, who, without a grain of reverence or pity in their perverted minds, are performing the sacred exteriors of duty to the relics of their departed partner in folly, but I am as much moved to sympathy from the very want of it in them, as I should be by the finest representation of a virtuous death-bed surrounded by real mourners, pious children, weeping friends,—perhaps more by the very contrast. What reflections does it not awake, of the dreadful heartless state in which the creature (a female too) must have lived, who in death wants the accompaniment of one genuine tear. That wretch who is removing the lid of the coffin to gaze upon the corpse with a face which indicates a perfect negation of all goodness or womanhood—the hypocrite parson and his

* Lines inscribed under the plate.

demure partner—all the fiendish group—to a thoughtful mind present a moral emblem more affecting than if the poor friendless carcass had been depicted as thrown out to the woods, where wolves had assisted at its obsequies, itself furnishing forth its own funeral banquet.

It is easy to laugh at such incongruities as are met together in this picture,—incongruous objects being of the very essence of laughter,—but surely the laugh is far different in its kind from that thoughtless species to which we are moved by mere farce and grotesque. We laugh when Ferdinand Count Fathom, at the first sight of the white cliffs of Britain, feels his heart yearn with filial fondness towards the land of his progenitors, which he is coming to fleece and plunder,—we smile at the exquisite irony of the passage,—but if we are not led on by such passages to some more salutary feeling than laughter, we are very negligent perusers of them in book or picture.

It is the fashion with those who cry up the great Historical School in this country, at the head of which Sir Joshua Reynolds is placed, to exclude Hogarth from that school, as an artist of an inferior and vulgar class. Those persons seem to me to confound the painting of subjects in common or vulgar life with the being a vulgar artist. The quantity of thought which Hogarth crowds into every picture would alone *unvulgarise* every subject which he might choose. Let us take the lowest of his subjects, the print called Gin Lane. Here is plenty of poverty and low stuff to disgust upon a superficial view; and accordingly a cold spectator feels himself immediately disgusted and repelled. I have seen many turn away from it, not being able to bear it. The same persons would perhaps have looked with great complacency upon Poussin's celebrated picture of the Plague at Athens.* Disease and Death and bewildering Terror, in *Athenian garments*, are endurable, and come, as the delicate critics express it, within the 'limits of pleasurable sensation.' But the scenes of their own St. Giles's, delineated by their own countryman, are too shocking to think of. Yet if we could abstract our minds from the fascinating colours of the picture, and forget the coarse execution (in some respects) of the print, intended as it was to be a cheap plate, accessible to the poorer sort of people, for whose instruction it was done, I

* At the late Mr. Hope's, in Cavendish Square.

think we could have no hesitation in conferring the palm of superior genius upon Hogarth, comparing this work of his with Poussin's picture. There is more of imagination in it— that power which draws all things to one—which makes things animate and inanimate, beings with their attributes, subjects, and their accessories, take one colour and serve to one effect. Everything in the print, to use a vulgar expression, *tells*. Every part is full of 'strange images of death.' It is perfectly amazing and astounding to look at. Not only the two prominent figures, the woman and the half-dead man, which are as terrible as anything which Michael Angelo ever drew, but everything else in the print, contributes to bewilder and stupefy,—the very houses, as I heard a friend of mine express it, tumbling all about in various directions, seem drunk—seem absolutely reeling from the effect of that diabolical spirit of frenzy which goes forth over the whole composition. To show the poetical and almost prophetical conception in the artist, one little circumstance may serve. Not content with the dying and dead figures, which he has strewed in profusion over the proper scene of the action, he shows you what (of a kindred nature) is passing beyond it. Close by the shell, in which by direction of the parish beadle, a man is depositing his wife, is an old wall, which, partaking of the universal decay around it, is tumbling to pieces. Through a gap in this wall are seen three figures, which appear to make a part in some funeral procession which is passing by on the other side of the wall, out of the sphere of the composition. This extending of the interest beyond the bounds of the subject could only have been conceived by a great genius. Shakspeare, in his description of the painting of the Trojan War, in his Tarquin and Lucrece, has introduced a similar device, where the painter made a part stand for the whole:—

> For much imaginary work was there,
> Conceit deceitful, so compact, so kind,
> That for Achilles' image stood his spear,
> Grip'd in an armed hand; himself behind
> Was left unseen, save to the eye of mind:
> A hand, a foot, a face, a leg, a head,
> Stood for the whole to be imagined.

This he well calls *imaginary work*, where the spectator must meet the artist in his conceptions half-way; and it is peculiar to the confidence of high genius alone to trust so much to spectators or readers. Lesser artists show everything distinct and full, as they require an object to be made out to themselves before they can comprehend it.

When I think of the power displayed in this (I will not hesitate to say) sublime print, it seems to me the extreme narrowness of system alone, and of that rage for classification, by which, in matters of taste at least, we are perpetually perplexing, instead of arranging, our ideas, that would make us concede to the work of Poussin above mentioned, and deny to this of Hogarth, the name of a grand serious composition.

We are for ever deceiving ourselves with names and theories. We call one man a great historical painter, because he has taken for his subjects kings or great men, or transactions over which time has thrown a grandeur. We term another the painter of common life, and set him down in our minds for an artist of an inferior class, without reflecting whether the quantity of thought shown by the latter may not much more than level the distinction which their mere choice of subjects may seem to place between them; or whether, in fact, from that very common life a great artist may not extract as deep an interest as another man from that which we are pleased to call history.

I entertain the highest respect for the talents and virtues of Reynolds, but I do not like that his reputation should overshadow and stifle the merits of such a man as Hogarth, nor that to mere names and classifications we should be content to sacrifice one of the greatest ornaments of England.

I would ask the most enthusiastic admirer of Reynolds, whether in the countenances of his Staring and Grinning Despair, which he has given us for the faces of Ugolino and dying Beaufort, there be anything comparable to the expression which Hogarth has put into the face of his brokendown rake in the last plate but one of the Rake's Progress,*

---

* The first perhaps in all Hogarth for serious expression. That which comes next to it, I think, is the jaded morning countenance of the debauchee in the second plate of the Marriage Alamode, which lectures on the vanity of pleasure as audibly as anything in Ecclesiastes.

where a letter from the manager is brought to him to say that his play 'will not do'? Here all is easy, natural, un-distorted, but withal what a mass of woe is here accumulated! —the long history of a mis-spent life is compressed into the countenance as plainly as the series of plates before had told it; here is no attempt at Gorgonian looks, which are to freeze the beholder—no grinning at the antique bed-posts—no face-making, or consciousness of the presence of spectators in or out of the picture, but grief kept to a man's self, a face retiring from notice with the shame which great anguish sometimes brings with it,—a final leave taken of hope,—the coming on of vacancy and stupefaction,—a beginning alien-ation of mind looking like tranquillity. Here is matter for the mind of the beholder to feed on for the hour together,— matter to feed and fertilise the mind. It is too real to admit one thought about the power of the artist who did it. When we compare the expression in subjects which so fairly admit of comparison, and find the superiority so clearly to remain with Hogarth, shall the mere contemptible difference of the scene of it being laid, in the one case, in our Fleet or King's Bench Prison, and, in the other, in the State Prison of Pisa, or the bedroom of a cardinal,—or that the subject of the one has never been authenticated, and the other is matter of history,—so weigh down the real points of the comparison, as to induce us to rank the artist who has chosen the one scene or subject (though confessedly inferior in that which constitutes the soul of his art) in a class from which we exclude the better genius (who has happened to make choice of the other) with something like disgrace?*

The Boys under Demoniacal Possession of Raphael and

---

* Sir Joshua Reynolds, somewhere in his Lectures, speaks of the *presumption* of Hogarth in attempting the grand style in painting, by which he means his choice of certain Scripture subjects. Hogarth's excursions into Holy Land were not very nu-merous, but what he has left us in this kind have at least this merit, that they have expression of *some sort or other* in them,—the Child Moses before Pharaoh's Daughter, for instance: which is more than can be said of Sir Joshua Reynolds's Repose in Egypt, painted for Macklin's Bible, where for a Madonna he has substituted a sleepy, insensible, unmotherly girl, one so little worthy to have been selected as the Mother of the Saviour, that she seems to have neither heart nor feeling to entitle her to be-come a mother at all. But indeed the race of Virgin Mary painters seems to have been cut up, root and branch, at the Reformation. Our artists are too good Protestants to give life to that admirable commixture of maternal tenderness with reverential awe and wonder approaching to worship, with which the Virgin Mothers of L. da Vinci and Raphael (themselves by their divine countenances inviting men to worship) contemplate the union of the two natures in the person of their Heaven-born Infant.

Domenichino, by what law of classification are we bound to assign them to belong to the great style in painting, and to degrade into an inferior class the Rake of Hogarth when he is the Madman in the Bedlam scene? I am sure he is far more impressive than either. It is a face which no one that has seen can easily forget. There is the stretch of human suffering to the utmost endurance, severe bodily pain brought on by strong mental agony, the frightful obstinate laugh of madness,—yet all so unforced and natural, that those who never were witness to madness in real life, think they see nothing but what is familiar to them in this face. Here are no tricks of distortion, nothing but the natural face of agony. This is high tragic painting, and we might as well deny to Shakspeare the honours of a great tragedian, because he has interwoven scenes of mirth with the serious business of his plays, as refuse to Hogarth the same praise for the two concluding scenes of the Rake's Progress, because of the Comic Lunatics* which he has thrown into the one, or the Alchymist that he has introduced in the other, who is paddling in the coals of his furnace, keeping alive the flames of vain hope within the very walls of the prison to which the vanity has conducted him, which have taught the darker lesson of extinguished hope to the desponding figure who is the principal person of the scene.

It is the force of these kindly admixtures which assimilates the scenes of Hogarth and of Shakspeare to the drama of real life, where no such thing as pure tragedy is to be found; but merriment and infelicity, ponderous crime and feather-light vanity, like twi-formed births, disagreeing complexions of one intertexture, perpetually unite to show forth motley spectacles to the world. Then it is that the poet or painter shows his art, when in the selection of these comic adjuncts he chooses such circumstances as shall relieve, contrast with, or fall into, without forming a violent opposition to his

---

* There are of madmen, as there are of tame,
All humour'd not alike. We have here some
So apish and fantastic, play with a feather;
And though 'twould grieve a soul to see God's image
So blemish'd and defac'd, yet do they act
Such antick and such pretty lunacies,
That, spite of sorrow, they will make you smile.
Others again we have, like angry lions,
Fierce as wild bulls, untameable as flies.

Honest Whore.

principal object. Who sees not that the Gravedigger in Hamlet, the Fool in Lear, have a kind of correspondency to, and fall in with, the subjects which they seem to interrupt: while the comic stuff in Venice Preserved, and the doggerel nonsense of the Cook and his poisoning associates in the Rollo of Beaumont and Fletcher, are pure, irrelevant, impertinent discords,—as bad as the quarrelling dog and cat under the table of the Lord and the Disciples at Emmaus of Titian?

Not to tire the reader with perpetual reference to prints which he may not be fortunate enough to possess, it may be sufficient to remark, that the same tragic cast of expression and incident, blended in some instances with a greater alloy of comedy, characterises his other great work, the Marriage Alamode, as well as those less elaborate exertions of his genius, the prints called Industry and Idleness, the Distrest Poet, etc., forming, with the Harlot's and Rake's Progresses, the most considerable if not the largest class of his productions, —enough surely to rescue Hogarth from the imputation of being a mere buffoon, or one whose general aim was only to *shake the sides*.

There remains a very numerous class of his performances, the object of which must be confessed to be principally comic. But in all of them will be found something to distinguish them from the droll productions of Bunbury and others. They have this difference, that we do not merely laugh at, we are led into long trains of reflection by them. In this respect they resemble the characters of Chaucer's Pilgrims, which have strokes of humour in them enough to designate them for the most part as comic, but our strongest feeling still is wonder at the comprehensiveness of genius which could crowd, as poet and painter have done, into one small canvas so many diverse yet co-operating materials.

The faces of Hogarth have not a mere momentary interest, as in caricatures, or those grotesque physiognomies which we sometimes catch a glance of in the street, and, struck with their whimsicality, wish for a pencil and the power to sketch them down; and forget them again as rapidly,—but they are permanent abiding ideas. Not the sports of nature, but her necessary eternal classes. We feel that we cannot part with any of them, lest a link should be broken.

It is worthy of observation, that he has seldom drawn a

mean or insignificant countenance.* Hogarth's mind was eminently reflective; and, as it has been well observed of Shakspeare, that he has transfused his own poetical character into the persons of his drama (they are all more or less *poets*) Hogarth has impressed a *thinking character* upon the persons of his canvas. This remark must not be taken universally. The exquisite idiotism of the little gentleman in the bag and sword beating his drum in the print of the Enraged Musician, would of itself rise up against so sweeping an assertion. But I think it will be found to be true of the generality of his countenances. The knife-grinder and Jew flute-player in the plate just mentioned, may serve as instances instead of a thousand. They have intense thinking faces, though the purpose to which they are subservient by no means required it; but indeed it seems as if it was painful to Hogarth to contemplate mere vacancy or insignificance.

This reflection of the artist's own intellect from the faces of his characters, is one reason why the works of Hogarth, so much more than those of any other artist, are objects of meditation. Our intellectual natures love the mirror which gives them back their own likenesses. The mental eye will not bend long with delight upon vacancy.

Another line of eternal separation between Hogarth and the common painters of droll or burlesque subjects, with whom he is often confounded, is the sense of beauty, which in the most unpromising subjects seems never wholly to have deserted him. 'Hogarth himself,' says Mr. Coleridge,† from whom I have borrowed this observation, speaking of a scene which took place at Ratzeburg, 'never drew a more ludicrous distortion, both of attitude and physiognomy, than this effect occasioned: nor was there wanting beside it one of those beautiful female faces which the same Hogarth, *in whom the satirist never extinguished that love of beauty which belonged to him as a poet*, so often and so gladly introduces as the central figure in a crowd of humorous deformities, which figure (such is the power of true genius) neither acts nor is meant

* If there are any of that description, they are in his Strolling Players, a print which has been cried up by Lord Oxford as the richest of his productions, and it may be, for what I know, in the mere lumber, the properties, and dead furniture of the scene, but in living character and expression it is (for Hogarth) lamentably poor and wanting; it is perhaps the only one of his performances at which we have a right to feel disgusted.
† *The Friend*, No. XVI.

to act as a contrast; but diffuses through all and over each of the group a spirit of reconciliation and human kindness; and even when the attention is no longer consciously directed to the cause of this feeling, still blends its tenderness with our laughter: and *thus prevents the instructive merriment at the whims of nature, or the foibles or humours of our fellow-men, from degenerating into the heart-poison of contempt or hatred.*' To the beautiful females in Hogarth, which Mr. C. has pointed out, might be added, the frequent introduction of children (which Hogarth seems to have taken a particular delight in) into his pieces. They have a singular effect in giving tranquillity and a portion of their own innocence to the subject. The baby riding in its mother's lap in the March to Finchley (its careless innocent face placed directly behind the intriguing time-furrowed countenance of the treason-plotting French priest), perfectly sobers the whole of that tumultuous scene. The boy mourner winding up his top with so much unpretending insensibility in the plate of the Harlot's Funeral (the only thing in that assembly that is not a hypocrite), quiets and soothes the mind that has been disturbed at the sight of so much depraved man and woman kind.

I had written thus far, when I met with a passage in the writings of the late Mr. Barry, which, as it falls in with the *vulgar notion* respecting Hogarth, which this Essay has been employed in combating, I shall take the liberty to transcribe, with such remarks as may suggest themselves to me in the transcription; referring the reader for a full answer to that which has gone before.

Notwithstanding Hogarth's merit does undoubtedly entitle him to an honourable place among the artists, and that his little compositions, considered as so many dramatic representations, abounding with humour, character, and extensive observations on the various incidents of low, faulty, and vicious life, are very ingeniously brought together, and frequently tell their own story with more facility than is often found in many of the elevated and more noble inventions of Raphael and other great men; yet it must be honestly confessed, that in what is called knowledge of the figure, foreigners have justly observed, that Hogarth is often so raw and unformed, as hardly to deserve the name of an artist. But this capital defect is not often perceivable, as examples of the naked and of elevated nature but rarely occur in his subjects, which are for the most part filled with characters that in their nature tend to deformity; besides his figures are small, and the jonctures, and other difficulties of drawing that might occur in their limbs, are artfully concealed with their clothes, rags, etc. But what would atone for all his defects, even if they were twice told, is his admirable fund of invention, ever inexhaustible in its resources; and his satire, which is always sharp and pertinent, and often highly moral, was (except in a few instances, where he weakly and meanly suffered his integrity to give way to his envy) seldom or never employed in a dishonest or unmanly way. Hogarth has been often imitated in his satirical vein, sometimes in his humorous: but very few have attempted to rival him in his moral walk. The line of art pursued by my very ingenious predecessor and brother Academician, Mr. Penny, is quite distinct from that of Hogarth, and is of a much more delicate and superior relish; he attempts the heart, and reaches it, whilst Hogarth's general aim is only to shake the sides; in other respects no comparison can be thought of, as Mr. Penny has all that knowledge of the figure and academical skill which the other wanted. As to Mr. Bunbury, who had so happily succeeded in the vein of humour and caricatura, he has for some time past altogether relinquished it, for the more amiable pursuit of beautiful nature: this, indeed, is not to be wondered at, when we recollet that he has, in Mrs. Bunbury, so admirable an exemplar of the most finished grace and beauty continually at his elbow. But (to say all that occurs to me on this subject) perhaps it may be reasonably doubted, whether the being much conversant with Hogarth's method of exposing meanness, deformity, and vice, in many of his works, is not rather a dangerous, or, at least, a worthless pursuit; which, if it does not find a false relish and a love of and search after satire and buffoonery in the spectator, is at least not unlikely to give him one. Life is short; and the little leisure of it is much better laid out upon that species of art which is employed about the amiable and the admirable, as it is more likely to be attended with better and nobler consequences to ourselves. These two pursuits in art may be compared with two sets of people with whom we might associate; if we give ourselves up to the Footes, the Kenricks, etc., we shall be continually busied and paddling in whatever is ridiculous, faulty, and vicious in life; whereas there are those to be found with whom we should be in the constant pursuit and study of all that gives a value and a dignity to human nature.

[Account of a Series of Pictures in the Great Room of the

Society of Arts, Manufactures, and Commerce, at the Adelphi, by James Barry, R. A., Professor of Painting to the Royal Academy; reprinted in the last quarto edition of his works.]

—— It must be honestly confessed, that in what is called knowledge of the figure, foreigners have justly observed, etc.

It is a secret well known to the professors of the art and mystery of criticism, to insist upon what they do not find in a man's works, and to pass over in silence what they do. That Hogarth did not draw the naked figure so well as Michael Angelo might be allowed, especially as 'examples of the naked,' as Mr. Barry acknowledges, 'rarely (he might almost have said never) occur in his subjects'; and that his figures under their draperies do not discover all the fine graces of an Antinoüs or an Apollo, may be conceded likewise; perhaps it was more suitable to his purpose to represent the average forms of mankind in the mediocrity (as Mr. Burke expresses it) of the age in which he lived: but that his figures in general, and in his best subjects, are so glaringly incorrect as is here insinuated, I dare trust my own eye so far as positively to deny the fact. And there is one part of the figure in which Hogarth is allowed to have excelled, which these foreigners seem to have overlooked, or perhaps calculating from its proportion to the whole (a seventh or an eighth, I forget which), deemed it of trifling importance; I mean the human face; a small part, reckoning by geographical inches, in the map of man's body, but here it is that the painter of expression must condense the wonders of his skill, even at the expense of neglecting the 'jonctures and other difficulties of drawing in the limbs,' which it must be a cold eye that, in the interest so strongly demanded by Hogarth's countenances, has leisure to survey and censure.

The line of art pursued by my very ingenious predecessor and brother Academician, Mr. Penny.

The first impression caused in me by reading this passage was an eager desire to know who this Mr. Penny was. This great surpasser of Hogarth in the 'delicacy of his relish,' and the 'line which he pursued,' where is he, what are his works, what has he to show? In vain I tried to recollect, till by happily putting the question to a friend who is more conversant in the works of the illustrious obscure than myself

I learnt that he was the painter of a Death of Wolfe which missed the prize the year that the celebrated picture of West on the same subject obtained it; that he also made a picture of the Marquis of Granby relieving a Sick Soldier; moreover, that he was the inventor of two pictures of Suspended and Restored Animation, which I now remember to have seen in the Exhibition some years since, and the prints from which are still extant in good men's houses. This then, I suppose, is the line of subjects in which Mr. Penny was so much superior to Hogarth. I confess I am not of that opinion. The relieving of poverty by the purse, and the restoring a young man to his parents by using the methods prescribed by the Humane Society, are doubtless very amiable subjects, pretty things to teach the first rudiments of humanity; they amount to about as much instruction as the stories of good boys that give away their custards to poor beggar-boys in children's books. But, good God! is this *milk for babes* to be set up in opposition to Hogarth's moral scenes, his *strong meat for men?* As well might we prefer the fulsome verses upon their own goodness to which the gentlemen of the Literary Fund annually sit still with such shameless patience to listen, to the satires of Juvenal and Persius; because the former are full of tender images of Worth relieved by Charity, and Charity stretching out her hand to rescue sinking Genius, and the theme of the latter is men's crimes and follies with their black consequences—forgetful meanwhile of those strains of moral pathos, those sublime heart-touches, which these poets (in *them* chiefly showing themselves poets) are perpetually darting across the otherwise appalling gloom of their subject-consolatory remembrancers, when their pictures of guilty mankind have made us even to despair for our species, that there is such a thing as virtue and moral dignity in the world, that her unquenchable spark is not utterly out—refreshing admonitions, to which we turn for shelter from the too great heat and asperity of the general satire.

And is there nothing analogous to this in Hogarth? nothing which 'attempts and reaches the heart?'—no aim beyond that of 'shaking the sides'?—If the kneeling ministering female in the last scene of the Rake's Progress, the Bedlam scene, of which I have spoken before, and have dared almost to parallel it with the most absolute idea of Virtue which Shakspeare has left us, be not enough to disprove the assertion; if the sad endings of the Harlot and the Rake, the passionate heart-bleeding entreaties for forgiveness which the adulterous wife is pouring forth to her assassinated and dying lord in the last scene but one of the Marriage Alamode,—if these be not things to touch the heart, and dispose the mind to a meditative tenderness: is there nothing sweetly conciliatory in the mild patient face and gesture with which the wife seems to allay and ventilate the feverish irritated feelings of her poor poverty-distracted mate (the true copy of the *genus irritabile*) in the print of the Distrest Poet? or if an image of maternal love be required, where shall we find a sublimer view of it than in that aged woman in Industry and Idleness (Plate V.) who is clinging with the fondness of hope not quite extinguished to her brutal vice-hardened child, whom she is accompanying to the ship which is to bear him away from his native soil, of which he has been adjudged unworthy: in whose shocking face every trace of the human countenance seems obliterated, and a brute beast's to be left instead, shocking and repulsive to all but her who watched over it in its cradle before it was so sadly altered, and feels it must belong to her while a pulse by the vindictive laws of his country shall be suffered to continue to beat in it. Compared with such things, what is Mr. Penny's 'knowledge of the figure and academical skill which Hogarth wanted'?

With respect to what follows concerning another gentleman, with the congratulations to him on his escape out of the regions of 'humour and caricatura,' in which it appears he was in danger of travelling side by side with Hogarth, I can only congratulate my country, that Mrs. Hogarth knew *her* province better than, by disturbing her husband at his palette, to divert him from that universality of subject, which has stamped him perhaps, next to Shakspeare, the most inventive genius which this island has produced, into the 'amiable pursuit of beautiful nature,' *i.e.*, copying *ad infinitum* the individual charms and graces of Mrs. H.

Hogarth's method of exposing meanness, deformity, and vice, paddling in whatever is ridiculous, faulty, and vicious.

A person unacquainted with the works thus stigmatised would be apt to imagine that in Hogarth there was nothing else to be found but subjects of the coarsest and most repulsive nature. That his imagination was naturally unsweet, and that he delighted in raking into every species of moral filth. That he preyed upon sore places only, and took a pleasure in exposing the unsound and rotten parts of human nature:—whereas, with the exception of some of the plates of the Harlot's Progress, which are harder in their character than any of the rest of his productions (the Stages of Cruelty I omit as mere worthless caricaturas, foreign to his general habits, the offspring of his fancy in some wayward humour), there is scarce one of his pieces where vice is most strongly satirised, in which some figure is not introduced upon which the moral eye may rest satisfied; a face that indicates goodness, or perhaps mere good-humouredness and carelessness of mind (negation of evil) only, yet enough to give a relaxation to the frowning brow of satire, and keep the general air from tainting. Take the mild, supplicating posture of patient Poverty in the poor woman that is persuading the pawnbroker to accept her clothes in pledge, in the plate of Gin Lane, for an instance. A little does it, a little of the *good* nature overpowers a world of *bad*. One cordial honest laugh of a Tom Jones absolutely clears the atmosphere that was reeking with the black putrefying breathings of a hypocrite Blifil. One homely expostulating shrug from Strap warms the whole air which the suggestions of a gentlemanly ingratitude from his friend Random had begun to freeze. One 'Lord bless us!' of Parson Adams upon the wickedness of the time, exorcises and purges off the mass of iniquity which the world-knowledge of even a Fielding could cull out and rake together. But of the severer class of Hogarth's performances, enough, I trust, has been said to show that they do not merely shock and repulse; that there is in them the 'scorn of vice' and the 'pity' too; something to touch the heart, and keep alive the sense of moral beauty; the 'lacrymæ rerum,' and the sorrowing by which the heart is made better. If they be bad things, then is satire and tragedy a bad thing; let us proclaim at once an age of gold, and sink the existence of vice and misery in our speculations: let us

—— wink, and shut our apprehensions up
From common sense of what men were and are:

let us *make believe* with the children, that everybody is good and happy; and, with Dr. Swift, write panegyrics upon the world.

But that larger half of Hogarth's works, which were painted more for entertainment than instruction (though such was the suggestiveness of his mind that there is always something to be learnt from them), his humorous scenes,—are they such as merely to disgust and set us against our species?

The confident assertions of such a man as I consider the late Mr. Barry to have been, have that weight of authority in them which staggers, at first hearing, even a long preconceived opinion. When I read his pathetic admonition concerning the shortness of life, and how much better the little leisure of it were laid out upon 'that species of art which is employed about the amiable and the admirable'; and Hogarth's 'method,' proscribed as a 'dangerous or worthless pursuit,' I began to think there was something in it; that I might have been indulging all my life a passion for the works of this artist, to the utter prejudice of my taste and moral sense; but my first convictions gradually returned, a world of good-natured English faces came up one by one to my recollection, and a glance at the matchless Election Entertainment, which I have the happiness to have hanging up in my parlour, subverted Mr. Barry's whole theory in an instant.

In that inimitable print (which in my judgment as far exceeds the more known and celebrated March to Finchley, as the best comedy exceeds the best farce that ever was written), let a person look till he be saturated, and when he has done wondering at the inventiveness of genius which could bring so many characters (more than thirty distinct classes of face) into a room and set them down at table together, or otherwise dispose them about, in so natural a manner, engage them in so many easy sets and occupations, yet all partaking of the spirit of the occasion which brought them together, so that we feel that nothing but an election time could have assembled them; having no central figure or principal group (for the hero of the piece, the Candidate, is properly set aside in the levelling indistinction of the day, one must look for him to find him), nothing to detain the eye from passing from part to part, where every part is alike instinct with life,—for here are no furniture faces, no figures brought in to fill up the scene like stage choruses, but all *dramatis personæ:* when he shall have done wondering at all these faces so strongly charactered, yet finished with the accuracy of the finest miniature; when he shall have done admiring the numberless appendages of the scene, those gratuitous doles which rich genius flings into the heap when it has already done enough, the over-measure which it delights in giving, as if it felt its stores were exhaustless; the dumb rhetoric of the scenery—for tables, and chairs, and joint-stools in Hogarth are living and significant things; the witticisms that are expressed by words (all artists but Hogarth have failed when they have endeavoured to combine two mediums of expression, and have introduced words into their pictures), and the unwritten numberless little allusive pleasantries that are scattered about; the work that is going on in the scene, and beyond it, as is made visible to the 'eye of mind,' by the mob which chokes up the doorway, and the sword that has forced an entrance before its master; when he shall have sufficiently admired this wealth of genius, let him fairly say what is the *result* left on his mind. Is it an impression of the vileness and worthlessness of his species? or is it not the general feeling which remains, after the individual faces have ceased to act sensibly on his mind, a *kindly one in favour of his species?* was not the general air of the scene wholesome? did it do the heart hurt to be among it? Something of a riotous spirit to be sure is there, some worldly-mindedness in some of the faces, a Doddingtonian smoothness which does not promise any superfluous degree of sincerity in the fine gentleman who has been the occasion of calling so much good company together; but is not the general cast of expression in the faces of the good sort? do they not seem cut out of the *good old rock*, substantial English honesty? would one fear treachery among characters of their expression? or shall we call their honest mirth and seldom-returning relaxation by the hard names of vice and profligacy? That poor country fellow, that is grasping his staff (which, from that difficulty of feeling themselves at home which poor men experience at a feast, he has never parted with since he came into the room), and is enjoying with a relish that seems to fit all the capacities of his soul the slender joke, which that facetious wag his neighbour is practising upon the gouty gentleman, whose eyes the effort to suppress pain has made as round as rings—does it shock the 'dignity of human nature' to look at that man, and to sympathise with him in the seldom-heard joke which has unbent his careworn, hard-working visage, and drawn iron smiles from it? or with that full-hearted cobbler, who is honouring with the grasp of an honest fist the unused palm of that annoyed patrician, whom the licence of the time has seated next him?

I can see nothing 'dangerous' in the contemplation of such scenes as this, or the Enraged Musician, or the Southwark Fair, or twenty other pleasant prints which come crowding in upon my recollection, in which the restless activities, the diversified bents and humours, the blameless peculiarities of men, as they deserve to be called, rather than their 'vices and follies,' are held up in a laughable point of view. All laughter is not of a dangerous or soul-hardening tendency. There is the petrifying sneer of a demon which excludes and kills Love, and there is the cordial laughter of a man which implies and cherishes it. What heart was ever made the worse by joining in a hearty laugh at the simplicities of Sir Hugh Evans or Parson Adams, where a sense of the ridiculous mutually kindles and is kindled by a perception of the amiable? That tumultuous harmony of singers that are roaring out the words, 'The world shall bow to the Assyrian throne,' from the opera of Judith, in the third plate of the series called the Four Groups of Heads; which the quick eye of Hogarth must have struck off in the very infancy of the rage for sacred oratorios in this country, while 'Music yet was young'; when we have done smiling at the deafening distortions, which these tearers of devotion to rags and tatters, these takers of heaven by storm, in their boisterous mimicry of the occupation of angels, are making,—what unkindly impression is left behind, or what more of harsh or contemptuous feeling, than when we quietly leave Uncle Toby and Mr. Shandy riding their hobby-horses about the room? The conceited, long-backed Sign-painter, that with all the self-applause of a Raphael or Correggio (the twist of body which his conceit has thrown him into has something of the Correggiesque in it), is contemplating the picture of a bottle, which he is drawing from an actual bottle that hangs beside him, in the print of Beer Street,—while we smile at the enormity of the self-delusion, can we help loving the good-humour and self-complacency of the fellow? would we willingly wake him from his dream?

I say not that all the ridiculous subjects of Hogarth have,

necessarily, something in them to make us like them; some are indifferent to us, some in their natures repulsive, and only made interesting by the wonderful skill and truth to nature in the painter; but I contend that there is in most of them that sprinkling of the better nature, which, like holy water, chases away and disperses the contagion of the bad. They have this in them, besides, that they bring us acquainted with the everyday human face,—they give us skill to detect those gradations of sense and virtue (which escape the careless or fastidious observer) in the countenances of the world about us; and prevent that disgust at common life, that *tædium quotidianarum formarum*, which an unrestricted passion for ideal forms and beauties is in danger of producing. In this, as in many other things, they are analogous to the best novels of Smollett or Fielding.

Charles Lamb's Autobiography

CHARLES LAMB, born in the Inner Temple, 10th of February, 1775; educated in Christ's Hospital; afterwards a clerk in the Accountants' Office, East-India House; pensioned off from that service, 1825, after thirty-three years' service; is now a gentleman at large; can remember few specialities in his life worth noting, except that he once caught a swallow flying (*teste sua manu*). Below the middle stature; cast of face slightly Jewish, with no Judaic tinge in his complexional religion; stammers abominably, and is therefore more apt to discharge his occasional conversation in a quaint aphorism, or a poor quibble, than in set and edifying speeches; has consequently been libelled as a person always aiming at wit; which, as he told a dull fellow that charged him with it, is at least as good as aiming at dulness. A small eater, but not drinker; confesses a partiality for the production of the juniper-berry; was a fierce smoker of tobacco, but may be resembled to a volcano burnt out, emitting only now and then a casual puff. Has been guilty of obtruding upon the public a tale, in prose, called 'Rosamund Gray'; a dramatic sketch, named 'John Woodvil'; a 'Farewell Ode to Tobacco,' with sundry other poems, and light prose matter, collected in two slight crown octavos, and pompously christened his works, though in fact they were his recreations. His true works may be found on the shelves of Leadenhall Street, filling some hundred folios. He is also the true Elia, whose Essays are extant in a little volume, published a year or two since, and rather better known from that name without a meaning than from anything he has done, or can hope to do, in his own name. He was also the first to draw the public attention to the old English dramatists, in a work called 'Specimens of English Dramatic Writers who lived about the Time of Shakspeare,' published about fifteen years since. In short, all his merits and demerits to set forth would take to the end of Mr. Upcott's book, and then not be told truly.

He died   18   , much lamented.

Witness his hand,

CHARLES LAMB.

18th April, 1827.

Elia on 'The Confessions of a Drunkard'

FROM THE 'LONDON MAGAZINE,' 1822

MANY are the sayings of Elia, painful and frequent his lucubrations, set forth for the most part (such his modesty!) without a name; scattered about in obscure periodicals and forgotten miscellanies. From the dust of some of these it is our intention occasionally to revive a tract or two that shall seem worthy of a better fate, especially at a time like the present, when the pen of our industrious contributor, engaged in a laborious digest of his recent Continental tour, may haply want the leisure to expatiate in more miscellaneous speculations. We have been induced, in the first instance, to reprint a thing which he put forth in a friend's volume some years since, entitled The Confessions of a Drunkard, seeing that Messieurs the Quarterly Reviewers have chosen to embellish their last dry pages with fruitful quotations therefrom; adding, from their peculiar brains, the gratuitous affirmation, that they have reason to believe that the describer (in his delineation of a drunkard, forsooth!) partly sat for his own picture. The truth is, that our friend had been reading among the essays of a contemporary, who has perversely been confounded with him, a paper in which Edax (or the

Great Eater) humorously complaineth of an inordinate appetite; and it struck him that a better paper—of deeper interest and wider usefulness—might be made out of the imagined experiences of a Great Drinker. Accordingly he set to work, and, with that mock fervour and counterfeit earnestness with which he is too apt to over-realise his descriptions, has given us—a frightful picture indeed, but no more resembling the man Elia than the fictitious Edax may be supposed to identify itself with Mr. L. its author. It is, indeed, a compound extracted out of his long observations of the effects of drinking upon all the world about him; and this accumulated mass of misery he hath centred (as the custom is with judicious essayists) in a single figure. We deny not that a portion of his own experiences may have passed into the picture; (as who, that is not a washy fellow, but must at some times have felt the after-operation of a too-generous cup?) but then how heightened! how exaggerated! how little within the sense of the Review, where a part, in its slanderous usage, must be understood to stand for the whole! But it is useless to expostulate with this Quarterly slime, brood of Nilus, watery heads with hearts of jelly spawned under the sign of Aquarius, incapable of Bacchus, and therefore cold, washy, spiteful, bloodless. Elia shall string them up one day, and show their colours,—or, rather, how colourless and vapid the whole fry,—when he putteth forth his long-promised, but unaccountably hitherto delayed, Confessions of a Water-Drinker.

A Character of the Late Elia

BY A FRIEND

FROM THE 'LONDON MAGAZINE,' 1823

THIS gentleman, who for some months past had been in a declining way, hath at length paid his final tribute to Nature. He just lived long enough (it was what he wished) to see his papers collected into a volume. The pages of the London Magazine will henceforth know him no more.

Exactly at twelve, last night, his queer spirit departed; and the bells of Saint Bride's rang him out with the old year. The mournful vibrations were caught in the dining-room of his friends T. and H.*; and the company, assembled there to welcome in another 1st of January, checked their carousals in mid-earth, and were silent. Janus wept. The gentle P——r,† in a whisper, signified his intention of devoting an elegy; and Allan C.,‡ nobly forgetful of his countrymen's wrongs, vowed a memoir to his *manes*, full and friendly, as a *Tale of Lyddalcross*.

To say truth, it is time he were gone. The humour of the thing, if there was ever much in it, was pretty well exhausted; and a two years and a half's existence has been a tolerable duration for a phantom.

I am now at liberty to confess, that much which I have heard objected to my late friend's writings was well founded. Crude they are, I grant you,—a sort of unlicked, incondite things,—villainously pranked in an affected array of antique modes and phrases. They had not been *his* if they had been other than such; and better it is that a writer should be natural in a self-pleasing quaintness, than to affect a naturalness (so called) that should be strange to him. Egotistical they have been pronounced by some who did not know that what he tells us as of himself was often true only (historically) of another; as in his Third Essay (to save many instances), where, under the *first person* (his favourite figure), he shadows forth the forlorn estate of a country boy placed at a London school, far from his friends and connections,—in direct opposition to his own early history. If it be egotism to imply and twine with his own identity the griefs and affections of another,—making himself many, or reducing many unto himself,—then is the skilful novelist, who all along brings in his hero or heroine, speaking of themselves, the greatest egotist of all; who yet has never, therefore, been accused of that narrowness. And how shall the intenser dramatist escape being faulty, who doubtless, under cover of passion uttered by another, oftentimes gives blameless vent to his most inward feelings, and expresses his own story modestly?

My late friend was in many respects a singular character. Those who did not like him hated him; and some, who once liked him, afterwards became his bitterest haters. The truth is, he gave himself too little concern about what he uttered,

---

* Taylor and Hessey, the publishers of the London Magazine.
† Procter, better known as Barry Cornwall.
‡ Cunningham.

and in whose presence. He observed neither time nor place, and would ever out with what came uppermost. With the severe religionist he would pass for a free-thinker; while the other faction set him down for a bigot, or persuaded themselves that he belied his sentiments. Few understood him; and I am not certain that at all times he quite understood himself. He too much affected that dangerous figure,—irony. He sowed doubtful speeches, and reaped plain, unequivocal hatred. He would interrupt the gravest discussion with some light jest; and yet, perhaps, not quite irrelevant in ears that could understand it. Your long and much talkers hated him. The informal habit of his mind, joined to an inveterate impediment of speech, forbade him to be an orator; and he seemed determined that no one else should play that part when he was present. He was *petit* and ordinary in his person and appearance. I have seen him sometimes in what is called good company, but, where he has been a stranger, sit silent, and be suspected for an odd fellow, till (some unlucky occasion provoking it) he would stutter out some senseless pun (not altogether senseless perhaps, if rightly taken), which has stamped his character for the evening. It was hit or miss with him; but, nine times out of ten, he contrived by this device to send away a whole company his enemies. His conceptions rose kindlier than his utterance, and his happiest *impromptus* had the appearance of effort. He has been accused of trying to be witty, when in truth he was but struggling to give his poor thoughts articulation. He chose his companions for some individuality of character which they manifested. Hence not many persons of science, and few professed *literati*, were of his councils. They were, for the most part, persons of an uncertain fortune; and as to such people, commonly, nothing is more obnoxious than a gentleman of settled (though moderate) income, he passed with most of them for a great miser. To my knowledge, this was a mistake. His *intimados*, to confess a truth, were, in the world's eye, a ragged regiment. He found them floating on the surface of society; and the colour, or something else, in the weed, pleased him. The burs stuck to him; but they were good and loving burs for all that. He never greatly cared for the society of what are called good people. If any of these were scandalised (and offences were sure to arise), he could not help it. When he has been remonstrated with for not making more concessions to the feelings of good people, he would retort by asking, What one point did these good people ever concede to him? He was temperate in his meals and diversions, but always kept a little on this side of abstemiousness. Only in the use of the Indian weed he might be thought a little excessive. He took it, he would say, as a solvent of speech. Marry—as the friendly vapour ascended, how his prattle would curl up sometimes with it! the ligaments, which tongue-tied him, were loosened, and the stammerer proceeded a statist!

I do not know whether I ought to bemoan or rejoice that my old friend is departed. His jests were beginning to grow obsolete, and his stories to be found out. He felt the approaches of age; and, while he pretended to cling to life, you saw how slender were the ties left to bind him. Discoursing with him latterly on this subject, he expressed himself with a pettishness which I thought unworthy of him. In our walks about his suburban retreat (as he called it) at Shacklewell, some children belonging to a School of Industry met us, and bowed and courtesied, as he thought, in an especial manner to *him*. 'They take me for a visiting governor,' he muttered earnestly. He had a horror, which he carried to a foible, of looking like anything important and parochial. He thought that he approached nearer to that stamp daily. He had a general aversion from being treated like a grave or respectable character, and kept a wary eye upon the advances of age that should so entitle him. He herded always, while it was possible, with people younger than himself. He did not conform to the march of time, but was dragged along in the procession. His manners lagged behind his years. He was too much of the boy-man. The *toga virilis* never sat gracefully on his shoulders. The impressions of infancy had burnt into him, and he resented the impertinence of manhood. These were weaknesses; but such as they were, they are a key to explicate some of his writings.

He left little property behind him. Of course, the little that is left (chiefly in India bonds) devolves upon his cousin Bridget. A few critical dissertations were found in his *escritoire*, which have been handed over to the editor of this magazine, in which it is to be hoped they will shortly appear, retaining his accustomed signature.

He has himself not obscurely hinted that his employment lay in a public office. The gentlemen in the export department of the East-India House will forgive me if I acknowledge the readiness with which they assisted me in the retrieval of his few manuscripts. They pointed out in a most obliging manner the desk at which he had been planted for forty years; showed me ponderous tomes of figures, in his own remarkably neat hand, which, more properly than his few printed tracts, might be called his 'Works.' They seemed affectionate to his memory, and universally commended his expertness in book-keeping. It seems he was the inventor of some ledger which should combine the precision and certainty of the Italian double entry (I think they called it) with the brevity and facility of some newer German system; but I am not able to appreciate the worth of the discovery. I have often heard him express a warm regard for his associates in office, and how fortunate he considered himself in having his lot thrown in amongst them. There is more sense, more discourse, more shrewdness, and even talent, among these clerks (he would say), than in twice the number of authors by profession that I have conversed with. He would brighten up sometimes upon the 'old days of the India House,' when he consorted with Woodroffe and Wissett, and Peter Corbet (a descendant and worthy representative, bating the point of sanctity, of old facetious Bishop Corbet); and Hoole, who translated Tasso; and Bartlemy Brown, whose father (God assoil him therefore!) modernised Walton; and sly, warm-hearted old Jack Cole (King Cole they called him in those days), and Campe and Fombelle, and a world of choice spirits, more than I can remember to name, who associated in those days with Jack Burrell (the *bon vivant* of the South-Sea House); and little Eyton (said to be a *fac-simile* of Pope,—he was a miniature of a gentleman), that was cashier under him; and Dan Voight of the Custom House, that left the famous library.

Well, Elia is gone,—for aught I know, to be reunited with them,—and these poor traces of his pen are all we have to show for it. How little survives of the wordiest authors! Of all they said or did in their lifetime, a few glittering words only! His Essays found some favourers, as they appeared separately. They shuffled their way in the crowd well enough singly: how they will *read*, now they are brought together, is a question for the publishers, who have thus ventured to draw out into one piece his 'weaved-up follies.'

PHIL-ELIA.

On the Inconveniences Resulting from Being Hanged

TO THE EDITOR OF 'THE REFLECTOR'

Sir,—I am one of those unhappy persons whose misfortunes, it seems, do not entitle them to the benefit of pure pity. All that is bestowed upon me of that kindest alleviator of human miseries comes dashed with a double portion of contempt. My griefs have nothing in them that is felt as sacred by the bystanders. Yet is my affliction, in truth, of the deepest grain—the heaviest task that was ever given to mortal patience to sustain. Time, that wears out all other sorrows, can never modify or soften mine. Here they must continue to gnaw as long as that fatal mark——

Why was I ever born? Why was innocence in my person suffered to be branded with a stain which was appointed only for the blackest guilt? What had I done, or my parents, that a disgrace of mine should involve a whole posterity in infamy? I am almost tempted to believe, that, in some pre-existent state, crimes to which this sublunary life of mine hath been as much a stranger as the babe that is newly born into it, have drawn down upon me this vengeance, so disproportionate to my actions on this globe.

My brain sickens, and my bosom labours to be delivered of the weight that presses upon it, yet my conscious pen shrinks from the avowal. But out it must——

O, Mr. Reflector! guess at the wretch's misery who now writes this to you, when, with tears and burning blushes, he is obliged to confess that he has been—HANGED——

Methinks I hear an involuntary exclamation burst from you, as your imagination presents to you fearful images of your correspondent unknown—*hanged!*

Fear not, Mr. Editor. No disembodied spirit has the honour of addressing you. I am flesh and blood, an unfortunate system of bones, muscles, sinews, arteries, like yourself.

Then, I presume, you mean to be pleasant.—That expression of yours, Mr. Correspondent, must be taken somehow in a metaphorical sense——

In the plainest sense, without trope or figure—Yes, Mr.

Editor! this neck of mine has felt the fatal noose,—these hands have tremblingly held up the corroborative prayer-book,—these lips have sucked the moisture of the last consolatory orange,—this tongue has chanted the doleful cantata which no performer was ever called upon to repeat, —this face has had the veiling night-cap drawn over it——

But for no crime of mine.—Far be it from me to arraign the justice of my country, which, though tardy, did at length recognize my innocence. It is not for me to reflect upon judge or jury, now that eleven years have elapsed since the erroneous sentence was pronounced. Men will always be fallible, and perhaps circumstances did appear at the time a little strong——

Suffice it to say, that after hanging four minutes (as the spectators were pleased to compute it,—a man that is being strangled, I know from experience, has altogether a different measure of time from his friends who are breathing leisurely about him,—I suppose the minutes lengthen as time approaches eternity, in the same manner as the miles get longer as you travel northward),—after hanging four minutes, according to the best calculation of the bystanders, a reprieve came, and I was cut DOWN——

Really I am ashamed of deforming your pages with these technical phrases—if I knew how to express my meaning shorter——

But to proceed.—My first care after I had been brought to myself by the usual methods (those methods that are so interesting to the operator and his assistants, who are pretty numerous on such occasions,—but which no patient was ever desirous of undergoing a second time for the benefit of science), my first care was to provide myself with an enormous stock or cravat to hide the place—you understand me;—my next care was to procure a residence as distant as possible from that part of the country where I had suffered. For that reason I chose the metropolis, as the place where wounded honour (I had been told) could lurk with the least danger of exciting inquiry, and stigmatised innocence had the best chance of hiding her disgrace in a crowd. I sought out a new circle of acquaintance, and my circumstances happily enabling me to pursue my fancy in that respect, I endeavoured, by mingling in all the pleasures which the town affords, to efface the memory of what I had undergone.

But, alas! such is the portentous and all-pervading chain of connexion which links together the head and members of this great community, my scheme of lying perdu was defeated almost at the outset. A countryman of mine, whom a foolish law-suit had brought to town, by chance met me, and the secret was soon blazoned about.

In a short time, I found myself deserted by most of those who had been my intimate friends. Not that any guilt was supposed to attach to my character. My officious country-man, to do him justice, had been candid enough to explain my perfect innocence. But, somehow or other, there is a want of strong virtue in mankind. We have plenty of the softer instincts, but the heroic character is gone. How else can I account for it, that of all my numerous acquaintance, among whom I had the honour of ranking sundry persons of education, talents, and worth, scarcely here and there one or two could be found who had the courage to associate with a man that had been hanged.

Those few who did not desert me altogether were persons of strong but coarse minds; and from the absence of all delicacy in them I suffered almost as much as from the superabundance of a false species of it in the others. Those who stuck by me were the jokers, who thought themselves entitled by the fidelity which they had shown towards me to use me with what familiarity they pleased. Many and unfeeling are the jests that I have suffered from these rude (because faithful) Achateses. As they passed me in the streets, one would nod significantly to his companion and say, pointing to me, Smoke his cravat, and ask me if I had got a wen, that I was so solicitous to cover my neck. Another would inquire, What news from *** Assizes? (which you may guess, Mr. Editor, was the scene of my shame), and whether the sessions was like to prove a maiden one? A third would offer to insure me from drowning. A fourth would tease me with inquiries how I felt when I was swinging, whether I had not something like a blue flame dancing before my eyes? A fifth took a fancy never to call me anything but *Lazarus*. And an eminent bookseller and publisher,—who, in his zeal to present the public with new facts, had he lived in those days, I am confident, would not have scrupled waiting upon the person himself last mentioned, at the most critical period of his existence, to solicit a *few facts relative to resusci-*

tation,—had the modesty to offer me——guineas per sheet, if I would write, in his Magazine, a physiological account of my feelings upon coming to myself.

But these were evils which a moderate fortitude might have enabled me to struggle with. Alas! Mr. Editor, the women,—whose good graces, I had always most assiduously cultivated, from whose softer minds I had hoped a more delicate and generous sympathy than I found in the men, —the women began to shun me—this was the unkindest blow of all.

But is it to be wondered at? How couldst thou imagine, wretchedest of beings, that that tender creature Seraphina would fling her pretty arms about that neck which previous circumstances had rendered infamous? That she would put up with the refuse of the rope, the leavings of the cord? Or that any analogy could subsist between the knot which binds true lovers, and the knot which ties malefactors?

I can forgive that pert baggage Flirtilla, who, when I complimented her one day on the execution which her eyes had done, replied, that, to be sure, Mr. * was a judge of those things. But from thy more exalted mind, Celestina, I expected a more unprejudiced decision. The person whose true name I conceal under this appellation, of all the women that I was ever acquainted with, had the most manly turn of mind, which she had improved by reading and the best conversation. Her understanding was not more masculine than her manners and whole disposition were delicately and truly feminine. She was the daughter of an officer who had fallen in the service of his country, leaving his widow, and Celestina, an only child, with a fortune sufficient to set them above want, but not to enable them to live in splendour. I had the mother's permission to pay may addresses to the young lady, and Celestina seemed to approve of my suit.

Often and often have I poured out my overcharged soul in the presence of Celestina, complaining of the hard and unfeeling prejudices of the world; and the sweet maid has again and again declared, that no irrational prejudice should hinder her from esteeming every man according to his intrinsic worth. Often has she repeated the consolatory assurance, that she could never consider as essentially ignominious an *accident*, which was indeed to be deprecated, but which might have happened to the most innocent of mankind.

Then would she set forth some illustrious example, which her reading easily furnished, of a Phocion or a Socrates unjustly condemned; of a Raleigh or a Sir Thomas More, to whom late posterity had done justice; and by soothing my fancy with some such agreeable parallel, she would make me almost to triumph in my disgrace, and convert my shame into glory.

In such entertaining and instructive conversations the time passed on, till I importunately urged the mistress of my affections to name the day for our union. To this she obligingly consented, and I thought myself the happiest of mankind. But how was I surprised one morning on the receipt of the following billet from my charmer:—

SIR,—You must not impute it to levity, or to a worse failing, ingratitude, if, with anguish of heart, I feel myself compelled by irresistible arguments to recall a vow which I fear I made with too little consideration. I never can be yours. The reasons of my decision, which is final, are in my own breast, and you must everlastingly remain a stranger to them. Assure yourself that I can never cease to esteem you as I ought.   CELESTINA.

At the sight of this paper, I ran in frantic haste to Celestina's lodgings, where I learned, to my infinite mortification, that the mother and daughter were set off on a journey to a distant part of the country, to visit a relation, and were not expected to return in less than four months.

Stunned by this blow, which left me without the courage to solicit an explanation by letter, even if I had known where they were (for the particular address was industriously concealed from me), I waited with impatience the termination of the period, in the vain hope that I might be permitted to have a chance of softening the harsh decision by a personal interview with Celestina after her return. But before three months were at an end, I learned from the newspapers that my beloved had—given her hand to another!

Heart-broken as I was, I was totally at a loss to account for the strange step which she had taken; and it was not till some years after that I learned the true reason from a female relation of hers, to whom it seems Celestina had confessed in confidence, that it was no demerit of mine that had caused her to break off the match so abruptly, nor any preference which she might feel for any other person, for she preferred me (she was pleased to say), to all mankind; but when she came to lay the matter closer to her heart, she found that she never should be able to bear the sight—(I give you her very words as they were detailed to me by her relation)—the sight of a man in a nightcap, who had appeared on a public platform—it would lead to such a disagreeable association of ideas! And to this punctilio I was sacrificed.

To pass over an infinite series of minor mortifications, to which this last and heaviest might well render me callous, behold me here, Mr. Editor! in the thirty-seventh year of my existence (the twelfth, reckoning from my re-animation), cut off from all respectable connexions; rejected by the fairer half of the community,—who in my case alone seem to have laid aside the characteristic pity of their sex; punished because I was once punished unjustly; suffering for no other reason than because I once had the misfortune to suffer without any cause at all. In no other country, I think, but this, could a man have been subject to such a lifelong persecution, when once his innocence had been clearly established.

Had I crawled forth a rescued victim from the rack in the horrible dungeons of the Inquisition,—had I heaved myself up from a half bastinado in China, or been torn from the just-entering, ghastly impaling stake in Barbary,—had I dropt alive from the knout in Russia, or come off with a gashed neck from the half-mortal, scarce-in-time-retracted cimeter of an executioneering slave in Turkey,—I might have borne about the remnant of this frame (the mangled trophy of reprieved innocence) with credit to myself, in any of those barbarous countries. No scorn, at least, would have mingled with the pity (small as it might be) with which what was left of me would have been surveyed.

The singularity of my case has often led me to inquire into the reasons of the general levity with which the subject of hanging is treated as a topic in this country. I say, as a topic: for let the very persons who speak so lightly of the thing at a distance be brought to view the real scene,—let the platform be *bonâ fide* exhibited, and the trembling culprit brought forth,—the case is changed; but as a topic of conversation, I appeal to the vulgar jokes which pass current in every street. But why mention them, when the politest authors have agreed in making use of this subject as a source of the ridiculous? Swift, and Pope, and Prior, are fond of recurring to it. Gay has built an entire drama upon this single foundation. The whole interest of the Beggar's Opera may be said to hang upon it. To such writers as Fielding and Smollett it is a perfect *bonne-bouche*.—Hear the facetious Tom Brown, in his Comical View of London and Westminster, describe the *Order of the Show at one of the Tyburn Executions* in his time:—'Mr. Ordinary visits his melancholy flock in Newgate by eight. Doleful procession up Holborn Hill about eleven. Men handsome and proper that were never thought so before, which is some comfort however. Arrive at the fatal place by twelve. Burnt brandy, women, and Sabbath-breaking, repented of. Some few penitential drops fall under the gallows. Sheriff's men, parson, pickpockets, criminals, all very busy. The last concluding peremptory psalm struck up. Show over by one.'—In this sportive strain does this misguided wit think proper to play with a subject so serious, which yet he would hardly have done if he had not known that there existed a predisposition in the habits of his unaccountable countrymen to consider the subject as a jest. But what shall we say to Shakspeare, who (not to mention the solution which the Grave-digger in Hamlet gives of his fellow-workman's problem), in that scene in Measure for Measure, where the Clown calls upon Master Barnardine to get up and be hanged, which he declines on the score of being sleepy, has actually gone out of his way to gratify this amiable propensity in his countrymen; for it is plain, from the use that was to be made of his head, and from Abhorson's asking, 'Is the axe upon the block, sirrah?' that beheading, and not hanging, was the punishment to which Barnardine was destined. But Shakspeare knew that the axe and block were pregnant with no ludicrous images, and therefore falsified the historic truth of his own drama (if I may so speak), rather than he would leave out such excellent matter for a jest as the suspending of a fellow-creature in mid-air has been ever esteemed to be by Englishmen.

One reason why the ludicrous never fails to intrude itself into our contemplations upon this mode of death, I suppose to be, the absurd posture into which a man is thrown who is condemned to dance, as the vulgar delight to express it, upon nothing. To see him whisking and wavering in the air,

As the wind you know will wave a man*; to behold the vacant carcass, from which the life is newly dislodged, shifting between earth and heaven, the sport of every gust; like a weathercock, serving to show from which point the wind blows; like a maukin, fit only to scare away birds; like a nest left to swing upon a bough when the bird is flown: these are uses to which we cannot without a mixture of spleen and contempt behold the human carcass reduced. We string up dogs, foxes, bats, moles, weasels. Man surely deserves a steadier death.

Another reason why the ludicrous associates more forcibly with this than with any other mode of punishment, I cannot help thinking to be, the senseless costume with which old prescription has thought fit to clothe the exit of malefactors in this country. Let a man do what he will to abstract from his imagination all idea of the whimsical, something of it will come across him when he contemplates the figure of a fellow-creature in the day-time (in however distressing a situation) in a nightcap. Whether it be that this nocturnal addition has something discordant with daylight, or that it is the dress which we are seen in at those times when we are 'seen,' as the Angel in Milton expresses it, 'least wise,'—this, I am afraid, will always be the case; unless, indeed, as in my instance, some strong personal feeling overpower the ludicrous altogether. To me, when I reflect upon the train of misfortunes which have pursued men through life, owing to that accursed drapery, the cap presents as purely frightful an object as the sleeveless yellow coat and devil-painted mitre of the San Benitos.—An ancestor of mine, who suffered for his loyalty in the time of the civil wars, was so sensible of the truth of what I am here advancing, that on the morning of execution, no entreaties could prevail upon him to submit to the odious dishabille, as he called it, but he insisted upon wearing and actually suffered in, the identical, flowing periwig which he is painted in, in the gallery belonging to my uncle's seat in ——shire.

Suffer me, Mr. Editor, before I quit the subject, to say a word or two respecting the minister of justice in this country; in plain words, I mean the hangman. It has always appeared to me that, in the mode of inflicting capital punishments with us, there is too much of the ministry of the human hand. The

* Hieronimo in the Spanish Tragedy.

guillotine, as performing its functions more of itself and sparing human agency, though a cruel and disgusting exhibition, in my mind has many ways the advantage over *our way*. In beheading, indeed, as it was formerly practised in England, and in whipping to death, as is sometimes practised now, the hand of man is no doubt sufficiently busy; but there is something less repugnant in these downright blows than in the officious barber-like ministerings of *the other*. To have a fellow with his hangman's hands fumbling about your collar, adjusting the thing as your valet would regulate your cravat, valuing himself on his menial dexterity—

I never shall forget meeting my rascal,—I mean the fellow who officiated for me,—in London last winter. I think I see him now,—in a waistcoat that had been mine,—smirking along as if he knew me——

In some parts of Germany, that fellow's office is by law declared infamous, and his posterity incapable of being ennobled. They have hereditary hangmen, or had at least, in the same manner as they had hereditary other great officers of state; and the hangmen's families of two adjoining parishes intermarried with each other, to keep the breed entire. I wish something of the same kind were established in England.

But it is time to quit a subject which teems with disagreeable images——

Permit me to subscribe myself, Mr. Editor, your unfortunate friend,　　　　　　　　　　　　　　　PENSILIS.

*Letter to an Old Gentleman whose education has been neglected**

TO THE EDITOR OF THE LONDON MAGAZINE —

DEAR SIR—I send you a bantering 'Epistle to an Old Gentleman whose Education is supposed to have been neglected.' Of course, it was *suggested* by some letters of your admirable Opium-Eater, the discontinuance of which has caused so much regret to myself in common with most of your readers. You will do me injustice by supposing that, in the remotest degree, it was my intention to ridicule those papers.

* From the *London Magazine*, 1825.

The fact is, the most serious things may give rise to an innocent burlesque; and, the more serious they are, the fitter they become for that purpose. It is not to be supposed that Charles Cotton did not entertain a very high regard for Virgil, notwithstanding he travestied that poet. Yourself can testify the deep respect I have always held for the profound learning and penetrating genius of our friend. Nothing upon earth would give me greater pleasure than to find that he has not lost sight of his entertaining and instructive purpose.—I am, dear sir, yours and *his* sincerely,   ELIA.

MY DEAR SIR—The question which you have done me the honour to propose to me, through the medium of our common friend, Mr. Grierson, I shall endeavour to answer with as much exactness as a limited observation and experience can warrant.

You ask,—or rather Mr. Grierson, in his own interesting language, asks for you,—'Whether a person at the age of sixty-three, with no more proficiency than a tolerable knowledge of most of the characters of the English alphabet at first sight amounts to, by dint of persevering application and good masters,—a docile and ingenuous disposition on the part of the pupil always presupposed,—may hope to arrive, within a presumable number of years, at that degree of attainments which shall entitle the possessor to the character, which you are on so many accounts justly desirous of acquiring, of a *learned man*.'

This is fairly and candidly stated,—only I could wish that on one point you had been a little more explicit. In the meantime, I will take it for granted, that by a 'knowledge of the alphabetic characters' you confine your meaning to the single powers only, as you are silent on the subject of the diphthongs and harder combinations.

Why, truly, sir, when I consider the vast circle of sciences,—it is not here worth while to trouble you with the distinction between learning and science,—which a man must be understood to have made the tour of in these days, before the world will be willing to concede to him the title which you aspire to,—I am almost disposed to reply to your inquiry by a direct answer in the negative.

However, where all cannot be compassed, a great deal that is truly valuable may be accomplished. I am unwilling to throw out any remarks that should have a tendency to damp a hopeful genius; but I must not, in fairness, conceal from you that you have much to do. The consciousness of difficulty is sometimes a spur to exertion. Rome—or rather, my dear sir, to borrow an illustration from a place as yet more familiar to you, Rumford—Rumford was not built in a day.

Your mind as yet, give me leave to tell you, is in the state of a sheet of white paper. We must not blot or blur it over too hastily. Or, to use an opposite simile, it is like a piece of parchment all bescrawled and bescribbled over with characters of no sense or import, which we must carefully erase and remove before we can make way for the authentic characters or impresses which are to be substituted in their stead by the corrective hand of science.

Your mind, my dear sir, again, resembles that same parchment, which we will suppose a little hardened by time and disuse. We may apply the characters; but are we sure that the ink will sink?

You are in the condition of a traveller that has all his journey to begin. And, again, you are worse off than the traveller which I have supposed; for you have already lost your way.

You have much to learn, which you have never been taught; and more, I fear, to unlearn, which you have been taught erroneously. You have hitherto, I daresay, imagined that the sun moves round the earth. When you shall have mastered the true solar system, you will have quite a different theory upon that point, I assure you. I mention but this instance. Your own experience, as knowledge advances, will furnish you with many parallels.

I can scarcely approve of the intention, which Mr. Grierson informs me you had contemplated, of entering yourself at a common seminary, and working your way up from the lower to the higher forms with the children. I see more to admire in the modesty than in the expediency of such a resolution. I own I cannot reconcile myself to the spectacle of a gentleman at your time of life, seated, as must be your case at first, below a tyro of four or five; for at that early age the rudiments of education usually commence in this country. I doubt whether more might not be lost in the point of fitness than would be gained in the advantages which you propose to yourself by this scheme.

You say you stand in need of emulation; that this incitement is nowhere to be had but at a public school; that you should be more sensible of your progress by comparing it with the daily progress of those around you. But have you considered the nature of emulation, and how it is sustained at those tender years which you would have to come in competition with? I am afraid you are dreaming of academic prizes and distinctions. Alas! in the university for which you are preparing, the highest medal would be a silver penny; and you must graduate in nuts and oranges.

I know that Peter, the great Czar—or Emperor—of Muscovy, submitted himself to the discipline of a dockyard at Deptford, that he might learn and convey to his countrymen the noble art of shipbuilding. You are old enough to remember him, or at least the talk about him. I call to mind also other great princes, who, to instruct themselves in the theory and practice of war, and set an example of subordination to their subjects, have condescended to enroll themselves as private soldiers; and, passing through the successive ranks of corporal, quartermaster, and the rest, have served their way up to the station at which most princes are willing enough to set out,—of general and commander-in-chief over their own forces. But—besides that there is oftentimes great sham and pretence in their show of mock humility—the competition which they stooped to was with their coevals, however inferior to them in birth. Between ages so very disparate as those which you contemplate, no salutary emulation can, I fear, subsist.

Again: in the other alternative, could you submit to the ordinary reproofs and discipline of a day-school? Could you bear to be corrected for your faults? Or how would it look to see you put to stand, as must be the case sometimes, in a corner?

I am afraid the idea of a public school in your circumstances must be given up.

But is it impossible, my dear sir, to find some person of your own age,—if of the other sex, the more agreeable, perhaps,—whose information, like your own, has rather lagged behind his years, who should be willing to set out from the same point with yourself? to undergo the same tasks?—thus at once inciting and sweetening each other's labours in a sort of friendly rivalry. Such a one, I think, it would not be difficult to find in some of the western parts of this island,—about Dartmoor, for instance.

Or what if, from your own estate,—that estate, which, unexpectedly acquired so late in life, has inspired into you this generous thirst after knowledge,—you were to select some elderly peasant, that might best be spared from the land, to come and begin his education with you, that you might till, as it were, your minds together,—one whose heavier progress might invite, without a fear of discouraging, your emulation? We might then see—starting from an equal post—the difference of the clownish and the gentle blood.

A private education, then, or such a one as I have been describing, being determined on, we must in the next place look out for a preceptor; for it will be some time before either of you, left to yourselves, will be able to assist the other to any great purpose in his studies.

And now, my dear sir, if, in describing such a tutor as I have imagined for you, I use a style a little above the familiar one in which I have hitherto chosen to address you, the nature of the subject must be my apology. *Difficile est de scientiis inscienter loqui;* which is as much as to say, that, 'in treating of scientific matters, it is difficult to avoid the use of scientific terms.' But I shall endeavour to be as plain as possible. I am not going to present you with the *ideal* of a pedagogue as it may exist in my fancy, or has possibly been realised in the persons of Buchanan and Busby. Something less than perfection will serve our turn. The scheme which I propose in this first or introductory letter has reference to the first four or five years of your education only; and, in enumerating the qualifications of him that should undertake the direction of your studies, I shall rather point out the *minimum,* or *least,* that I shall require of him, than trouble you in the search of attainments neither common nor necessary to our immediate purpose.

He should be a man of deep and extensive knowledge. So much at least is indispensable. Something older than yourself, I could wish him, because years add reverence.

To his age and great learning, he should be blessed with a temper and a patience willing to accommodate itself to the imperfections of the slowest and meanest capacities. Such a one, in former days, Mr. Hartlib appears to have been; and such, in our days, I take Mr. Grierson to be: but our friend, you know, unhappily has other engagements. I do not demand a consummate grammarian; but he must be a thorough master of vernacular orthography, with an insight into the accentualities and punctualities of modern Saxon or English. He must be competently instructed (or how shall he instruct you?) in the tetralogy, or four first rules, upon which not only arithmetic, but geometry, and the pure mathematics themselves, are grounded. I do not require that he should have measured the globe with Cook or Ortelius; but it is desirable that he should have a general knowledge (I do not mean a very nice or pedantic one) of the great division of the earth into four parts, so as to teach you readily to name the quarters. He must have a genius capable in some degree of soaring to the upper element, to deduce from thence the not much dissimilar computation of the cardinal points, or hinges, upon which those invisible phenomena, which naturalists agree to term *winds*, do perpetually shift and turn. He must instruct you, in imitation of the old Orphic fragments (the mention of which has possibly escaped you), in numeric and harmonious responses, to deliver the number of solar revolutions within which each of the twelve periods of the *Annus Vulgaris*, or common year, is divided, and which doth usually complete and terminate itself. The intercalaries, and other subtle problems, he will do well to omit, till riper years, and course of study, shall have rendered you more capable thereof. He must be capable of embracing all history, so as, from the countless myriads of individual men who have peopled this globe of earth,—*for it is a globe,*—by comparison of their respective births, lives, deaths, fortunes, conduct, prowess, etc., to pronounce, and teach you to pronounce, dogmatically and catechetically, who was the richest, who was the strongest, who was the wisest, who was the meekest, man that ever lived; to the facilitation of which solution, you will readily conceive, a smattering of biography would in no inconsiderable degree conduce. Leaving the dialects of men (in one of which I shall take leave to suppose you by this time at least superficially instituted), you will learn to ascend with him to the contemplation of that unarticulated language which was before the written tongue; and, with the aid of the elder Phrygian or Æsopic key, to interpret the sounds by which the animal tribes communicate their minds, evolving moral instruction with delight from the dialogue of cocks, dogs, and foxes. Or, marrying theology with verse, from whose mixture a beautiful and healthy offspring may be expected, in your own native accents (but purified), you will keep time together to the profound harpings of the more modern or Wattsian hymnics.

Thus far I have ventured to conduct you to a 'hillside, whence you may discern the right path of a virtuous and noble education; laborious indeed at the first ascent, but else so smooth, so green, so full of goodly prospects and melodious sounds on every side, that the harp of Orpheus was not more charming.'*

With my best respects to Mr. Grierson, when you see him, I remain, dear sir, your obedient servant, ELIA.

---

* Milton's Tractate on Education, addressed to Mr. Hartlib.

LETTERS

To Samuel Taylor Coleridge
May 27, 1796.

DEAR COLERIDGE—Make yourself perfectly easy about May.
I paid his bill when I sent your clothes. I was flush of money,
and am so still to all the purposes of a single life; so give
yourself no further concern about it. The money would be
superfluous to me if I had it.

When Southey becomes as modest as his predecessor,
Milton, and publishes his Epics in duodecimo, I will read
'em; a guinea a book is somewhat exorbitant, nor have I the
opportunity of borrowing the work. The extracts from it in
the *Monthly Review*, and the short passages in your *Watchman*,
seem to me much superior to any thing in his partnership
account with Lovell. Your poems I shall procure forthwith.
There were noble lines in what you inserted in one of your
Numbers from *Religious Musings;* but I thought them elaborate. I am somewhat glad you have given up that paper: it
must have been dry, unprofitable, and of 'dissonant mood'
to your disposition. I wish you success in all your under-
takings, and am glad to hear you are employed about the
Evidences of Religion. There is need of multiplying such books
a hundredfold in this philosophical age, to *prevent* converts to
atheism, for they seem too tough disputants to meddle with
afterwards.

Le Grice is gone to make puns in Cornwall. He has got a
tutorship to a young boy living with his mother, a widow
lady. He will, of course, initiate him quickly in 'whatsoever
things are honest, lovely, and of good report.' He has cut
Miss Hunt completely: the poor girl is very ill on the
occasion; but he laughs at it, and justifies himself by saying,
'she does not see me laugh.' Coleridge, I know not what
suffering scenes you have gone through at Bristol. My life has
been somewhat diversified of late. The six weeks that finished
last year and began this, your very humble servant spent
very agreeably in a madhouse, at Hoxton. I am got somewhat rational now, and don't bite any one. But mad I was;
and many a vagary my imagination played with me, enough

to make a volume, if all were told. My Sonnets I have extended to the number of nine since I saw you, and will some day communicate to you. I am beginning a poem in blank verse, which, if I finish, I publish. White is on the eve of publishing (he took the hint from *Vortigern*) 'Original letters of Falstaff, Shallow,' etc.; a copy you shall have when it comes out. They are without exception the best imitations I ever saw. Coleridge, it may convince you of my regards for you when I tell you my head ran on you in my madness, as much almost as on another person, who I am inclined to think was the more immediate cause of my temporary frenzy.

The Sonnet I send you has small merit as poetry; but you will be curious to read it when I tell you it was written in my prison-house in one of my lucid intervals.

TO MY SISTER

If from my lips some angry accents fell,
    Peevish complaint, or harsh reproof unkind,
    'Twas but the error of a sickly mind
And troubled thoughts, clouding the purer well
    And waters clear of Reason; and for me,
    Let this my verse the poor atonement be—
    My verse, which thou to praise wert e'er inclined
Too highly, and with a partial eye to see
No blemish. Thou to me didst ever show
    Kindest affection; and would'st oft-times lend
    An ear to the desponding love-sick lay,
Weeping my sorrows with me, who repay
    But ill the mighty debt of love I owe,
    Mary, to thee, my sister and my friend.

With these lines, and with that sister's kindest remembrances to C——, I conclude.

Your sincerely,   LAMB.

Your *Conciones ad Populum* are the most eloquent politics that ever came in my way.

Write when convenient—not as a task, for there is nothing in this letter to answer.

We cannot send our remembrances to Mrs. C., not having seen her, but believe me our best good wishes attend you both.

My civic and poetic compliments to Southey if at Bristol. Why, he is a very Leviathan of Bards!—the small minnow, I!

June 10, 1796.

With *Joan of Arc* I have been delighted, amazed. I had not presumed to expect any thing of such excellence from Southey. Why, the poem is alone sufficient to redeem the character of the age we live in from the imputation of degenerating in Poetry, were there no such beings extant as Burns, and Bowles, Cowper, and ——: fill up the blank how you please; I say nothing. The subject is well chosen. It opens well. To become more particular, I will notice in their order a few passages that chiefly struck me on perusal. Page 26, 'Fierce and terrible Benevolence!' is a phrase full of grandeur and originality. The whole context made me feel *possessed*, even like Joan herself. Page 28, 'It is most horrible with the keen sword to gore the finely-fibred human frame,' and what follows, pleased me mightily. In the 2nd Book, the first forty lines in particular are majestic and high-sounding. Indeed the whole vision of the Palace of Ambition and what follows are supremely excellent. Your simile of the Laplander,

> . . . . . 'by Niemi lake
> Or Balda Zhiok, or the mossy stone
> Of Solfar-kapper,'

will bear comparison with any in Milton for fulness of circumstance and lofty pacedness of versification. Southey's similes, though many of 'em are capital, are all inferior. In one of his books, the simile of the oak in the storm occurs, I think, four times. To return: the light in which you view the heathen deities is accurate and beautiful. Southey's personifications in this book are so many fine and faultless pictures. I was much pleased with your manner of accounting for the reason why monarchs take delight in war. At the 447th line you have placed Prophets and Enthusiasts cheek by jowl, on too intimate a footing for the dignity of the former. Necessarian-like-speaking, it is correct. Page 98, 'Dead is the Douglas! cold thy warrior frame, illustrious Buchan,' etc., are of kindred excellence with Gray's 'Cold is Cadwallo's tongue,' etc. How famously the Maid baffles the Doctors, Seraphic and Irrefragable, 'with all their trumpery!' Page 126, the procession, the appearances of the Maid, of the Bastard Son of Orleans and of Tremouille, are full of fire and fancy, and exquisite melody of versification. The personifications from line 303 to 309, in the heat of the battle, had better been omitted; they are not very striking, and only encumber. The converse which Joan and Conrade hold on the banks of the Loire is altogether beautiful. Page 313, the conjecture that in dreams 'all things are that seem,' is one of those conceits which the Poet delights to admit into his creed; a creed, by the way, more marvellous and mystic than ever Athanasius dreamed of. Page 315, I need only *mention* those lines ending with 'She saw a serpent gnawing at her heart!' They are good imitative lines, 'he toiled and toiled, of toil to reap no end, but endless toil and never-ending woe.' Page 347, Cruelty is such as Hogarth might have painted her. Page 361, all the passage about Love (where he seems to confound conjugal love with creating and preserving love) is very confused, and sickens me with a load of useless personifications; else that ninth Book is the finest in the volume—an exquisite combination of the ludicrous and the terrible: I have never read either, even in translation, but such as I conceive to be the manner of Dante or Ariosto. The tenth Book is the most languid. On the whole, considering the celerity wherewith the poem was finished, I was astonished at the infrequency of weak lines. I had expected to find it verbose. Joan, I think, does too little in battle; Dunois perhaps the same; Conrade too much. The anecdotes interspersed among the battles refresh the mind very agreeably, and I am delighted with the very many passages of simple pathos abounding throughout the poem; passages which the author of 'Crazy Kate' might have written. Has not Master Southey spoke very slightly, in his Preface, and disparagingly of Cowper's Homer? What makes him reluctant to give Cowper his fame? And does not Southey use too often the expletives 'did,' and 'does?' They have a good effect at times, but are too inconsiderable, or rather become blemishes, when they mark a style. On the whole, I expect Southey one day to rival Milton: I already deem him equal to Cowper, and superior to all living poets besides. What says Coleridge? The 'Monody on Henderson' is *immensely good:* the rest of that little volume is *readable, and above mediocrity.* I proceed to a more pleasant task; pleasant because the poems are yours; pleasant because you impose the task on me; and pleasant, let me add, because it will confer a whimsical importance on me to sit in judgment upon your rhymes. First, though, let me thank you again and again, in my own and my sister's name, for your invitations. Nothing could give us more pleasure than to come, but (were there no other reasons) while my brother's leg is so bad it is out of the question. Poor fellow! he is very feverish and light-headed; but Cruikshanks has pronounced the symptoms favourable, and gives us every hope that there will be no need of amputation: God send, not! We are necessarily confined with him all the afternoon and evening till very late, so that I am stealing a few minutes to write to you.

Thank you for your frequent letters: you are the only correspondent, and I might add, the only friend I have in the world. I go nowhere, and have no acquaintance. Slow of speech, and reserved of manners, no one seeks or cares for my society; and I am left alone. Allen calls very occasionally, as though it were a duty rather, and seldom stays ten minutes. Then judge how thankful I am for your letters! Do not, however, burthen yourself with the correspondence. I trouble you again so soon, only in obedience to your injunctions. Complaints apart, proceed we to our task. I am called away to tea; thence must wait upon my brother; so must delay till tomorrow. Farewell!—*Wednesday*.

Thursday.—I will first notice what is new to me. Thirteenth page: 'The thrilling tones that concentrate the soul' is a nervous line; and the first six lines of page 14 are very pretty; the twenty-first effusion is a perfect thing. That in the manner of Spenser is very sweet, particularly at the close: the thirty-fifth effusion is most exquisite; that line in particular, 'And, tranquil, muse upon tranquillity.' It is the very reflex pleasure that distinguishes the tranquillity of a thinking being from that of a shepherd, a modern one I would be understood to mean, a Damœtas, one that keeps other people's sheep. Certainly, Coleridge, your letter from Shurton Bars has less merit than most things in your volume; personally, it may chime in best with your own feelings, and therefore you love it best. It has, however, great merit. In your fourth epistle, *that* is an exquisite paragraph, and fancy-full, of 'A stream there is which rolls in lazy flow,' etc., etc. 'Murmurs sweet undersong 'mid jasmine bowers' is a sweet line; and so are the three next. The concluding simile is far-fetched—'tempest-honoured' is a quaintish phrase. Of the Monody on Henderson I will here only notice these lines, as superlatively excellent. That energetic one, 'Shall I not praise thee, scholar, Christian, friend,' like to that beautiful climax of Shakspeare's 'King, Hamlet, Royal Dane, Father;' 'yet memory turns from little men to thee,' 'And sported careless round their fellow child.' The whole, I repeat it, is immensely good.

Yours is a poetical family. I was much surprised and pleased to see the signature of Sara to that elegant composition, the fifth epistle. I dare not *criticise* the *Religious Musings*: I like not to select any part, where all is excellent. I can only admire, and thank you for it in the name of a Christian, as well as a lover of good poetry: only let me ask, Is not that thought and those words in Young, 'stands in the sun,'—or is it only such as Young, in one of his *better moments*, might have writ?—

> 'Believe thou, O my soul,
> Life is a vision, shadowy of Truth;
> And vice, and anguish, and the wormy grave,
> Shapes of a dream!'

I thank you for these lines in the name of a necessarian, and for what follows in the next paragraph, in the name of a child fancy. After all, you cannot, nor ever will, write any thing with which I shall be so delighted as what I have heard yourself repeat. You came to town, and I saw you at a time when your heart was yet bleeding with recent wounds. Like yourself, I was sore galled with disappointed hope. You had

> . . . 'many an holy lay
> That, mourning, soothed the mourner on his way.'

I had ears of sympathy to drink them in, and they yet vibrate pleasant on the sense. When I read in your little volume, your nineteenth effusion, or the twenty-eighth or twenty-ninth, or what you call the 'Sigh,' I think I hear *you* again. I image to myself the little smoky room at the *Salutation and Cat*, where we have sat together through the winter nights, beguiling the cares of life with Poesy. When you left London I felt a dismal void in my heart. I found myself cut off, at one and the same time, from two most dear to me. 'How blest with ye the path could I have trod of quiet life!' In your conversation you had blended so many pleasant fancies that they cheated me of my grief. But in your absence the tide of melancholy rushed in again, and did its worst mischief by

overwhelming my reason. I have recovered, but feel a stupor
that makes me indifferent to the hopes and fears of this life.
I sometimes wish to introduce a religious turn of mind; but
habits are strong things, and my religious fervours are confined, alas! to some fleeting moments of occasional solitary
devotion. A correspondence, opening with you, has roused
me a little from my lethargy, and made me conscious of
existence. Indulge me in it: I will not be very troublesome.
At some future time I will amuse you with an account, as
full as my memory will permit, of the strange turn my frenzy
took. I look back upon it at times with a gloomy kind of
envy; for, while it lasted, I had many, many hours of pure
happiness. Dream not, Coleridge, of having tasted all the
grandeur and wildness of fancy till you have gone mad! All
now seems to me vapid, comparatively so. Excuse this selfish
digression. Your 'Monody' is so superlatively excellent, that
I can only wish it perfect, which I can't help feeling it is not
quite. Indulge me in a few conjectures. What I am going to
propose would make it more compressed, and, I think, more
energetic, though I am sensible at the expense of many
beautiful lines. Let it begin 'Is this the land of song-ennobled
line?' and proceed to 'Otway's famish'd form;' then, 'Thee,
Chatterton,' to 'blaze of Seraphim;' then, 'clad in Nature's
rich array,' to 'orient day;' then, 'but soon the scathing
lightning,' to 'blighted land;' then, 'sublime of thought,' to
'his bosom glows;' then

> 'But soon upon his poor unshelter'd head
> Did Penury her sickly mildew shed :
> Ah! where are fled the charms of vernal Grace,
> And Joy's wild gleams that lighten'd o'er his face?'

Then 'youth of tumultuous soul' to 'sigh,' as before. The rest
may all stand down to 'gaze upon the waves below.' What
follows now may come next as detached verses, suggested by
the Monody, rather than a part of it. They are indeed, in
themselves, very sweet:

> 'And we, at sober eve, would round thee throng
> Hanging, enraptured, on thy stately song,'

in particular, perhaps. If I am obscure, you may understand
me by counting lines. I have proposed omitting twenty-four
lines. I feel that thus compressed it would gain energy, but

think it most likely you will not agree with me; for who shall go to bring opinions to the bed of Procrustes, and introduce among the sons of men a monotony of identical feelings? I only propose with diffidence. Reject, if you please, with as little remorse as you would the colour of a coat or the pattern of a buckle, where our fancies differed. The lines 'Friend to the Friendless,' etc., which you may think rudely disbranched from the Chatterton, will patch in with the Man of Ross, where they were at once at home, with two more which I recollect,

'And o'er the dowried virgin's snowy cheek
Bade bridal Love suffuse his blushes meek,'

very beautiful.

The 'Pixies' is a perfect thing; and so are the 'Lines on the Spring,' page 28. The 'Epitaph on an Infant,' like a Jack-o'-lantern, has danced about (or like Dr. Forster's scholars) out of the *Morning Chronicle* into the *Watchman*, and thence back into your Collection. It is very pretty, and you seem to think so; but, may be, o'erlooked its chief merit, that of filling up a whole page. I had once deemed Sonnets of unrivalled use that way; but your Epitaphs, I find, are the more diffuse. 'Edmund' still holds its place among your best verses. 'Ah! fair delights' to 'roses round,' in your Poem called 'Absence,' recall (none more forcibly) to my mind the tones in which *you recite it*. I will not notice, in this tedious (to you) manner, verses which have been so long delightful to me, and which you already know my opinion of. Of this kind are Bowles, Priestley, and that most exquisite and most Bowles-like of all, the nineteenth effusion. It would have better ended with 'agony of care:' the last two lines are obvious and unnecessary, and you need not now make fourteen lines of it: now it is rechristened from a Sonnet to an Effusion. Schiller might have written the twentieth Effusion: 'tis worthy of him in any sense. I was glad to meet with those lines you sent me, when my sister was so ill: I had lost the copy, and I felt not a little proud at seeing my name in your verse. The 'Complaint of Ninathoma' (first stanza in particular) is the best, or only good imitation, of Ossian I ever saw, your 'Restless Gale' excepted. 'To an Infant' is most sweet. Is not 'foodful,' though, very harsh? Would not 'dulcet' fruit be less harsh, or some other friendly bi-syllable? In 'Edmund,' 'Frenzy, fierce-eyed child,' is not so well as 'frantic,' though that is an epithet adding nothing to the meaning. Slander *couching* was better than 'squatting.' In the 'Man of Ross' it *was* a better line thus:

'If 'neath this roof thy wine-cheer'd moments pass,'

than as it stands now. Time nor nothing can reconcile me to the concluding five lines of 'Kosciusko:' call it anything you will but sublime. In my twelfth effusion I had rather have seen what I wrote myself, though they bear no comparison with your exquisite lines—

'On rose-leaf'd beds, amid your faery bowers,' etc.

I love my Sonnets because they are reflected images of my own feelings at different times. To instance, in the thirteenth—

'How reason reel'd,' etc.,

are good lines, but must spoil the whole with me, who know it is only a fiction of yours, and that the 'rude dashings' did in fact not 'rock me to repose.' I grant the same objection applies not to the former Sonnet; but still I love my own feelings: they are dear to memory, though they now and then wake a sigh or a tear. 'Thinking on divers things fore-done,'' I charge you, Coleridge, spare my ewe lambs; and though a gentleman may borrow six lines in an epic poem (I should have no objection to borrow five hundred, and without acknowledging), still, in a sonnet, a personal poem, I do not 'ask my friend the aiding verse.' I would not wrong your feelings by proposing any improvements (did I think myself capable of suggesting 'em) in such personal poems as 'Thou bleedest, my poor heart!'—'od so,—I am caught—I have already done it; but that simile I propose abridging, would not change the feeling or introduce any alien ones. Do you understand me? In the twenty-eighth, however, and in the 'Sigh,' and that composed at Clevedon, things that come from the heart direct, not by the medium of the fancy, I would not suggest an alteration. When my blank verse is finished, or any long fancy-poems, *propino tibi alterandum, cut-up-andum, abridgandum*, just what you will with it; but spare my ewe lambs! That to 'Mrs. Siddons,' now, you were wel-come to improve, if it had been worth it; but I say unto you again, Coleridge, spare my ewe lambs! I must confess were

they mine, I should omit, *in editione secundâ*, Effusions two and
three, because satiric, and below the dignity of the poet of
Religious Musings, fifth, seventh, half of the eighth, that
'Written in early youth,' as far as 'thousand eyes,'—though
I part not unreluctanly with that lively line—

'Chaste joyance dancing in her bright blue eyes,'

and one or two more just thereabouts. But I would substitute
for it that sweet poem called 'Recollection,' in the fifth
Number of the *Watchman;* better, I think, than the remainder
of this poem, though not differing materially; as the poem
now stands it looks altogether confused. And do not omit
those lines upon the 'Early Blossom,' in your sixth Number
of the *Watchman:* and I would omit the tenth Effusion or,
what would do better, alter and improve the last four lines.
In fact, I suppose, if they were mine, I should *not* omit 'em.
But your verse is, for the most part, so exquisite, that I like
not to see aught of meaner matter mixed with it. Forgive
my petulance, and often, I fear, ill-founded criticisms; and
forgive me that I have, by this time, made your eyes and
head ache with my long letter; but I cannot forego hastily
the pleasure and pride of thus conversing with you. You did
not tell me whether I was to include the *Conciones ad Populum*
in my remarks on your poems. They are not unfrequently
sublime: and I think you could not do better than to
turn 'em into verse, if you have nothing else to do. Allen,
I am sorry to say, is a *confirmed* Atheist. Stoddart, a cold-
hearted, well-bred, conceited disciple of Godwin, does him
no good. His wife has several daughters (one of 'em as old
as himself). Surely there is something unnatural in such a
marriage.

How I sympathise with you on the dull duty of a reviewer,
and heartily damn with you Ned Evans and the Prosodist.
I shall, however, wait impatiently for the articles in the
Critical Review, next month, because they are *yours*. Young
Evans (W. Evans, a branch of a family you were once so
intimate with) is come into our office, and sends his love to
you! Coleridge, I devoutly wish that Fortune, who has made
sport with you so long, may play one freak more,—throw
you into London, or some spot near it, and there snug-ify
you for life. 'Tis a selfish, but natural wish for me, cast as
I am 'on life's wide plain, friendless.' Are you acquainted

with Bowles? I see, by his last Elegy (written at Bath), you are near neighbours.—*Thursday.*

'And I can think I can see the groves again—was it the voice of thee—turns not the voice of thee, my buried friend —who dries with her dark locks the tender tear,' are touches as true to Nature as any in his other Elegy, written at the Hot Wells, about poor Russell, etc. You are doubtless acquainted with it.

I do not know that I entirely agree with you in your stricture upon my Sonnet 'To Innocence.' To men whose hearts are not quite deadened by their commerce with the world, innocence (no longer familiar) becomes an awful idea. So I felt when I wrote it. Your other censures (qualified and sweetened, though, with praises somewhat extravagant) I perfectly coincide with; yet I choose to retain the word 'lunar.' Indulge a 'lunatic' in his loyalty to his mistress the Moon. I have just been reading a most pathetic copy of verses on Sophia Pringle, who was hanged and burnt for coining. One of the strokes of pathos (which are very many, all somewhat obscure), is 'She lifted up her guilty forger to heaven.' A note explains, by 'forger,' her right hand, with which she forged or coined the base metal. For 'pathos' read *bathos.* You have put me out of conceit with my blank verse by your *Religious Musings.* I think it will come to nothing. I do not like 'em enough to send 'em. I have just been reading a book which I may be too partial to, as it was the delight of my childhood; but I will recommend it to you: it is Izaak Walton's *Compleat Angler.* All the scientific part you may omit in reading. The dialogue is very simple, full of pastoral beauties, and will charm you. Many pretty old verses are interspersed. This letter, which would be a week's work reading only, I do not wish you to answer it in less than a month. I shall be richly content with a letter from you some day early in July; though, if you get anyhow *settled* before then, pray let me know it immediately; 'twould give me so much satisfaction. Concerning the Unitarian chapel, the salary is the only scruple that the most rigid moralist would admit as valid. Concerning the tutorage, is not the salary low, and absence from your family unavoidable? London is the only fostering soil for genius. Nothing more occurs just now; so I will leave you, in mercy, one small white spot empty below, to repose your eyes upon, fatigued as they must be with the wilderness of words they have by this time painfully travelled through. God love you, Coleridge, and prosper you through life; though mine will be loss if your lot is to be cast at Bristol, or at Nottingham, or anywhere but London. Our loves to Mrs. C——. C. L.

Friday, 10th June 1796.

July 5, 1796.

LET US PROSE

What can I do till you send word what priced and placed house you should like? Islington, possibly, you would not like; to me 'tis classical ground. Knightsbridge is a desirable situation for the air of the parks. St. George's Fields is convenient for its contiguity to the Bench. Choose! But are you really coming to town? The hope of it has entirely disarmed my petty disappointment of its nettles; yet I rejoice so much on my own account, that I fear I do not feel enough pure satisfaction on yours. Why, surely, the joint editorship of the [*Morning*] *Chronicle* must be a very comfortable and secure living for a man. But should not you read French, or do you? and can you write sufficient with moderation, as 'tis called, when one suppresses the one half of what one feels or could say on a subject, to chime in the better with popular luke-warmness? White's 'Letters' are near publication. Could you review 'em, or get 'em reviewed? Are you not connected with the *Critical Review?* His frontispiece is a good conceit: Sir John learning to dance to please Madame Page, in dress of doublet, etc., from the upper half; and modern pantaloons, with shoes, etc., of the eighteenth century, from the lower half; and the whole work is full of goodly quips and rare fancies, 'all deftly masqued like hoar antiquity'—much superior to Dr. Kenrick's *Falstaff's Wedding*, which you may have seen. Allen sometimes laughs at superstition, and religion, and the like. A living fell vacant lately in the gift of the Hospital: White informed him that he stood a fair chance for it. He scrupled and scrupled about it, and at last, to use his own words, 'tampered' with Godwin to know whether the thing was honest or not. Godwin said nay to it, and Allen rejected the living! Could the blindest poor papist have bowed more servilely to his priest or casuist? Why sleep the *Watchman's* answers to that Godwin? I beg you will not delay to alter, if you mean to keep, those last lines I sent you. Do that, and read these for your pains:—

TO THE POET COWPER

Cowper, I thank my God that thou art heal'd!
Thine was the sorest malady of all;
And I am sad to think that it should light
Upon thy worthy head! But thou art heal'd,
And thou art yet, we trust, the destined man,
Born to reanimate the lyre, whose chords
Have slumber'd, and have idle lain so long;
To the immortal sounding of whose strings
Did Milton frame the stately-pacèd verse;
Among whose wires with light finger playing,
Our elder bard, Spenser, a gentle name,
The lady Muses' dearest darling child,
Elicited the deftest tunes yet heard
In hall or bower, taking the delicate ear
Of Sidney and his peerless Maiden Queen.

Thou, then, take up the mighty epic strain,
Cowper, of England's Bards, the wisest and the best.

1796.

I have read your climax of praises in those three Reviews. These mighty spouters out of panegyric waters have, two of 'em, scattered their spray even upon me, and the waters are cooling and refreshing. Prosaically, the *Monthly* reviewers have made indeed a large article of it, and done you justice. The *Critical* have, in their wisdom, selected not the very best specimens, and notice not, except as one name on the muster-roll, the *Religious Musings*. I suspect Master Dyer to have been the writer of that article, as the substance of it was the very remarks and the very language he used to me one day. I fear you will not accord entirely with my sentiments of Cowper, as *expressed* above (perhaps scarcely just), but the poor gentleman has just recovered from his lunacies, and that begets pity, and pity love, and love admiration; and then it goes hard with people, but they lie! Have you read the Ballad called 'Leonora,' in the second Number of the *Monthly Magazine?* If you have!!!! There is another fine song, from the same author (Burger), in the third Number, of scarce inferior merit; and (vastly below these) there are some happy specimens of English hexameters, in an imitation of Ossian, in the fifth Number. For your Dactyls—I am sorry you are so sore about 'em—a very Sir Fretful! In good troth, the Dactyls are good Dactyls, but their measure is naught. Be not yourself 'half anger, half agony,' if I pronounce your darling lines not to be the best you ever wrote—you have written much.

Have a care, good Master poet, of the Statute *de Contumeliâ*. What do you mean by calling Madame Mara 'harlot' and other naughty things? The goodness of the verse would not save you in a Court of Justice. But are you really coming to town? Coleridge, a gentleman called in London lately from Bristol, and inquired whether there were any of the family of a Mr. Chambers living: this Mr. Chambers, he said, had been the making of a friend's fortune, who wished to make some return for it. He went away without seeing her. Now, a Mrs. Reynolds, a very intimate friend of ours, whom you have seen at our house, is the only daughter, and all that survives, of Mr. Chambers; and a very little supply would be of service to her, for she married very unfortunately, and has parted with her husband. Pray find out this Mr. Pember (for that was the gentelman's friend's name); he is an attorney, and lives at Bristol. Find him out, and acquaint him with the circumstances of the case, and offer to be the medium of supply to Mrs. Reynolds, if he chooses to make her a present. She is in very distressed circumstances. Mr. Pember, attorney, Bristol. Mr. Chambers lived in the Temple; Mrs. Reynolds, his daughter, was my schoolmistress, and is in the room at this present writing. This last circumstance induced me to write so soon again. I have not further to add. Our loves to Sara. C. LAMB.

Thursday.

August 14, 1800.

My head is playing all the tunes in the world, ringing such peals! It has just finished the 'Merry Christ Church Bells,' and absolutely is beginning 'Turn again, Whittington,' Buz, buz, buz, bum, bum, bum, wheeze, wheeze, wheeze, fen, fen, fen, tinky, tinky, tinky, *cr'annch.* I shall certainly come to be condemned at last. I have been drinking too much for two days running. I find my moral sense in the last stage of a consumption, and my religion getting faint. This is disheartening; but I trust the devil will not overpower me. In the midst of this infernal larum, Conscience is barking and yelping as loud as any of them. I have sat down to read over again your satire upon me in the *Anthology*, and I think I do begin to spy out something like beauty and design in it. I perfectly accede to all your alterations, and only desire that you had cut deeper, when your hand was in.

In sober truth, I cannot see any great truth in the little dialogue called 'Blenheim.' It is rather novel and pretty, but the thought is very obvious and is but poor prattle, a thing of easy imitation. *Pauper vult videri et est.*

In the next edition of the *Anthology* (which Phœbus avert, and those nine other wandering maids also!) please to blot out 'gentle-hearted,' and substitute drunken dog, ragged head, seld-shaven, odd-eyed, stuttering, or any other epithet which truly and properly belongs to the gentleman in question. And for Charles read Tom, or Bob, or Richard for mere delicacy. Hang you, I was beginning to forgive you, and believe in earnest that the lugging in of my proper name was purely unintentional on your part, when looking back for further conviction, stares me in the face, 'Charles Lamb of the *India House.*' *Now* I am convinced it was all done in malice, heaped sack-upon-sack, congregated, studied malice. You dog! your 141st page shall not save you. I own I was just ready to acknowledge that there is a something not unlike good poetry in that page, if you had not run into the unintelligible abstraction—fit about the matter of the Deity's making spirits perceive his presence. God, nor created thing alive can receive any honour from such thin show-box attributes. By the by, where did you pick up that scandalous piece of private history about the angel and the Duchess of Devonshire? If it is a fiction of your own, why truly it was a very modest one *for you.* Now I do affirm, that 'Lewti' is a very beautiful poem. I *was* in earnest when I praised it. It describes a silly species of one not the wisest of passions. *Therefore* it cannot deeply affect a disenthralled mind. But such imagery, such novelty, such delicacy, and such versification never got into an *Anthology* before. I am only sorry that the cause of all the passionate complaint is not greater than the trifling circumstance of Lewti being out of temper one day. 'Gaulberto' certainly has considerable originality, but sadly wants finishing. It is, as it is, one of the very best in the book. Next to 'Lewti' I like the 'Raven,' which has a good deal of humour. I was pleased to see it again, for you once sent it me, and I have lost the letter which contained it. Now I am on the subject of Anthologies, I must say I am sorry the old pastoral way has fallen into disrepute. The gentry which now indite sonnets are certainly the legitimate descendants of the ancient shepherds. The same simpering face of description, the old family face, is visibly continued in the line. Some of their ancestors' labours are yet to be found in Allan Ramsay's and Jacob Tonson's Miscellanies. But miscellanies decaying, and the old pastoral way dying of mere want, their successors (driven from their paternal acres) now-a-days settle and lie upon Magazines and Anthologies. This race of men are uncommonly addicted to superstition. Some of them are idolators, and worship the moon. Others deify qualities, as Love, Friendship, Sensibility; or bare accidents, as Solitude. Grief and Melancholy have their respective altars and temples among them, as the heathens builded theirs to Mors, Febris, Pallor, etc. They all agree in ascribing a peculiar sanctity to the number 14. One of their own legislators affirmeth, that whatever exceeds that number 'encroacheth upon the province of the elegy'—*vice versa*, whatever 'cometh short of that number abutteth upon the premises of the epigram.' I have been able to discover but few *images* in their temples, which, like the caves of Delphos of old, are famous for giving *echoes*. They impute a religious importance to the letter O, whether because by its roundness it is thought to typify the moon, their principal goddess, or for its analogies to their own labours, all ending where they began, or for whatever other high and mystical reference, I have never been able to discover, but I observe they never begin their invocations to their gods without it, except indeed one insignificant sect among them, who use the Doric A, pronounced like Ah! broad, instead. These boast to have restored the old Dorian mood.

Now I am on the subject of poetry, I must announce to you, who doubtless in your remote part of the island have not heard tidings of so great a blessing, that George Dyer hath prepared two ponderous volumes full of poetry and criticism. They impend over the town, and are threatened to fall in the Winter. The first volume contains every sort of poetry, except personal satire, which George, in his truly original prospectus, renounceth for ever, whimsically foisting the intention in between the price of his book and the proposed number of subscribers. (If I can, I will get you a copy of his *handbill*.) He has tried his *vein* in every species besides—the Spenserian, Thomsonian, Masonic, and Akensidish more especially. The second volume is all criticism; wherein he demonstrates to the entire satisfaction of the literary world, in a way that must silence all reply for ever, that the Pastoral was introduced by Theocritus, and polished by Virgil and Pope; that Gray and Mason (who always hunt in couples in George's brain) have a good deal of poetical fire and true lyric genius; that Cowley was ruined by excess of wit (a warning to all moderns); that Charles Lloyd, Charles Lamb, and William Wordsworth, in later days, have struck the true chords of poesy. O George, George! with a head uniformly wrong, and a heart uniformly right, that I had power and might equal to my wishes: then I would call the gentry of thy native island, and they should come in troops, flocking at the sound of thy prospectus trumpet, and crowding who shall be first to stand in thy list of subscribers! I can only put twelve shillings into thy pocket (which, I will answer for them, will not stick there long), out of a pocket almost as bare as thine. Is it not a pity so much fine writing should be erased? But, to tell the truth, I began to scent that I was getting into that sort of style which Longinus and Dionysius Halicarnassus aptly call 'the affected.'   C. L.

To Thomas Manning

December 27, 1800.

AT length George Dyer's phrenitis has come to a crisis; he is raging and furiously mad. I waited upon the heathen, Thursday was a se'nnight. The first symptom which struck my eye, and gave me incontrovertible proof of the fatal truth, was a pair of nankeen pantaloons four times too big for him, which the said Heathen did pertinaciously affirm to be new.

They were absolutely ingrained with the accumulated dirt of ages; but he affirmed them to be clean. He was going to visit a lady that was nice about those things, and that's the reason he wore nankeen that day. And then he danced, and capered, and fidgeted, and pulled up his pantaloons, and hugged his intolerable flannel vestment closer about his poetic loins. Anon he gave it loose to the zephyrs which plentifully insinuate their tiny bodies through every crevice, door, window, or wainscot, expressly formed for the exclusion of such impertinents. Then he caught at a proof sheet, and catched up a laundress's bill instead—made a dart at Bloom-field's Poems, and threw them in agony aside. I could not bring him to one direct reply; he could not maintain his jumping mind in a right line for the tithe of a moment by Clifford's Inn clock. He must go to the printer's immediately: (the most unlucky accident!) he had struck off five hundred impressions of his Poems, which were ready for delivery to subscribers, and the Preface must all be expunged. There were eighty pages of Preface, and not till that morning had he discovered that in the very first page of said Preface he had set out with a principle of Criticism fundamentally wrong, which vitiated all his following reasoning. The Preface must be expunged, although it cost him £30, the lowest calculation, taking in paper and printing! In vain have his real friends remonstrated against this Midsummer madness. George is as obstinate as a Primitive Christian, and wards and parries off all our thrusts with one unanswerable fence:—'Sir, 'tis of great consequence that the *world* is not *misled!*'

As for the other Professor, he has actually begun to dive into Tavernier and Chardin's *Persian* Travels for a story, to form a new drama for the sweet tooth of this fastidious age. Hath not Bethlehem College a fair action for non-residence against such professors? Are poets so *few* in *this age*, that He must write poetry? *Is morals* a subject so exhausted, that he must quit that line? Is the metaphysic well (without a bottom) drained dry?

If I can guess at the wicked pride of the Professor's heart, I would take a shrewd wager that he disdains ever again to dip his pen in *Prose*. Adieu, ye splendid theories! Farewell, dreams of political justice! Lawsuits, where I was council for Archbishop Fenelon *versus* my own mother, in the famous fire cause!

Vanish from my mind, professors, one and all! I have metal more attractive on foot.

Man of many snipes,—I will sup with thee (Deo volente, et diabolo nolente), on Monday night, the 5th of January, in the new year, and crush a cup to the infant century.

A word or two of my progress: Embark at six o'clock in the morning. with a fresh gale, on a Cambridge one-decker; very cold till eight at night; land at St. Mary's lighthouse, muffins and coffee upon table (or any other curious production of Turkey, or both Indies), snipes exactly at nine, punch to commence at ten, with *argument;* difference of opinion is expected to take place about eleven; perfect unanimity, with some haziness and dimness, before twelve. *N.B.*—My single affection is not so singly wedded to snipes; but the curious and epicurean eye would also take a pleasure in beholding a delicate and well-chosen assortment of teals, ortolans, the unctuous and palate-soothing flesh of geese, wild and tame, nightingales' brains, the sensorium of a young sucking pig, or any other Christmas dish, which I leave to the judgment of you and the cook of Conville.

C. LAMB.

February 15, 1802.

Apropos, I think you wrong about my play. All the omissions are right. And the supplementary scene, in which Sandford narrates the manner in which his master is affected, is the best in the book. It stands where a hodge-podge of German puerilities used to stand. I insist upon it that you like that scene. Love me, love that scene. I will now transcribe the 'Londoner' (No. 1), and wind up all with affection and humble servant at the end.

To the Editor of 'The Reflector'

MR. REFLECTOR,—I was born under the shadow of St. Dunstan's steeple, just where the conflux of the eastern and western inhabitants of this twofold city meet and justle in friendly opposition at Temple Bar. The same day which gave me to the world, saw London happy in the celebration of her great annual feast. This I cannot help looking upon as a lively omen of the future great goodwill which I was destined to bear toward the city, resembling in kind that solicitude which every Chief Magistrate is supposed to feel for whatever concerns her interests and well-being. Indeed I consider myself in some sort a speculative Lord Mayor of London: for though circumstances unhappily preclude me from the hope of ever arriving at the dignity of a gold chain and Spital Sermon, yet thus much will I say of myself in truth, that Whittington with his Cat (just emblem of vigilance and a furred gown) never went beyond me in affection which I bear to the citizens.

I was born, as you have heard, in a crowd. This has begot in me an entire affection for that way of life, amounting to an almost insurmountable aversion from solitude and rural scenes. This aversion was never interrupted or suspended, except for a few years in the younger part of my life, during a period in which I had set my affections upon a charming young woman. Every man, while the passion is upon him, is for a time at least addicted to groves and meadows and purling streams. During this short period of my existence, I contracted just familiarity enough with rural objects to understand tolerably well ever after the *poets*, when they declaim in such passionate terms in favour of a country life.

For my own part, now the fit is past, I have no hesitation in declaring, that a mob of happy faces crowding up at the pit door of Drury Lane Theatre, just at the hour of six, gives me ten thousand sincerer pleasures, than I could ever receive from all the flocks of silly sheep that ever whitened the plains of Arcadia or Epsom Downs.

This passion for crowds is nowhere feasted so full as in London. The man must have a rare *recipe* for melancholy who can be dull in Fleet Street. I am naturally inclined to hypochondria, but in London it vanishes, like all other ills. Often, when I have felt a weariness or distaste at home, have I rushed out into her crowded Strand, and fed my humour, till tears have wetted my cheek for unutterable sympathies with the multitudinous moving picture, which she never fails to present at all hours, like the scenes of a shifting pantomime.

The very deformities of London, which give distaste to others, from habit do not displease me. The endless succession of shops where *Fancy miscalled Folly* is supplied with perpetual gauds and toys, excite in me no puritanical aversion. I gladly behold every appetite supplied with its proper food. The obliging customer, and the obliged tradesman—things which live by bowing, and things which exist but for homage—do not affect me with disgust; from habit I perceive nothing but urbanity, where other men, more refined, discover meanness: I love the very smoke of London, because it has been the medium most familiar to my vision. I see grand principles of honour at work in the dirty ring which encompasses two combatants with fists, and principles of no less eternal justice in the detection of a pick-pocket. The salutary astonishment with which an execution is surveyed, convinces me more forcibly than a hundred volumes of abstract polity, that the universal instinct of man in all ages has leaned to order and good government.

Thus an art of extracting morality from the commonest incidents of a town life is attained by the same well-natured alchymy with which the Foresters of Arden, in a beautiful country,

> Found tongues in trees, books in the running brooks,
> Sermons in stones, and good in everything.

Where has spleen her food but in London! Humor, Interest, Curiosity, suck at her measureless breasts without a possibility of being satiated. Nursed amid her noise, her crowds, her beloved smoke, what have I been doing all my life, if I have not lent out my heart with usury to such scenes!—I am, Sir, your faithful servant,   A. LONDONER.

'What is all this about?' said Mrs. Shandy. 'A story of a cock and a bull,' said Yorick: and so it is; but Manning will take good-naturedly what *God will send him* across the water: only I hope he won't *shut* his *eyes*, and *open* his *mouth*, as the children say, for that is the way to *gape*, and not to *read*. Manning, continue your laudable purpose of making me your register. I will render you back all your remarks; and *I, not you*, shall have received usury by having read them. In the meantime, may the great Spirit have you in his keeping, and preserve our Englishman from the inoculation of frivolity and sin upon French earth.

Allons—or what is it you say, instead of *good-bye?*

Mary sends her kind remembrance, and covets the remarks equally with me.   C. LAMB.

January 2, 1810.

DEAR MANNING—When I last wrote to you I was in lodgings. I am now in chambers, No. 4, Inner Temple Lane, where I should be happy to see you any evening. Bring any of your friends, the Mandarins, with you. I have two sitting-rooms: I call them so *par excellence*, for you may stand, or loll, or lean, or try any posture in them, but they are best for sitting; not squatting down Japanese fashion, but the more decorous use of the haunches which European usage has consecrated. I have two of these rooms on the third floor, and five sleeping, cooking, etc., rooms, on the fourth floor. In my best room is a choice collection of the works of Hogarth, an English painter of some humour. In my next best are shelves containing a small but well-chosen library. My best room commands a court, in which there are trees and a pump, the water of which is excellent cold, with brandy, and not very insipid without. Here I hope to set up my rest, and not quit till Mr. Powell, the undertaker, gives me notice that I may have possession of my last lodging. He lets lodgings for single gentlemen. I sent you a parcel of books by my last, to give you some idea of the state of European literature. There comes with this two volumes, done up as letters, of minor poetry, a sequel to 'Mrs. Leicester'; the best you may suppose mine; the next best are my coadjutor's. You may amuse yourself in guessing them out; but I must tell you mine are but one-third in quantity of the whole. So much for a very delicate subject. It is hard to speak of one's self, etc. Holcroft had finished his life when I wrote to you, and Hazlitt has since finished his life; I do not mean his own life, but he has finished a life of Holcroft, which is going to press. Tuthill is Dr. Tuthill. I continue Mr. Lamb. I have published a little book for children on titles of honour; and to give them some idea of the difference of rank and gradual rising, I have made a little scale, supposing myself to receive the following various accessions of dignity from the king, who is the fountain of honour—As at first, 1, Mr. C. Lamb; 2, C. Lamb, Esq.; 3, Sir C. Lamb, Bart.; 4, Baron Lamb, of Stamford; 5, Viscount Lamb; 6, Earl Lamb; 7, Marquis Lamb; 8, Duke Lamb. It would look like quibbling to carry it on further, and especially as it is not necessary for children to go beyond the ordinary titles of sub-regal dignity in our own country; otherwise I have sometimes in my dreams imagined myself still advancing, as 9th, King Lamb; 10th, Emperor Lamb; 11th, Pope Innocent; higher than which is nothing upon earth. Puns I have not made many (nor punch munch) since the date of my last; one I cannot help relating. A constable in Salisbury Cathedral was telling me that eight people dined at the top of the spire of the cathedral; upon which I remarked, that they must be very sharp set. But in general I cultivate the reasoning part of my mind more than the imaginative. I am stuffed out so with eating turkey for dinner, and another turkey for supper yesterday (Turkey in Europe and Turkey in Asia), that I can't jog on. It is New Year here; that is, it was New Year half a year back, when I was writing this. Nothing puzzles me more than time and space; and yet nothing puzzles me less, for I never think about them. The Persian ambassador is the principal thing talked of now. I sent some people to see him worship the sun on Primrose Hill, at half-past six in the morning, 28th November; but he did not come, which makes me think the old fire-worshippers are a sect almost extinct in Persia. The Persian ambassador's name in Shaw Ali Mirza. The common people call him Shaw Nonsense. While I think of it, I have put three letters, besides my own three, into the India Post for you, from your brother, sister, and some gentleman whose name I forget. Will they, have they, did they come safe? The distance you are at, cuts up tenses by the root. I think you said you did not know Kate * * * * * * * * *. I express her by nine stars, though she is but one. You must have seen her at her father's. Try and remember her. Coleridge is bringing out a paper in weekly Numbers, called the *Friend*, which I would send if I could; but the difficulty I had in getting the packets of books out to you before, deters me; and you'll want something new to read when you come home. It is chiefly intended to puff off Wordsworth's poetry; but there are some noble things in it by the by. Except Kate, I have had no vision of excellence this year, and she passed by like the Queen on her coronation day; you don't know whether you saw her or not. Kate is fifteen: I go about moping, and sing the old pathetic ballad I used to like in my youth—

> 'She's sweet fifteen,
> I'm *one year more*.'

Mrs. Bland sang it in boy's clothes the first time I heard it. I sometimes think the lower notes in my voice are like Mrs. Bland's. That glorious singer, Braham, one of my lights, is fled. He was for a season. He was a rare composition of the Jew, the gentleman, and the angel; yet all these elements mixed up so kindly in him, that you could not tell which preponderated; but he is gone, and one Phillips is engaged instead. Kate is vanished, but Miss B—— is always to be met with!

> 'Queens drop away, while blue-legg'd Maukin thrives;
> And courtly Mildred dies while country Madge survives.'

That is not my poetry, but Quarles's; but haven't you observed that the rarest things are the least obvious? Don't show anybody the names in this letter. I write confidentially, and wish this letter to be considered as *private*. Hazlitt has written a *grammar* for Godwin. Godwin sells it bound up with a treatise of his own on language; but the *gray mare is the better horse*. I don't allude to Mrs. Godwin, but to the word *grammar*, which comes near to *gray mare*, if you observe, in sound. That figure is called paronomasia in Greek. I am sometimes happy in it. An old woman begged of me for charity. 'Ah! sir,' said she, 'I have seen better days.' 'So have I, good woman,' I replied; but I meant, literally, days not so rainy and overcast as that on which she begged: she meant more prosperous days. Mr. Dawe is made associate of the Royal Academy. By what law of association I can't guess. Mrs. Holcroft, Miss Holcroft, Mr. and Mrs. Godwin, Mr. and Mrs. Hazlitt, Mrs. Martin and Louisa, Mrs. Lum, Capt. Burney, Mrs. Burney, Martin Burney, Mr. Rickman, Mrs. Rickman, Dr. Stoddart, William Dollin, Mr. Thompson, Mr. and Mrs. Norris, Mr. Fenwick, Mrs. Fenwick, Miss Fenwick, a man that saw you at our house one day, and a lady that heard me speak of you; Mrs. Buffam that heard Hazlitt mention you, Dr. Tuthill, Mrs. Tuthill, Colonel Harwood, Mrs. Harwood, Mr. Collier, Mrs. Collier, Mr. Sutton, Nurse, Mr. Fell, Mrs. Fell, Mr. Marshall, are very well, and occasionally inquire after you.

I remain yours ever,   CH. LAMB.

To William Wordsworth

September 28, 1805.

MY DEAR WORDSWORTH (or Dorothy rather, for to you appertains the biggest part of this answer by right)—I will not again deserve reproach by so long a silence. I have kept deluding myself with the idea that Mary would write to you, but she is so lazy (or, which I believe is the true state of the case, so diffident), that it must revert to me as usual. Though she writes a pretty good style, and has some notion of the force of words, she is not always so certain of the true orthography of them; and that, and a poor handwriting (in this age of female calligraphy), often deters her, where no other reason does.

We have neither of us been very well for some weeks past. I am very nervous, and she most so at those times when I am; so that a merry friend, adverting to the noble consolation we were able to afford each other, denominated us, not unaptly, Gum-boil and Tooth-Ache, for they used to say that a gum-boil is a great relief to a tooth-ache.

We have been two tiny excursions this Summer, for three or four days each, to a place near Harrow, and to Egham, where Cooper's Hill is: and that is the total history of our rustications this year. Alas! how poor a round to Skiddaw and Helvellyn, and Borrowdale, and the magnificent sesquipedalia of the year 1802! Poor old Molly! to have lost her pride, that 'last infirmity of noble minds,' and her cow. Fate need not have set her wits to such an old Molly. I am heartily sorry for her. Remember us lovingly to her; and in particular remember us to Mrs. Clarkson in the most kind manner.

I hope, by 'southwards,' you mean that she will be at or near London, for she is a great favourite of both of us, and we feel for her health as much as possible for any one to do. She is one of the friendliest, comfortablest women we know, and made our little stay at your cottage one of the pleasantest times we ever past. We were quite strangers to her. Mr. C. is with you too; our kindest separate remembrances to him. As to our special affairs, I am looking about me. I have done nothing since the beginning of last year, when I lost my newspaper job; and having had a long idleness, I must do something, or we shall get very poor. Sometimes I think of a farce, but hitherto all schemes have gone off; an idle brag or two of an evening, vapouring out of a pipe, and going off in the morning; but now I have bid farewell to my 'sweet enemy,' Tobacco, I shall perhaps set nobly to work. Hang work!

I wish that all the year were holiday; I am sure that indolence—indefeasible indolence—is the true state of man, and business the invention of the old Teazer, whose interference doomed Adam to an apron and set him a hoeing. Pen and ink, and clerks and desks, were the refinements of this old torturer some thousand years after, under pretence of 'Commerce allying distant shores, promoting and diffusing knowledge, good,' etc. etc.

I wish you may think this a handsome farewell to my 'Friendly Traitress.' Tobacco has been my evening comfort and my morning curse for these five years; and you know how difficult it is from refraining to pick one's lips even, when it has become a habit. This poem is the only one which I have finished since so long as when I wrote 'Hester Savory.' I have had it in my head to do it these two years, but tobacco stood in its own light when it gave me headaches that prevented my singing its praises. Now you have got it, you have got all my store, for I have absolutely not another line. No more has Mary. We have nobody about us that cares for poetry; and who will rear grapes when he shall be the sole eater? Perhaps if you encourage us to show you what we may write, we may do something now and then before we absolutely forget the quantity of an English line for want of practice. The 'Tobacco,' being a little in the way of Wither (whom Southey so much likes), perhaps you will somehow convey it to him with my kind remembrances. Then, everybody will have seen it that I wish to see it, I having sent it to Malta.

I remain, dear W. and D., yours truly,   C. LAMB.

June 26, 1806.

MARY is just stuck fast in 'All's Well that Ends Well.' She complains of having to set forth so many female characters in boys' clothes. She begins to think Shakspeare must have wanted—imagination! I, to encourage her (for she often faints in the prosecution of her great work), flatter her with telling her how well such a play and such a play is done. But she is stuck fast, and I have been obliged to promise to assist her. To do this it will be necessary to leave off tobacco. But I had some thoughts of doing that before, for I sometimes think it does not agree with me. Wm. Hazlitt is in town. I took him to see a very pretty girl, professedly, where there were two young girls (the very head and sum of the girlery was two young girls); they neither laughed, nor sneered, nor giggled, nor whispered—but they were young girls—and he sat and frowned blacker and blacker, indignant that there should be such a thing as youth and beauty, till he tore me away before supper, in perfect misery, and owned he could not bear young girls; they drove him mad. So I took him home to my old nurse, where he recovered perfect tranquillity. Independent of this, and as I am not a young girl myself, he is a great acquisition to us. He is, rather imprudently I think, printing a political pamphlet on his own account, and will have to pay for the paper, etc. The first duty of an author, I take it, is never to pay anything. But *non cuivis contigit adire Corinthum*. The managers, I thank my stars, have settled that question for me.

Yours truly,   C. LAMB.

Accountant's Office, April 26, 1816.

DEAR W.—I have just finished the pleasing task of correcting the revise of the poems and letter. I hope they will come out faultless. One blunder I saw and shuddered at. The hallucinating rascal had printed *battered* for *battened*, this last not conveying any distinct sense to his gaping soul. The Reader (as they call 'em) had discovered it, and given it the marginal brand, but the substitutory *n* had not yet appeared. I accompanied his notice with a most pathetic address to the printer not to neglect the correction. I know how such a blunder would 'batter at your peace.' With regard to the works, the Letter I read with unabated satisfaction. Such a thing was wanted—called for. The parallel of Cotton with Burns I heartily approve. Izaak Walton hallows any page in which his reverend name appears. 'Duty archly bending to purposes of general benevolence' is exquisite. The poems I endeavoured not to understand, but to read them with my eye alone, and I think I succeeded. (Some people will do that when they come out, you'll say.) As if I were to luxuriate to-morrow at some picture gallery I was never at before, and going by to-day by chance, found the door open, and had but five minutes to look about me, peeped in; just such a *chastised* peep I took with my mind at the lines my luxuriating eye was coursing over unrestrained, not to anticipate another day's fuller satisfaction. Coleridge is printing 'Christabel,' by Lord Byron's recommendation to Murray, with what he calls a vision, 'Kubla Khan,' which said vision he repeats so enchantingly that it irradiates and brings heaven and elysian bowers into my parlour while he sings or says it; but there is an observation, 'Never tell thy dreams,' and I am almost afraid that 'Kubla Khan' is an owl that won't bear daylight. I fear lest it should be discovered by the lantern of typography and clear reducing to letters no better than nonsense or no sense. When I was young I used to chant with ecstasy 'MILD ARCADIANS EVER BLOOMING,' till somebody told me it was meant to be nonsense. Even yet I have a lingering attachment to it, and I think it better than 'Windsor Forest,' 'Dying Christian's Address,' etc. Coleridge has sent his tragedy to D[rury] L[ane] T[heatre]. It cannot be acted this season; and by their manner of receiving, I hope he will be able to alter it to make them accept it for next. He is, at present, under the medical care of a Mr. Gillman (Killman?) a Highgate apothecary, where he plays at leaving off laud—m. I think his essentials not touched: he is very bad; but then he wonderfully picks up another day, and his face, when he repeats his verses, hath its ancient glory; an archangel a little damaged. Will Miss H. pardon our not replying at length to her kind letter? We are not quiet enough; Morgan is with us every day, going betwixt Highgate and the Temple. Coleridge is absent but four miles, and the neighbourhood of such a man is as exciting as the presence of fifty ordinary persons. 'Tis enough to be within the whiff and wind of his genius for us not to possess our souls in quiet. If I lived with him or the Author of the *Excursion*, I should, in a very little time, lose my own identity, and be dragged along in the current of other people's thoughts, hampered in a net. How cool I sit in this office, with no possible interruption further than what I may term *material!* There is not as much metaphysics in thirty-six of the people here as there is in the first page of Locke's 'Treatise on the Human Understanding,' or as much poetry as in any ten lines of the 'Pleasures of Hope,' or more natural 'Beggar's Petition.' I never entangle myself in any of their speculations. Interruptions, if I try to write a letter even, I have dreadful. Just now, within four lines, I was called off for ten minutes to consult dusty old books for the settlement of obsolete errors. I hold you a guinea you don't find the chasm where I left off, so excellently the wounded sense closed again and was healed.

N.B.—Nothing said above to the contrary, but that I hold the personal presence of the two mentioned potent spirits at a rate as high as any; but I pay dearer. What amuses others robs me of myself: my mind is positively discharged into their greater currents, but flows with a willing violence. As to your question about work, it is far less oppressive to me than it was, from circumstances. It takes all the golden part of the day away, a solid lump, from ten to four; but it does not kill my peace as before. Some day or other I shall be in a taking again. My head aches, and you have had enough. God bless you!   C. LAMB.

To Mrs. Wordsworth

East India House,
February 18, 1818.

MY DEAR MRS. WORDSWORTH—I have repeatedly taken pen in hand to answer your kind letter. My sister should more properly have done it, but she having failed, I consider myself answerable for her debts. I am now trying to do it in the midst of commercial noises, and with a quill which seems more ready to glide into arithmetical figures and names of gourds, cassia, cardamoms, aloes, ginger, or tea, than into kindly responses and friendly recollections. The reason why I cannot write letters at home is, that I am never alone. Plato's—(I write to W. W. now)—Plato's double-animal parted never longed more to be reciprocally re-united in the system of its first creation than I sometimes do to be but for a moment single and separate. Except my morning's walk to the office, which is like treading on sands of gold for that reason, I am never so. I cannot walk home from office but some officious friend offers his unwelcome courtesies to accompany me. All the morning I am pestered. I could sit and gravely cast up sums in great books, or compare sum with sum, and write 'paid' against this, and 'unpaid' against t'other, and yet reserve in some corner of my mind 'some darling thoughts all my own,'—faint memory of some passage in a book, or the tone of an absent friend's voice—a snatch of Miss Burrell's singing, or a gleam of Fanny Kelly's divine plain face. The two operations might be going on at the same time without thwarting, as the sun's two motions (earth's, I mean), or as I sometimes turn round till I am giddy, in my back parlour, while my sister is walking longitudinally in the front; or as the shoulder of veal twists round with the spit, while the smoke wreathes up the chimney. But there are a set of amateurs of the Belles Lettres —the gay science—who come to me as a sort of rendezvous, putting questions of criticism, of British Institutions, Lalla Rookhs, etc.—what Coleridge said at the lecture last night— who have the form of reading men, but, for any possible use reading can be to them, but to talk of, might as well have been Ante-Cadmeans born, or have lain sucking out the sense of an Egyptian hieroglyph as long as the pyramids will last, before they should find it. These pests worrit me at business, and in all its intervals, perplexing my accounts, poisoning my little salutary warming-time at the fire, puzzling my paragraphs if I take a newspaper, cramming in between my own free thoughts and a column of figures, which had come to an amicable compromise but for them. Their noise ended, one of them, as I said, accompanies me home, lest I should be solitary for a moment; he at length takes his welcome leave at the door; up I go, mutton on table, hungry as hunter, hope to forget my cares, and bury them in the agreeable abstraction of mastication; knock at the door, in comes Mr. Hazlitt, or Mr. Martin Burney, or Morgan Demigorgon, or my brother, or somebody, to prevent my eating alone—a process absolutely necessary to my poor wretched digestion. O the pleasure of eating alone! eating my dinner alone! let me think of it. But in they come, and make it absolutely necessary that I should open a bottle of orange; for my meat turns into stone when any one dines with me, if I have not wine. Wine can mollify stones; then *that* wine turns into acidity, acerbity, misanthropy, a hatred of my interrupters—(God bless 'em! I love some of 'em dearly), and with the hatred, a still greater aversion to their going away. Bad is the dead sea they bring upon me, choking and deadening, but worse is the deader dry sand they leave me on, if they go before bed-time. Come never, I would say to these spoilers of my dinner; but if you come, never go! The fact is, this interruption does not happen very often; but every time it comes by surprise, that present bane of my life, orange wine, with all its dreary stifling consequences, follows. Evening company I should always like had I any mornings, but I am saturated with human faces (*divine* forsooth!) and voices all the golden morning; and five evenings in a week would be as much as I should covet to be in company; but I assure you that is a wonderful week in which I can get two, or one to myself. I am never C. L., but always C. L. and Co. He who thought it not good for man to be alone, preserve me from the more prodigious monstrosity of being never by myself! I forget bed-time, but even there these sociable frogs clamber up to annoy me. Once a week, generally some singular evening that, being alone, I go to bed at the hour I ought always to be a-bed; just close to my bedroom window is the club-room of a public-house, where a set of singers, I take them to be chorus-singers of the two theatres (it must be *both of them*), begin their orgies. They are a set of fellows (as I conceive) who, being limited by their talents to the burthen of the song at the play-houses, in revenge have got the common popular airs by Bishop, or some cheap composer, arranged for choruses; that is, to be sung all in chorus. At least I never can catch any of the text of the plain song, nothing but the Babylonish choral howl at the tail on't. 'That fury being quenched'— the howl, I mean—a burden succeeds of shouts and clapping, and knocking of the table. At length overtasked nature drops under it, and escapes for a few hours into the society of the sweet silent creatures of dreams, which go away with mocks and mows at cockcrow. And then I think of the words Christabel's father used (bless me, I have dipt in the wrong ink!) to say every morning by way of variety when he awoke:

'Every knell, the Baron saith,
Wakes us up to a world of death'—

or something like it. All I mean by this senseless interrupted tale, is, that by my central situation I am a little over-companied. Not that I have any animosity against the good creatures that are so anxious to drive away the happy solitude from me. I like 'em, and cards, and a cheerful glass; but I mean merely to give you an idea, between office confinement and after-office society, how little time I can call my own. I mean only to draw a picture, not to make an inference. I would not that I know of have it otherwise. I only wish sometimes I could exchange some of my faces and voices for the faces and voices which a late visitation brought most welcome, and carried away, leaving regret, but more pleasure, even a kind of gratitude, at being so often favoured with that kind northern visitation. My London faces and noises don't hear me—I mean no disrespect, or I should explain myself, that instead of their return 220 times a year, and the return of W. W., etc., seven times in 104 weeks, some more equal distribution might be found. I have scarce room to put in Mary's kind love, and my poor name,

C. LAMB.

W. H. goes on lecturing against W. W. and making copious use of quotations from said W. W. to give a zest to said lectures. S. T. C. is lecturing with success. I have not heard either him or H., but I dined with S. T. C. at Gillman's a Sunday or two since, and he was well and in good spirits. I mean to hear some of the course; but lectures are not much to my taste, whatever the lecturer may be. If *read*, they are dismal flat, and you can't think why you are brought together to hear a man read his works, which you could read so much better at leisure yourself. If delivered extempore, I am always in pain lest the gift of utterance should suddenly fail the orator in the middle, as it did me at the dinner given in honour of me at the London tavern. 'Gentlemen,' said I, and there I stopped; the rest my feelings were under the necessity of supplying. Mrs. Wordsworth *will* go on, kindly haunting us with visions of seeing the lakes once more, which never can be realised. Between us there is a great gulf, not of inexplicable moral antipathies and distances, I hope, as there seemed to be between me and that gentleman concerned in the Stamp Office, that I so strangely recoiled from at Haydon's. I think I had an instinct that he was the head of an office. The dear abstract notion of the East India Company, as long as she is unseen, is pretty, rather poetical; but as she makes herself manifest by the persons of such beasts, I loathe and detest her as the scarlet what-do-you-call-her of Babylon. I thought, after abridging us of all our red-letter days, they had done their worst; but I was deceived in the length to which the heads of offices, those true liberty-haters, can go. They are the tyrants; not Ferdinand, nor Nero. By a decree passed this week, they have abridged us of the immemorially-observed custom of going at one o'clock of a Saturday, the little shadow of a holiday left us. Dear W. W., be thankful for liberty.

To Robert Southey

London, May 6, 1815.

DEAR SOUTHEY—I have received from Longman a copy of *Roderick*, with the Author's Compliments, for which I much thank you. I don't know where I shall put all the noble presents I have lately received in that way: the *Excursion*, Wordsworth's two last vols., and now *Roderick*, have come pouring in upon me like some irruption from Helicon. The story of the brave Maccabee was already, you may be sure, familiar to me in all its parts. I have, since the receipt of your present, read it quite through again, and with no diminished pleasure. I don't know whether I ought to say that it has given me more pleasure than any of your long poems. *Kehama* is doubtless more powerful, but I don't feel that firm footing in it that I do in *Roderick:* my imagination goes sinking and floundering in the vast spaces of unopened-before systems and faiths; I am put out of the pale of my old sympathies; my moral sense is almost outraged; I can't believe, or with horror am made to believe, such desperate chances against Omnipotence, such disturbances of faith to the centre; the more potent the more painful the spell. Jove, and his brotherhood of gods, tottering with the giant assailings, I can bear, for the soul's hopes are not struck at in such contests; but your Oriental almighties are too much types of the intangible prototype to be meddled with without shuddering. One never connects what are called the attributes with Jupiter.—I mention only what diminishes my delight at the wonder-workings of *Kehama*, not what impeaches its power, which I confess with trembling; but *Roderick* is a comfortable poem. It reminds me of the delight I took in the first reading of the *Joan of Arc*. It is maturer and better than *that*, though not better to me now than that was then. It suits me better than *Madoc*. I am at home in Spain and Christendom. I have a timid imagination, I am afraid. I do not willingly admit of strange beliefs, or out-of-the-way creeds or places. I never read books of travels, at least not farther than Paris or Rome. I can just endure Moors, because of their connection as foes with Christians; but Abyssinians, Ethiops, Esquimaux, Dervises, and all that tribe, I hate. I believe I fear them in some manner. A Mahometan turban on the stage, though enveloping some well-known face (Mr. Cook or Mr. Maddox, whom I see another day good Christian and English waiters, innkeepers, etc.), does not give me pleasure unalloyed. I am a Christian, Englishman, Londoner, *Templar*. God help me when I come to put off these snug relations, and to get abroad into the world to come! I shall be like *the crow on the sand*, as Wordsworth has it; but I won't think on it: no need, I hope, yet.

The parts I have been most pleased with, both on first and second readings, perhaps, are Florinda's palliation of Roderick's crime, confessed to him in his disguise—the retreat of the Palayos family first discovered—his being made king—'For acclamation one form must serve *more solemn for the breach of old observances.*' Roderick's vow is extremely fine, and his blessing on the vow of Alphonso:

> 'Towards the troop he spread his arms,
> As if the expanded soul diffused itself,
> And carried to all spirits *with the act*
> Its affluent inspiration.'

It struck me forcibly that the feeling of these last lines might have been suggested to you by the Cartoon of Paul at Athens. Certain it is that a better motto or guide to that famous attitude can nowhere be found. I shall adopt it as explanatory of that violent but dignified motion.

I must read again Landor's *Julian*. I have not read it for some time. I think he must have failed in Roderick, for I remember nothing of him, nor of any distinct character as a character—only fine-sounding passages. I remember thinking also he had chosen a point of time after the event, as it were, for Roderick survives to no use; but my memory is weak, and I will not wrong a fine poem by trusting to it.

The notes to your poem I have not read again: but it will be a take-downable book on my shelf, and they will serve sometimes at breakfast, or times too light for the text to be duly appreciated. Though some of 'em—one of the serpent penance—is serious enough, now I think on't. Of Coleridge I hear nothing, nor of the Morgans. I hope to have him like a reappearing star, standing up before me some time when least expected in London, as has been the case whilere.

I am *doing* nothing (as the phrase is) but reading presents, and walk away what of the day hours I can get from hard occupation. Pray accept once more my hearty thanks, and expression of pleasure for your remembrance of me. My sister desires her kind respects to Mrs. S. and to all at Keswick.

Yours truly,

C. LAMB.

The next present I look for is the *White Doe*.

Have you seen Mat. Betham's *Lay of Marie?* I think it very delicately pretty as to sentiment, etc.

R. Southey, Esq.,
    Keswick, near Penrith,
        Cumberland.

August 9, 1815.

DEAR SOUTHEY—Robinson is not on the circuit, as I erroneously stated in a letter to W. W., which travels with this, but is gone to Brussels, Ostend, Ghent, etc. But his friends, the Colliers, whom I consulted respecting your friend's fate, remember to have heard him say Father Pardo had effected his escape (the cunning greasy rogue!), and to the best of their belief is at present in Paris. To my thinking, it is a small matter whether there be one fat friar more or less in the world. I have rather a taste for clerical executions, imbibed

451

from early recollections of the fate of the excellent Dodd. I hear Buonaparte has sued his habeas corpus, and the twelve judges are now sitting upon it at the Rolls.

Your boute-feu (bonfire) must be excellent of its kind. Poet Settle presided at the last great thing of the kind in London, when the pope was burnt in form. Do you provide any verses on this occasion? Your fear for Hartley's intellectuals is just and rational. Could not the Chancellor be petitioned to remove him? His lordship took Mr. Betty from under the paternal wing. I think at least he should go through a course of matter-of-fact with some sober man after the mysteries. Could not he spend a week at Poole's before he goes back to Oxford? Tobin is dead. But there is a man in my office, a Mr. Hedges, who proses it away from morning to night, and never gets beyond corporal and material verities. He'd get these crack-brain metaphysics out of the young gentleman's head as soon as any one I know. When I can't sleep o' nights, I imagine a dialogue with Mr. Hedges, upon any given subject, and go prosing on in fancy with him, till I either laugh or fall asleep. I have literally found it answer. I am going to stand godfather; I don't like the business; I cannot muster up decorum for these occasions; I shall certainly disgrace the font. I was at Hazlitt's marriage, and had like to have been turned out several times during the ceremony. Anything awful makes me laugh. I misbehaved once at a funeral. Yet I can read about those ceremonies with pious and proper feelings. The realities of life only seem the mockeries. I fear I must be cured along with Hartley, if not too inveterate. Don't you think Louis the Desirable is in a sort of quandary?

After all, Buonaparte is a fine fellow, as my barber says and I should not mind standing bareheaded at his table to do him service in his fall. They should have given him Hampton Court or Kensington, with a tether extending forty miles round London. Qu. Would not the people have ejected the Brunswicks some day in his favour? Well, we shall see.
C. LAMB.

To Bernard Barton

India House,
September 11, 1822.

DEAR SIR—You have misapprehended me sadly, if you suppose that I meant to impute any inconsistency in your writing poetry with your religious profession. I do not remember what I said, but it was spoken sportively, I am sure—one of my levities, which you are not so used to as my older friends. I probably was thinking of the light in which your so indulging yourself would appear to Quakers, and put their objection in my own foolish mouth. I would eat my words (provided they should be written on not very coarse paper) rather than I would throw cold water upon your, and my once, harmless occupation.

I have read 'Napoleon' and the rest with delight. I like them for what they are, and for what they are not. I have sickened on the modern rhodomontade and Byronism, and your plain Quakerish beauty has captivated me. It is all wholesome cates; ay, and toothsome too; and withal Quakerish. If I were George Fox, and George Fox licenser of the press, they should have my absolute *imprimatur*. I hope I have removed the impression.

I am, like you, a prisoner to the desk. I have been chained to that galley thirty years,—a long shot. I have almost grown to the wood. If no imaginative poet, I am sure I am a figurative one. Do 'Friends' allow puns? *verbal* equivocations? They are unjustly accused of it; and I did my little best in the 'Imperfect Sympathies' to vindicate them. I am very tired of clerking it, but have no remedy. Did you see a Sonnet to this purpose in the *Examiner?*—

> '*Who* first invented work, and bound the free
> And holy-day rejoicing spirit down
> To the ever-haunting importunity
> Of business, in the green fields and the town,
> To plough, loom, anvil, spade; and oh, most sad,
> To that dry drudgery at the desk's dead wood?
> Who but the being unblest, alien from good,
> Sabbathless Satan! he who his unglad

453

> Task ever plies, 'mid rotatory burnings,
> That round and round incalculably reel;
> For wrath Divine hath made him like a wheel
> In that red realm from which are no returnings;
> Where, toiling and turmoiling, ever and aye,
> He and his thoughts keep pensive worky-day.'

I fancy the sentiment exprest above will be nearly your own. The expression of it probably would not so well suit with a follower of John Woolman. But I do not know whether diabolism is a part of your creed, or where indeed to find exposition of your creed at all. In feelings and matters not dogmatical, I hope I am half a Quaker. Believe me, with great respect, yours, C. LAMB.

I shall always be happy to see or hear from you.

To Mr. H. C. Robinson

Colebrooke Row, Islington,
Saturday, January 20, 1827.

DEAR ROBINSON—I called upon you this morning, and found that you were gone to visit a dying friend. I had been upon a like errand. Poor Norris has been lying dying for now almost a week, such is the penalty we pay for having enjoyed a strong constitution. Whether he knew me or not, I know not; or whether he saw me through his poor glazed eyes; but the group I saw about him I shall not forget. Upon the bed, or about it, were assembled his wife and two daughters, and poor deaf Richard, his son, looking doubly stupefied. There they were, and seemed to have been sitting all the week. I could only reach out a hand to Mrs. Norris. Speaking was impossible in that mute chamber. By this time I hope it is all over with him. In him I have a loss the world cannot make up. He was my friend and my father's friend all the life I can remember. I seem to have made foolish friendships ever since. Those are friendships which outlive a second generation. Old as I am waxing, in his eyes I was still the child he first knew me. To the last he called me Charley. I have none to call me Charley now. He was the last link that bound me to the Temple. You are but of yesterday. In him seem to have died the old plainness of manners and singleness of heart. Letters he knew nothing of, nor did his reading extend beyond the pages of the *Gentleman's Magazine*. Yet there was a pride of literature about him from being amongst books (he was librarian), and from some scraps of doubtful Latin which he had picked up in his office of entering students, that gave him very diverting airs of pedantry. Can I forget the erudite look with which, when he had been in vain trying to make out a black-letter text of Chaucer in the Temple Library, he laid it down and told me that—'in those old books, Charley, there is sometimes a deal of very indifferent spelling;' and seemed to console himself in the reflection! His jokes, for he had his jokes, are now ended; but they were old trusty perennials, staples that pleased after *decies repetita*, and were always as good as new. One song he had, which was reserved for the night of Christmas Day, which we always spent in the Temple. It was an old thing, and spoke of the flat bottoms of our foes, and the possibility of their coming over in darkness, and alluded to threats of an invasion many years blown over; and when he came to the part—

'We'll still make 'em run, and we'll still make 'em sweat,
In spite of the Devil and *Brussels Gazette*,'

his eyes would sparkle as with the freshness of an impending event. And what is the *Brussels Gazette* now? I cry while I enumerate these trifles. 'How shall we tell them in a stranger's ear?' His poor good girls will now have to receive their afflicted mother in an unsuccessful hovel in an obscure village in Herts, where they have been long struggling to make a school without effect; and poor deaf Richard, and the more helpless for being so, is thrown on the wide world.

My first motive in writing, and indeed in calling on you, was to ask if you were enough acquainted with any of the Benchers to lay a plain statement before them of the circumstances of the family. I almost fear not, for you are of another hall. But if you can oblige me and my poor friend, who is now insensible to any favours, pray exert yourself. You cannot say too much good of poor Norris and his poor wife.

Yours ever,   CHARLES LAMB.

To C. Cowden Clarke

[*December* 1828.]

MY DEAR THREE C.'s—The way from Southgate to Colney
Hatch thro' the unfrequentedest Blackberry paths that ever
concealed their coy bunches from a truant Citizen, we have
accidentally fallen upon—the giant Tree by Chestnut we
have missed, but keep your chart to go by, unless you will be
our conduct. At present I am disabled from further flights
than just to skirt round Clay Hill, with a peep at the fine
backwoods, by strained tendons, got by skipping a skipping
rope at 53—*hei mihi non sum qualis;* but do you know, now
you come to talk of walks, a ramble of four hours or so—
there and back—to the willow and lavender plantations at
the south corner of Northaw Church by a well dedicated to
Saint Claridge, with the clumps of finest moss rising hillock
fashion, which I counted to the number of two hundred and
sixty, and are called 'Claridge's covers,' the tradition being
that that saint entertained so many angels or hermits there,
upon occasion of blessing the waters? The legends have set
down the fruits spread upon that occasion, and in the 'Black
Book of St. Albans,' some are named which are not supposed
to have been introduced into this island until a century
later. But waiving the miracle, a sweeter spot is not in ten
counties round; you are knee—deep in clover, that is to say,
if you are not above a middling man's height; from this
paradise, making a day of it, you go to see the ruins of an old
convent at March Hall, where some of the painted glass is
yet whole and fresh.

If you do not know this, you do not know the capabilities
of this country; you may be said to be a stranger to Enfield.
I found it out one morning in October, and so delighted was
I that I did not get home before dark, well a-paid.

I shall long to show you the Clump Meadows, as they are
called—we might do that without reaching March Hall;
when the days are longer we might take both, and come
home by Forest Cross, so skirt over Pennington and the
cheerful little village of Churchley to Forty Hill.

But these are dreams till summer; meanwhile we should be most glad to see you for a lesser excursion—say Sunday next, you and *another*, or if more, best on a week-day with a notice, but o' Sundays, as far as a leg of mutton goes, most welcome.

We can squeeze out a bed. Edmonton coaches run every hour, and my pen has run out its quarter. Heartily farewell.

To B. W. Procter

January 22, 1829.

DON'T trouble yourself about the verses. Take 'em coolly as they come. Any day between this and Midsummer will do. Ten lines the extreme. There is no mystery in my incognita. She has often seen you, though you may not have observed a silent brown girl, who for the last twelve years has rambled about our house in her Christmas holidays. She is Italian by name and extraction. Ten lines about the blue sky of her country will do, as 'tis her foible to be proud of it.—Item: I have made her a tolerable Latinist. She is called Emma Isola. I approve heartily of your turning your four vols. into a lesser compass. 'Twill Sybillise the gold left. I shall, I think, be in town in a few weeks, when I will assuredly see you. I will put in here Loves to Mrs. Procter and the anti-Capulets, because Mary tells me I omitted them in my last. I like to see my friends here. I have put my lawsuit into the hands of an Enfield practitioner, a plain man, who seems perfectly to understand it, and gives me hopes of a favourable result.

Rumour tells us that Miss Holcroft is married. Who is Badman, or Bed'em? Have I seen him at Montacute's? I hear he is a great chymist. I am sometimes chymical myself. A thought strikes me with horror. Pray heaven he may not have done it for the sake of trying chymical experiments upon her,—young female subjects are so scarce. Louisa would make a capital shot. Aren't you glad about Burke's case? We may set off the Scotch murders against the Scotch novels: Hare, the Great Un-hanged!

M. B. is richly worth your knowing. He is on the top scale of my friendship ladder, on which an angel or two is still climbing, and some, alas! descending. I am out of the literary world at present. Pray, is there anything new from the admired pen of the author of the *Pleasures of Hope?* Has Mrs. He-mans (double masculine) done anything pretty lately? Why sleeps the lyre of Hervey, and of Alaric Watts? Is the muse of L. E. L. silent? Did you see a sonnet of mine in Blackwood's last? Curious construction! Elaborata facilitas! And now I'll tell. 'Twas written for the *Gem*, but the editors declined it, on the plea that it would *shock all mothers;* so they published the 'Widow,' instead. I am born out of time. I have no conjecture about what the present world calls delicacy. I thought *Rosamund Gray* was a pretty modest thing. Hessey assures me that the world would not bear it. I have lived to grow into an indecent character. When my sonnet was rejected, I exclaimed, 'Damn the age! I will write for Antiquity.'

Erratum in Sonnet:—Last line but something, for 'tender,' read *tend*. The Scotch do not know our law terms; but I find some remains of honest, plain, old writing lurking there still. They were not so mealy-mouthed to refuse my verses. Maybe 'tis their oatmeal.

Blackwood sent me £20 for the drama. Somebody cheated me out of it next day; and my new pair of breeches, just sent home, cracking at first putting on, I exclaimed in my wrath, 'All tailors are cheats, and all men are tailors.' Then I was better.

C. L.

To Mr. Gillman

November 30, 1829.

DEAR G.—The excursionists reached home, and the good town of Enfield, a little after four, without slip or dislocation. Little has transpired concerning the events of the back-journey, save that on passing the house of 'Squire Mellish, situate a stone-bow's cast from the hamlet, Father Westwood, with a good-natured wonderment, exclaimed, 'I cannot think what is gone of Mr. Mellish's rooks. I fancy they have taken flight somewhere, but I have missed them two or three years past.' All this while, according to his fellow-traveller's report, the rookery was darkening the air above with un-diminished population, and deafening all ears but his with their cawings. But Nature has been gently withdrawing such phenomena from the notice of two of Thomas West-wood's senses, from the time he began to miss the rooks. T. Westwood has passed a retired life in this hamlet, of thirty or forty years, living upon the minimum which is consistent with gentility, yet a star among the minor gentry, receiving the bows of the tradespeople, and courtesies of the alms-women, daily. Children venerate him not less for his external show of gentry, than they wonder at him for a gentle rising endorsation of the person, not amounting to a hump, or if a hump, innocuous as the hump of the buffalo, and coronative of as mild qualities. 'Tis a throne on which patience seems to sit,—the proud perch of a self-respecting humility, stooping with condescension. Thereupon the cares of life have sate, and rid him easily. For he has thrid the *angustiæ domûs* with dexterity. Life opened upon him with comparative brilliancy. He set out as a rider or traveller for a wholesale house, in which capacity he tells of many hair-breadth escapes that befell him; one especially, how he rode a mad horse into the town of Devizes; how horse and rider arrived in a foam, to the utter consternation of the expostu-lating hostlers, inn-keepers, etc. It seems it was sultry weather, piping hot; the steed tormented into frenzy with gad-flies, long past being road-worthy; but safety and the interest of the house he rode for were incompatible things; a fall in serge cloth was expected, and a mad entrance they made of it. Whether the exploit was purely voluntary, or partially; or whether a certain personal defiguration in the man part of this extraordinary centaur (non-assistive to partition of natures) might not enforce the conjunction, I stand not to inquire. I look not with 'skew eyes into the deeds of heroes. The hosier that was burnt with his shop, in Field Lane, on Tuesday night, shall have past to heaven for me like a Marian Martyr, provided always that he consecrated the fortuitous incremation with a short ejaculation in the exit, as much as if he had taken his state degrees of martyr-dom *informâ* in the market vicinage. There is adoptive as well as acquisitive sacrifice. Be the animus what it might, the fact is indisputable, that this composition was seen flying all abroad, and mine host of Daintry may yet remember its passing through his town, if his scores are not more faithful than his memory. After this exploit (enough for one man), Thomas Westwood seems to have subsided into a less hazardous occupation: and in the twenty-fifth year of his age we find him a haberdasher in Bow Lane: yet still retentive of his early riding (though leaving it to rawer stomachs), and Christmasly at night sithence to this last, and shall to his latest Christmas, hath he, doth he, and shall he, tell after supper the story of the insane steed and the desperate rider. Save for Bedlam or Luke's no eye could have guessed that melting day what house he rid for. But he reposes on his bridles, and after the ups and downs (metaphoric only) of a life behind the counter—hard riding sometimes, I fear, for poor T. W.—with the scrapings together of the shop, and *one anecdote*, he hath finally settled at Enfield; by hard economising, gardening, building for himself, hath reared a mansion; married a daughter; qualified a son for a counting-house; gotten the respect of high and low; served for self or substitute the greater parish offices; hath a special voice at vestries; and, domiciliating us, hath reflected a portion of his house-keeping respectability upon your humble servants. We are greater, being his lodgers, than when we were substantial renters. His name is a passport to take off the sneers of the native Enfielders against obnoxious foreigners. We are endenizened. Thus much of T. Westwood have I thought fit to acquaint you, that you may see the exemplary reliance upon Providence with which I entrusted so dear a charge as my own sister to the guidance of a man that rode the mad horse into Devizes. To come from his heroic character, all the amiable qualities of domestic life concentre in this tamed Bellerophon. He is excellent over a glass of grog; just as pleasant without it; laughs when he hears a joke, and when (which is much oftener) he hears it not; sings glorious old sea-songs on festival nights; and but upon a slight acquaintance of two years, Coleridge, is as dear a deaf old man to us as old Norris (rest his soul!) was after fifty. To him and his scanty literature (what there is of it, *sound*) have we flown from the metropolis and its damn'd annualists, reviewers, authors, and the whole muddy ink press of that stagnant pool.

Now, Gillman again, you do not know the treasure of the Fullers. I calculate on having massy reading till Christmas. All I want here is books of the true sort, not those things in boards that moderns mistake for books, what they club for at book-clubs.

I did not mean to cheat you with a blank side, but my eye smarts, for which I am taking medicine, and abstain, this day at least, from any aliments but milk porridge, the innocent taste of which I am anxious to renew after a half-century's disacquaintance. If a blot fall here like a tear, it is not pathos, but an angry eye.

Farewell, while my *specilla* are sound.

Yours and yours, C. LAMB.

To Mr. Moxon

October 24, 1831.

To address an abdicated monarch is a nice point of breeding. To give him his lost titles is to mock him; to withhold 'em is to wound him. But his minister, who falls with him, may be gracefully sympathetic. I do honestly feel for your diminution of honours, and regret even the pleasing cares which are part and parcel of greatness. Your magnanimous submission, and the cheerful tone of your renunciation, in a letter which, without flattery, would have made an 'ARTICLE,' and which, rarely as I keep letters, shall be preserved, comfort me a little. Will it please, or plague you, to say that when your parcel came I damn'd it? for my pen was warming in my hand at a ludicrous description of a Landscape of an R.A., which I calculated upon sending you tomorrow, the last day you gave me. Now any one calling in, or a letter coming, puts an end to my writing for the day. Little did I think that the mandate had gone out, so destructive to my occupation, so relieving to the apprehensions of the whole body of R.A.'s; so you see I had not quitted the ship while a plank was remaining.

To drop metaphors, I am sure you have done wisely. The very spirit of your epistle speaks that you have a weight off your mind. I have one on mine; the cash in hand, which, as —— less truly says, burns in my pocket. I feel queer at returning it (who does not?), you feel awkward at retaking it (who ought not). Is there no middle way of adjusting this fine embarrassment? I think I have hit upon a medium to skin the sore place over, if not quite to heal it. You hinted that there might be something under £10, by and by, accruing to me—*Devil's Money* (you are sanguine, say £7 : 10s.); that I entirely renounce, and abjure all future interest in: I insist upon it; and 'by him I will not name,' I won't touch a penny of it. That will split your loss, one half, and leave me conscientious possessor of what I hold. Less than your assent to this, no proposal will I accept of.

The Rev. Mr. ——, whose name you have left illegible (is it *Seagull?*) never sent me any book on Christ's Hospital, by which I could dream that I was indebted to him for a dedication. Did G. D. send his penny tract to me to convert me to Unitarianism? Dear, blundering soul! why I am as old a one-Goddite as himself. Or did he think his cheap publication would bring over the Methodists over the way here? However, I'll give it to the pew-opener, in whom I have a little interest, to hand over to the clerk, whose wife she sometimes drinks tea with, for him to lay before the deacon, who exchanges the civility of the hat with him, for to transmit to the minister, who shakes hands with him out of chapel, and he, in all odds, will —— with it.

I wish very much to see you. I leave it to you to come how you will; we shall be very glad (we need not repeat) to see your sister, or sisters, with you; but for you, individually, I will just hint that a dropping in to tea, unlooked for, about five, stopping bread-and-cheese and gin-and-water, is worth a thousand Sundays. I am naturally miserable on a Sunday; but a week-day evening and supper is like old times. Set out *now*, and give no time to deliberation.

P.S.—The second volume of 'Elia' is delightful (ly bound, I mean), and quite cheap. Why, man, 'tis a unique!

If I write much more I shall expand into an article, which I cannot afford to let you have so cheap. By the by, to show the perverseness of human will, while I thought I *must* furnish one of those accursed things monthly, it seemed a labour above Hercules's 'Twelve' in a year, which were evidently monthly contributions. Now I am emancipated, I feel as if I had a thousand Essays swelling within me. False feelings both!

Your ex-Lampoonist, or Lamb-punnist, from Enfield, October 24, or 'last day but one for receiving articles that can be inserted.'

To Mr. and Mrs. Moxon

August 1833.

DEAR MR. AND MRS. MOXON—Time very short. I wrote to Miss Fryer, and had the sweetest letter about you, Emma, that ever friendship dictated. 'I am full of good wishes, I am crying with good wishes,' she says; but you shall see it.

Dear Moxon—I take your writing most kindly, and shall, most kindly, your writing from Paris.

I want to crowd another letter to Miss Fryer into the little time after dinner, before post time. So with twenty thousand congratulations,

Yours,   C. L.

I am calm, sober, happy. Turn over for the reason. I got home from Dover Street, by Evans, *half as sober as a judge*. I am turning over a new leaf, as I hope you will now.

[*The turn of the leaf presented the following from Miss Lamb:*]

MY DEAR EMMA AND EDWARD MOXON—Accept my sincere congratulations, and imagine more good wishes than my weak nerves will let me put into good set words. The dreary blank of *unanswered questions* which I ventured to ask in vain was cleared up on the wedding-day by Mrs. W. taking a glass of wine, and, with a total change of countenance, begging leave to drink Mr. and Mrs. Moxon's health. It restored me from that moment, as if by an electrical stroke, to the entire possession of my senses. I never felt so calm and quiet after a similar illness as I do now. I feel as if all tears were wiped from my eyes, and all care from my heart.

MARY LAMB.

[*At the foot of this letter is the following by Charles:*]
Wednesday.

DEARS, AGAIN—Your letter interrupted a seventh game at picquet which *we* were having, after walking to Wright's and purchasing shoes. We pass our time in cards, walks, and reading. We attack Tasso soon.

C. L.

Never was such a calm, or such a recovery. 'Tis her own words undictated.

POEMS

The Old Familiar Faces

I HAVE had playmates, I have had companions,
In my days of childhood, in my joyful school-days—
All, all are gone, the old familiar faces.

I have been laughing, I have been carousing,
Drinking late, sitting late, with my bosom cronies—
All, all are gone, the old familiar faces.

I loved a love once, fairest among women;
Closed are her doors on me, I must not see her—
All, all are gone, the old familiar faces.

I have a friend, a kinder friend has no man;
Like an ingrate, I left my friend abruptly;
Left him, to muse on the old familiar faces.

Ghost-like I paced round the haunts of my childhood.
Earth seem'd a desert I was bound to traverse,
Seeking to find the old familiar faces.

Friend of my bosom, thou more than a brother,
Why wert not thou born in my father's dwelling?
So might we talk of the old familiar faces—

How some they have died, and some they have left me,
And some are taken from me; all are departed;
All, all are gone, the old familiar faces.

A Vision of Rrepentance

I SAW a famous fountain, in my dream,
  Where shady pathways to a valley led;
A weeping willow lay upon that stream,
  And all around the fountain brink were spread
Wide-branching trees, with dark green leaf rich clad,
Forming a doubtful twilight—desolate and sad.

467

The place was such, that whoso enter'd in,
   Disrobèd was of every earthly thought,
And straight became as one that knew not sin,
   Or to the world's first innocence was brought;
Enseem'd it now, he stood on holy ground,
In sweet and tender melancholy wrapt around.

A most strange calm stole o'er my soothèd sprite;
   Long time I stood, and longer had I stayed,
When lo! I saw, saw by the sweet moon-light,
   Which came in silence o'er that silent shade,
Where, near the fountain, SOMETHING like DESPAIR
Made, of that weeping willow, garlands for her hair.

And eke with painful fingers she inwove
   Many an uncouth stem of savage thorn—
'The willow garland, *that* was for her love,
   And *these* her bleeding temples would adorn.'
With sighs her heart nigh burst, salt tears fast fell,
As mournfully she bended o'er that sacred well.

To whom when I addrest myself to speak,
   She lifted up her eyes, and nothing said;
   And, gath'ring up her loose attire, she fled
To the dark covert of that woody shade,
And in her going seem'd a timid gentle maid.

Revolving in my mind what this should mean,
   And why that lovely lady plainèd so;
Perplex'd in thought at that mysterious scene,
   And doubting if 'twere best to stay or go,
I cast mine eyes in wistful gaze around,
When from the shades came slow a small and plaintive sound.

> 'PSYCHE am I, who love to dwell
> In these brown shades, this woody dell
> Where never busy mortal came,
> Till now, to pry upon my shame.
>
> 'At thy feet what thou dost see
> The waters of repentance be,
> Which, night and day, I must augment
> With tears, like a true penitent,

'If haply so my day of grace
Be not yet past; and this lone place,
O'er-shadowy dark, excludeth hence
All thoughts but grief and penitence.'

'Why dost thou weep, thou gentle maid!
And wherefore in this barren shade
Thy hidden thoughts with sorrow feed?
Can thing so fair repentance need?'

'O! I have done a deed of shame,
And tainted is my virgin fame,
And stain'd the beauteous maiden white
In which my bridal robes were dight.'

'And who the promised spouse? declare:
And what those bridal garments were.'

'Severe and saintly righteousness
Composed the clear white bridal dress;
JESUS, the Son of Heaven's high King,
Bought with His blood the marriage ring.

'A wretched sinful creature, I
Deem'd lightly of that sacred tie,
Gave to a treacherous WORLD my heart,
And play'd the foolish wanton's part.

Soon to these murky shades I came,
To hide from the sun's light my shame.
And still I haunt this woody dell,
And bathe me in that healing well,
Whose waters clear have influence
From sin's foul stains the soul to cleanse;
And, night and day, I them augment,
With tears, like a true penitent,
Until, due expiation made,
And fit atonement fully paid,
The Lord and Bridegroom me present,
Where in sweet strains of high consent,
God's throne, the Seraphim
Shall chant the ecstatic marriage hymn.'

'Now Christ restore thee soon'—I said,
And thenceforth all my dream was fled.

469

A Farewell to Tobacco

MAY the Babylonish curse
Straight confound my stammering verse,
If I can a passage see
In this word-perplexity,
Or a fit expression find,
Or a language to my mind
(Still the phrase is wide or scant)
To take leave of thee, GREAT PLANT!
Or in any terms relate
Half my love, or half my hate:
For I hate, yet love, thee so,
That, whichever thing I show,
The plain truth will seem to be
A constrain'd hyperbole,
And the passion to proceed
More from a mistress than a weed.

Sooty retainer to the vine,
Bacchus' black servant, negro fine;
Sorcerer, that mak'st us dote upon
Thy begrimed complexion,
And, for thy pernicious sake,
More and greater oaths to break
Than reclaimèd lovers take
'Gainst women: thou thy siege dost lay
Much too in the female way,
While thou suck'st the lab'ring breath
Faster than kisses or than death.

Thou in such a cloud dost bind us,
That our worst foes cannot find us,
And ill fortune, that would thwart us,
Shoots at rovers, shooting at us;
While each man, through thy height'ning steam,
Does like a smoking Etna seem,
And all about us does express
(Fancy and wit in richest dress)
A Sicilian fruitfulness.

Thou through such a mist dost show us,
That our best friends do not know us,
And, for those allowèd features,
Due to reasonable creatures,
Liken'st us to fell Chimeras,
Monsters that, who see us, fear us;
Worse than Cerberus or Geryon,
Or, who first loved a cloud, Ixion.

Bacchus we know, and we allow
His tipsy rites. But what art thou,
That but by reflex canst show
What his deity can do,
As the false Egyptian spell
Aped the true Hebrew miracle?
Some few vapours thou may'st raise,
•The weak brain may serve to amaze,
But to the reins and nobler heart
Canst nor life nor heat impart.

Brother of Bacchus, later born,
The old world was sure forlorn
Wanting thee, that aidest more
The god's victories than before
All his panthers, and the brawls
Of his piping Bacchanals.
These, as stale, we disallow,
Or judge of *thee* meant: only thou
His true Indian conquest art;
And, for ivy round his dart,
The reformèd god now weaves
A finer thyrsus of thy leaves.

Scent to match thy rich perfume
Chemic art did ne'er presume
Through her quaint alembic strain,
None so sov'reign to the brain.
Nature, that did in thee exel,
Framed again no second smell.
Roses, violets, but toys
For the smaller sort of boys,
Or for greener damsels meant;
Thou art the only manly scent.

Stinking'st of the stinking kind,
Filth of the mouth and fog of the mind,
Africa, that brags her foison,
Breeds no such prodigious poison,
Henbane, nightshade, both together,
Hemlock, aconite——

                Nay, rather
Plant divine, of rarest virtue;
Blisters on the tongue would hurt you.
'Twas but in a sort I blamed thee;
None e'er prosper'd who defamed thee;
Irony all, and feign'd abuse,
Such as perplex'd lovers use,
At a need, when, in despair
To paint forth their fairest fair,
Or in part but to express
That exceeding comeliness
Which their fancies doth so strike,
They borrow language of dislike;
And, instead of Dearest Miss,
Jewel, Honey, Sweetheart, Bliss,
And those forms of old admiring,
Call her Cockatrice and Siren,
Basilisk, and all that's evil,
Witch, Hyena, Mermaid, Devil,
Ethiop, Wench, and Blackamoor,
Monkey, Ape, and twenty more;
Friendly Trait'ress, loving Foe,—
Not that she is truly so,
But no other way they know
A contentment to express,
Borders so upon excess,
That they do not rightly wot
Whether it be pain or not.

Or, as men, constrain'd to part
With what's nearest to their heart,
While their sorrow's at the height,
Lose discrimination quite,
And their hasty wrath let fall,
To appease their frantic gall,
On the darling thing whatever,
Whence they feel it death to sever,

Though it be, as they, perforce,
Guiltless of the sad divorce.

For I must (nor let it grieve thee,
Friendliest of plants, that I must) leave thee.
For thy sake, TOBACCO, I
Would do anything but die,
And but seek to extend my days
Long enough to sing thy praise.
But, as she, who once hath been
A king's consort, is a queen
Ever after, nor will bate
Any tittle of her state,
Though a widow, or divorced,
So I, from my converse forced,
The old name and style retain,
A right Katherine of Spain;
And a seat, too, 'mongst the joys
Of the blest Tobacco Boys;
Where, though I, by sour physician,
Am debarr'd the full fruition
Of thy favours, I may catch
Some collateral sweets, and snatch
Sidelong odours, that give life
Like glances from a neighbour's wife;
And still live in the by-places
And the suburbs of thy graces;
And in thy borders take delight,
An unconquer'd Canaanite.

On an Infant dying as soon as born

I SAW where in the shroud did lurk
A curious frame of Nature's work.
A flow'ret crushed in the bud,
A nameless piece of Babyhood,
Was in her cradle-coffin lying;
Extinct, with scarce the sense of dying:
So soon to exchange the imprisoning womb
For darker closets of the tomb!
She did but ope an eye, and put
A clear beam forth, then straight up shut

For the long dark: ne'er more to see
Through glasses of mortality.
Riddle of destiny, who can show
What thy short visit meant, or know
What thy errand here below?
Shall we say, that Nature blind
Check'd her hand, and changed her mind,
Just when she had exactly wrought
A finish'd pattern without fault?
Could she flag, or could she tire,
Or lack'd she the Promethean fire
(With her nine moons' long workings sicken'd)
That should thy little limbs have quicken'd?
Limbs so firm, they seem'd to assure
Life of health and days mature:
Woman's self in miniature!
Limbs so fair, they might supply
(Themselves now but cold imagery)
The sculptor to make Beauty by.
Or did the stern-eyed Fate descry,
That babe, or mother, one must die;
So in mercy left the stock,
And cut the branch; to save the shock
Of young years widow'd; and the pain,
When Single State comes back again
To the lone man who, 'reft of wife,
Thenceforward drags a maimed life?
The ecomomy of Heaven is dark;
And wisest clerks have miss'd the mark,
Why Human Buds, like this, should fall,
More brief than fly ephemeral,
That has his day; while shrivell'd crones
Stiffen with age to stocks and stones;
And crabbed use the conscience sears
In sinners of an hundred years.
Mother's prattle, mother's kiss,
Baby fond, thou ne'er wilt miss.
Rites, which custom does impose,
Silver bells and baby clothes;
Coral redder than those lips,
Which pale death did late eclipse;
Music framed for infant's glee,
Whistle never tuned for thee;
Though thou want'st not, thou shalt have them,

Loving hearts were they which gave them.
Let not one be missing; nurse,
See them laid upon the hearse
Of infant slain by doom perverse.
Why should kings and nobles have
Pictured trophies to their grave;
And we, churls, to thee deny
Thy pretty toys with thee to lie,
A more harmless vanity?

The Christening

ARRAY'D—a half-angelic sight—
In vests of pure Baptismal white,
The Mother to the Font doth bring
The little helpless nameless thing,
With hushes soft and mild caressing,
At once to get—a name and blessing.
Close by the babe the Priest doth stand,
The Cleansing Water at his hand,
Which must assoil the soul within
From every stain of Adam's sin.
The Infant eyes the mystic scenes,
Nor knows what all this wonder means;
And now he smiles, as if to say
'I am a Christian made this day';
Now frighted clings to Nurse's hold,
Shrinking from the water cold,
Whose virtues, rightly understood,
Are, as Bethesda's waters, good.
Strange words—The World, The Flesh, The Devil—
Poor Babe, what can it know of Evil?
But we must silently adore
Mysteriouc truths, and not explore.
Enough for him, in after-times,
When he shall read these artless rhymes,
If, looking back upon this day
With quiet conscience, he can say—
'I have in part redeem'd the pledge
Of my Baptismal privilege;
And more and more will strive to flee
All which my Sponsors kind did then renounce for me.'

To Martin Charles Burney, Esq.

FORGIVE me, BURNEY, if to thee these late
And hasty products of a critic pen,
Thyself no common judge of books and men,
In feeling of thy worth I dedicate.
My *verse* was offered to an older friend;
The humbler *prose* has fallen to thy share:
Nor could I miss the occasion to declare,
What spoken in thy presence must offend—
That, set aside some few caprices wild,
Those humorous clouds that flit o'er brightest days,
In all my threadings of this worldly maze
(And I have watched thee almost from a child),
From self-seeking, envy, low design,
I have not found a whiter soul than thine.

To the Editor of the 'Every-Day Book'

I LIKE you, and your book, ingenious Hone!
  In whose capacious all-embracing leaves
The very marrow of tradition's shown;
  And all that history—much that fiction—weaves.

By every sort of taste your work is graced.
  Vast stores of modern anecdote we find,
With good old story quaintly interlaced—
  The theme as various as the reader's mind.

Rome's lie-fraught legends you so truly paint—
  Yet kindly,—that the half-turn'd Catholic
Scarcely forbears to smile at his own saint,
  And cannot curse the candid heretic.

Rags, relics, witches, ghosts, fiends, crowd your page;
  Our fathers' mummeries we well-pleased behold,
And, proudly conscious of a purer age,
  Forgive some fopperies in the times of old.

Verse-honouring Phœbus, Father of bright *Days*,
  Must needs bestow on you both good and many,
Who, building trophies of his Children's praise,
  Run their rich Zodiac through, not missing any.

Dan Phœbus loves your book—trust me, friend Hone—
    The title only errs, he bids me say:
For while such art, wit, reading, there are shown,
    He swears, 'tis not a work of *every day*.

Written at Cambridge

I WAS not train'd in Academic bowers,
And to those learned streams I nothing owe
Which copious from those twin fair founts do flow;
Mine have been anything but studious hours.
Yet can I fancy, wandering mid thy towers,
Myself a nursling, Granta, of thy lap;
My brow seems tightening with the Doctor's cap,
And I walk *gowned;* feel unusual powers.
Strange forms of logic clothe my admiring speech,
Old Ramus' ghost is busy at my brain;
And my skull teems with notions infinite.
Be still, ye reeds of Camus, while I teach
Truths which transcend the searching School-men's vein,
And half had stagger'd that stout Stagirite!

BIBLIOGRAPHY

1797   *Poems by S. T. Coleridge to which are now added Poems by Charles Lamb and Charles Lloyd.*

1798   *Blank Verse* by Charles Lamb and Charles Lloyd.

1802   *John Woodvil. A Tragedy.*

1809   *Poetry for Children, Entirely Original.*

Miscellaneous Prose Works:—

1798   *A Tale of Rosamund Gray and Old Blind Margaret.*

1807   *Tales from Shakespeare* (With Mary Lamb).

1807   *Mrs. Leicester's School, or the History of Several Young Ladies.*

1808   *The Adventures of Ulysses.*

1811   *Beauty and the Beast, or A Rough Outside with a Gentle Heart.*

1823   *Elia.* Essays which have Appeared Under that Signature in the *London Magazine.*

1833   *Last Essays of Elia.*

1835   *Collected Edition of both series by Moxon.*

Also numerous other editions of the essays.

Letters of Charles Lamb:—

1837   Edited by T. N. Talfourd with sketch of his life.

1848   *Final Memorials.* Edited by T. N. Talfourd.

1886   *Letters.* Edited by W. C. Hazlitt.

1905   *Letters.* Edited by E. V. Lucas.

1935   *Letters of Charles Lamb to which are added those of his Sister Mary.* Edited by E. V. Lucas.

Collected Editions:—

The Works of Charles Lamb. Edited by T. N. Talfourd, five parts (1840).

Complete Correspondence and Works. Edited by T. Purnell, 4 vols. (1870).

Life, Letters and Writings. Edited by P. Fitzgerald, 6 vols. (1875, 1895, 1924).

Works. Edited by E. V. Lucas, 7 vols. (1903–5).

The following contain information on the Lamb's Lives and Works:—

Charles Lamb: A Memoir by B. W. Proctor (1866).

Charles Lamb: His Friends, his Haunts and His Books by Percy Fitzgerald (1866).

Charles Lamb by Alfred Ainger (1882).

The Lambs: Their Lives, Their Friends, and Their Correspondence by W. C. Hazlitt (1897).

Life by E. V. Lucas (1921).

Charles Lamb: His Life recorded by his Contemporaries compiled by Edmund Blunden (1934).

Charles Lamb by O. Williams (1934).

Lamb Always Elia by E. C. Johnson (. . . .).

The Lambs by Katharine Anthony (1949).